The First Global Prosecutor

The establishment of the International Criminal Court (ICC) gave rise to the first permanent Office of the Prosecutor, with independent powers of investigation and prosecution. Elected in 2003 for a nine-year term as the ICC's first prosecutor, Luis Moreno Ocampo established policies and practices about when and how to investigate, when to pursue prosecution, and how to obtain the cooperation of sovereign nations. He laid a foundation for the Office of the Prosecutor's involvement with the United Nations Security Council, state parties, nongovernmental organizations, victims, the accused, witnesses, and the media.

This volume of essays presents the first sustained examination of this unique office and offers a rare look into international justice. The contributors, who include legal scholars as well as practitioners of international law, explore the range of options available to the Office of the Prosecutor, the particular choices the first prosecutor made, and issues ripe for consideration as Moreno Ocampo's successor, Fatou B. Bensouda, assumes her duties. Bensouda's term also offers the perfect opportunity to examine the first prosecutor's singular efforts to strengthen international justice in all its facets.

Martha Minow is the Morgan and Helen Chu Dean and Professor of Law at Harvard Law School.

C. Cora True-Frost is assistant professor of law at the Syracuse University College of Law.

Alex Whiting is Professor of Practice at Harvard Law School.

Law, Meaning, and Violence

The scope of Law, Meaning, and Violence is defined by the wide-ranging scholarly debates sig-naled by each of the words in the title. Those debates have taken place among and between lawyers, anthropologists, political theorists, sociologists, and historians, as well as literary and cultural crit-ics. This series is intended to recognize the importance of such ongoing conversations about law, meaning, and violence as well as to encourage and further them.

Series Editors: Martha Minow, Harvard Law School
                    Austin Sarat, Amherst College

RECENT TITLES IN THE SERIES

The First Global Prosecutor: Promise and Constraints,
    edited by Martha Minow, C. Cora True-Frost, and Alex Whiting

Hybrid Justice: The Extraordinary Chambers in the Courts of Cambodia,
    by John D. Ciorciari and Anne Heindel

The Justice of Mercy, by Linda Ross Meyer

Dying Inside: The HIV/AIDS Ward at Limestone Prison,
    by Benjamin Fleury-Steiner with Carla Crowder

Sacred Violence: Torture, Terror, and Sovereignty, by Paul W. Kahn

Punishment and Political Order, by Keally McBride

Lives of Lawyers Revisited: Transformation and Resilience in the Organizations of Practice,
    by Michael J. Kelly

Among the Lowest of the Dead: The Culture of Capital Punishment,
    by David Von Drehle

Punishing Schools: Fear and Citizenship in American Public Education,
    by William Lyons and Julie Drew

Suing the Gun Industry: A Battle at the Crossroads of Gun Control and Mass Torts,
    edited by Timothy D. Lytton

Transformative Justice: Israeli Identity on Trial, by Leora Bilsky

Jurors' Stories of Death: How America's Death Penalty Invests in Inequality,
    by Benjamin Fleury-Steiner

The Jurisprudence of Emergency: Colonialism and the Rule of Law, by Nasser Hussain

Communities and Law: Politics and Cultures of Legal Identities, by Gad Barzilai

From Noose to Needle: Capital Punishment and the Late Liberal State,
    by Timothy V. Kaufman-Osborn

The Limits to Union: Same-Sex Marriage and the Politics of Civil Rights,
    by Jonathan Goldberg-Hiller

Pain, Death, and the Law, edited by Austin Sarat

Bad Boys: Public Schools in the Making of Black Masculinity, by Ann Arnett Ferguson

Whispered Consolations: Law and Narrative in African American Life,
    by Jon-Christian Suggs

Laws of the Postcolonial, edited by Eve Darian-Smith and Peter Fitzpatrick

The First Global Prosecutor

Promise and Constraints

*Edited by Martha Minow, C. Cora True-Frost,
and Alex Whiting*

UNIVERSITY OF MICHIGAN PRESS

Ann Arbor

Published in the United States of America by the
University of Michigan Press
Manufactured in the United States of America
♾ Printed on acid-free paper

2018   2017   2016   2015   4   3   2   1

A CIP catalog record for this book is available from the British Library.

Library of Congress Cataloging-in-Publication Data

The first global prosecutor : promise and constraints / Edited by Martha Minow, C. Cora True-Frost, and Alex Whiting.
        pages   cm. — (Law, meaning, and violence)
    Includes bibliographical references and index.
    ISBN 978-0-472-07251-4 (hardcover : alk. paper) — ISBN 978-0-472-05251-6
(pbk. : alk. paper) — ISBN 978-0-472-12086-4 (e-book)
    1. Prosecution (International law)   2. International criminal courts.   3. International criminal law.   I. Minow, Martha, 1954– editor.   II. True-Frost, C. Cora, editor.
III. Whiting, A. (Alex), editor.
    KZ7230.F57   2015
      345'.01262—dc23

                                                                    2014040568

Note on cover image: This building of the International Criminal Court headquarters in The Hague will always be identified with the first Prosecutor since Luis Moreno Ocampo worked in it during his entire tenure; the second Prosecutor, Fatou Bensounda, will witness during her term the move of the Court from this location to its new, permanent premises.

Contents

The Impacts of the Prosecutor's Work

Prologue

The Prosecutor's Use of Legal Policies

Luis Moreno Ocampo

This book provides a critical analysis of the policies of the Office of the Prosecutor of the International Criminal Court (ICC) and offers a unique perspective on one of the most innovative international endeavors to end impunity for and prevent massive atrocities. It is a result of Professors Martha Minow, Alex Whiting, and C. Cora True-Frost's unique efforts to innovate in legal analysis by expanding the scholarly focus to take into account emerging supranational legal systems.

The Importance of Developing Policies to Confront Atrocity Crimes

After the Holocaust, the international community still did not have an effective policy to stop the commission of genocide, crimes against humanity, or war crimes. International leaders promised over and over that those crimes would never happen again, only to see them occur again and again before our eyes. The Cold War, combined with regional and domestic conflicts, produced millions of victims in Latin America, Africa, Eastern Europe, and Asia, including the Khmer Rouge killings, the execution of innocent civilians in Srebrenica, the machete- and rape-driven Rwandan genocide, and the millions of civilians who died during the Congo wars. Against this background, the Rome Statute deserves our attention because it is the most ambitious and comprehensive global effort to deal with those massive atrocities.

In addition, the need to find new policies to confront international crimes has been exacerbated by technological development. The age-old problem of dealing with mass atrocities was transformed as perpetrators acquired new capabilities. In the Internet era, organizations that commit massive crimes respect no borders: weapons supply, communications, funding, and political support always rely on international connections. As a consequence, the classic legal focus on national systems is missing the fact that this type of crime cannot be controlled by the territorial state alone or, even worse, that in some cases national authorities are the ones committing these crimes using the state apparatus. The Republic of Uganda and the Democratic Republic of the Congo are recent examples of the first situation; Darfur and Libya in 2011 are examples of the second. Countering these forces is an emerging global civil society demanding global action. Whether through activists in Libya or a nongovernmental organization (NGO) such as San Diego's Invisible Children, citizens are learning to use Facebook and YouTube to expose crimes and demand worldwide action to stop them.

These are the challenges faced by the supranational criminal justice system created by the Rome Statute. The Rome Statute represents an innovative collective effort to prevent and manage mass violence: a network of national states integrated under the principle of complementarity with a court of last resort. The International Criminal Court is the most visible node of the new system and will decide on the individual responsibility of the accused, but to end impunity for the most serious crimes, the entire network has to perform.

For this reason, an exclusive focus on courtroom activities will conceal other activities needed to stop and punish massive atrocities. To achieve such goals, the international community has to agree on additional actions, including political, humanitarian, military, and judicial measures. Political leaders, diplomats, army officers, humanitarian workers, conflict managers, and NGOs should harmonize their practices with this new framework of "no impunity" promoted by the Rome Statute. How are they aligning their goals with the new legal obligations? That is the crucial question.

The variety of actors involved shows the complexity of the decision-making process required. It also explains the international community's difficulties in reacting efficiently to the growing global demand for an end to mass crimes. Just to decide on the intervention of the Court in Darfur or Libya, the debate included the fifteen members of the U.N. Security Council, national leaders, NGOs, and regional organizations such as the African Union and the Arab League. The ratification of the Rome Statute by more than 120 states created a new dynamic that is influencing the decision-making process amid conflicts. For example, in 2005, nine of the fifteen members of the Security Council were state parties to the statute, and as a consequence, as soon as the United Kingdom and France started to promote the referral of the Darfur situation to the International Criminal Court, they had a majority vote in the Council. I believe that producing systematic knowledge about these new and complex supranational institutions, about the ways in which they influence and are influenced by others, is the current challenge for legal scholars.

The Origins of the Book

In 2009, Jonathan Fanton, then-president of the MacArthur Foundation, and Christopher Stone, then chair of the Hauser Center for nonprofit organizations at Harvard University, promoted the idea of focusing on the emerging global justice system. They started to plan a conference to help states, the U.N. and regional international organizations, NGOs, and other actors involved better articulate and align their strategies.[1] They organized a preparatory meeting in May 2009 to discuss the concept and invited Professor Martha Minow to present her views.

After the meeting, Minow decided to contribute to these efforts by teaching a seminar to discuss the Rome Statute. She realized that a focus on the Office of the Prosecutor's policies provided a unique entry point into this groundbreaking institution. A few months later, she was appointed the dean of the Harvard Law School. I thought that her new obligations would mean that she would not have enough time for the project. However, Martha persisted and even developed the idea further, creating an experimental laboratory to develop a new academic approach and integrating scholars from different disciplines with practitioners. She also brought along Alex Whiting, a former prosecutor at the ICTY and assistant U.S. attorney who was then an assistant clinical professor at Harvard Law School. C. Cora True-Frost, an assistant professor at Syracuse University who previously worked in East Timor and Sierra Leone and led the NGO Working Group on Women, Peace, and Security at the U.N. Headquarters, later joined. Martha invited the Office of the Prosecutor to present its policies and elucidate the challenges it was facing, and she convened Harvard professors including Christopher Stone, Catharine MacKinnon, Robert H. Mnookin, Jack Goldsmith, and Philip Heymann, along with students, to discuss the office's decisions and policies and to make recommendations. She also included other participants in the international decision-making process, among them Jorge Urbina, Costa Rica's ambassador to the U.N., and Richard Williamson, U.S. president George W. Bush's special envoy for Sudan, who shared their own experiences as diplomats dealing with massive crimes. To go even further, Martha organized a follow-up conference with leading experts from other universities, including Julie Rose O'Sullivan, Máximo Langer, and Leila Nadya Sadat. This lab was sustained for more than three years and produced a cutting-edge course for students, made new data available to academics, and provided the Office of the Prosecutor with an invaluable place to review its decisions. This important book is one of the many results of these efforts.

The Policies of the Office of the Prosecutor

As the first prosecutor of the International Criminal Court, I am very grateful for Minow, Whiting, and True-Frost's work because they provided us with an opportunity to refine our thinking. During my mandate, I had to make daily decisions on problems that no previous national or international prosecutor had ever faced.

Where and how to trigger the jurisdiction of the Court? The Office of the Prosecutor received hundreds of requests to use its *proprio motu* powers to open an investigation into the Iraq War. These requests exposed the most important difference between the International Criminal Court and the previous ad hoc tribunals. States defined the situations to be investigated in the International Military Tribunal at Nuremberg, the Tokyo Tribunal, the International Criminal Tribunal for the Former Yugoslavia (ICTY), and the International Criminal Tribunal for Rwanda (ICTR); in such courts the prosecutor was responsible only for selecting the suspects and the criminal incidents. Under the Rome Statute, the prosecutor must also identify the situations that should be presented before the Court. As a consequence, the Rome Statute introduces the prosecutor and the Court as a new autonomous actor in the international relations arena. The prosecutor's responsibility includes two critical duties: the prosecutor shall refrain from opening investigations when national authorities conduct genuine proceedings but shall trigger the jurisdiction of the Court when states are unable or unwilling to fulfill their obligations.

In addition, some particular cases raise issues not clearly defined by the law. For example, should the Office of the Prosecutor consider the Palestinian National Authority as a "state" that could accept the jurisdiction of the Court for crimes committed in Palestine?

The need to investigate ongoing crimes presents peculiar challenges. How to protect witnesses in Darfur when the territorial state was attacking those living there? How to harmonize the Office of the Prosecutor's obligations to respect the confidentiality required by the information providers[8] and guaranteed by article 54(3)(e) of the statute with its obligation to disclose information material to the defense of Thomas Lubanga?

My duty was to decide these extremely complex issues, applying an innovative law adopted by more than 120 states from around the world. To represent the will of those states when they defined the office's mandate, we had to limit ourselves to applying the statute without stretching the interpretation of its norms. As Roscoe Pound said, "It is the work of lawyers to make the law in action conform to the law in the books."[2] It was clear to us that if the prosecutor were not perceived as respecting the law, the entire Rome Statute's legitimacy might be undermined. To avoid that possibility and build a solid institutional basis from the beginning, we made public our policies[3] and regularly explained our legal decisions.

During my swearing-in, I expressed the three basic concepts of our mandate. First, as mentioned in its preamble, the Rome Statute's final objective is to prevent future crimes and protect the victims.[4] Second, the office emphasized the need to fully respect complementarity and to consider states' actions as an indicator of the Rome Statute's success: "The absence of trials by the ICC, as a consequence of the effective functioning of national systems, would be a major success."[5] Third, to avoid misunderstandings and build consensus, we promised a continuous dialogue with all of our stakeholders. This started the following day, when we held our first public hearing, and it continued during my entire tenure.[6]

In September 2003, we made public our main operational policies: (a) the promotion of genuine national proceedings, a policy that we called "positive complementarity"; (b) investigations and prosecutions focused on those who bear the greatest responsibility in accordance with the evidence collected; and (c) the maximization of the office's contribution to the prevention of future crimes while operating a system of low costs. This policy allowed the office to fulfill its independent mandate within a limited budget.[7]

We sought to show our respect for the legal limits, thereby increasing the predictability of the office's activities and motivating or influencing other actors to adjust their conduct accordingly.

Nevertheless, as investigations and cases progressed in strict compliance[8] with the announced policies, the Office of the Prosecutor's commitment to transparency and its adherence to its legal mandate produced a peculiar outcome; they became an explosive formula fueling public debates. Although regard for the limits of the law should be a normal practice for a prosecutor, many political actors and international relations and legal experts resisted such a basic idea for the prosecutor of the International Criminal Court. Even strong supporters of the independence of the office at the Rome Conference in 1998 believed that the prosecutor should make decisions based on different grounds—for example, respecting local views on immunity for leaders such as Joseph Kony and stopping the proceedings against him, or delaying the request for arrest warrants against Saif Gaddafi to allow states to negotiate with him. Other actors, including the Sudanese president Omar al-Bashir, indicted for genocide, crimes against humanity, and war crimes, had a personal interest in escaping from justice. He and his followers attacked the Court, abusing the history of Africa's colonial past. They replaced the narrative about crimes committed in Darfur with allegations that the Court was biased against Africa. In 2009, Muammar Gaddafi, president of the African Union, understood the importance of undermining the Court to continue committing crimes to stay in power, so at the Sirte summit, he personally imposed an African Union resolution calling on member states to refuse to cooperate with the International Criminal Court. Many journalists repeated these arguments without further analysis and increased these controversies. In this context, Minow's lab provided a space to reflect on our policies and understand these reactions.

The Harvard Lab and the Chapters of the Book

During the lab's lifetime, we presented our main policies and practices.[9] In addition to our September 2003 policy paper and the public documents on the "interests of justice," "victims," and "preliminary examination," we discussed several other aspects of the office, including gender crimes, public information, selection of cases and positive complementarity, protection of witnesses and persons at risk, and disclosure and investigative methods. All of them were debated during three years both in classrooms and during special workshops with different experts. Some of them are further discussed in this book.

The Rome Statute and Gender Crimes

Professor Catharine MacKinnon was the natural choice to discuss gender crimes during the lab. The Rome Statute defines persecution against a group on gender grounds as a crime against humanity and establishes specific obligations for the prosecutor's office to investigate gender crimes. MacKinnon pioneered the concept of sexual crimes being gendered and has been developing this idea in both her theoretical work and her law practice since the mid-1970s. She is a law professor at the University of Michigan and Harvard, and she was the first special gender adviser of the Office of the Prosecutor. She conducted training at the office, helped develop policies and prepare cases, and assisted us in the analysis of gender crimes committed in our cases. Through her participation in the lab, she further helped us refine and explain our approach to gender crimes. In this book, Jessica Lynn Corsi's chapter explores how the actions of the Office of the Prosecutor are influencing the instruction of state and nonstate actors' fighting forces in the prohibition of sexual violence in conflict.

In 2003, Stone helped the Office of the Prosecutor define its structure and produce a strategic plan, and he continued advising us on strategic issues until 2011. After being appointed Guggenheim Professor of the Practice of Criminal Justice at the Kennedy School of Government and chair of the Hauser Center for nonprofit organizations, he combined his unique knowledge of the prosecutor's office with his expertise on the dynamics of civil society organizations to present an analysis of the connection between the different parts of the Rome Statute network. During the lab, he presented his ideas on how NGOs and members of civil society could take advantage of the office's preliminary examination process to promote national justice efforts. He organized events to put his ideas into practice and invited NGOs from different countries—including Kenya, Afghanistan, Colombia, and Georgia, which were under preliminary examination at the time—to discuss and explore efforts to promote justice at the national level. Stone's chapter reflects that fundamental concept: the prevention and punishment of massive atrocities requires a collective effort involving the alignment of many actors.

The Investigative Role of the Prosecutor

For the past twenty years, I have been learning from Heymann about the role of prosecutor. He combines his valuable work as prosecutor and deputy U.S. attorney general with deep knowledge of organized transnational crime, including terrorism, and criminal law enforcement experiences in Guatemala, South Africa, and Argentina. During the lab, he commented on the differences between a national prosecutor with strong powers and many tools with which to investigate crimes and an international prosecutor who has to request assistance from states and international organizations for each investigative step, highlighting the difficulties of the International Criminal Court's investigations. Also on this issue, Whiting's chapter situates the investigative challenges faced by the prosecutor within the broader dynamics of the institution and its relationship to state power.

The Jurisdictional System of the Rome Statute

Langer, a professor at the University of California at Los Angeles who produced a critical analysis of the efficiency of the court proceedings at the ICTY and is becoming the global expert on universal jurisdiction, joined one of the seminars. There, he helped make clear the differences between universal jurisdiction and the International Criminal Court's jurisdiction accepted by those territorial states that ratified the treaty. In his chapter, he argues that the Court has more state-consent, political, procedural, rational, and functional legitimacy than statutes and proceedings based on universal jurisdiction.

The Rome Statute's jurisdiction is based on the free decision of sovereign states that ratified the treaty and does not reach the territory of those states that did not. According to Langer, this respect for the will of states provides a robust jurisdictional basis for the International Criminal Court but at the same time could create a public perception of double standards. More than sixty states—among them Israel, Iran, India, China, the United States, Sri Lanka, Iraq, Burma, Cuba, Nicaragua, and Zimbabwe—did not ratify the Rome Statute and are therefore beyond the jurisdiction of the Court unless the Security Council decides otherwise. To join or not join the ICC is a decision of sovereign states that requires political debate, in the same way that referring a situation to the Court is the exclusive prerogative of the Security Council, the highest international authority in terms of peace and security. Those are not issues that could be solved in the judicial arena.

The Role of Diplomats and Political Leaders

Urbina also provided his insights to the participants in the Harvard lab. He explained how the active role of Costa Rica as a nonpermanent member of the Security Council during negotiations on the Darfur conflict combined principles with self-interest. He said, "Costa Rica has no army, we rely on international law to defend our land and our people"; and he added, "ensuring respect for international law is a central part of our defense system, and of course strengthening international law in Darfur will increase our protection. We should not wait until we have a conflict in Costa Rica." Costa Rica, like many small countries, has a different national interest than big countries with powerful armies. Just like Botswana, the Netherlands, and other small nations with big principles, Costa Rica has the ability to influence the international community's decision-making process. In June 2008, Bruno Stagno Ugarte, the Costa Rican minister of foreign affairs, traveled to New York to be part of the Security Council meeting on the occasion of my briefing on the situation in Darfur. He was going to propose a presidential statement to support the Court's activities and demand the execution of the arrest warrants against Ahmed Harun and Ali Kushayb. During an informal bilateral meeting in preparation for the session, other ambassadors advised him not to do so; some even said it was a naive enterprise, while others called it a mission impossible. There was no consensus, no major power in the lead.

Costa Rica's leadership in making a formal request for a presidential statement provided incentives to the other eight members of the Security Council and state parties to the Rome Statute to support the motion. The United States also supported it. But the consensus required by a presidential statement still did not exist. Normally this would have been the end of the endeavor.

But Costa Rica insisted, firmly asserting that with ten votes it could request more than a statement: it could request a Security Council resolution, and any country that wanted to veto it was welcome to do so. In the end, on June 24, 2008, a presidential statement by the fifteen members of the Security Council was approved by consensus. Thus, Costa Rica, a country with no army, mobilized the entire Council and produced an unexpected outcome.

One of Williamson's contributions to the seminar was to show other aspects of the process by which decisions are made at the international community level. After the arrest warrant request against President al-Bashir, President Bush decided to ignore his reservations about the ICC and focus on the need to bring the perpetrators of the genocide in Darfur to justice. During the last six months of his term in office, Bush took a strong stand, announcing that he would veto any Security Council attempt to use article 16 of the Rome Statute to suspend the ICC investigations of President al-Bashir. Ambassador Williamson worked to win over other Security Council members such as France and the United Kingdom. He also worked with the joint African Union–U.N. chief mediator for Darfur, Dijbril Bassole, to promote negotiations to end the commission of crimes, bringing the Arab League and Qatari authorities into the effort. At a 2013 event on Darfur held in Washington, Ambassador Williamson expressed that he did not support the ICC's existence and that al-Bashir's indictment was inconvenient, but that the indictment allowed Williamson to reach an agreement with Sudan to deploy U.N.AMID peacekeepers and increase humanitarian assistance. Ambassador Williamson thus showed how the framework established by the Court's activities could create leverage. In the wake of his unexpected death in December 2013, the world will miss his wisdom.

The Shadow of the Court

Ambassador Williamson's and Ambassador Urbina's participation exposed the impact of the Rome Statute on the work of those involved in diplomatic activities. Following a concept developed by Mnookin in another context, Minow has suggested labeling those activities the "shadow" of the Court.[10] In 1978, Mnookin coauthored "Bargaining in the Shadow of the Law," which examined the impact of Court decisions on divorce cases. He argued that while family courts make rulings on specific cases brought before them, many other couples and lawyers later use those rulings to resolve their disputes and work out their own agreements. Accordingly, the majority of cases never reach the courts but instead are solved in the "shadow of the law." One court ruling on divorce affects a multiplicity of cases, and this phenomenon may well be considered as the most important impact of a family court, or any court. The "shadow" metaphor provided a clear image to express the role of our office and of the Court. A court isolated in the Hague could never end impunity around the world; its impact depends on the size of its "shadow"—that is, on the activities of diplomats such as Ambassadors Williamson and Urbina and of NGOs as presented by Stone. We at the office regularly evoked the concept of the shadow of the Court,[11] and U.N. secretary-general Ban Ki-moon later used this image during his May 2010 address to the Review Conference on the ICC: "The era of impunity is over. . . . Now we have the ICC, permanent, increasingly powerful, casting a long shadow."[12]

Peace and Justice: Defining the "Interests of Justice"

In 2007, the office presented its policy paper on the "interests of justice," affirming that peace and political considerations are the exclusive responsibility of the Security Council.[13] In his chapter, Professor Mnookin strongly disagrees with our interpretation of article 53 of the Rome Statute, which enumerates the reasons for which the prosecutor may determine that no reasonable basis exists to proceed with an investigation. He believes that by focusing only on the enforcement of law, our understanding of article 53 is too narrowly conceived. He proposes that the prosecutor should act as a diplomat representing the Court and must constantly assess the potential long-run political impact of her actions and concludes that the tension between peace and justice is real and cannot simply be wished away.

Professor Cora True-Frost disagrees with Mnookin when she considers that the central job of the prosecutor is to act as an international civil servant, exercising prosecutorial discretion to impart the lesson that there will be no impunity for massive crimes. She concludes that in this regard, the prosecutor must maintain independent discretion by applying the law while engaging the Council as an institutional—but not political—ally. Implicit in her view is the idea that states, not the prosecutor, will have to adjust over the long term; in light of this, she proposes some guidelines to be adopted by the office to help the members of the Security Council internalize the lesson that there will be no impunity for such grave crimes.

I think this is the most critical issue.[14] The Court is part of a new global trend that makes it no longer acceptable for leaders to commit massive atrocities to gain or retain power. This is the lesson learned after the Holocaust and the basis for the end of dictatorships in Latin America, the fall of the Berlin Wall, the request for changes in South Africa, and the Arab Spring. It is a challenge to the old dictators, but it also presents a challenge for those who manage conflict in international relations.

Consolidating this new trend requires answering the question of whether the Court should firmly hold to legal limits and force other actors to adjust to the law or take political factors into consideration when making decisions. This is a crucial debate about the controversial relation between the limits established by legal systems and the political actors' appetite for a lack of restrictions.

The Role of the Prosecutor as an International Actor

In his chapter, David Scheffer provides another insight into the complex decision-making process of diplomacy. He recognizes that during the United Nations talks about the Rome Statute, where he was head of the U.S. delegation, he and other senior U.S. government officials presented very negative assessments about the proposed *proprio motu* power of the prosecutor; however, he acknowledges that the original concerns about having a prosecutor who could open investigations for political reasons have dissipated. He notes that the Office of the Prosecutor has not taken into consideration political requests and has developed protocols that proved to be of far greater sophistication than the totally unregulated political decisions by either a state party or the Security Council.[15] He concludes—and I fully agree—that this is the merit of the Court's constitutional design.

So I wonder if we have managed to keep politics out of the decisions about which situations to investigate, should political questions be reintroduced to stop or advance specific cases by arguing a conflict exists between peace and justice?

End of Impunity for Leaders Who Commit Crimes against Humanity

Sovereignty as a legal principle providing immunity to those committing massive atrocities using state power was challenged after the First World War and ended at Nuremberg. There, during the first trial before the International Military Tribunal, the concept of "crimes against humanity" was developed in relation to aggression, affirming that no government has legal competence to commit such crimes. In the subsequent Nuremberg trials before the American Military Tribunals, the concept was further refined and included attacks by the Nazi regime against German citizens labeled as anarchists, Jews, or gypsies, establishing that national leaders have no immunity for attacking their own citizens. The chapter by Sadat, a professor at Washington University School of Law and director of its Crimes against Humanity Initiative, provides a comprehensive review of the recent evolution of the concept of crimes against humanity and its prominence in ICC cases.

The Courtroom Dynamic and the Legitimacy of the Court

O'Sullivan brings to this project her exceptional combination of experiences as prosecutor, private lawyer, law professor, and author of a seminal book on international criminal law. She also spent more than two months at the ICC to understand better the Court's dynamic. Through her participation in the lab and more thoroughly in her chapter, she presents an innovative and profound analysis of the main legal debates about the relation between the Office of the Prosecutor and the judges. She explores how the entire Court discussed the activities of the office and the appropriate scope of the Chambers' supervisory powers, highlighting the crucial role of the Appeals Chambers as dispassionate referees between the Office of the Prosecutor, the Pre-Trial Chamber, and the Trial Chamber. She concludes that these public contests may have created heated debates, but they have also strengthened the legitimacy of the prosecution function as well as the institution as a whole.

Judge Patricia M. Wald, former U.S. federal and ICTY judge, does not entirely share O'Sullivan's optimism, and her chapter summarizes many of the challenges in the relationship between the judges and the prosecutor. She reminds us that because the prosecutor is not part of any government, the office must establish priorities and the criminal philosophy of the prosecutor's administration. Judge Wald also notes that the prosecutor and the eighteen judges come from different legal cultures and traditions. Domestic judges generally trust prosecutors to follow familiar and established rules of the road, but the ICC's road wasn't laid out until the journey was already under way. Judge Wald mentions additional problems that increase the tensions between international judges and prosecutors: at international tribunals, witnesses have likely been interviewed by prosecutors only through translators and years before the trial. Furthermore, Judge Wald believes that the ban on witness proofing by the Pre-Trial and Trial Chambers can lead to recanting of testimony at trial, with attendant confusion and delay.

Institutional Analysis

Professor Jens Meierhenrich focuses on the crucial and underresearched topic of the institutional development of the Office of the Prosecutor. He focuses on (1) the establishment of the Jurisdiction, Complementarity, and Cooperation Division; (2) the introduction of joint teams; (3) the creation of the Executive Committee; and (4) the drafting of the confidential Operational Manual of the Office of the Prosecutor. He also highlights the complexity of the ICC as an evolving international organization comprised of numerous distinct yet interrelated bureaucracies. In his chapter, Meierhenrich opens the door for a fascinating further exploration of how a complex institution such as the ICC can interconnect with state party bureaucracies, human rights advocates, and the Security Council to create a global justice system.

Preventing Mass Violence through Education

Minow's chapter focuses on the importance of educational policies in preventing massive violence. She highlights that the ICC, as a creature of a treaty that creates a body of member states, could provide a focal point for a mass movement for conflict-prevention education because the Assembly of States Parties offers a potential venue for sharing information, devising and testing educational programs, and fostering competition among states to deliver better programs. In short, these states form a community with appointed representatives and have already signed on to the project of preventing genocide, crimes against humanity, war crimes, and the crime of aggression. The Assembly offers a ready-made forum for ongoing prevention efforts. She suggests that the prosecutor should organize an international conference to share information and learn about educational alternatives with either a simple program of information exchange or a more ambitious undertaking in which member nations would compete to demonstrate the most effective approaches. In her view, the prosecutor could mobilize educators and funders to create educational resources to be shared or provide a platform for educators in member states to exchange ideas about organizing the curricula and other matters. She proposes that the new prosecutor take up education as a means to advance the vision of preventing mass violence.

The ideas presented by Minow further pursue a current trend in the Office of the Prosecutor's work. In its Prosecutorial Strategy for 2009–12, the office identified education as one of the fundamental means of maximizing the Court's contribution to the prevention of future crimes.[16] On September 21, 2012, the new prosecutor, Fatou Bensouda, presented her ideas during a high-level strategic meeting organized in New York by Her

Highness Sheikha Moza bint Nasser, UNESCO envoy for basic and higher education and chair of Education above All. Prosecutor Bensouda focused on a "legal response to the protection of education during insecurity and armed conflict," saying, "We see in particular the importance of contributing, together with many other actors, including our 121 States Parties, to developing and strengthening global citizenship and promoting educational initiatives to include children in conflict-affected areas who are excluded from education, and improve peace and justice education for children whose education does not include these subjects."[17]

Final Considerations

Understanding the Rome Statute's justice system will require connecting different fields, in particular international relations, global security, and international and criminal law. The Harvard Lab opened a path in this direction, and this book follows that path. The next challenge is to maintain and deepen this cross-discipline dialogue so that we can keep learning from one another. In this sense, I conclude by quoting what Telford Taylor, one of the main Nuremberg prosecutors, told me in 1988 when we met at his office at Columbia University: "The main lesson I learned at Nuremberg was that the worst crimes were committed by ordinary people. Most of the Nazi officers were normal people, they loved their families, they were personally honest and they were very scrupulously recording their own crimes, denying the horrors they committed. The idea that they were evil and monsters provides comfort. Because if they are ordinary citizens it means that the horrors could be repeated."

How do ordinary citizens become massive killers? Minow's chapter provides an important clue to understanding the mechanism. She says, "War, atrocity, genocide, torture, rape—these may seem to be names of the problem, but in fact, they are manifestations of an underlying problem. That underlying problem is the easy availability of denigrating conceptions of 'other people' as an outlet for fear and insecurity and a resource for unscrupulous leaders to manipulate." I could not agree more.

In all my cases, I witnessed a common tactic to promote massive crimes. It is not about evil or monsters; it is about promoting solidarity against "other people." The first step requires convincing my community that it is under attack and that defending it requires killing the enemies, the "other people." When the solution of eliminating the enemies becomes a common narrative, it is then easy to implement it. Rwanda is one of the clearest examples, but it is not the only one. In Argentina, the enemies were the "capitalists" or the "communists"; in Darfur, they were "Fur," "Masalit," or "Zaghawa"; and for Muammar Gaddafi, the enemies were anyone opposed to his will.

The Rome Statute proposes the law as a global narrative to neutralize this mechanism. The law will define a way to protect citizens from all over the world; it is creating a global community living in a worldwide legal system enforced either by national states or by the International Criminal Court. Leaders will not be allowed to use massive atrocities to retain or to gain power; protecting their communities will not be accepted as an alibi for committing crimes. There will be no more enemies to kill, no more "other people." Those individuals who commit atrocious attacks against a community will be investigated and prosecuted.

NOTES

I thank my research assistant, Florencia Montal, and my former professional assistant at the Office of the Prosecutor, Joanna Frivet, for their contributions.

1. Memorandum from Christopher Stone to Participants in the Preparatory Meeting for the Sept. 2009 Consultative Conference on International Criminal Court (May 5, 2009) (on file with author) ("The aim of the conference was to further strengthen international criminal justice by taking seriously the conception of these institutions and networks as a "system of justice. Yet the networks on which this 'system' depends—networks among states, among NGOs, among international bodies—are unevenly developed and only tenuously connected to one another. If the system of international criminal justice is to continue to mature over the next decade, these networks, too, must be strengthened and aligned.").

2. Roscoe Pound, *Law in Books & Law in Action: Historical Causes of Divergence between the Nominal & Actual Law,* 36 AM. L. REV. 12 (1910), *quoted in* Mahnoush H. Arsanjani & W. Michael Reisman, *The Law-in-Action of the International Criminal Court,* 99 AM. J. INT'L L. 385 (2005).

3. On June 16–17, 2003, immediately after the swearing in ceremony for the prosecutor, the office organized a public hearing to listen to the different stakeholders, including states' representatives, NGOs, and academics, on strategic issues. In Sept. 2003, the Office of the Prosecutor published its main policies. In addition, the office established biannual meetings with NGOs and civil society and issued more specific policy papers on the interests of justice, on victims' participation, and on preliminary examinations. The office also presented a report on the first three years of its work (Three Year Report, June 2006), and the Prosecutorial Strategy for 2006–9 and 2009–12. (International Criminal Court, *Office of the Prosecutor: Policies & Strategies,* http://www.icc-cpi.int/en_menus/icc/structure%20of%20the%20court/office%20of%20the%20prosecutor/policies%20and%20strategies/Pages/documents.aspx. A confidential operational manual, defining in detail the activities of each member of the office, was issued in 2010.

4. International Criminal Court, *Statement Made by Mr. Luis Moreno Ocampo at the Ceremony for the Solemn Undertaking of the Chief Prosecutor of the ICC* (June 16, 2003), http://www.icc-cpi.int/nr/rdonlyres/d7572226-264a-4b6b-85e3-2673648b4896/ 143585/ 030616_moreno_ocampo_english.pdf (accessed Feb. 3, 2014):

> Our common mission is to ensure that the most serious crimes of concern to humanity are investigated and punished thus contributing to the protection of millions of individuals. . . .
>
> Please allow me to conclude with a reference to the victims. To protect them is the objective of our mission. We must learn the lesson. On my first visit to the Holocaust Museum in Washington, I received a copy of a passport of a young [P]olish boy. He had emigrated from Warsaw with his family, escaping the atrocities of the First World War. In the 1930's, all of them returned to their home and were exterminated during the Nazi occupation.
>
> In the junta trials in my own country, I met a woman whose parents were killed in the Nazi concentration camps. She wanted to have a peaceful life by emigrating to Argentina. Her sons were abducted and disappeared during the military dictatorship.
>
> The attack on the Twin Towers in Manhattan is just another tragic demonstration that the security offered by a State will not be sufficient to guarantee the life and freedom of their citizens if the international community is not based on the rule of law.
>
> The threat posed by the development of weapons of mass-destruction and the evolution of communication systems require, more than ever before, the urgent development of the institutions designed to prevent massive violence and hate. The International Criminal Court is one of the first new answers to these new threats.
>
> We must learn: there is no safe haven for life and freedom if we fail to protect the rights of any person in any country of the world.

5. *Id.:* "The Court is complementary to national systems. This means that whenever there is genuine State action, the Court cannot and will not intervene. But States not only have the right, but also the primary responsibility to prevent, control and prosecute atrocities. Complementarity protects national sovereignty and at the same time promotes state action. The effectiveness of the International Criminal Court should not be measured by the number of cases that reach it. On the contrary, complementarity implies that the absence of trials before this Court, as a consequence of the regular functioning of national institutions, would be a major success."

6. *Id.:*

> There are so many divergent interests in the world today that there is not even consensus about the basic goal of punishing genocide. An international criminal court totally independent and impartial brings hope, but at the same time raises reasonable fears and misunderstandings. . . .
>
> To face this challenge, the Office of the Prosecutor will undertake a participatory dialogue both in the policy-setting process and in the actual implementation of its policies. This process will start tomorrow with the first public hearing

of the Office to discuss the policies and regulations, and will continue through further meetings and informal consultations.

7. International Criminal Court, *Office of the Prosecutor Policy Paper* (Sept. 2003), http://www.icc-cpi.int/NR/rdonlyres/1FA7C4C6-DE5-42B7-8B25-60AA962ED8B6/143594/030905_Policy_Paper.pdf.

8. *Address to the Assembly of States Parties by Prosecutor of the International Criminal Court Mr. Luis Moreno Ocampo*, (Dec. 12, 2011), available at http://www.icc-cpi.int/iccdocs/asp_docs/ASP10/Statements/ASP10-ST-ProsecutorLMO-ENG.pdf. There were no national proceedings before the office triggered the jurisdiction of the Court in the territory of four state parties: Uganda, Democratic Republic of Congo, Central African Republic, and Kenya. There were none following the Security Council referrals in Darfur and Libya or the acceptance of jurisdiction by the Côte d'Ivoire. The respect for national efforts is also apparent from the preliminary examinations conducted in Colombia, Guinea, and Georgia as well as in the office's policy of inviting the territorial state to refer the situation before using *proprio motu* powers. All the cases presented were against the top leaders of the organizations involved in the commission of the crimes, including three heads of state.

9. All the members of the office worked in the preparation of the policies. Silvia Fernandez de Gurmendi led the preparation of the 2003 policy paper, supported by Gavin Hood and Darryl Robinson and Elizabeth Willmhurst as an external consultant. The policy on the interests of justice was extensively discussed internally by the same persons, with additional important contributions from Paul Seils, Fabricio Guariglia, and Rod Rastan, and externally during a seminar at Cape Town organized by Juan Mendez and Louis Bickford from the International Center for Transitional Justice. Beatrice Le Fraper du Hellen took the lead in the preparation of the policy papers on victims' participation and preliminary examinations supported by the entire office. A draft was discussed extensively in meetings with states and NGOs at the Hague and New York. Deputy prosecutor Fatou Bensouda and Beatrice Le Fraper du Hellen, Michel De Smedt, and Sara Criscitelli as members of the executive committed led the adoption of the operational manual. It reflects the practices of the entire office and was assembled under the direction of the Shamila Batohi and Hans Bevers of the Legal Advisory Section with input from all the staff. Yayoi Yamaguchi as member of the Legal Advisory Section supported the first course in Jan. 2010. Olivia Swaak-Goldman, head of the International Relations Task Force, co-taught the course in Jan. 2012.

10. Robert H. Mnookin & Lewis Kornhauser, *Bargaining in the Shadow of the Law: The Case of Divorce*, 88 YALE L. J. 950 (1978).

11. *See* International Criminal Court, *Prosecutor's Address at the Council of Foreign Relations* (Feb. 4, 2010), http://www.icc-cpi.int/NR/rdonlyres/A80CDDDD-8A9A-432E-97CE-F6EAD700B5AE/281527/100204ProsecutorsspeechforCFR.pdf.

12. Ban Ki-moon, U.N. Secretary-General, *Address to the Review Conference on the International Criminal Court: An Age of Accountability, Kampala, Uganda* (May 31, 2010), http://www.un.org/sg/selected-speeches/statement_full.asp?statID=829 ("The old era of impunity is over. In its place, slowly but surely, we are witnessing the birth of a new Age of Accountability. It began, many decades ago, with Nuremberg and the Tokyo Tribunals. It gained strength with the international criminal tribunals for Rwanda and the former Yugoslavia, as well as the so-called "hybrid" tribunals in Sierra Leone,

Cambodia and Lebanon. Now we have the ICC, permanent, increasingly powerful, casting a long shadow.").

13. International Criminal Court, *Office of the Prosecutor: Interests of Justice Policy Paper,* at 4 (Sept. 2007), http://www.icc-cpi.int/NR/rdonlyres/772C95C9-F54D-4321-BF09-73422BB23528/143640/ICCOTPInterestsOfJustice.pdf.

14. The issue was further discussed during an international conference organized by Mnookin, Confronting Evil: Interdisciplinary Perspectives, Harvard University, Mahindra Humanities Center, Cambridge, Mass. (Apr. 19–20, 2013).

15. International Criminal Court, *Office of the Prosecutor: Draft Policy Paper on Preliminary Examinations* (Nov. 2013), http://www.icc-cpi.int/en_menus/icc/press%20and%20media/press%20releases/Documents/OTP%20Preliminary%20Examinations/OTP%20-%20Policy%20Paper%20Preliminary%20Examinations%20%202013.pdf; International Criminal Court, *Office of the Prosecutor: The Interests of Justice 1* (Sept. 2007), http://www.icc-cpi.int/NR/rdonlyres/772C95C9-F54D-4321-BF09-73422BB23528/143640/ICCOTPInterestsOfJustice.pdf.

16. International Criminal Court, *Office of the Prosecutor: Prosecutorial Strategy 2009–2012* (Feb. 1, 2010), http://www.icc-cpi.int/NR/rdonlyres/66A8DCDC-3650-4514-AA62-D229D1128F65/281506/OTPProsecutorialStrategy20092013.pdf.

17. Fatou Bensouda, International Criminal Court Prosecutor, *Talking Points* (on file with author). She also announced that with the U.N.-mandated University for Peace Center at the Hague, the office would organize a one-day strategic meeting on Oct. 18, 2012, in the Hague on "Sharing Educational Experiences to Promote and Increase Education for Peace and Justice." The meeting allowed interested organizations to exchange strategies, best practices, and content proposals, which would then be compiled and shared with the ministries of education of the 121 states parties to the Rome Statute for their consideration and possible inclusion in their national curricula systems. *See* International Criminal Court, *Press Release: Education to Build a Culture of Peace & Justice: Key Stakeholders Convene for ICC/OTP-UPEACE Co-Hosted Exchange* (Oct. 10, 2012), http://www.icc-cpi.int/en_menus/icc/press%20and%20media/press%20releases/Pages/pr842.aspx.

The Prosecutor Casts a Shadow

Convenor, Collaborator, and Law Enforcer

Martha Minow, C. Cora True-Frost, and Alex Whiting

> "Constraint offers an unparalleled opportunity for growth and innovation."
>
> —Scott Dadich, in *Wired*[1]

Holding individuals legally responsible for war, war crimes, crimes against humanity, and genocide remains a relatively new idea, and a permanent international commitment to pursue the idea started only as this new century began. Crucial to the scope and operations of the International Criminal Court (ICC or Court) is the role of the prosecutor. The creation of an independent prosecutor was the most controversial issue in the negotiations behind the Court, and decisions of the prosecutor from the start have been the target of considerable critique and criticism. This book provides the first sustained assessment of the initial decade of the first permanent Office of the Prosecutor (OTP). Having a prosecutor with international scope raises a host of issues in both international law and international affairs. This book analyzes the legal, practical, and institutional challenges faced by the first prosecutor, Luis Moreno Ocampo. In the process of examining the foundation laid by Moreno Ocampo, the book explores how the OTP has become a dynamic force in building international criminal justice norms.

Focusing on this new office after its first occupant has finished his tour of duty and as the second prosecutor makes her own mark on the Court offers timely and enduring opportunities for reflection and growth in supranational international criminal law. In April 2003, the states parties to the Rome Statute[2] elected Moreno Ocampo to serve a nine-year term as

HARVARD LAW SCHOOL
J.D. Admissions

Dear Linda,

I thought that you'd enjoy having a copy of this book to start off your legal library.

Enjoy!

Jessica Soban
Associate Dean for Strategic Initiatives
and Admissions

the first prosecutor at the ICC. Renowned for his experiences as a prosecutor in the trials of the juntas in Argentina, Moreno Ocampo also participated in many corruption prosecutions and in a notable case against army commanders accused of malpractice during the Malvinas/Falklands War, served as private inspector general for large companies, and represented the victims in the extradition of a former Nazi officer for trial. He developed expertise in media and brought resolution of private disputes to public attention through television. He drew on all of these experiences in his work as the first prosecutor of the International Criminal Court.

Setting up the OTP required establishing policies and practices regarding when and how to investigate international crimes, when and on what grounds to initiate prosecutions, how to undertake cooperation with domestic nations to secure evidence and indictees, and how to relate to and interact with the United Nations Security Council, states parties, nongovernmental organizations (NGOs), victims, the accused, and the media. The prosecutor had to craft a coherent practice out of multiple and diverse legal systems as well as negotiate for the Court a place in the global context, all in the course of his quest to prosecute grave crimes. The chapters in this book explore many of the choices Moreno Ocampo made during his tenure and examine issues ripe for future consideration.

As the Court enters a new era with its second prosecutor, it is particularly important to look back to examine the prosecutor's proactive role in pursuing collaboration with and mobilizing the support of member states, international organizations, and NGOs to strengthen the future of the international justice project. One persistent theme in these chapters arises from a distinctive feature of the ICC itself. Although the OTP enjoys considerable independence and discretion, it is also highly constrained: the Court and thus the OTP depend on the actions and inactions of the states in which perpetrators and evidence lie. Vital to the success of the Court is the assistance of nations, including some, like the United States, that are not parties—for example, to develop investigations and secure witnesses—and the collaboration of other institutions, including the United Nations, NGOs, academic institutions, and media organizations. These constraints influenced many of the prosecutor's most-criticized choices even as they required the prosecutor to be concerned with strengthening states' perceptions of the Court.

Constrained and lacking authority to make arrests or order production of documents or witnesses, the OTP nonetheless has markedly broader geographical and temporal authority than its predecessors possessed. The Rome Statute creates a role for the prosecutor as catalyst and negotiator, authorized and expected to build commitment to the norms and practices of international criminal justice. The prosecutors of the ad hoc tribunals appointed by the United Nations Security Council[3] and the prosecutors of the hybrid tribunals appointed by varying combinations of authority of the United Nations and the host country[4] have had limited mandates to investigate and prosecute persons responsible for serious violations of international humanitarian law committed within defined time periods and past conflicts. By contrast, the OTP has the authority under article 13 to initiate prosecutions in situations within an essentially global jurisdiction concerning events occurring after July 2002.[5]

At the same time, the prosecutor's power is limited both by the many tasks the OTP faces as well as the tools it possesses to achieve its goals. The prosecutor's dependence on the cooperation of states parties (as well as non–states parties) to investigate and to enforce the Court's decisions has often meant that investigations are nearly impossible and enforcement is not forthcoming. A notorious example is the still-outstanding warrant for the arrest of Omar al-Bashir, and the failure of many member states to enforce the arrest warrant, as well as states parties' invitations to al-Bashir to visit, in violation of their obligations under international law. Moreover, the prosecutor has sometimes struggled to gather sufficient evidence to support cases in the various situations under investigation. These constraints inform this book, as the contributors acknowledge and confront the consequences of these restrictions for the prosecutor's work.

This book asks whether the limitations of the prosecutor's powers also suggest strengths—as the limitations necessarily require cooperation with a wide array of other actors and institutions, affording surprising opportunities for building coalitions and advancing international criminal law norms. This question owes much to the extensive literature and debate regarding the power of soft law, but the unique situation faced by the prosecutor is the coupling of the hard law in the Rome Statute with the soft power of the prosecutor and the Court to build support for its determinations, sometimes forcing the prosecutor to play the role of activist or judicial entrepreneur. The need to build support has been amply criticized. But perhaps in requiring the prosecutor and the Court more broadly to encourage member states and other actors to support the Court's determinations, the statute requires innovation and at times strengthens the hand and work of the prosecutor. The relatively small OTP must enlist the support and resources of national entities, both governmental and nongovernmental, to survive. If the prosecutor's mission is adopted by other entities, the result may well enhance the prosecutor's work and serve as "force multipliers" for the Court. In other words, by requiring collaboration and cooperation among member states, the Rome Statute both limits the powers of the prosecutor and forces authorities beyond the prosecution office to become engaged in the international criminal justice project.

In this way, the Rome Statute opens the door for norm advocates to promote enforcement of international criminal law norms by articulating the legal standards, even as it does not couple these standards with resources that enable the prosecutor and the Court to enforce them. The limitations on the prosecutor's power and resources underscore the significance of each instance when the Court secures the collaboration it requires. Perhaps paradoxically, a more powerful OTP—one with authority for unilateral, top-down determinations and enforcement—would face far greater criticism and resistance than is evident in current critiques of the OTP's selectivity of situations and cases. Some contributors to this book explore, then, whether the vulnerability of the prosecutor and the Court itself may strengthen the legitimacy and impact of its actions over the long term, though Alex Whiting rightly notes that evidence indicates that the states have failed to be motivated to support the prosecutor's aggressive pursuit of accountability.

The essays collected in this book reflect a special mix of theorists' and practitioners' perspectives, offering a detailed examination of both the promise and constraints presented and faced by the OTP. The result is a window into international justice and new opportunities to advance knowledge and practice, allowing deep study of the ICC's most dynamic organ, the OTP. In returning to the theme of the power of vulnerability and the necessity of coalition building it requires, the authors explore enduring questions about the proper relationships between law and politics as well as arguments reflecting competing views about the structures and processes of the Court and the prosecutor. We hope that the resulting analysis will serve as a valuable tool not only for understanding the significance of an independent international prosecutor for the future of international justice but also for lending insight at the comparative level, as the OTP's features are explored in relation to many of the member states' systems.

The book is divided into three parts: "Foundations for Prosecuting," "The Prosecutor's Interactions with Other International Actors," and "The Impacts of the Prosecutor's Work." The book opens with a preface written by Moreno Ocampo in which he describes his work and how he came to understand how the OTP could maximize its impact in the world by establishing new rules to which actors would have to adjust, including through developing prosecutorial policies that would form a framework for future practice.

Part 1 examines the foundations for the OTP's supranational prosecutions: the legal constraints on the prosecutor, the internal policies established by the prosecutor, and the institutional structure within which the prosecutor must operate. In this section, David Scheffer, who served as the U.S. ambassador at large for war crimes between 1997 and 2001, argues that Moreno Ocampo's prosecutorial strategy has demonstrated to the international community—in particular, opponents of the Rome Statute provisions making the prosecutor independent—that the alarm about *proprio motu* (independently initiated)[6] investigations and prosecutions was misplaced. Next, Professor Leila Nadya Sadat analyzes the ways in which the expanded subject matter jurisdiction of crimes against humanity can and should offer opportunities for the prosecutor to reach different types of crimes. Professor Robert H. Mnookin critiques the prosecutor's decision to interpret the authority in article 53 to decline prosecution if it would "not serve the interests of justice" as completely excluding considerations of peace and reconciliation. Instead, Mnookin argues, the prosecutor should take advantage of his discretion to determine the timing of prosecutions as well as the complementarity provisions of the statute to allow him to consider both justice and peace imperatives. Jens Meierhenrich in turn argues that the winding road of institutional development in the OTP has given rise to virtuous as well as pathological dynamics in the investigation and prosecution of international crimes. In the final chapter in part 1, Alex Whiting argues that the prosecutor, dependent on state cooperation for investigations, has tried to build a functioning court and motivate support for the OTP's work by bringing cases forward, but the states have not always followed his lead.

Part 2 scrutinizes many of the vital relationships between the prosecutor and other international actors in international law and diplomacy. Professor Julie Rose O'Sullivan analyzes Moreno Ocampo's approach toward the balance of power between his office and the judges of the ICC, arguing that his respectful and careful stance has helped to enhance the independent role of the judges and reputation of the Court as a whole. Judge Patricia Wald, former chief judge of the Court of Appeals for the District of Columbia Circuit and former judge of the International Criminal Tribunal of Yugoslavia, then engages Professor O'Sullivan's argument about the relationship between the prosecutor and the ICC judges, offering guidelines for future success in this and other areas. Next, Professor Máximo Langer addresses the question of how the prosecutor's mandate relates to domestic actors' attempts to prosecute under universal jurisdiction theories. He argues that the ICC prosecutor has more legitimacy than domestic prosecutors might have in asserting universal jurisdiction as a basis for proceeding against a defendant, but he also contends that universal jurisdiction continues to serve an important gap-filling function because of the ICC's limited resources. Part 2 closes with Professor C. Cora True-Frost's examination of the evolving relationship between the U.N. Security Council and the prosecutor, and argues that the prosecutor framed his role as that of an impartial international civil servant, compelled to apply the law and disregard politics. By protecting his independence while treating the Council as an institutional ally, he helped facilitate increased engagement between the Council and the ICC.

The final part of the book examines the impacts the prosecutor's actions have already had and suggests ways in which the second prosecutor might increase the OTP's future reach. Professor Christopher Stone, president of the Open Society Foundation, describes how the prosecutor has used preliminary examinations to advance a policy of "positive complementarity," an innovative approach to the Rome Statute that seeks actively to promote accountability for international crimes at the domestic level. Preliminary examinations, which the prosecutor can commence and end, have the potential to motivate both domestic state actors and civil society. Stone explores the different strategies that the prosecutor can use during preliminary examinations to promote national activity and the ways in which local NGOs can be empowered by the ICC's attention. Jessica Lynn Corsi then examines the effects of ICC prosecutions on the conduct of rebel leaders in the Central African Republic with a particular focus on preventing sexual violence—an area of priority for the first prosecutor and pursued in addition by his successors.[7] Finally, Dean Martha Minow advances the idea that in addition to investigations and prosecutions of perpetrators, education can offer more effective tools than prosecutions in achieving the Court's objective of prevention. In this light, Minow argues that the prosecutor should spearhead the development of education initiatives within the Assembly of States Parties, focusing in particular on young people and profiting from recent learning in the field of education that could be shared among the states and implemented as part of national strategies to prevent mass atrocities.

The chapters combine to form a critical inquiry into both the promise offered and constraints faced by the OTP. Perhaps the constraints on this new prosecutor in this new Court afford genuine chances for building and extending human rights.

NOTES

1. Dadich, *Design under Constraint: How Limits Boost Creativity,* WIRED (Feb. 23, 2009), wired.com/cultural/design/magazine/17-03/dp_intro.

2. Rome Statute of the International Criminal Court, Adopted by the United Nations Diplomatic Conference of Plenipotentiaries on the Establishment of an International Criminal Court, July 17, 1998, U.N. Doc. A/CONF. 183/9 (hereinafter Rome Statute).

3. *See* U.N. S.C. Res. 955, U.N. Doc. S/RES/955 (Nov. 8, 1994); U.N. S.C. Res. 827, U.N. Doc. S/RES 827 (May 25, 1993).

4. *See* Statute of the Special Court for Sierra Leone, Annexed to the Agreement between the United Nations and the Government of Sierra Leone on the Establishment of a Special Court for Sierra Leone of 16 January 2002, www.sc-sl.org; EAST-WEST CENTER, THE SERIOUS CRIMES TRIALS IN EAST TIMOR: AN OVERVIEW 8 (2005).

5. *See* Rome Statute, art. 13.

6. Rome Statute, arts. 13(c), 15, 53(1).

7. In June 2014, Fatou Bensouda, the second ICC prosecutor, released the *Policy Paper on Sexual and Gender-Based Crimes,* the first document of its kind publicly produced for an international court or tribunal. See http://www.icc-cpi.int/iccdocs/otp/OTP-Policy-Paper-on-Sexual-and-Gender-Based-Crimes--June-2014.pdf.

Foundations for Prosecuting

False Alarm about the *Proprio Motu* Prosecutor

David Scheffer

The role of the *proprio motu* (independent) prosecutor at the International Criminal Court (ICC or the Court) is a study in both liberty and constraints. The liberty flows from the power to "initiate investigations *proprio motu* on the basis of information on crimes within the jurisdiction of the Court."[1] The constraints come in different forms. Perhaps foremost, they arise from the requirement of the Pre-Trial Chamber to authorize the commencement of any such *proprio motu* investigation.[2] Additionally, nonstatutory constraints arise in the form of political and financial considerations that may affect how a prosecutor perceives investigatory opportunities. Finally, the internal guidelines established for the preliminary examinations that the prosecutor undertakes to initiate investigations *proprio motu* (also used to consider referrals of situations by states parties or the U.N. Security Council) have standards of evidence and judgment built into the decision-making processes that will determine the prosecutor's willingness to approach the Pre-Trial Chamber for authorization to officially commence an investigation.

Following more than a decade of practice by the ICC, the concept of the *proprio motu* prosecutor has achieved normality and acceptability, belying the prognostications preceding the conclusion of the Rome Statute in July 1998. As the head of the U.S. delegation to the United Nations talks finalizing the Rome Statute and many of its key supplemental documents, I, along with other senior U.S. government officials, delivered many such negative assessments about the proposed *proprio motu* prosecutor. Having lost that battle in Rome, the United States signed the Rome Statute on December 31, 2000. We bore witness to the activation of the Court on July 1, 2002, following the deposit of more than sixty ratifying instruments, and then to more than ten years of the Court's operations. During that time, Luis Moreno Ocampo, the Court's first prosecutor, undertook his *proprio motu* responsibilities with sufficient discretion and procedural integrity to deflate a great deal of the concern that had occupied so much diplomatic and governmental deliberations in connection with the Rome Statute.

It is fitting for a book about the first global prosecutor to return briefly to the Clinton administration's arguments during final negotiations for the Rome Statute, which called into question the proposed independent role of the prosecutor in triggering investigations before the ICC. The fact that so many of those arguments were not validated during the first ten years of the Court's operations should demonstrate the merit of the constitutional design of the Court and now encourage proponents of U.S. ratification of the Rome Statute, for this was a pillar of Washington's criticism of certain aspects of the treaty in 1998.

The U.S. position was set forth in the official June 22, 1998, "Statement of the United States Delegation Expressing Concerns Regarding the Proposal for a *Proprio Motu* Prosecutor: The Concerns of the United States Regarding the Proposal for a *Proprio Motu* Prosecutor" ("U.S. delegation statement").[3] Many of the points expressed therein had been articulated in diplomatic meetings and public settings for months prior to the Rome Conference. For example, U.S. opposition to a *proprio motu* prosecutor was included among other priority issues for the country's delegation in Rome. These issues also included the retention of both the Security Council's referral power and its oversight role of state party referrals, the need for nonparty states to consent to the ICC's jurisdiction except where the Security Council had referred the situation to the Court, an acceptable definition and jurisdictional filter for the crime of aggression, the right to make reservations to the treaty, sufficient access to funding, and the professional qualifications for the selection of judges.

Significantly, however, by early June 1998 we had decided within the Clinton administration to highlight our objection to the *proprio motu* prosecutor at the beginning of the Rome Conference. We believed that we had a strong legal and political case on this issue and that it would resonate more broadly with governments than would our much-criticized position supporting the Security Council's referral power and its oversight of state party referrals. Unlike Washington's advocacy of Security Council dominance of the referral power, which attracted few allies, a larger number of governments were skeptical of the *proprio motu* prosecutor proposal.

Bill Richardson, the U.S. permanent representative to the United Nations, was the top U.S. diplomat to address the opening session of the U.N. Plenipotentiaries Conference on the Establishment of an International Criminal Court in Rome on June 17, 1998. Central to U.S. strategy was Ambassador Richardson's opening salvo condemning the *proprio motu* prosecutor proposal. He devoted three paragraphs to criticizing the proposal, which exceeded the space devoted to any other concern about the Court:

> With the best intentions of international justice in mind, some have proposed granting a prosecutor the right to initiate investigations and seek indictments against anyone in any place. Although we respect the views of those who advocate this proposal, we believe that it is unrealistic and unwise. It will overload the limits of the Court's design, leading to greater confusion and controversy. It will, in fact, weaken rather than strengthen the Court. This Court cannot and should not address every crime that goes unpunished, no matter how horrific or atrocious it may be.
>
> To be sure, the United States regards all violations of human rights and international humanitarian law as reprehensible. But we must not turn an International Criminal Court or its prosecutor into a human rights ombudsman open to, and responsible for responding to, any and all complaints from any source. If we do, the Court will be flooded with every imaginable complaint, hindering its investigation into the most serious crimes and undermining its scope and relevance. The only way the office of the prosecutor could manage such an onrush would be by making decisions that inevitably will be regarded as political.
>
> At best, the proposal for a self-initiating prosecutor is premature. We should first give the Court the opportunity to establish its credibility. If we move too quickly, we may create a Court that will appear sound on paper but collapse under the weight of its own mandate. At the same time, however, we support giving maximum independence and discretion to the prosecutor in his or her proper sphere. When a State Party to the treaty or the Security Council refers a situation to the jurisdiction of the Court, the prosecutor should be free to investigate the situation within the context of the overall referral. This would ensure that the prosecutor has the necessary backing to get the job done and the necessary independence to do it.[4]

This, then, was the core U.S. position that drove our public and private discussions for several weeks thereafter. Ultimately, however, the argument failed to attract significant support at the Rome Conference, a reality discussed later in this chapter.

On June 22, 1998, several days after Ambassador Richardson's plenary address, the U.S. delegation issued its statement on the *proprio motu* prosecutor.[5] The early authors of the statement were Department of Justice prosecutors, who also served on my delegation. As a result, the statement reflected their skepticism of an independent prosecutor who could initiate investigations of situations without any check or oversight by either the U.N. Security Council (other than through what became article 16 of the Rome Statute) or states parties of the Court. In part, this skepticism was a product of political realities unfolding in the United States at the end of the 1990s. An independent prosecutor, Kenneth W. Starr, was aggressively investigating President Bill Clinton in 1998 over the Whitewater matter and the Monica Lewinsky affair.[6] The Clinton administration thus had very little enthusiasm for even the concept of independent prosecutors, whom Washington had come to see as highly politicized vultures. The notion that the administration would warmly embrace a permanent independent prosecutor for the ICC during such a tumultuous year at home was fanciful, to say the least. Conversely, domestic events in Washington should not be viewed as the sole cause of opposition to the *proprio motu* prosecutor.

The U.S. delegation's statement amplified the concerns set forth in Ambassador Richardson's address. A review of its primary points, juxtaposed with events involving the Office of the Prosecutor (OTP) during the Court's first decade, should demonstrate that the U.S. delegation at the time exaggerated, albeit it in good faith, the consequences of a *proprio motu* prosecutor at the ICC.

The initial point, which was not directly relevant to the proposal for a *proprio motu* prosecutor, was noncontroversial and had been universally accepted by the time of the Rome Conference: "No one, not the Security Council, not States, not any entity nor individual, should be able to control the direction of the Prosecutor's investigation by referring a particular case against a particular person. That is why the United States has and will continue to press for the formula that referrals from States and the Security Council must be referrals of overall situations. It must lie with the Prosecutor to determine whether a crime has been committed and by whom; the referral mechanism cannot purport to limit the Prosecutor's decisions on such matters."[7]

This position—prosecutorial discretion and independence once a situation has been referred to the Court by either a state party or the Security Council—was a pillar of Moreno Ocampo's discretionary power throughout the first decade of the Court's existence. His use of that discretionary power under such referrals was seriously challenged only twice: first, when he indicted Sudanese president Omar al-Bashir for atrocity crimes, including genocide, in Darfur,[8] and second, when he indicted Libyan leader Muammar Gaddafi only a few months after the Security Council referred the Libyan situation to the Court.[9] President al-Bashir's indictment triggered fierce opposition from the African Union and Arab League.[10] But the prosecutor withstood those challenges thanks in large measure to the unwillingness of the United States, France, and the United Kingdom, as permanent members of the Security Council, to accede to the African Union's request that the Council adopt a chapter VII enforcement resolution to suspend the indictment for at least one year pursuant to article 16 of the Rome Statute. The second challenge came in response to Moreno Ocampo's relatively speedy indictment of Gaddafi, which stood in contrast to the seemingly more deliberate pace taken by investigators for the U.N. Human Rights Council.[11] Both indictments attracted criticism as supposed examples of double standards and "selective justice" aimed at Africa.[12]

Even where Moreno Ocampo made contentious decisions, perhaps best exemplified in his targeting of al-Bashir (at all) and Gaddafi (so early), most states parties as well as the United States (as a nonparty state and permanent member of the Security Council facilitating the Court's jurisdictional reach into Sudan and Libya), stood by him in the exercise of this discretionary power to select targets of investigation and seek indictments in individual cases. There will always be scholarly and political scrutiny of how the prosecutor actually exercises such discretion case by case, but in 1998, at least, there was no debate over the necessity for independence and discretion in the context of a referral by the Security Council or a state party.

The objections to a *proprio motu* prosecutor in the U.S. delegation statement centered on several primary grounds, all of which have been largely debunked during the first decade of the Court's operations. First, the United States stressed a threshold requirement (often understood as magnitude or gravity of crimes) for the work of the Court. The Rome Statute's preamble mandates that the Court "exercise jurisdiction only over the most serious crimes of concern to the international community as a whole."[13] The U.S. delegation statement continued,

It is essential that there be some screen to distinguish between crimes which do rise to the level of concern to the international community and those which do not. The only rational and workable proposal to date—even if it may fall short of the perfect—is to look to States, and in appropriate cases the Security Council, to speak for what is "of concern to the international community as a whole." For the United States, it is inappropriate and ultimately unworkable to suggest that this role is better vested in a single individual, the ICC Prosecutor.[14]

As it turned out, Moreno Ocampo developed protocols to guide how the gravity or magnitude of a crime should impact the threshold question of whether to investigate. These protocols proved to be far more sophisticated than the totally unregulated political decisions by either a state party or the Security Council.[15] With respect to state party referrals, there was no gravity or threshold test demonstrated publicly by Uganda, the Democratic Republic of the Congo, the Central African Republic, or Mali in their self-referrals to the Court. The Security Council did rely on the Commission of Inquiry report on Darfur, which addressed magnitude issues,[16] before referring Darfur to the Court in February 2005,[17] but the Council did not impose any particular test on itself in reviewing that report. In the end, its decision was politically grounded and depended on a contentious American abstention (thus avoiding a veto), which had little to do with gravity issues and everything to do with raw political calculations by the George W. Bush administration at the time and the political pressure it was encountering both at home and abroad.[18]

The Security Council's referral of the Libyan situation to the Court in February 2011 was based not on a high threshold of atrocity crimes having been scaled but rather on a relatively small number of attacks by the Libyan military on civilians and the credible prospect that many more would be launched against the civilian population of Benghazi.[19] One doubts that the prosecutor, using his *proprio motu* power, could have initiated a formal investigation of Libya if it were a state party, with the approval of the Pre-Trial Chamber at that particular moment in the emerging civil war. He doubtless would have had to wait until many weeks if not months later to make an airtight case to the judges based on his own internal guidelines.

In contrast, the prosecutor relied on internal guidelines relating to gravity of criminal conduct to persuade the Pre-Trial Chamber to authorize his *proprio motu* investigations in the Kenya and Côte d'Ivoire situations, and the judges looked to the prosecutor to persuade them on that point. Rigorous legal standards were applied, or at least there is a strong argument that they played an important role in the process.[20]

The gravity requirement is central to *proprio motu* preliminary examinations undertaken by the OTP, which are exercises based on information delivered to the OTP and not on state party or Security Council referrals.[21] Indeed, some may criticize the OTP for applying too rigorous a standard of gravity when preliminarily examining these situations. When the prosecutor declined to investigate British military operations in Iraq, he relied in his report, inter alia, on a finding that the requisite gravity required by the Rome Statute had not been established.[22] The same guiding principles were applied to his refusal to initiate an investigation of alleged atrocity crimes in Venezuela.[23]

No one would seriously question whether the threshold requirement was met in each of the state party referrals to the Court, but they were not subjected to any rigorous legal standards as part of the initial referral. As part of the preliminary discussions between the prosecutor and the relevant state party prior to the self-referral, Moreno Ocampo may have offered advice about the requirements expected under the Rome Statute. Legal criteria on gravity would have been applied at later stages, during the preparation of indictments and in decisions and judgments by the Court in connection with cases arising from each self-referred situation.

Thus, a conclusion contrary to that speculated by the U.S. delegation can be drawn following the experience of the OTP and the Court during the first operational decade. Paradoxically, the prosecutor applied rigorous legal standards for the gravity test while undertaking his *proprio motu* responsibilities, whereas state party and Security Council referrals demonstrated uneven attention to legal standards. Nonetheless, Moreno Ocampo reviewed situations referred by the Security Council and states parties to determine whether prosecutions should be brought. Thus, legal standards were applied by the prosecutor following the actual referral.

In fact, these referrals were largely guided by political factors, including negotiated decisions leading either to Council resolutions or state party self-referrals. Luckily, the referrals pertained to atrocity crimes that fairly obviously met the magnitude requirements of the Rome Statute for adjudication of atrocity crimes. But the screen called for by the U.S. delegation to distinguish "between crimes which do rise to the level of concern to the international community and those which do not" was created and applied rigorously by the prosecutor in the performance of his *proprio motu* responsibilities. The process, guided by the prosecutor, has become a very workable and rational methodology, contrary to U.S. concerns expressed in June 1998.

The second issue addressed in the U.S. delegation statement concerned the political will of states: "We reject as entirely cynical the notion that the community of States is so lacking in moral and political courage that when faced with an atrocity meriting the attention of the Court, not one State will respond. Indeed, quite the opposite has been demonstrated by the United States and other States which have worked hard to establish and support the work of the *ad hoc* tribunals, and which are in Rome to facilitate future prosecutions through the establishment of a permanent court."[24] In an unexpected way, this view proved somewhat true during the Court's first decade. Four state parties (Uganda, the Democratic Republic of the Congo, the Central African Republic, and Mali) self-referred their situations to the International Criminal Court.[25] The self-referrals were not necessarily acts of altruism or devotion to the principles of international criminal law, for they likely reflected political calculations to isolate opposition militia through the medium of international criminal prosecutions.[26]

In contrast, as of mid-2013, only one state party has referred a situation to the Court that concerns a nonparty state. In May 2013, the Union of the Comoros referred the Israel Defense Forces for their 2010 attack on a Comoros-registered vessel that was in international waters on its way to supplying humanitarian assistance to the residents of Gaza.[27] That referral has remained under preliminary examination by the OTP. As of mid-2014, no other state party has referred another state party to the Court. This is particularly surprising given that the state party–to–state party referral was one of the most anticipated referral mechanisms during the negotiations leading to the Rome Statute. The expectation that a state party would refer its fellow members also underpinned the U.S. delegation's contention. Although, in hindsight, U.S. negotiators would not have dismissed the possibility of a state party self-referral, the entire argument was premised on the presumed political will of at least one state party referring to the Court an atrocity crimes situation occurring in another state party or on the major powers agreeing within the Security Council to refer the situation to the Court under U.N. Charter chapter VII authority. The latter occurred twice—Darfur and Libya—by mid-2012 and thus bore some truth. But no state party stepped forward to refer alleged atrocity crimes situations in Afghanistan, Honduras, South Korea, Iraq, Nigeria, Colombia, Georgia, Guinea, or Venezuela—all of which have been at some point under preliminary examination by the prosecutor exercising the *proprio moto* authority but any one of which could be easily referred by a state party and perhaps accelerate serious consideration at the Court.

Given the geopolitical divisions among the Security Council's permanent members concerning the situation in Syria, it is not terribly surprising that they and their nonpermanent colleagues failed between early 2011 and at least mid-2014 to refer Syria to the Court for investigation and prosecution.[28] While this inaction may yet be remedied, the refusal or inability to refer the atrocities under way in Syria, a nonparty state, reflect a signal failure by the Security Council on the scales of justice regardless of the political factors at play. Similar Council inaction following the violent uprisings in Yemen and Bahrain during 2011 further undermined presumptions of courage within that body.

The third argument addressed in the U.S. delegation statement concerned the "overly simplistic" theory that states parties and the Security Council would politicize the prosecutor under the weight of governmental partisanism and self-interest, while a *proprio motu* prosecutor would act only with strict impartiality as he or she sifts through information received from presumably unbiased individuals and organizations. U.S. negotiators thought quite differently, believing that it "would be naïve to ignore the considerable political pressure that organizations will bring to bear on the Prosecutor in advocating that he or she take on the cause which they champion."[29]

In practice, however, the sheer volume of applications arriving at the OTP from a multitude of different sources (within civil society and from international and regional organizations) may have insulated the OTP from undue influence by any particular group, be it the major powers, nongovernmental organizations, or individual complainants. A good example, however, of where political factors (including statehood status) and the objective determination on the facts presented controversial challenges for the OTP may be evident in the OTP's preliminary examination of Operation Cast Lead and the admissibility of claims by Palestinian authorities.[30]

There remains considerable truth in the fourth position presented by the U.S. delegation—that is, "the extent to which State and Security Council referral in fact has a 'political' component which is beneficial, if not essential, to the work of the Prosecutor. In making referrals, States are expressing political will and political support for the Prosecutor and his work; they are signaling to other States the level of their concern about the situation at issue and their commitment to stand behind and assist the Prosecutor both directly, and in his or her dealings with other States, including those likely to be hostile to the Prosecutor's investigation." The alternative, a *proprio motu* prosecutor, elicits the fear that "it will become too easy for States Parties to abdicate their responsibilities and simply leave it to individuals, organizations and the Prosecutor himself to initiate cases without the starting foundation of political will and commitment only States can provide. The Prosecutor then can become isolated, and abandoned to deal in a difficult international arena without the clear, continuing involvement of States Parties in affirming his or her work."[31]

Given the large number of situations under preliminary examination pursuant to the *proprio motu* authority of the prosecutor, such inquiries likely would have progressed more rapidly and efficiently if investigations had been initiated by a state party or Security Council referral and certainly would have done so in the presence of the tangible support of the referring government or the Council itself. But the picture was mixed during the Court's first decade. Governments that self-referred situations offered less-than-full cooperation to the OTP. The Security Council offered very little postreferral assistance to the OTP in either the Darfur or Libya referrals and did not use its chapter VII authority to pry loose cooperation by either the Sudanese government under President Omar al-Bashir or the Libyan government under either Gaddafi or the post-Gaddafi leadership. Nor did the Security Council see fit to recommend to the General Assembly any financial assistance to the ICC in connection with the two referrals.[32]

In sum, the kind of political support that the U.S. delegation statement assumed would be forthcoming in the event of a state party referral or a Security Council referral was often unimpressive or nonexistent during the first ten years. In practice, the prosecutor must rely on the Assembly of States Parties and its budgetary authority to ensure sufficient support for the OTP's responsibilities. The Assembly is not a referring body under the Rome Statute and thus cannot be equated with the state party or the Security Council that refers a situation and then either supports that referral (financially, logistically, politically, perhaps even militarily) or refrains from such support. Unfortunately, the latter predicament has proven to be far more common than the former.

The fourth prong of U.S. objections to a *proprio motu* prosecutor rested on the presumption that legal criteria in examining situations would quickly give way to questions of policy as the prosecutor is flooded with complaints from individuals and organizations that cannot be screened in advance by a state party or the Security Council, as would be the case if they alone had the power of referral. As the U.S. delegation's statement speculated, "If the Prosecutor has authority—and indeed the responsibility—to pursue all facially credible allegations coming from individuals or organizations, there will surely be many more complaints than the Prosecutor can possibly handle. Without the screen of a State and Security Council mechanism, the volume of complaints will expand significantly, including those that will prove to be [an] inappropriate basis for prosecution. . . . In sum, the *proprio motu* proposal risks routinely drawing the Prosecutor into making difficult public policy decisions which the Prosecutor is neither well-equipped nor inclined to make. In our view, these initial public policy decisions are best made by political bodies, freeing the Prosecutor to deal for the most part with the law and facts."[33]

Though logically premised, these concerns were simply not borne out by the work of the OTP during its first decade. The prosecutor survived considerable criticism over the years, although the OTP's credibility surely suffered under the weight of various allegations. Indeed, other chapters in this book reveal much of that criticism and the fate of the OTP's credibility. Nonetheless, there is no evidence during the first ten years that critics intimidated the prosecutor into abandoning legal standards of review for raw policy judgments based on lobbying pressure. That evidence may come to light someday, but there is little doubt that the OTP has managed the incoming applications cautiously and conservatively, with dominant reliance on standards of legal review.

The final issue raised in the U.S. delegation statement also had a logical premise, but it, too, did not result in the feared consequences: "The United States is deeply concerned by the tremendous resources implications of the *proprio motu* proposal and the extent to which it will transform the nature of the Prosecutor's office. One need only look at the volume of complaints lodged with human rights organizations to understand how debilitating it will be to make the Prosecutor responsive to all possible allegations of conduct coming within the framework of the statute."[34] The high volume of communications lodged with the then U.N. Human Rights Commission's Resolution 1503 procedures under the first optional protocol of the International Covenant on Civil and Political Rights (ICCPR) and with other international and regional human rights bodies were ominously noted. At that time, however, we overlooked the reality that human rights abuses far outnumber atrocity crimes in certain regions. The latter is a particularly gross or severe violation of human rights and thus necessarily makes up only a fraction of the wide range of human rights violations that confront the other bodies. Similarly, we also failed to recognize that jurisdictional and gravity requirements would disqualify a large number of the applications submitted to the ICC, thereby enhancing the prosecutor's ability to pursue truly significant and jurisdictionally qualified situations. By the end of 2011, the prosecutor had received a total of 9,332 applications since the Court's creation on July 1, 2002,[35] an average of about 983 applications per year. Comparable numbers in 2011 alone included 605 petitions before the U.N. Human Rights Council[36] and 116 submissions before the Human Rights Committee of the ICCPR.[37] In contrast, 64,500 filings occurred before the European Court of Human Rights during 2011.[38]

Despite the considerable political capital that the U.S. delegation invested in opposing a *proprio motu* prosecutor, by the third week of the Rome Conference, it was becoming evident that governments were supporting the proposal in sufficient numbers to make its inclusion in the Rome Statute inevitable. My own rough calculation during the conference showed that forty-five countries favored the idea by July 13, 1998, and most of them had confirmed their support before July 2. Early on, the United States was joined in opposition to the proposal by France, Japan, Russia, Mexico, China, Singapore, India, Israel, Indonesia, Kenya, and Uruguay. But France, Mexico, and Japan fairly quickly reversed their positions and came to support a *proprio motu* prosecutor. The fact that Iran, Nigeria, Pakistan, Syria, and Qatar expressed their opposition to the *proprio motu* prosecutor proposal later in the Rome Conference proved unpersuasive, as the like-minded countries supporting the idea would not be influenced by these particular countries, most of which would not join the Court any time soon.

In my testimony before the Senate Foreign Relations Committee on July 23, 1998, I repeated American opposition to the *proprio motu* prosecutor at the Rome Conference, even if this opposition was not emphasized in my prepared testimony. As time progressed, the issue faded from U.S. official statements. In 2000, I submitted several key proposals to the continuing negotiations preparing the supplemental documents and agreements to the Rome Statute.[39] They attracted important support among key governments and showed promise for affirmative votes in the session planned for 2001. One such proposal would have required the prosecutor to follow guidelines prepared by the participating governments to ensure nonpolitical decision making within the OTP.[40] The United States already had joined consensus in approving the Rules of Procedure and Evidence and the Elements of Crimes for the Rome Statute, and I believed that such a proposal would help tamp down lingering concerns in the Pentagon and on Capitol Hill. Fortunately, the proposal to establish such guidelines for the prosecutor was lined up for formal consideration in 2001. But the arrival of the George W. Bush administration on January 20, 2001, ended official American participation in the negotiations, and the proposal died as a consequence of the subsequent lack of U.S. government interest.[41]

The exercise of *proprio motu* powers by the prosecutor has not proven to be the dangerous and politically dominated exercise once feared. That reality can be credited to Luis Moreno Ocampo, and his staff, who developed standards of legal review and generally executed a cautious methodology during the Court's first decade. It appears that at least for now, the deep U.S. skepticism toward the idea of an a *proprio motu* prosecutor probably will not be validated. Despite good-faith predictions about what would come to pass, the reality proved otherwise. And that is good news.

NOTES

1. Rome Statute of the International Criminal Court, art. 15, ¶¶1–2, July 17, 1998, 2187 U.N.T.S. 90.

2. *Id.*, at art. 15, ¶¶3–5.

3. *Is a U.N. International Criminal Court in the U.S. National Interest?: Hearing before the Subcomm. on Int'l Operations of the S. Comm. on Foreign Relations,* 105th Cong. 147–50 (1998) (hereinafter *Senate Hearing*).

4. Ambassador Bill Richardson, U.S. Permanent Representative to the United Nations, *Statement at the U.N. Plenipotentiaries Conference on the Establishment of an International Criminal Court,* U.S. U.N. Press Release #108 (98) (June 17, 1998).

5. *Senate Hearing, supra* note 3.

6. For the ultimate results of that investigation, see the *Starr Report to Congress, H.R. Rep. No.* 105-310 (1998).

7. *Senate Hearing, supra* note 3, at 148.

8. Prosecutor v. al-Bashir, Case No. ICC-02/05-01/09, Second Warrant of Arrest for Omar Hassan Ahmad al-Bashir (July 12, 2010), http://www.icc-cpi.int/iccdocs/doc/doc907140.pdf.

9. Situation in the Libyan Arab Jamahiriya, Case No. ICC-01/11, Warrant of Arrest for Muammar Mohammed Abu Minyar Gaddafi (June 27, 2012), http://www.icc-cpi.int/iccdocs/doc/doc1099321.pdf.

10. *See* DAVID SCHEFFER, ALL THE MISSING SOULS: A PERSONAL HISTORY OF THE WAR CRIMES TRIBUNALS 415–17 (2012); *AU Chief Condemns Bashir Warrants: African Leaders Attack International Criminal Court over Moves against Sudan President,* AL JAZEERA (July 27, 2010), http://www.aljazeera.com/news/africa/2010/07/2010726423699861.html; *Arab Leaders Reject Arrest Warrant against Sudan's Bashir,* FRANCE 24 (Mar. 31, 2009), http://www.france24.com/en/20090330-arab-leaders-reject-arrest-warrant-against-sudans-bashir-.

11. Marc Lynch, *Cherif Bassiouni: The FP Interview,* FOREIGN POLICY (Apr. 18, 2012), http://lynch.foreignpolicy.com/posts/2012/04/18/cherif_bassiouni_the_fp_interview; Assia Boundaoui, *War Crimes Investigator,* PRI'S THE WORLD (July 27, 2011), http://

www.theworld.org/2011/07/war-crimes-investigator/ (radio interview with Mahmoud Cherif Bassiouni) ("The problem is that you sometimes also have to debunk many of the allegations that are made which are exaggerated. For example recently there's been all sorts of allegations that there is a policy of mass rape that the Gaddafi regime has established. Well we don't know that, we found no basis for that. As people get so attached to well was there or wasn't there a policy of mass rape, we are ignoring the fact that 15,000 people have been killed. We're ignoring the fact that some of these crimes are still ongoing. Not to say that it's not important, it is important if it's there. But it's not important if it's made up."). *See generally* Human Rights Council, *Report of the International Commission of Inquiry to Investigate All Alleged Violations of International Human Rights Law in the Libyan Arab Jamahiriya*, U.N. Doc. A/HRC/17/44 (June 1, 2011), http://www2.ohchr.org/english/bodies/hrcouncil/docs/17session/A.HRC.17.44_AUV.pdf.

12. For a comprehensive set of essays by leading scholars on this issue, see Online Forum, *Is the International Criminal Court (ICC) Targeting Africa Inappropriately?*, SANELA DIANA JENKINS HUMAN RIGHTS PROJECT AT UCLA SCHOOL OF LAW, http://iccforum.com/africa#Bassiouni.

13. *See* Rome Statute of the International Criminal Court, pmbl., July 17, 1998, 2187 U.N.T.S. 90.

14. *Senate Hearing, supra* note 3, at 148.

15. *See* Office of the Prosecutor, ICC, *Draft Policy Paper on Preliminary Examinations* (Oct. 4, 2010), http://www.icc-cpi.int/NR/rdonlyres/E278F5A2-A4F9-43D7-83D2-6A2C9CF5D7D7/282515/OTP_Draftpolicypaperonpreliminaryexaminations04101.pdf (hereinafter *Draft Policy Paper on Preliminary Examinations*); Office of the Prosecutor, ICC, *The Interests of Justice* 1 (Sept. 2007), http://www.icc-cpi.int/NR/rdonlyres/772C95C9-F54D-4321-BF09-73422BB23528/143640/ICCOTPInterestsOfJustice.pdf.

16. *See* Int'l Comm'n of Inquiry on Darfur, *Rep. to the Secretary-General* (Jan. 25, 2005), http://www.un.org/news/dh/sudan/com_inq_darfur.pdf.

17. S.C. Res. 1593, ¶1, U.N. Doc. S/RES/1593 (Mar. 31, 2005).

18. *See* Warren Hoge, *U.N. Votes to Send Any Sudan War Crimes Suspects to World Court*, N.Y. TIMES, Apr. 1, 2005, http://travel.nytimes.com/2005/04/01/international/africa/01sudan.html?scp=15&sq=United+States+Darfur&st=nyt.

19. *See* Office of the Prosecutor, ICC, *Statement of the Prosecutor on the Opening of the Investigation into the Situation in Libya* (Mar. 3, 2011), http://www.icc-cpi.int/NR/rdonlyres/035C3801-5C8D-4ABC-876B-C7D946B51F22/283045/Statement Libya_03032011.pdf.

20. *See Situation in the Republic of Côte d'Ivoire, Case No. ICC-02/11-14, Decision Pursuant to Article 15 of the Rome Statute on the Authorization of an Investigation into the Situation in the Republic of Côte d'Ivoire*, ¶¶23–25, 52–56, 62, 120, 174, 184, 201–06 (Oct. 3, 2011), http://www.icc-cpi.int/iccdocs/doc/doc1240553.pdf; *Situation in the Republic of Kenya, Case No. ICC-01/09-19, Decision Pursuant to Article 15 of the Rome Statute on the Authorization of an Investigation into the Situation in the Republic of Kenya*, ¶¶52, 55–70, 90–99, 188–200 (Mar. 31, 2010), http://www.icc-cpi.int/iccdocs/doc/doc854287.pdf.

21. *See Draft Policy Paper on Preliminary Examinations, supra* note 15, at ¶¶67–72.

22. *See* Office of the Prosecutor, ICC, *OTP Response to Communications Received Concerning Iraq* 8–9 (Feb. 9, 2006), http://www.icc-cpi.int/NR/rdonlyres/04D143C8–

19FB-466C-AB77-4CDB2FDEBEF7/143682/OTP_letter_to_senders_re_Iraq_9_February_2006.pdf (by Luis Moreno Ocampo).

23. *See* Office of the Prosecutor, ICC, *OTP Response to Communications Received Concerning Venezuela,* at 3–4 (Feb. 9, 2006), http://www.icc-cpi.int/NR/rdonlyres/4E2BC725-6A63-40B8-8CDC-ADBA7BCAA91F/143684/OTP_letter_to_senders_re_Venezuela_9_February_2006.pdf (by Luis Moreno Ocampo).

24. *See Senate Hearing, supra* note 3, at 148.

25. *See ICC Prosecutor Fatou Bensouda on the Malian State Referral of the Situation in Mali since January 2012,* Press Release ICC-OTP-20120718-PR829 (July 18, 2012); *Prosecutor Receives Referral Concerning Central African Republic,* Press Release ICC-20050107-86 (Jan. 7, 2005); *Prosecutor Receives Referral of the Situation in the Democratic Republic of Congo,* Press Release ICC-OTP-20040419-50 (Apr. 19, 2004); *President of Uganda Refers Situation Concerning the Lord's Resistance Army (LRA) to the ICC,* Press Release ICC-20040129-44 (Jan. 29, 2004).

26. *See* Mahnoush H. Arsanjani & W. Michael Reisman, *The Law-in-Action of the International Criminal Court,* 99 AM. J. INT'L L. 385 (2005).

27. *See Letter on Behalf of Union of the Comoros to Fatou Bensouda, Prosecutor, ICC* (May 14, 2013) (referring incident under art. 14 to the ICC), http://www.icc-cpi.int/iccdocs/otp/Referral-from-Comoros.pdf; see further at http://www.icc-cpi.int/en_menus/icc/situations%20and%20cases/situations/situation-ICC-01-13/Pages/default.aspx.

28. An effort by three permanent members of the Security Council—the United States, France, and the United Kingdom—to refer the situation in Syria to the International Criminal Court in May 2014 failed when Russia and China vetoed the proposed Chapter VII resolution. *See* Somini Sengupta, *China and Russia Block Referral of Syria to Court,* N.Y. TIMES, May 22, 2014, A3, available at http://www.nytimes.com/2014/05/23/world/middleeast/syria-vote-in-security-council.html?module=Search&mabReward=relbias%3Ar%2C{%222%22%3A%22RI%3A15%22%2C%221%22%3A%22RI%3A7%22}.

29. *Senate Hearing, supra* note 3, at 148.

30. *See* Office of the Prosecutor, ICC, *Situation in Palestine* (Apr. 3, 2012), http://www.icc-cpi.int/NR/rdonlyres/C6162BBF-FEB9-4FAF-AFA9-836106D2694A/284387/SituationinPalestine030412ENG.pdf.

31. *Senate Hearing, supra* note 3, at 148–49.

32. *See generally* DAVID KAYE, THE COUNCIL & THE COURT: IMPROVING SECURITY COUNCIL SUPPORT OF THE INTERNATIONAL CRIMINAL COURT (International Justice Clinic, University of California School of Law, Irvine) (2013).

33. *Senate Hearing, supra* note 3, at 149.

34. *Id.*

35. *See* Office of the Prosecutor, ICC, *Rep. on Preliminary Examination Activities,* at 5 (Dec. 13, 2011), http://www.icc-cpi.int/NR/rdonlyres/63682F4E-49C8-445D-8C13-F310A4F3AEC2/284116/OTPReportonPreliminaryExaminations13December2011.pdf.

36. *See* Office of the U.N. High Comm'r for Human Rights, *United Nations Special Procedures: Facts & Figures 2011,* at 9 (May 2012), http://www.ohchr.org/Documents/HRBodies/SP/Facts_Figures2011.pdf.

37. *See Individual Human Rights Complaints Handled by the U.N.: Few & Very Far*

Between, HUMAN RIGHTS VOICES, http://www.eyeontheun.org/print/default.asp?http://www.eyeontheun.org/facts.asp?1=1&p=54.

38. *See* Eur. Court of Human Rights, *Analysis of Statistics 2011,* at 4 (Jan. 2012), http://www.echr.coe.int/NR/rdonlyres/11CE0BB3-9386-48DC-B012-AB2C046FEC7C/0/STATS_EN_2011.PDF.

39. *See* Working Group on a Relationship Agreement between the United Nations and the International Criminal Court, *Proposal Submitted by the United States of America,* U.N. Doc. PCNICC/2000/DP.1 (2000) (hereinafter *U.S. Proposal PCNICC/2000/DP.1*); Working Group on a Relationship Agreement between the United Nations and the International Criminal Court, *Proposal Submitted by the United States of America,* U.N. Doc. PCNICC/2000/WGICC-UN/DP.17 (2000); Working Group on Rules of Procedure and Evidence, *Proposal Submitted by the United States of America Concerning Rules of Procedure & Evidence Relating to Part 13 of the Statute (Final Clauses),* U.N. Doc. PCNICC/2000/WGRPE(13)/DP.1 (2000); Preparatory Commission for the International Criminal Court, *Addendum: Finalized Draft Text of the Rules of Procedure & Evidence,* U.N. Doc. PCNICC/2000/INF/3/Add.1 (2000), http://www.coalitionfortheicc.org/documents/RulesofProcEvidenceEng.pdf.

40. *See* U.S. Proposal PCNICC/2000/DP.1, *supra* note 39: "The United States of America proposes for the consideration of the Preparatory Commission the development of factors for the Court that may be relevant for the investigation, prosecution and surrender of suspects, including the context within which an alleged crime has occurred and a State's contribution to international peace and security."

41. *See* Scheffer, *supra* note 10, at 235, 247.

Crimes against Humanity

Limits, Leverage, and Future Concerns

Leila Nadya Sadat

Crimes against humanity, one of the three offenses incorporated into the Rome Statute for the International Criminal Court (ICC), have been perhaps the most ubiquitous and horrific atrocities committed in modern times. Yet an understanding of their theoretical basis and their application to particular cases remains elusive. Part of the confusion is a problem of labeling: what was prosecuted as *crimes against humanity* at Nuremberg (the widespread and systematic persecution of and destruction of European Jewry) is now codified and prosecuted as the crime of *genocide,* leaving modern crimes against humanity law to cover other kinds of widespread or systematic human rights abuses that do not have as their objective the destruction of a racial, religious, national, or ethnic group.[1] Since Nuremberg, the focus has been on protecting civilians from victimization by their own governments as well as from the depredations of other states. Crimes against humanity law also applies to attacks on civilians in peacetime, not just in war, and modern understandings of this crime do not require the attack to be carried out by a state but apply to the actions of nonstate actors as well.[2] The expansive ambit of crimes against humanity makes it a powerful weapon in a prosecutor's arsenal, allowing him or her to reach atrocity crimes prior to the onset of war or genocide and avoiding difficult questions about whether an offense was committed in international or noninternational armed conflict. Moreover, as the Libya situation demonstrated, this renders crimes against humanity law a potential tool for mass atrocity prevention because the legal threshold for intervention is lowered. For the same reason, the idea of crimes against humanity can be threatening to states, which have studiously avoided its comprehensive codification since World War II other than its inclusion in the ICC Statute in 1998.[3]

This chapter briefly traces the evolution of crimes against humanity in international criminal law before exploring the ICC prosecutor's early use of this category of offense and the Court's jurisprudence to date. It grows out of a larger study on the application and interpretation of crimes against humanity in international criminal law, the preliminary findings of which offer valuable insights into the importance of such charges to the work of the ICC.[4] Although the Court's first trial and judgment was a war crimes case, the first ICC prosecutor, Luis Moreno Ocampo, relied heavily on crimes against humanity to carry out his mandate in all of the situations currently before the Court, as has his successor, Fatou Bensouda. Indeed, in the Côte d'Ivoire, Kenya, and Libya situations, crimes against humanity provided the only possible basis for the Court's jurisdiction *ratione materiae*.

The definition of crimes against humanity in article 7 of the Rome Statute differs from the definitions of crimes against humanity in the statutes of earlier international criminal tribunals. Although it expands the list of predicate acts considerably, the *chapeau,* or contextual elements of the crime, contain limits expressly rejected by earlier tribunals—in particular, the requirement that crimes against humanity be committed pursuant to a "state or organizational policy."[5] These limits presumably provided comfort to states during the statute's negotiation and adoption by ensuring that only the most egregious cases would be taken up by the ICC; the restrictions thus effectuated a triage between "ordinary crimes" of murder or rape, for example, and international crimes representing "the most serious crimes of concern to the international community as a whole."[6] These substantive limits are fortified by the procedural constraints embedded in the ICC Statute that empower the Court's Pre-Trial Chambers to impose rigorous procedural checks on prosecutorial action and discretion. The combination of these substantive and procedural constraints should narrow the application of crimes against humanity as a category of offense to only the clearest situations of atrocity crimes. This could mean that some mass atrocity cases will not succeed in the Court, even where a strong argument could be made that they fall within the Court's jurisdiction. This could shore up the perceived legitimacy of the ICC's intervention by rendering the Court's interventions predictable and limited, but it may not create the strong antidote to impunity that at least some observers hoped the Court would provide. The ICC Prosecutor is at the center of this debate and must judiciously decide which cases are likely to succeed and which ones are less promising. As we have already seen in the situations before the Court, the ICC prosecutor has an extraordinarily difficult mandate that is likely to upset or even infuriate those on the receiving end of the Court's arrest warrants and indictments. Faithfulness to text and responsiveness to the procedural limits on his or her power while aggressively and vigorously pursuing his or her independent mandate may be critical not only to the prosecutor's success but also to the Court's overall standing and legitimacy.

Codification of Crimes against Humanity in the ICC Statute—Promise and Constraints

Until the conclusion of the Rome Statute, no codification of crimes against humanity existed in a multilateral specialized convention.[7] Instead, various texts adopted by states, the Security Council, and the International Law Commission contained different elaborations of the crime.[8] Moreover, before the ICC Statute's negotiation in 1998, there was little in the way of constructive practice or precedent emerging either from the ad hoc tribunals, which had decided very few cases, or from the Special Court for Sierra Leone (SCSL), which had not yet been established. Thus, with a couple of exceptions, the experience of those tribunals—experience that may help shape the ICC prosecutor's approach to these cases—was largely unavailable to the negotiators at Rome. These exceptions included lessons from the International Criminal Tribunals for the Former Yugoslavia and Rwanda (ICTY and ICTR, respectively) about the importance of prosecuting sex and gender crimes,[9] early decisions from the *Tadić* case,[10] and the trial (but not the decision) in *Akayesu*.[11] Thus, the negotiators at Rome had not only to codify the jurisdictional and procedural rules of the Court but also, in the case of crimes against humanity, to define the crime.

In terms of *chapeau* or threshold elements, the armed conflict nexus (found in the ICTY Statute) was eliminated. The discriminatory intent requirement (present in the ICTR and later in the Extraordinary Chambers in the Courts in Cambodia [ECCC] Statutes) was also discarded.[12] Finally, the Rome Statute employs the rubric "widespread *or* systematic" (as opposed to "*and* systematic"), following the provisions of the SCSL, ECCC and ICTR Statutes.[13] Additional acts were added as well: like the SCSL, the ICC Statute includes additional provisions on crimes of sexual violence (but adds the idea that they must be of "comparable gravity" to the other crimes involving sexual violence set forth in article 7(1)(g)), expands considerably the ambit of persecution in article 7(1)(h) beyond the narrow grounds of ethnic, racial, religious, political and national found in the ICTR and the ECCC Statutes,[14] and includes enforced disappearance of persons and the crime of apartheid as new specific acts constituting crimes against humanity. The Rome Conference rejected appeals from some governments to add economic and environmental crimes, preferring the list to track crimes already found in other international instruments, or clearly understood to be predicate acts of crimes against humanity under customary international law.

Article 7 of the Rome Statute contains four separate preconditions that must be satisfied before jurisdiction attaches in a particular case in which crimes against humanity are charged. The Elements of Crimes, adopted after the Rome Statute pursuant to article 9 of the ICC Treaty, refer to these as "context" elements.[15] These are the commission of the crime (1) as part of a "widespread or systematic attack";[16] (2) against a civilian population;[17] (3) with knowledge of the attack directed against any civilian population;[18] (4) and involving "a course of conduct involving the multiple commission of acts . . . against any civilian population pursuant to or in furtherance of a State or organization policy to commit such attack."[19]

The addition of this fourth "policy" element was presumably intended to avoid the possibility that an isolated attack on civilians could be considered a crime against humanity under the Rome Statute. Yet the element's addition was controversial.[20] Although the French courts required the existence of a "common plan" in their interpretation of the Nuremberg Charter,[21] as did some of the decisions under Control Council Law No. 10,[22] no subsequent ad hoc tribunal statute had included a similar element, and at least to this author, the French interpretation was questionable as a matter of textual interpretation.[23] Likewise, it is unclear what the term *organizational* means in article 7(2)(a),[24] and the term is not defined by the statute.

Additional jurisprudence from the ICTY and ICTR was available to the Preparatory Commission, which was established following the Rome Conference and charged with elaborating the statute's Elements of Crimes, although it is unclear how much those decisions influenced the drafters. During the negotiation of the Elements, crimes against humanity— particularly the contextual or *chapeau* elements—emerged as some of the more controversial elements of the Commission's work.[25] The Elements supply subsidiary means of interpretation to the Court regarding the interpretation and application of article 7 and regarding crimes against humanity, and they are prefaced by three paragraphs setting forth general principles for their interpretation. In particular, the first preambular paragraph references the need to construe article 7 strictly, consistently with article 22 of the Rome Statute.

One sees not only in the text of article 7 but also in the preambular paragraphs of the Elements an intent to clarify the application of article 7 by the ICC and in particular to rely on article 22's strict rules of construction to keep the Court faithful to the text of the statute. Perhaps the negotiators were also concerned about possible overreach by an ICC prosecutor who was yet to be named. Yet the Elements offer little assistance in the understanding of article 7, for they fail to define critical terms such as *civilian population* and *widespread* or *systematic* attacks and offer very little guidance as to the meaning of *state or organizational policy*. Thus, the job of definition, interpretation, and application of article 7 falls by default to the prosecutor in the first instance and to the Court's judiciary on review. This was apparently by design: in the words of one observer, "Most delegations quickly agreed that [the definition of *civilian population*] was too complex a subject and an evolving area in the law, better left for resolution in case-law."[26]

The Importance of Crimes against Humanity to the Work of the ICC Prosecutor

At the ad hoc criminal tribunals, crimes against humanity charges were an important prosecutorial tool, covering cases that might not be proven as genocide, cases taking place when no armed conflict was ongoing, and cases involving particularly heinous acts—especially (but not limited to) sexual and gender-based violence as well as persecutions, where war crimes charges seemed insufficient to encompass a particular factual situation. The ability to use persecution as an overarching crime was critical to the ICTY to capture the idea of ethnic cleansing, for example, and the SCSL used crimes against humanity—as well as war crimes—as a rubric to capture some of the special horrors of the atrocities committed during that conflict. All of the ad hoc tribunals (and particularly the ICTY, the SCSL and the Nuremberg and Tokyo Tribunals) were created as a response to the commission of atrocities that had been linked to armed conflict in some way. This was less true of the Rwanda and Khmer Rouge tribunals, where an argument can be made that the atrocities took place in peacetime, but in each case, the ad hoc tribunal sought to prosecute cases after massive atrocities had already been committed. Conversely, at the ICC, a permanent court operating in real time, it is possible to imagine a much broader scope of application for crimes against humanity charges, and one might expect crimes against humanity to emerge as a crucial weapon in the ICC prosecutor's arsenal.

These assumptions are borne out by a look at the Court's work in its first few years. Crimes against humanity have been charged in all of the situations before the ICC. In cases involving armed conflict, the crimes against humanity charges often track war crimes charges or target persecution or sexual violence. In the Côte d'Ivoire, Libya, and Kenya situations, the crimes against humanity charges constitute the only basis on which the Court can exercise its jurisdiction, given the absence of an armed conflict sufficient to trigger the Court's war crimes jurisdiction (at least at the outset of the referral) and the implausibility of alleging genocide. This suggests that crimes against humanity may emerge as an important tool of genocide prevention, applicable before atrocity levels spin completely out of control to rein in a situation that is degrading into conflict or overwhelming levels of atrocity crimes.

As of February 2013, eight situations were before the ICC (Central African Republic, Côte d'Ivoire, Darfur, Democratic Republic of Congo, Kenya, Libya, Mali, and Uganda),[27] in seven of which charges had been brought against a total of thirty individuals. In total, the prosecution has charged these thirty persons with 137 counts of crimes against humanity (44.6 percent of total counts), 3 counts of genocide (1.0 percent), and 167 counts of war crimes (54.4 percent). The three situations in which only crimes against humanity charges have been brought (Côte d'Ivoire, Kenya, and Libya), account for eleven of those thirty accused (37 percent).[28] In contrast, at the ICTY and ICTR, only two accused at each tribunal were charged solely with crimes against humanity (1.2 and 2.2 percent, respectively, of all accused). This difference between the practice at the ad hoc international criminal tribunals and at the ICC is stunning. It suggests that the prosecutor—who, after all, is the engine driving the cases brought to the Court—has indeed seen the ICC as a "crimes against humanity court."

The situations now before the Court can be subdivided into three general categories: cases in which crimes against humanity are charged and have been committed during armed conflict (Central African Republic, the Democratic Republic of the Congo, and Uganda); cases in which allegations of genocide have surfaced but crimes against humanity may provide a "safer" and more winnable alternative for the prosecution, giving the difficulty of establishing the *dolus specialis* for genocide (Sudan); and cases involving crimes against humanity only (Côte d'Ivoire, Kenya, and Libya).

Crimes against Humanity during War

These situations are the least controversial for the ICC prosecutor. Not only do they involve self-referrals (the territorial state itself asked the ICC to intervene) but they harken back to the Nuremberg conceptualization of crimes against humanity as crimes linked to or committed in armed conflict. They are also similar in kind to the cases brought before the ad hoc international criminal tribunals. Even so, the ICC's Pre-Trial Chambers have exercised more control over the ICC prosecutor than judges did at its predecessor institutions.

The first case undertaken was referred by Uganda's president in December 2003[29] and involved the "situation concerning the Lord's Resistance Army," an armed group led by Joseph Kony that was operating in northern Uganda and had since 2002 brutalized the region's civilian inhabitants. In accepting Uganda's self-referral, the prosecutor notified Ugandan authorities that he would interpret the scope of the referral "consistently with the Rome Statute" and would therefore analyze crimes in northern Uganda "by whomever committed."[30] However, these cases have not involved charges against government officials and therefore have not threatened those in power in the states referring the cases (which has not, however, stopped their leaders from criticizing the ICC for taking the cases).[31] The prosecutor subsequently received referrals from the Democratic Republic of the Congo[32] and from the Central African Republic.[33]

Elsewhere, I have written extensively about the contributions made by the Court's early jurisprudence in these situations and the cases brought under them to our understanding of crimes against humanity.[34] These matters show a preoccupation by the Pre-Trial and Trial Chambers with cabining the prosecutor's discretion in terms of both the ability to cumulatively charge and of subtly narrowing the application of article 7 by cumulating the elements of "widespread" "systematic" and "organizational policy";[35] requiring attacks to be "thoroughly organized";[36] holding that "article 7 of the Statute affords rights and protections to 'any civilian population' regardless of their nationality, ethnicity or other distinguishing feature"[37] and thus suggesting an effort to relink crimes against humanity to genocide;[38] narrowing the definition of *civilian population*,[39] and requiring at the confirmation stage quite extensive evidence regarding the existence of a "state or organizational policy."[40] In the *Bemba* case, for example, the Pre-Trial Chamber rejected several charges as subsumed by others and limited the theory of individual criminal responsibility the prosecutor could use in attempting to link Bemba to the crimes committed, in what appears to be a significant departure from the practice at the ad hoc tribunals and an effort to cabin the prosecutor's freedom of action.[41]

Genocide or Crimes against Humanity? Referral of the Situation in Darfur by the Security Council

On September 18, 2004, responding to public concern about mass atrocities reportedly occurring in the Darfur region of what is now North Sudan, the Security Council established a commission of inquiry to investigate. The five-member commission, chaired by the late Antonio Cassese, concluded that the government of Sudan and the Janjaweed militias operating in Darfur[42] were responsible for serious violations of humanitarian law and human rights, including "indiscriminate attacks, killing of civilians, torture, enforced disappearances, destruction of villages, rape and other forms of sexual violence, pillaging and forced displacement."[43] The commission found that these acts had been committed on a widespread and systematic basis and that they could therefore be characterized as crimes against humanity. On the question of whether acts of genocide had been committed, the commission found that the government of Sudan had not "pursued a policy of genocide"[44] but added that a finding that no genocidal policy was pursued and implemented did not mean that offenses "no less serious and heinous," such as crimes against humanity and war crimes, had not taken place.[45]

The Darfur situation was referred to the ICC by the Security Council at the commission's suggestion,[46] and the prosecutor's office opened an investigation, issuing arrest warrants and/or summonses for seven individuals. The first warrants were issued by Pre-Trial Chamber I on April 27, 2007, against state minister for humanitarian affairs Ahmad Muhammad Harun and alleged Janjaweed leader Ali Muhammad Ali Abd-al-Rahman (Ali Kushayb) for war crimes and crimes against humanity. The charging pattern is similar to that exhibited in the three "self-referral" cases discussed previously, with crimes against humanity sometimes used independently of war crimes for elements of social harm such as persecution and to provide an alternative theory of liability for many crimes such as murder, rape, and inhumane treatment. The war crimes counts, as in the earlier cases, attempt to capture other elements of the attacks, such as property destruction (including food stores and mosques) and pillaging as well as attacks on the civilian population.[47]

The third and perhaps most controversial warrant issued by the Court was directed against Sudanese president Omar Hassan Ahmad al-Bashir.

Pre-Trial Chamber I issued a first warrant on March 4, 2009, on seven counts of war crimes and crimes against humanity[48] but declined to issue the warrant on genocide charges, with a majority concluding that "the existence of reasonable grounds to believe that the [government of Sudan] acted with a *dolus specialis*/specific intent to destroy in whole or in part the Fur, Masalit and Zaghawa groups is not the only reasonable conclusion that can be drawn therefrom."[49] Judge Anita Ušacka dissented, disagreeing with the legal and evidentiary standards applied by the majority on the genocide charges, and the prosecution was given leave to appeal.[50] The Appeals Chamber reversed, agreeing with Judge Ušacka that the majority had imposed a higher standard of proof at the arrest warrant stage than article 58 of the statute required,[51] and ordered reconsideration of the case. The Pre-Trial Chamber subsequently found that there were reasonable grounds to believe that al-Bashir was "criminally responsible . . . for charges of genocide . . . under article 58 of the Statute, to have been committed by the [government of Sudan] forces as part of the [government of Sudan] counter-insurgency campaign."[52]

The genocide charges largely track the crimes against humanity counts, so in some ways, it did not matter what the Court finally held regarding the ability of the prosecution to allege genocide. However, in terms of public opinion and even state responsibility under the genocide convention, a finding of genocide by the Court could be important. President al-Bashir has challenged the legality of the warrant against him and has tried to muster African Union support by arguing that he has been singled out as an African leader for unfair—even discriminatory—treatment by the Court. He continues to be received as a head of state by some African countries, and, along with the Kenyan Parliament's recent vote to withdraw from the ICC's jurisdiction,[53] the al-Bashir arrest warrant raises the specter of continued heated debates about the appropriateness and effectiveness of the ICC's intervention in Africa.[54]

Only Crimes against Humanity

Three situations have been brought to the Court in which only crimes against humanity have been charged: Côte d'Ivoire, Kenya, and Libya. All have involved the indictment of a head of state as well as violence between governments and their political opponents. Kenya and Côte d'Ivoire involve the invocation of the prosecutor's *proprio motu* powers under article 15 of the ICC Statute—in the case of Côte d'Ivoire, pursuant to the request of the situation country, but in the case of Kenya, over the target country's strong objections. Although the Libya and Côte d'Ivoire situations raise interesting questions of law and policy, this chapter will focus on the disagreement in the Kenya situation as to whether the situation really warranted ICC intervention.

Crimes against humanity were the only charge levied by the prosecutor regarding the violence that gripped Kenya between December 2007 and February 2008, following its presidential election.[55] The violence was investigated by an international commission of enquiry (the Waki Commission),[56] which had turned over materials including documents it had collected as well as a sealed envelope containing a list of suspects it had identified as allegedly most responsible for the violence.[57]

In its decision on the prosecutor's application to open an investigation under article 15 of the statute, Pre-Trial Chamber II set forth the legal requirements for the "contextual elements" of crimes against humanity, including the "civilian population" requirement, the "state or organizational policy" requirement, and the "widespread or systematic" nature of the attack. An article 15 decision such as this cannot be particularly factually intensive as, at this point in the proceedings, the prosecution is seeking authorization to open an investigation, not to charge specific individuals. Pre-Trial Chamber II concluded that the relevant evidentiary and legal standard was whether a "reasonable basis to proceed" existed under article 53 (initiation of an investigation), which is "the lowest evidentiary standard provided for in the Statute." Thus, the majority concluded that "in evaluating the available information provided by the Prosecutor, the Chamber must be satisfied that there exists a sensible or reasonable justification for a belief that a crime falling within the jurisdiction of the Court 'has been or is being committed.'"[58]

Judge Hans-Peter Kaul took issue with the majority, suggesting that the standard should be higher, particularly with regard to the "contextual elements of crimes against humanity," as these "decisive" elements trigger the "jurisdiction of the Court [and] elevate[] the acts concerned, which otherwise would fall exclusively under the responsibility of national jurisdictions, to international crimes."[59] Because he did not agree that the reasonable basis standard had been satisfied, particularly with regard to the notion of "State or organizational policy," he would not have authorized the prosecutor to proceed.

Pre-Trial Chamber II set out its views on the contextual elements of crimes against humanity, essentially following its earlier decisions.[60] The discussion of the "policy" element in both the majority opinion and Judge Kaul's dissent, however, may constitute the most significant contribution of the Court's early jurisprudence to the definition of crimes against humanity at the ICC. The Kenya situation presented a different scenario than the situations already before the Court. Kenya had held closely contested national elections on December 27, 2007, that pitted incumbent president Mwai Kibaki of the Party of National Unity (PNU) against the main opposition candidate, Raila Odinga of the Orange Democratic Movement (ODM). On December 30, 2007, Kenya's Electoral Commission declared that President Kibaki had been reelected, triggering a series of "violent demonstrations and targeted attacks in several locations within Kenya."[61] During the violence, there were a "reported 1,133 to 1,220 killings of civilians, more than 900 documented acts of rape and other forms of sexual violence, with many more unreported, the internal displacement of 350,000 persons, and 3,560 reported acts causing serious injury."[62] The violence took place in six of the country's eight regions, particularly in heavily populated areas, including Nairobi, the Rift Valley, and the Nyanza and Western provinces.[63] According to human rights groups, the Waki Commission, and the prosecution's application, the brutality took place in waves during which "gangs of young men armed with traditional weapons" targeted specific groups from "other tribes perceived as political opponents."[64] Attacks were initiated by groups associated with both the ODM and the PNU, retaliatory attacks occurred, and evidence showed that the police had committed massacres and torture.[65] During the initial phase of the violence, attacks appeared largely to target PNU supporters; subsequent attacks were directed at ethnic groups perceived to be affiliated with the ODM; and the police attacks appeared to have been directed toward people perceived as opposing their own ethnic affiliation or otherwise against gang members.[66]

The majority noted that the ad hoc tribunals eventually abandoned the "policy requirement" but nonetheless "deem[ed] it useful and thus appropriate to consider their definition of the concept in earlier cases."[67] Relying on this jurisprudence as well as the work of the International Law Commission, the majority gave the language a reading that was criticized by Judge Kaul, but one that is, in the view of this author, supported by both the text of the statute and its negotiating history. Referencing the ICTY Trial Chamber's opinion in *Blaškić*, the majority noted that the plan to commit the attack may be inferred from the commission of "a series of events," including a variety of factors.[68]

The majority also read *state* and *organizational* disjunctively, a view supported by the authentic texts in Arabic, French, Russian, and Spanish.[69] This, as well as the work of the International Law Commission, led the majority to reject the notion that only "State-like organizations may qualify." Rather, the majority focused on "whether a group has the capability to perform acts which infringe on basic human values.[70] Thus, not only did the organization not need to be "State-like," but the policy need not have been conceived at the highest level of the state, meaning that "regional or even local organs of the State could satisfy the requirement of a State policy."[71]

Judge Kaul disagreed.[72] He argued that "even though the constitutive elements of statehood need not be established those 'organizations" should partake of some characteristics of a State . . . turn[ing] the private 'organization' into an entity which may act like a State or has quasi-State abilities," and he set out certain characteristics of quasi-states.[73] Finding that there was no "organization" satisfying his criteria, he concluded that the evidence adduced suggested "chaos, anarchy, a collapse of State authority in most parts of the country and almost total failure of law enforcement agencies," but not a crime against humanity.[74] His opinion evinces a preoccupation with not "marginalizing" or "downgrading" the notion of crimes against humanity[75] and implies that the majority's view might "infringe upon State sovereignty," "broaden the scope of ICC intervention almost indefinitely," and "turn the ICC . . . in [sic] a hopelessly overstretched, inefficient international court, with related risks for its standing and credibility."[76]

The majority and dissenting opinions in the Kenya case offer very different views of the ICC's mandate. The majority focused principally on the gravity of the harm, the brutality of the violence, its widespread and systematic nature, and the preliminary stage of the proceedings. Examining the precedents available, it concluded that sufficient evidence of a policy had been presented to allow the investigation to proceed, and given the complete absence of real guidance on this question, looked to the resolution of similar questions before other courts and the work of the International Law Commission on the question of nonstate actors and crimes against humanity. The majority's guiding principle was faithfulness to the ICC's mandate to "protect human values." Judge Kaul rejected this approach, suggesting that a pure textual and historical exegesis could provide the appropriate test.[77]

Some commentators have welcomed Judge Kaul's exacting approach.[78] However, just as he implicitly suggests the majority might have been picking and choosing authorities, his opinion largely ignores the work of the International Law Commission (which had prepared the original draft of the ICC's statute as well as the *Draft Code of Crimes*) and a substantial body of work suggesting that a policy element may be *one* way to distinguish between ordinary and international crimes—and thereby confer international jurisdiction—but is not the *only way* to do so. Indeed, *jurisdiction* can be conferred because particular interests of the international community have been injured (*l'ordre public international*), because of the scale of the harm (gravity), or because the problem is incapable of solution by individual states.[79] History may offer an understanding of the origins of crimes against humanity but cannot properly serve as a comprehensive guide to the idea's current application. This particularly holds true for crimes against humanity because the original notion of crimes against humanity elaborated at Nuremberg was essentially codified *not* in a crimes against humanity convention (for no such convention exists) but was closer to the content of the genocide convention (which does not contain a policy element).

The prosecutor's investigations into the Kenyan situation resulted in summonses for six individuals, three each from the PNU and the ODM, which comprise the current government. The three suspects affiliated with the ODM (Ruto, Kosgey, and Sang) were charged in one case, while the three affiliated with the PNU (Muthaura, Kenyatta and Ali) were charged in a separate case. The Appeals Chamber rejected Kenya's challenge to admissibility,[80] and confirmation hearings were held.[81] Pre-Trial Chamber II issued two lengthy opinions on January 23, 2012, confirming charges against four of the accused and declining to confirm charges against two suspects, Henry Kosgey (case 1) and Mohammed Hussein Ali (case 2).[82] The two opinions reprise the Court's earlier holdings, including the innovation that the civilian population must constitute a "group distinguishable by nationality, ethnicity or other distinguishing feature"[83] and the idea that "State or organizational policy" did not exclude nonstate actors as potential policymakers and perpetrators.[84] Indeed, perhaps in response to the criticism of Judge Kaul in the earlier Kenya case, *Ruto* provides a particularly helpful explanation and analysis of which groups could satisfy the "organizational policy" requirement.[85] In *Ruto,* the Pre-Trial Chamber found that the accused had established a "network of perpetrators belonging to the Kalenjin community" to implement a policy of attacks against PNU supporters and that the network included "eminent ODM political representatives, representatives of the media, former members of the Kenyan police and army, Kalenjin elders and local leaders."[86] This network, in the view of the majority, satisfied the criteria of article 7. Judge Kaul was unconvinced[87] that the network was an "amorphous," ethnically driven group, opining that "members of a tribe . . . do not form a state-like 'organization,' unless they meet additional prerequisites."[88] Finally, he concluded by noting that he believed that the crimes that had been committed should be prosecuted—but by Kenyan, not international courts.[89]

Although the majority view has prevailed at the Court for the time being, there is no doubt that Judge Kaul's dissent struck a chord with many observers concerned about the possibility that the prosecutor was overreaching, and potentially expanding the jurisdiction of the Court beyond the framework envisioned by article 7. It is also not clear what the Appeals Chamber will ultimately do in the case, and other Chambers of the Court have suggested that the jurisprudence on this question is unsettled.[90] The current prosecutor has had to dismiss one of the cases on the basis of insufficient evidence,[91] and the Kenyan Parliament recently voted to withdraw from the ICC Statute.[92] This is perhaps to be expected; after all, the ICC is a Court operating in real time with the power to indict high-ranking government officials (including heads of state) for their actions, assuming the Court's jurisdiction is properly invoked. At the same time, the threats to the Court now emanating from the African Union may imperil its existence, suggesting that a more cautious approach to jurisdiction over cases may be warranted.

Conclusion

During the negotiation of the ICC statute, states were obliged to contemplate the possibility of their citizens' future liability. Moreover, as a permanent and independent court, the ICC, unlike the ad hoc tribunals, could potentially apply the law of the statute to a universe as of yet undetermined and even unimagined situations. The importance that many states and NGOs placed on providing the prosecutor with *proprio motu* powers caused the negotiators in Rome to place substantial procedural checks upon the prosecutor's freedom of action, checks that the Court's current judiciary are exercising with vigor. In addition, in codifying crimes against humanity in particular, the one crime for which there was no preexisting treaty instrument, states were relatively cautious: the requirement of a "state or organizational policy" was added; the classic requirement of an "attack" on a civilian population was retained; and the acts were limited largely to violent attacks on corporal integrity (and similar offenses), not expanded to cover environmental or economic crimes, as some states had urged. At the same time, the armed conflict nexus (which had been found in the ICTY Statute) was eliminated; the statute employs the rubric "widespread or systematic" (as opposed to "and systematic," a dispute that had arisen in the ICTR); no discriminatory intent element was included in the *chapeau* or contextual elements of the crime; and the list of acts constituting a possible crimes against humanity was expanded.

The Elements of Crimes underscore the need to construe article 7 narrowly and with fidelity to the ICC Statute. In spite of Judge Kaul's dissents in the Kenya case, which suggest otherwise, in the view of this author, the early case law of the Court evinces a desire on the part of the judges to be faithful to the text of article 7 and relatively conservative in their reading— even too much so at times. If one combines the judicial tendency to read the statute narrowly and, in contrast, to see its own role as quite expansive, particularly with regard to the searching review exercised by the Pre-Trial Chambers of the Court even in very early stages of the proceedings, it seems quite possible that the ICC's crimes against humanity jurisprudence may be narrower than that of the ad hoc tribunals. Of course, it is difficult to tell at this stage, given that no judgments for crimes against humanity have been rendered and that the Appeals Chamber has not ruled on many of the open questions in this area.

The question remains whether a restrictive approach to law and procedure hurts or helps the prosecutor (the subject of this volume), and the Court more generally. Crimes against humanity charges at the ICC certainly will be just as important as they were at the ad hoc tribunals, both quantitatively and qualitatively. Moreover, crimes against humanity will often be the *only* offense applicable, as in the Libya situation, the Kenya situation, and at least currently in the situation in Côte d'Ivoire. Thus, the ICC, even more than the ad hoc tribunals, is largely going to be a "crimes against humanity" court. To put it another way, successful prosecutions for crimes against humanity will be critical for the Court to fulfill its mandate to end impunity for international crimes that shock the conscience of humankind and are vital to the deterrent element of the Court's work. Conversely, *misuse* of crimes against humanity charges by the prosecutor could hurt the Court by calling into question the appropriateness of ICC action in borderline cases.

The ICC definition, particularly in its requirement that the crimes be committed pursuant to a "state or organizational policy," is generally more restrictive than the definition developed in the jurisprudence of the ad hoc tribunals, and the ICC prosecutor will need to be vigilant to guard against a tendency for the ICC to use the policy element of the *chapeau* to limit the application of crimes against humanity so severely that it becomes, like genocide, a crime so difficult to prove that its overall utility becomes severely limited. This danger is not purely hypothetical. Were the Court to adopt the view of Judge Kaul in his dissent to the decision of Pre-Trial Chamber II authorizing an investigation into the Kenyan situation, it could considerably hobble the utility of crimes against humanity as a rubric for addressing mass atrocities. Judge Kaul's use of history as a guiding principle would give the Court an easy and arguably principled way to effectuate a triage between potential mass atrocities that are "in" and "out" of the crimes against humanity rubric by requiring that the organization was either a state or "statelike." Yet it would exclude situations of mass atrocities committed by other organizations and ignore the evolution of crimes against humanity's definition over the decades following the Nuremberg judgment.[93]

In the view of this author, the majority in the Kenya case has support in text, in the negotiating history of the statute, and as a matter of policy (and international legal principles). Yet while I do not share Judge Kaul's legal conclusions, his thoughtful dissent may signal a need for the prosecutor to use crimes against humanity charges only where their applicability to a particular situation is clear, not in borderline cases about which there is much dispute. Judicious self-restraint on the prosecutor's part, combined with the limits in the statute itself, may help the ICC to retain its legitimacy by limiting its ambit only to cases that clearly appear to merit international intervention and sanction. Indeed, the procedural and substantive constraints in the ICC Statute may ultimately assist the ICC prosecutor considerably as he or she endeavors to exercise an extraordinarily difficult mandate that is likely to upset or even infuriate those on the receiving end of the Court's arrest warrants and indictments. Faithfulness to text and responsiveness to the procedural limits on the prosecutor's power—even while aggressively and vigorously pursuing his or her independent mandate—may be critical not only to the prosecutor's success but also to the Court's overall standing and legitimacy.

NOTES

1. *See* Leila Nadya Sadat, *Crimes against Humanity in the Modern Age*, 107 AM. J. INT'L L. 334 (2013).

2. *See* Prosecutor v. Tadić, Case No. IT-94-1-A, Judgment, ¶¶238–72 (July 15, 1999), http://www.icty.org/x/cases/tadic/acjug/en/tad-aj990715e.pdf. This is the position taken by article 7 of the ICC Statute. *See also* M. CHERIF BASSIOUNI, CRIMES AGAINST HUMANITY: HISTORICAL EVOLUTION & CONTEMPORARY APPLICATION (2011).

3. *See, e.g.,* FORGING A CONVENTION FOR CRIMES AGAINST HUMANITY (Leila Nadya

Sadat ed., 2d ed., 2013); M. Cherif Bassiouni, *"Crimes against Humanity": The Need for a Specialized Convention,* 31 COLUM. J. TRANSNAT'L L. 457 (1994).

4. *See* Sadat, *supra* note 1.

5. *See* Rome Statute of the International Criminal Court, art. 7, July 17, 1998, 2187 U.N.T.S. 90 (hereinafter Rome Statute). *See also* LEILA NADYA SADAT, THE INTERNATIONAL CRIMINAL COURT & THE TRANSFORMATION OF INTERNATIONAL LAW (2002).

6. *See* Rome Statute, *supra* note 5, pmbl., cl. 4.

7. An initiative spearheaded by the author is currently endeavoring to fill this gap. *See* Sadat, *supra* note 3 and accompanying text.

8. *See, e.g., Affirmation of the Principles of International Law Recognized by the Charter of the Nuremberg Tribunal,* G.A. Res. 95(1), U.N. Doc. A/RES/95(1) (Dec. 11, 1946); International Law Commission, *Report on the Formulation of Nürnberg Principles,* Prepared by the Special Rapporteur, Mr. J. Spiropoulos (A/CN.4/22, 12 Apr. 1950, *reproduced in* YEARBOOK OF THE INTERNATIONAL LAW COMMISSION, 1950, vol. 2). Crimes against humanity were incorporated in the Israeli legal system in several ways. *See, e.g.,* Nazis and Nazi Collaborators (Punishment) Law of 1950, 5710-1950, 4 LSI 154 (Isr.); CrimC (Jer) 40/61 Attorney General of the Government of Israel v. Eichmann (1961); CrimA 366/61 Eichmann v. Attorney General 17 IsrSC 2033 (1962). Before Mar. 1, 1994, crimes against humanity were incorporated in the French legal system through Law 64-1326 of Dec. 26, 1964 by reference to the Nuremberg Principles; Public Prosecutor v. Barbie (France) Trial Judgment, Assize Court of Rhône (July 4, 1987); Public Prosecutor v. Touvier (France) Trial Judgment, Assize Court of Yvelines (Apr. 20, 1994). *See also* Leila Nadya Sadat, *The Nuremberg Paradox,* 58 AM. J. COMP. L. 151 (2010). For Canada, see R. v. Finta, (1993) 1 S.C.R. 1138 (Can.); Mugesera v. Canada, (2005) 2 S.C.R. 100 (Can.). *See also* Statute of the International Criminal Tribunal for the Former Yugoslavia, S.C. Res. 1166, U.N. Doc. S/RES/1166, at art. 5 (May 13, 1998) (hereinafter ICTY Statute); International Criminal Tribunal for Rwanda, S.C. Res. 955, U.N. SCOR, 49th sess., U.N. Doc. S/RES/955, at art. 3 (Nov. 8, 1994) (hereinafter ICTR Statute); Statute of the Special Court for Sierra Leone, S.C. Res. 1315, U.N. Doc. S/RES/955 (Aug. 14, 2000) (authorizing the U.N. secretary-general to negotiate an agreement with Sierra Leone to create a special court); UNTAET, On the Amendment of UNTAET Regulation No.2000/11 on the Organization of Courts in East Timor and UNTAET Regulation No.2000/30 on the Transitional Rules of Criminal Procedure, §9, UNTAET/REG/2001/25 (Sept. 14, 2001) (hereinafter East Timor Statute); G.A. Res. 57/228, 57th Sess., U.N. Doc. A/RES/57/228, at art. 5 (Dec. 18, 2002) (hereinafter ECCC Statute). *See also supra* note 3.

9. *See generally* KELLY DAWN ASKIN, WAR CRIMES AGAINST WOMEN: PROSECUTION IN INTERNATIONAL WAR CRIMES TRIBUNALS (1997).

10. *See* Prosecutor v. Tadić, Case No. IT-94-1-T, Decision on the Defense Motion for Interlocutory Appeal on Jurisdiction (Int'l Crim Trib. for the Former Yugoslavia Oct. 2, 1995), http://www.icty.org/x/cases/tadic/acdec/en/51002.htm; Prosecutor v. Tadić, Case No. IT-94-1-T, Opinion and Judgment (Int'l Crim Trib. for the Former Yugoslavia May 7, 1997), http://www.icty.org/x/cases/tadic/tjug/en/tad-tsj70507JT2-e.pdf.

11. *See* Prosecutor v. Akayesu, Case No. ICTR-96-4-T, Judgment (Sept. 2, 1998), http://www.unictr.org/Portals/0/Case/English/Akayesu/judgement/akay001.pdf.

12. *See* Prosecutor v. Tadić, Case No. IT-94-1-T, Judgment, ¶¶650–52 (Int'l Crim. Trib. for the Former Yugoslavia May 7, 1997), *rev'd,* Prosecutor v. Tadić, Case No. IT-94-

1-A, Judgment, ¶305 (Int'l Crim. Trib. for the Former Yugoslavia July 15, 1999), http:// www.icty.org/x/cases/tadic/acjug/en/tad-aj990715e.pdf. The French delegation had advocated on behalf of this position, perhaps relying on France's own jurisprudence after World War II. *See* Darryl Robinson, *The Elements of Crimes against Humanity,* in THE INTERNATIONAL CRIMINAL COURT: ELEMENTS OF CRIMES & RULES OF PROCEDURE & EVIDENCE 63 (Roy S. Lee ed., 2001). This linkage is reinserted, however, in the definition of persecution under article 7(1)(h).

13. *See* Rodney Dixon, *Article 7: Crimes against Humanity,* in COMMENTARY ON THE ROME STATUTE OF THE INTERNATIONAL CRIMINAL COURT, 123 (Otto Triffterer ed., 1999). The French text of the ICTR Statute used *and,* but the tribunal viewed this as a drafting error.

14. The statute reads "persecution against any identifiable group or collectivity on political, racial, national, ethnic, cultural, religious, gender . . . or other grounds that are universally recognised as impermissible under international law," thereby considerably broadening the ambit of the provision's protections. However, it adds that the persecution must be "in connection with any referred to in this paragraph or any crime within the jurisdiction of the Court," which appears, like the judgment of the International Military Tribunal as well as the case law from the ICTY and ICTR, to reintroduce the idea that the crime of persecution must be accompanied by war or other acts of violence. *See* Ken Roberts, *The Law of Persecution before the International Criminal Tribunal for the Former Yugoslavia,* 15 LEIDEN J. INT'L L. 623, 632 (2002); Prosecutor v. Kupreškić, Case No. IT-95-16-T, Judgment, ¶¶573–581 (Int'l Crim. Trib. for the Former Yugoslavia Jan. 14, 2000), http://www.icty.org/x/cases/kupreskic/tjug/en/kup-tj000114e.pdf.

15. However, some should arguably be considered as jurisdictional in character, meaning that once they have been proven as regards a particular situation, they should not be reestablished *ab initio* with respect to each accused. *See, e.g.,* SADAT, *supra* note 5, at 146–48.

16. *See* Rome Statute, *supra* note 5, art. 7(1).

17. *Id.* Some delegations supported deletion of the words *civilian population* during the Rome Conference as too limiting, but this traditional limit on the ambit of crimes against humanity remained.

18. *Id.*

19. *Id.* art. 7(2)(a).

20. For a discussion of the negotiating history of article 7, see Sadat, *supra* note 1.

21. This requirement was articulated in the *Barbie* case and followed in subsequent decisions. *See* Prosecutor v. Klaus Barbie (Fr.), Judgment of June 3, 1988, Cour de cassation [Cass.] [supreme court for judicial matters] crim., 1988 J.C.P. IIG, No. 21,149 (Report of Counselor Angevin).

22. *See* Guénaël Mettraux, *Crimes against Humanity & the Question of a "Policy" Element,* in FORGING A CONVENTION FOR CRIMES AGAINST HUMANITY 142, 162–66 (Leila Nadya Sadat ed., 2011).

23. *See* Leila Nadya Sadat, *The Application of the Nuremberg Principles by the French Court of Cassation: From Touvier to Barbie & Back Again,* 32 COLUM. J. TRANSNAT'L L. 289, 361–63 (1994) (discussing the need for a "common plan" in the French case law). *But see* M. CHERIF BASSIOUNI, CRIMES AGAINST HUMANITY: HISTORICAL EVOLUTION & CONTEMPORARY APPLICATION 47 (2011) (noting that state policy is an essential characteristic of crimes against humanity).

24. The recollection of this author is that it was intended at least to address actions taken by various nonstate entities in a case involving a state's disintegration into component parts or situations in which no clear central authority exists. *See* Author's notes, Rome Diplomatic Conference.

25. *See* Robinson, *supra* note 12, at 58.

26. *Id.* at 78.

27. The official ICC website tracks the current situations and cases. *See All Situations,* ICC WEBSITE, http://www.icc-cpi.int/en_menus/icc/situations%20and%20cases/situations/Pages/situations%20index.aspx.

28. *See* Sadat, *supra* note 1, at 373.

29. *See* ICC, *President of Uganda Refers Situation Concerning the Lord's Resistance Army (LRA) to the ICC* (Jan. 29, 2004), http://www.icc-cpi.int/en_menus/icc/Pages/default.aspx (follow "Press and Media" link; then follow "Press Releases" link; then follow "2004" link).

30. *See* Luis Moreno Ocampo, Chief Prosecutor, to President Philippe Kirsch (June 17, 2004) (on file with author). No charges have been brought against any government officials, although allegations of war crimes and torture have been made against Ugandan government officials. *See, e.g.,* Human Rights Watch, *State of Pain: Torture in Uganda* (Mar. 2004) (alleging cases of torture and arbitrary detention); Payam Akhaven, *The Lord's Resistance Army Case: Uganda's Submission of the First State Referral to the International Criminal Court,* 99 AM. J. INT'L L. 403, 403–4 (2005). *See also* International Crisis Group, *Building a Comprehensive Peace Strategy for Northern Uganda,* Africa Briefing No. 27 (June 23, 2005), http://www.crisisgroup.org/en/regions/africa/horn-of-africa/uganda/B027-building-a-comprehensive-peace-strategy-for-northern-uganda.aspx.

31. H. E. Yoweri Kaguta Museveni, President of the Republic of Uganda, *Statement at the 68th United Nations General Assembly* (Sept. 24, 2013), http://www.statehouse.go.ug/media/speeches/2013/09/25/statement-he-yoweri-kaguta-museveni-president-republic-uganda-68th-united-.

32. *See* ICC, *Prosecutor Receives Referral of the Situation in the Democratic Republic of Congo* (Apr. 19, 2004), http://www.icc-cpi.int/en_menus/icc/Pages/default.aspx (follow "Press and Media" link; then follow "Press Releases" link; then follow "2004" link).

33. *See* ICC, *Prosecutor Receives Referral Concerning Central African Republic* (Jan. 7, 2005), http://www.icc-cpi.int/en_menus/icc/Pages/default.aspx (follow "Press and Media" link; then follow "Press Releases" link; then follow "2005" link).

34. *See* Sadat, *supra* note 1, at 357–61.

35. *See* Prosecutor v. Katanga, Case No. ICC-01/04–01/07, Decision on the Confirmation of Charges, ¶396 (Sept. 30, 2008), http://www.icc-cpi.int/iccdocs/doc/doc571253.pdf.

36. *Id.*

37. *Id.* at ¶399.

38. This dictum has been expanded in later confirmation decisions of the Court. *See, e.g.,* Prosecutor v. Francis Kirimi Muthaura et al., Case No. ICC-01/09-02/11, Decision on the Confirmation of Charges Pursuant to Article 61(7)(a) and (6) of the Rome Statute, ¶110 (Jan. 23, 2012), http://www.icc-cpi.int/iccdocs/doc/doc1314543.pdf (hereinafter Muthaura Confirmation of Charges Decision).

39. *Id.* at ¶78.

40. *See* Prosecutor v. Callixte Mbarushimana, Case No. ICC-01/04-01/10, Decision on the Confirmation of Charges (Dec. 16, 2011), http://www.icc-cpi.int/iccdocs/doc/doc1286409.pdf. *See also* Prosecutor v. Bemba, Case No. ICC-01/05-01/08, Decision Pursuant to Article 61(7)(a) and (b) of the Rome Statute on the Charges of the Prosecutor against Jean-Pierre Bemba Gombo (June 15, 2009), http://www.icc-cpi.int/iccdocs/doc/doc699541.pdf.

41. Of interest is the Chamber's searching review of the prosecution's evidence in terms of Bemba's individual criminal responsibility for the crimes alleged to have been committed by Movement for the Liberation of the Congo (MLC) troops. The Chamber found that Bemba could not be charged as a co-perpetrator under article 25(3)(a) but could only be charged under article 28(a) with command responsibility as a military commander. *See* Prosecutor v. Bemba, No. ICC-01/05-01/08, Decision Pursuant to Article 61(7)(a) and (b) of the Rome Statute on the Charges of the Prosecutor against Jean-Pierre Bemba Gombo, at ¶446 (June 15, 2009), http://www.icc-cpi.int/iccdocs/doc/doc699541.pdf.

42. *See* Int'l Comm. of Inquiry on Darfur, U.N.S.C., *Report to the Secretary-General* 2–3 (Jan. 25, 2005), http://www.un.org/news/dh/sudan/com_inq_darfur.pdf. *See also id.* ¶¶98–139 (discussing the Janjaweed).

43. *Id.* at 3.

44. *Id.* at 4. The ICC's Elements of Crimes provide that "the conduct [must take] place in the context of a manifest pattern of similar conduct directed against that group or was conduct that could itself effect such destruction." *See* ICC, Elements of Crimes, art. 6(a)(4) (2011) (defining genocide by killing). This, however, seems more of a "widespread and systematic" requirement than a requirement of policy and in any event is not found in the definition of genocide in article II of the Genocide Convention.

45. *See* Int'l Comm. of Inquiry on Darfur, *supra* note 42, ¶¶489–522 (describing issue of genocide).

46. *See* S.C. Res. 1593, ¶1, U.N. Doc. S/RES/1593 (Mar. 31, 2005).

47. *See* Prosecutor v. Harun and Kushayb, Case No. ICC-02/05-01/07, Warrant of Arrest for Ahmad Harun (Apr. 27, 2007), http://www.icc-cpi.int/iccdocs/doc/doc279813.pdf; Prosecutor v. Harun and Kushayb, Case No. ICC-02/05/01/07, Warrant of Arrest for Ali Kushayb (Apr. 27, 2007), http://www.icc-cpi.int/iccdocs/doc/doc279860.PDF.

48. *See* Prosecutor v. Omar Hassan Ahmad al-Bashir, Case No. ICC-02/0 5-01/09, *Decision on the Prosecution's Application for a Warrant of Arrest against Omar Hassan Ahmad al-Bashir,* ¶249 (Mar. 4, 2009), http://www.icc-cpi.int/iccdocs/doc/doc639096.pdf.

49. *Id.* at ¶205.

50. *See* Prosecutor v. Omar Hassan Ahmad al-Bashir, Case No. ICC-02/05-01/09, Decision on the Prosecutor's Application for Leave to Appeal the "Decision on the Prosecution's Application for a Warrant of Arrest against Omar Hassan Ahmad al-Bashir," (June 24, 2009), http://www.icc-cpi.int/iccdocs/doc/doc702324.pdf.

51. *See* Prosecutor v. Omar Hassan Ahmad al-Bashir, Case No. ICC-02/05-01/09-OA, Judgment on the Appeal of the Prosecutor against the "Decision on the Prosecution's Application for a Warrant of Arrest against Omar Hassan Ahmad al-Bashir," (Feb. 3, 2010), http://www.icc-cpi.int/iccdocs/doc/doc817795.pdf.

52. *See* Prosecutor v. Omar Hassan Ahmad al-Bashir, Case No. ICC-02/05-01/09,

Second Decision on the Prosecution's Application for a Warrant of Arrest, ¶43 (July 12, 2010), http://www.icc-cpi.int/iccdocs/doc/doc907142.pdf.

53. *See* Nicholas Kulish, *Kenyan Lawmakers Vote to Leave International Court*, N.Y. TIMES, Sept. 5, 2013, http://www.nytimes.com/2013/09/06/world/africa/kenyan-lawmakers-vote-to-leave-international-court.html?_r=0.

54. *See* African Union, *On the Decisions of Pre-Trial Chamber I of the International Criminal Court (ICC) Pursuant to Article 87(7) of the Rome Statute on the Alleged Failure by the Republic of Chad & the Republic of Malawi to Comply with the Cooperation Requests Issued by the Court with Respect to the Arrest & Surrender of President Omar Hassan al-Bashir of the Republic of Sudan* (Jan. 9, 2012), http://www.au.int/en/sites/default/files/PR-%20002-%20ICC%20English.pdf. The fourth case in the Sudan situation involved three individuals accused of attacks on African Union peacekeepers. They received summonses to appear and did so; because all three cases involve only war crimes, they add little to this essay, although one of the cases was dismissed by Pre-Trial Chamber I. *See* Prosecutor v. Bahar Idriss Abu Garda, Case No. ICC-02/05-02/09, Decision on the Confirmation of the Charges (Feb. 8, 2010), http://www.icc-cpi.int/iccdocs/doc/doc819602.pdf. On Apr. 23, 2010, Pre-Trial Chamber I issued a decision rejecting the prosecutor's application to appeal the decision. The other two are currently awaiting trial.

55. *See* Situation in the Republic of Kenya, Case No. ICC-01/09, Request for Authorization of an Investigation Pursuant to Article 15 (Nov. 26, 2009), http://www.icc-cpi.int/iccdocs/doc/doc785972.pdf.

56. *See* ICC, *Waki Commission List of Names in the Hands of ICC Prosecutor* (July 16, 2009), http://www.icc-cpi.int/Pages/default.aspx (follow "Press and Media" link; then follow "Press Releases" link; then follow "2009" link) .

57. The prosecutor received this information on July 16, 2009, following meetings with the Kenyan government and failed efforts to establish a specially constituted tribunal to conduct proceedings in Kenya.

58. *See* Situation in the Republic of Kenya, Case No. ICC-01/09, Decision Pursuant to Article 15 of the Rome Statute on the Authorization of an Investigation into the Situation in the Republic of Kenya, ¶35 (Mar. 31, 2010), http://www.icc-cpi.int/iccdocs/doc/doc854287.pdf (hereinafter Kenya Article 15 Decision).

59. *Id.* at app. ¶18 (Kaul, J., dissenting).

60. *Id.* at ¶80.

61. *See* Situation in the Republic of Kenya, Case No. ICC-01/09, Request for Authorization of an Investigation Pursuant to Article 15, ¶4 (Nov. 26, 2009), http://www.icc-cpi.int/iccdocs/doc/doc785972.pdf.

62. *Id.* at ¶56.

63. *Id.*

64. *Id.* at ¶74.

65. *Id.* at ¶¶104–6.

66. *Id.* at ¶114. There is little information on the police attacks and their organization in the opinion or the prosecutor's request for authorization. Clearly, however, the police attacks severely worsened the scope and gravity of the violence and aggravated the attacks by rival groups.

67. *See* Kenya Article 15 Decision, *supra* note 58, ¶86.

68. *Id.* at ¶87(citing Prosecutor v. Blaškić, Case No. ICTY-95-14-T, Judgment, ¶205 [Mar. 3, 2000]).

69. *Id.* at ¶90, n.82. The French text provides, "en application ou dans la poursuite de la politique d'un État ou d'une organisation ayant pour but une telle attaque." *See* Rome Statute, *supra* note 5, art. 7(2)(a).

70. *See* Kenya Article 15 Decision, *supra* note 58, ¶90. The Chamber quoted with approval language from M. Di Filippo, as well as the writings of other scholars, to the effect that purely private criminal organizations could satisfy the "organizational policy" requirement. *See* M. Di Filippo, *Terrorist Crimes & International Cooperation: Critical Remarks on the Definition & Inclusion of Terrorism in the Category of International Crimes*, 19 EUR. J. INT'L. L. 533 (2008).

71. *See* Kenya Article 15 Decision, *supra* note 58, ¶89.

72. The dissent argued that the ICTY case law could not guide the Chamber's analysis, apparently reading article 21 of the Court's statute (on applicable law) more narrowly than the majority, particularly with regard to the use of case law from other tribunals. His view seems narrower than international law requires, as judicial decisions may be accorded subsidiary value in ascertaining rules of customary international law. *See* Statute of the International Court of Justice, art. 38(1)(d). Indeed, the ICC has often looked to the jurisprudence of the ICTY—i.e., in the *Lubanga* confirmation decision regarding the definition of international armed conflict, for example at ¶¶205–11 (adopting the overall control test).

73. *See* Kenya Article 15 Decision, *supra* note 58, app. ¶52 (Kaul, J., dissenting).

74. *Id.* at app. ¶82 (Kaul, J, dissenting).

75. *Id.* at app. ¶9 (Kaul, J., dissenting).

76. *Id.* at app. ¶10 (Kaul, J., dissenting).

77. One section of the dissent suggests that the principles in the Vienna Convention on the Law of Treaties (VCLOT) supports—indeed, mandates—Kaul's position. It is undoubtedly true that the VCLOT requires reference to the "ordinary meaning to be given to the terms of the treaty in their context and in the light of [the treaty's] object and purpose." *See* Vienna Convention on the Law of Treaties art. 31, May 22, 1969, 1155 U.N.T.S. 331. This much is uncontroversial. Yet given that the plain meaning cannot be derived solely from the text, under VCLOT, reference must be made to the "object and purpose" of the treaty. In the view of this author, the dissent's reading of article 7(2)(a) would lead to a result inconsistent with other sections both of article 7 (by effectively reinserting a link to armed conflict which had been deleted by the drafters) and undermine the broader purpose of the statute's crimes against humanity provision, which tends toward the protection of "civilian populations."

78. *See, e.g.,* Claus Kress, *On the Outer Limits of Crimes against Humanity: The Concept of Organization within the Policy Requirement: Some Reflections on the March 2010 ICC Kenya Decision*, 23 LEIDEN J. INT'L L. 855 (2010); Charles C. Jalloh, *Situation in the Republic of Kenya*, 105 AM. J. INT'L L. 540 (2011); William A. Schabas, *Prosecuting Dr. Strangelove, Goldfinger, & the Joker at the International Criminal Court: Closing the Loopholes*, 23 LEIDEN J. INT'L. L. 847 (2010); *but see* Darryl Robinson, *Essence of Crimes against Humanity Raised by Challenges at ICC*, EJIL: TALK!, Sept. 27, 2011, http://www.ejiltalk.org/essence-of-crimes-against-humanity-raised-by-challenges-at-icc/#more-3782.

79. *See, e.g.,* Sadat, *supra* note 23. *See also* Antonio Cassese, *Crimes against Humanity*, in THE ROME STATUTE OF THE INTERNATIONAL CRIMINAL COURT 357 (A. Cassese, P. Gaeta, J. Jones eds., 2001) ("Crimes of this category are characterized either by their se-

riousness and their savagery . . . or by their magnitude, or by the fact that they were part of a system designed to spread terror, or that they were a link in a deliberately-pursued policy against certain groups") (internal citations omitted).

80. *See* Prosecutor v. Ruto, Kosgey, and Sang, Case No. ICC-01/09-01/11 OA, Judgment on the Appeal of the Republic of Kenya against the Decision of Pre-Trial Chamber II of 30 May 2011 Entitled "Decision on the Application by the Government of Kenya Challenging the Admissibility of the Case Pursuant to Article 19(2)(b) of the Statute (Aug. 30, 2011), http://www.icc-cpi.int/iccdocs/doc/doc1223118.pdf (hereinafter Ruto, Kosgey, and Sang Judgment). *See also* Prosecutor v. Muthaura, Kenyatta, and Ali, Case No. ICC-01/09-02/11 OA, Judgment on the Appeal of the Republic of Kenya against the Decision of Pre-Trial Chamber II of 30 May 2011 Entitled "Decision on the Application by the Government of Kenya Challenging the Admissibility of the Case Pursuant to Article 19(2)(b) of the Statute" (Aug. 30, 2011), http://www.icc-cpi.int/iccdocs/doc/doc1223134.pdf.

81. Reports of the confirmation hearings suggested that the accused ably defended themselves. *See, e.g., Confirmation of Charges Hearing in the Case of Ruto et al.,* INTERNATIONAL CRIMINAL COURT: KENYA MONITOR (Sept. 1, 2011), http://www.icckenya.org/2011/09/confirmation-of-charges-hearing-in-the-case-of-ruto-et-al-begins/; Steven Kay, *Uhuru Kenyatta Defence Team Respond to ICC Prosecutor. Kenyatta Gives Live Evidence,* INT'L CRIMINAL LAW BUREAU (Sept. 30, 2011), http://www.internationallawbureau.com/index.php/uhuru-kenyatta-defence-team-respond-to-the-icc-prosecutor-kenyatta-gives-live-evidence/. They also suggested that support among Kenyans for the ICC's intervention appears quite strong. *See, e.g.,* Henry Wanyama, *Kenyans Still Support ICC Trials, Says Poll,* KENYA STAR (Apr. 6, 2011), http://www.the-star.co.ke/news/article-67399/kenyans-still-support-icc-trials-says-poll.

82. *See* Prosecutor v. Ruto, Kosgey, and Sang, Case No. ICC-01/09-01/11, Decision on the Confirmation of Charges Pursuant to Article 61(7)(a) and (b) of the Rome Statute (Jan. 23, 2012), http://www.icc-cpi.int/iccdocs/doc/doc1314535.pdf (hereinafter Ruto, Kosgey, and Sang Confirmation of Charges); Prosecutor v. Muthaura, Kenyatta, and Ali, Case No. ICC-1/09-02/11, Decision on the Confirmation of Charges Pursuant to Article 61(7) (a) and (b) of the Rome Statute (Jan. 23, 2012), http://www.icc-cpi.int/iccdocs/doc/doc1314543.pdf.

83. *See* Ruto, Kosgey, and Sang Confirmation of Charges, *supra* note 82, at ¶164; Muthaura Confirmation of Charges Decision, *supra* note 38, at ¶110.

84. *See* Muthaura Confirmation of Charges Decision, *supra* note 38, at ¶¶111–14.

85. *See* Ruto, Kosgey, and Sang Confirmation of Charges, *supra* note 82, at ¶¶184–208.

86. *Id.* at ¶182.

87. *Id.* at app. ¶12 (Kaul, J., dissenting). Judge Kaul made similar findings in his dissent to the *Muthaura* case, finding that the "Mungiki" was a criminal gang but not one falling within the meaning of "organization" in article 7. *See* Muthaura Confirmation of Charges Decision, *supra* note 38, app. ¶¶15–21 (Kaul, J., dissenting).

88. *See* Ruto, Kosgey, and Sang Confirmation of Charges, *supra* note 82, app. ¶12 (Kaul, J., dissenting). Judge Kaul also noted that he believes article 54 requires an investigation to be substantially complete prior to confirmation of the charges rather than following the confirmation hearing. *Id.* at app. ¶52.

89. *Id.* at app. ¶¶59–60.

90. *Id.* at app. ¶99.

91. *See* Fatou Bensouda, ICC Prosecutor, Statement on the Notice to Withdraw Charges against Mr. Muthaura (Mar. 11, 2013), http://www.icc-cpi.int/en_menus/icc/press%20and%20media/press%20releases/Pages/OTP-statement-11-03-2013.aspx.

92. *See* Kulish, *supra* note 53.

93. The same concern arises in other decisions by the Court's Pre-Trial Chambers, such as the decision to dismiss the proceedings in the *Mbarushimana* case based on a narrow reading of article 7.

Rethinking the Tension between Peace and Justice

The International Criminal Prosecutor as Diplomat

Robert H. Mnookin

Imagine you are the prosecutor of the International Criminal Court (ICC). The war-torn country of Afghanistan is hobbling toward a fragile cease-fire. The president of Afghanistan and the Taliban have struck a tentative deal, which a war-weary American government supports. The Taliban will renounce al-Qaeda and terrorism. All remaining NATO combat troops will leave Afghanistan. The peace accord contemplates regional power sharing and national reconciliation. Mullah Omar and other exiled Taliban leaders will be allowed to return to the country and participate openly in Afghan politics. An essential element of the deal is a general amnesty, in which all combatants, including Mullah Omar, will receive immunity in Afghan courts from prosecution for crimes committed during the hostilities.

You suspect that during the civil war, combatants on all sides, including members of the Taliban and various warlords supporting the Karzai government, may have committed war crimes and crimes against humanity, as defined by the Rome Statute of the International Criminal Court.[1] American and United Nations diplomats informally tell you that prosecutorial actions on your part are likely to derail the fragile peace process and risk plunging the ravaged country back into deadly civil war. How would you respond? To what extent, if any, should you, as a responsible prosecutor charged with enforcement of the Rome Statute, consider the potential impact your actions may have on efforts to end armed conflict and promote national reconciliation?

For Afghanistan and other countries struggling to move beyond violent conflict, there may be a tension between the pursuit of peace and the pursuit of justice. The pursuit of peace often requires a negotiated resolution of armed conflict. The prospect of criminal prosecution may cause offenders to fight to the bitter end if they believe a negotiated "peace" means they will be exposed to severe criminal sanctions. The pursuit of justice often requires that the victims of heinous war crimes are heard and the guilty are punished.

History demonstrates that this tension is not hypothetical. Foregone justice—for example, amnesty from imprisonment—is often "the price for getting rid of tyrants and their associates" and "one of the techniques for ending civil wars or enabling transitions from authoritarian to democratic governments."[2] As Alexander Hamilton recognized more than two centuries ago, "In seasons of insurrection or rebellion, there are often critical moments, when a well-timed offer of pardon to the insurgents or rebels may restore tranquility to the commonwealth."[3] Conversely, allowing perpetrators to bargain for immunity offends our sense of justice and hardly serves deterrence. How should the prosecutor manage this tension?

The prosecutor appears to ignore the tension and honor only the demands of justice. A 2007 policy paper interpreting article 53 of the Rome Statute provides that the prosecutor may decline to investigate or prosecute an accused when doing so is not "in the interests of justice."[4] The announced policy precludes any consideration under article 53 of the potential impact of prosecutorial decisions on peacemaking efforts. Instead, the policy paper indicates that the prosecutor should be exclusively concerned with the pursuit of justice, narrowly conceived as the enforcement of law.[5] The policy paper then goes on to suggest that under the Rome Statute generally, the possible impact of a prosecution on ongoing peace processes is irrelevant and that broader issues of morality, politics, and peacemaking are not to be taken into account when deciding whether to initiate an investigation or begin a prosecution.[6] Instead, according to the policy paper, issued by Luis Moreno Ocampo (the first ICC prosecutor), these broader issues are the responsibility of the Security Council.[7] Moreno Ocampo's successor, Fatou Bensouda, has since reaffirmed this reading of the Rome Statute.[8]

I reject the suggestion that the prosecutor has an absolute obligation to investigate and prosecute crimes irrespective of the impact of those actions on peace negotiations. Even if one accepts the prosecutor's narrow reading of the article 53 provision, the broader suggestion that considerations of peacemaking and politics are irrelevant to the exercise of prosecutorial discretion under the remainder of the Rome Statute is unwise. The prosecutor is a political actor embedded in international politics, a diplomat representing the interests of both the ICC and the party states and their citizens. In that role, the prosecutor must constantly assess the effect her (and since the current prosecutor is female, I will refer to the prosecutor with feminine pronouns throughout) actions will have on both the Court and its member states. She cannot ignore the tension between the pursuit of peace and the pursuit of justice but instead must diplomatically manage this tension. I suggest how this might best be accomplished.

The first part of this chapter assesses the prosecutor's arguments in the policy paper relating to article 53 against the broader purposes of the Rome Statute and the prosecutor's underlying interests and institutional role. I suggest that managing that the tension between peace and justice does not as a general proposition require a categorical either/or choice of one value to the exclusion of the other. In the second and third sections, I reject the broad suggestion that the Rome Statute entirely precludes the prosecutor from taking account of political and peace-related considerations in the exercise of her prosecutorial discretion. A close examination of the prosecutorial process specified by the Rome Treaty demonstrates that the prosecutor has largely unfettered discretion to control timing—the choice of *when* to begin an investigation or prosecution. These discretionary timing decisions can take into consideration the impact of prosecutorial action on peace processes and reconciliation. The prosecutor can also forge an accommodation between the interests of peace and justice through the use of article 17's complementarity provision. In the fourth part of the chapter, I develop four guidelines from these insights to assist the prosecutor when she is confronted with a tension between peace and justice. The chapter then offers some conclusions.

The Rome Statute, the Interests of Justice Provision, and the Tension between Peace and Justice

The Rome Statute provides a framework for the investigation, prosecution, and punishment of genocide, war crimes, and crimes against humanity.[9] The prosecutor may only investigate and prosecute crimes that fall within the jurisdiction of the International Criminal Court,[10] and the crimes that have allegedly occurred in Afghanistan appear to meet the statute's jurisdictional standards.[11]

Parties to the Rome Conference did not overlook the tension between peace and justice; in fact, they hotly debated the extent to which political considerations should temper the decision to prosecute genocide, war crimes, and crimes against humanity. The United States argued in Rome that prosecutions should be limited to cases referred to the prosecutor by the Security Council.[12] This would have provided a robust political check on the power of the prosecutor and would have limited her ability to pursue the alleged war crimes in Afghanistan if the United States objected. But this view did not win the day because "the prevailing parties in Rome believed that the Security Council—and in particular the opportunistic votes of veto-wielding permanent members—was part of the problem."[13] Instead, they provided a much more limited political check: the Security Council may vote to delay prosecutions for twelve months.[14] The absence of Security Council or Great Power veto came at a high cost: the United States, Russia, and China all declined to sign the Rome Statute and grant the prosecutor jurisdiction over their territory, for fear that there were insufficient political checks on the power of the prosecutor to act.

As enacted, the Rome Statute thus created an Office of the Prosecutor with the power to investigate and prosecute crimes without having to obtain prior approval of the Security Council. This does not mean that the prosecutor is not subject to a variety of "softer" political constraints, including diplomatic pressure. The Office of the Prosecutor has limited financial resources and must rely on appropriations for its annual budget.[15] The prosecutor also lacks a police force and must therefore rely on the cooperation of states during the investigation and prosecution of crimes. But the significant point is that state parties lack significant means under the Rome Statute to force the prosecutor to drop a prosecution because they believe that an investigation or prosecution (the pursuit of justice) will undermine the pursuit of peace.

That the Rome Statute limits the power of *states* to override prosecutions that interfere with peacemaking processes does not mean that the statute necessarily precludes the *prosecutor* from considering the interests of peace in the exercise of her prosecutorial discretion. What guidance does the statute itself offer? The statute mentions the word *peace* only once, in the preamble, and is silent on whether the prosecutor should consider peacemaking processes while exercising prosecutorial discretion. One section of the Rome Statute, however, expressly acknowledges that the prosecutor might sometimes choose not to investigate or prosecute a crime when doing so is not in the "interests of justice."

Article 53 of the Rome Statute

Article 53 of the Rome Statute explicitly provides that the prosecutor may decline to investigate or prosecute crimes squarely within the ICC's jurisdiction because he believes pursuing the crime does not serve "the interests of justice." The prosecutor may decline to *investigate* a crime if, "taking into account the gravity of the crime and the interests of victims, there are nonetheless substantial reasons to believe that an investigation would not serve *the interests of justice.*"[16] The language with respect to a decision not to *prosecute* is more open ended: in determining the "interests of justice," the prosecutor may "tak[e] into account *all the circumstances,*" including not only "the gravity of the crime [and] the interests of victims" but also "the age or infirmity of the alleged perpetrator, and his or her role in the alleged crime."[17]

The words of article 53 are hardly self-defining. On the one hand, there is no reference to peacemaking or reconciliation. On the other hand, considerations of peacemaking might be included in the "interests" of justice or "all the circumstances." Article 53 might be read broadly enough to permit the prosecutor to defer an investigation or prosecution that might obstruct peace and reconciliation efforts and lead to "many more civilian deaths."[18]

This ambiguity appears to have been a deliberate choice.[19] The parties to the Rome Convention could not agree on the Court's role in cases where crimes are within the Court's jurisdiction, but a party state decides not to pursue criminal prosecutions. A number of delegations argued that the Statute should be flexible and not require the prosecutor to pursue every crime within the Court's jurisdiction.[20] But other delegations opposed considering the interests of peace out of principle: to them, it was unthinkable that those who commit genocide might get away without punishment.[21] They argued that permitting an exception to prosecution would swallow the rule.[22] Any "attempt at definition would have broken down at the Rome Conference, given profound disagreements about how the prosecutor should be governed in situations like that posed where a peace process requires justice to take a back seat."[23] At an impasse, the parties opted for "creative ambiguity."[24]

The Prosecutor's Policy Paper on the Interests of Justice

Against this background, the prosecutor issued the 2007 policy paper.[25] The policy paper categorically stated that considerations of peacemaking or reconciliation would not be taken into account in the exercise of prosecutorial discretion under the "interests of justice" provision of article 53. In doing so, the policy paper also suggested that these considerations would not influence the exercise of prosecutorial discretion under the statute as a whole.[26]

The prosecutor begins the policy paper by claiming that the Rome Statute establishes a "presumption in favour of investigation or prosecution" of crimes within the Court's jurisdiction. The Rome Statute embraces the idea that the best way to prevent the most serious crimes of concern to the international community is to end impunity for those crimes.[27] According to the prosecutor, Rome has established the prosecution of genocide, war crimes, and crimes against humanity (subject to the interests of justice inquiry) as a nonnegotiable legal requirement.[28] According the policy paper, the prosecutor should "only in exceptional circumstances" decide to defer investigation or prosecution based on a determination that prosecutorial action would not serve the interests of justice.[29]

The policy paper then turns squarely to giving some meaning to the "interests of justice" inquiry. Article 53 lists three factors that the prosecutor may consider under the interests of justice: the gravity of the crime, the interests of the victim, and the interests of the accused. Gravity, the paper argues, focuses squarely on the nature, scale, and manner of the crime.[30] To evaluate the interests of the victim, the prosecutor must consider both victims' interest in seeing justice done and their need for "safety, physical and psychological well-being, dignity and privacy."[31] As for the accused, the policy paper emphasizes that investigations must focus on those leaders "bearing the greatest degree of responsibility" for the crimes.[32] But even these leaders may be spared prosecution if, for example, they are terminally ill or have themselves been victims of human rights violations.[33]

After putting aside issues of complementarity,[34] the policy paper turns to its most contentious question: may the prosecutor consider issues of peace when deciding whether to investigate and prosecute crimes? The paper suggests a categorical rule excluding any consideration of the impact of the prosecutor's actions on peace processes because of the Rome Statute's deterrence goal and because of the prosecutor's institutional role. Although peace processes are important, the paper argues that the Office of the Prosecutor, as an institution responsible for enforcing the Rome Statute, has a mandate to be concerned exclusively with the pursuit of justice, narrowly conceived as the enforcement of law. After noting that under article 16, the Security Council may defer ICC action for up to twelve months at a time,[35] the policy paper emphatically states, "The broader matter of international peace and security is not the responsibility of the prosecutor; it falls within the mandate of other institutions."[36]

As suggested earlier, this was not the only plausible reading of the interests of justice language in article 53. The drafters did agree to the goal of ending genocide, war crimes, and crimes against humanity. But there was no agreement that criminal *investigations and prosecutions* must be exclusive means to achieve that end.[37] Article 53 might have been interpreted to contemplate that the prosecutor will consider each situation on a case-by-case basis, perhaps declining to prosecute if the political demands are pressing enough.[38] Some commentators go so far as to say that the prosecutor's policy paper interpretation of the Rome Statute is *contrary to* the framers' intent and that the policy paper is "trying to impose a literal approach to legal interpretation on an expression that was intended to leave the exercise of prosecutorial discretion unfettered."[39]

Why would a prosecutor want to constrain its own discretion when the language of the statute did not require it? The policy paper might best be understood as a self-imposed commitment device to strengthen the prosecutor's bargaining position. The policy paper ties the hands of the prosecutor and would eliminate her discretion to use the "interests of justice" provision of article 53(2)(c) to consider trading a grant of immunity for peace. Thomas Schelling has described how commitment strategies that remove a party's freedom of action increase their bargaining power.[40]

That the prosecutor would want to adopt a public posture that claims to preclude consideration of peacemaking efforts is understandable from this perspective. If the prosecutor acknowledged in the policy paper that her office would take into account the impact of prosecutorial decisions on peacemaking, this would both mitigate deterrence and give her less leverage to encourage state parties to undertake prosecutions. To acknowledge a willingness to consider peacemaking invites external pressure and even negotiations.[41]

Plea-bargaining and deal-making with accused criminals is common in American jurisdictions but not in most civil law jurisdictions. Moreover, the possibility of a grant of immunity might well vitiate deterrence: would-be war criminals might figure that even if they didn't win the war, they could bargain for immunity when they sued for peace. The incentive effects might be very perverse. A cruel dictator in the midst of a civil war might accelerate his atrocities to make the demands for peace so great that the criminals receive immunity in exchange for abdicating power.

By establishing a credible threat that she will prosecute war criminals, the prosecutor also makes it more likely that member states will investigate and punish these crimes, thus conserving the international prosecutor's scarce resources. The decisions of member states to pursue crimes are made in the prosecutor's "shadow,"[42] and Moreno Ocampo has recognized the importance of this "shadow effect."[43] If a member state knows the prosecutor is likely to investigate or prosecute crimes, the state is probably more likely to investigate and prosecute. Essentially, Moreno Ocampo has indicated that his goal is to stand tall to cast a long shadow.[44]

Another consideration not mentioned in the policy paper may also have influenced the prosecutor. The prosecutor's decisions not to investigate or prosecute pursuant to article 53 are subject to judicial review by the Pre-Trial Chamber. If the prosecutor declines to investigate or prosecute "solely" because he believes pursuing the crime is not in the interests of justice, the Chamber may review the decision of its own initiative. The Chamber's powers in this area are great because it may effectively countermand the prosecutor's decision. According to the statute, the prosecutor's decision not to prosecute because of the interests of justice is "effective only if confirmed by the Pre-Trial Chamber."[45] By refusing to rely on the interests of justice provision, the prosecutor insulates his decisions from review by the Pre-Trial Chamber.

On balance, these considerations might well justify reading article 53 narrowly, to preclude consideration of peacemaking under that provision. But the policy paper ignores two constraints that as a practical matter must inform the prosecutor's decision-making. The first has to do with resource constraints. The prosecutor cannot investigate or prosecute every war crime or crime against humanity that is covered by the Rome Statute, just as a United States attorney cannot prosecute every crime falling within his jurisdiction. As Attorney General Robert Jackson explained about the federal prosecutor in the United States, "One of the greatest difficulties of the position of prosecutor is that he must pick his cases, because no prosecutor can even investigate all of the cases in which he receives complaints."[46] The exercise of prosecutorial discretion is unavoidable.

Regarding the question of choosing prosecutorial targets, Moreno Ocampo has suggested that efforts will be directed primarily toward those leaders who bear the greatest responsibility for the crimes,[47] implicitly acknowledging that other guilty parties will not be prosecuted. This shows a willingness to sacrifice or trade some "justice" to conserve prosecutorial resources and perhaps promote reconciliation.

The second constraint relates to the fact that the prosecutor lacks enforcement powers.[48] As noted earlier, the prosecutor has no police force. The support of relevant member states is indispensable in gaining access to relevant witnesses, evidence, and suspects. As a practical matter, an investigation or prosecution is unlikely to succeed without such support. And any investigation or prosecution undertaken without regard for the interests of peace is unlikely to succeed when important state parties refuse to cooperate because they believe the prosecutor's actions would jeopardize a vital interest in peacemaking.

What is most troubling is not the policy paper's conclusion with respect to article 53 but its more sweeping rhetoric that appears to suggest that the prosecutor must choose between peacemaking or justice—i.e., one value to the exclusion of the other. A "peace versus justice" frame suggests a zero-sum, either/or choice—that more of one means less of the other. This is a gross simplification.

Prosecutions may inhibit or inflame conflict.[49] Sometimes pursuing criminal sanctions through an adversarial adjudicatory process may facilitate a more peaceful transition in a war-torn society.[50] But at other times, transitions require political actors to bargain, compromise, and forgo a certain amount of justice. Perhaps most important, an all-or-nothing trade-off between the pursuit of justice and the pursuit of peace usually does not exist. A society may honor the policies said to underlie either concept to a greater or lesser degree, and it may be possible to have some of each. The prosecutor would do well to keep this in mind when deciding whether and when to pursue crimes.

I believe that the prosecutor cannot ignore the tension between peace and justice and forge ahead with investigations and prosecutions without considering the impact her actions will have on ongoing peace processes. Instead, I believe the prosecutor must diplomatically manage this tension. Despite the prosecutor's insistence to the contrary, the Rome Statute provides the prosecutor with ample tools to consider the interests of peace. Although I would not have shut the door so firmly to using article 53 to import peace considerations, I can understand why the prosecutor took this position. Nonetheless, I strongly reject the broader suggestion that considerations of peacemaking and politics are irrelevant to the exercise of prosecutorial discretion under the remainder of the Rome Statute and the implication that the prosecutor has an obligation to investigate and prosecute crimes irrespective of its impact on peace negotiations.

Timing as a Tool for Considering the Interests of Peace

One powerful tool the prosecutor has to manage the tension between peace and justice is her power to decide *when* to commence an investigation or prosecution. The prosecutor has no absolute obligation to investigate and prosecute crimes, and once investigations and prosecutions have commenced, she has ample power to delay them. This is because of the prosecutor's resource constraints, the limited power of external bodies like the Security Council to force her to act, and the discretionary nature of the judgments the prosecutor must make in deciding whether a crime within her jurisdiction has been committed. When the immediate pursuit of crimes might threaten peace processes, the prosecutor should defer investigations and prosecutions until the future.

I begin with the obvious: given the limited financial resources available to the prosecutor, not all offenders can be investigated or prosecuted; choices must be made. Resource constraints are often particularly acute in the context of international criminal prosecutions,[51] and the ICC is no exception. The ICC's total budget for 2012 was €108.8M ($142M),[52] enough to conduct only a limited number of investigations and prosecutions. Investigations into genocide, war crimes, and crimes against humanity require substantial resources, and the prosecutor's budget is insufficient to investigate and prosecute every crime within the Court's jurisdiction. According to one estimate, the prosecutor's budget permits her to conduct only three meaningful investigations at a time.[53] Indeed, the ICC budget submissions explicitly suggest that the prosecutor should manage her limited resources by engaging in a rotating investigation system, beginning new cases only as the investigation of older ones wrap up.[54] One way to mitigate this constraint is to urge state parties to investigate, with an implicit warning that the prosecutor may initiate future actions if member states do not act on their own.

The structure of the Rome Statute also permits and in many cases requires delay. The Rome Statute does not impose on the prosecutor an affirmative duty to prosecute every crime within her jurisdiction. The statute contains a variety of "provisions mandating time-consuming procedures but none encouraging haste."[55] And just as the Security Council and other political actors cannot prevent the prosecutor from investigating and prosecuting certain crimes, so, too, do they lack formal mechanisms to force the prosecutor to investigate and prosecute. To illustrate this point, I consider the three stages of investigation and prosecution, and I demonstrate that the prosecutor has substantial discretion to weigh concerns about the impact her actions will have on the pursuit of peace and reconciliation. The first stage involves a determination that a "situation" exists that warrants a preliminary examination. The second stage involves the initiation of an "investigation," which requires approval by the Pre-Trial Chamber of the Court. The third stage involves the actual prosecution in the trial itself.

Stage 1: Defining a Situation

The prosecutor's first task is to consider whether there exists a "situation" that merits a "preliminary examination" into whether some person or group has committed crimes within the prosecutor's jurisdiction. Under the Rome Statute, a "situation" can arise in three ways: (1) referral by a state party that suspects a violation of the Rome Statute may have occurred in its country; (2) referral by the United Nations Security Council; or (3) on the prosecutor's own initiative (*proprio motu*).[56] When there is a referral from either a state party or the Security Council, the prosecutor is *obligated* to conduct a preliminary examination. But absent a referral, the prosecutor has unreviewable discretion to decide whether to act *proprio motu* to initiate a "preliminary examination."[57] And even when the prosecutor is obligated to conduct a preliminary examination, the prosecutor has unreviewable discretion to decide the extent to which she will devote financial and human resources to a particular preliminary examination, so she can effectively stall an investigation that she believes is not in the interests of peace.

Stage 2: Initiating an Investigation

After conducting the preliminary examination, the prosecutor may request authorization to investigate from the Pre-Trial Chamber if she believes that "there is a reasonable basis to proceed with an investigation."[58] If the prosecutor determines that "there is no reasonable basis to proceed," however, she need not initiate an investigation.[59] This broad standard permits the prosecutor substantial discretion to decline to pursue crimes, including for the reason that the pursuit of a crime will not further the interests of peace.

The prosecutor's decision not to prosecute is also not subject to significant judicial review. If the prosecutor's decision not to investigate is based on any reason other than the "interests of justice" exception of article 53, the Pre-Trial Chamber may review only at the request of the Security Council or the referring state party. The Chamber's power is very limited: it lacks the power to reverse the prosecutor's determination and may only "ask the Prosecutor to reconsider that decision."[60] If the prosecutor's decision is based *solely* on the "interests of justice" exception, the Pre-Trial Chamber has broader powers of review: it may review that decision on its own initiative, and it has the power to reverse the prosecutor's decision.[61] This means that the prosecutor can effectively insulate from review her decision not to prosecute crimes by framing her decision as not based *solely* on the interests of justice.

Stage 3: Halting a Prosecution after an Investigation Has Begun

Even after an investigation has been initiated and approved by the Pre-Trial Chamber, the prosecutor can decide not to prosecute the crimes. The statute makes plain that after a formal investigation has been approved, the prosecutor must notify the Pre-Trial Chamber *and* the state party or the Security Council of a decision not to prosecute, providing reasons for her decision. But the Pre-Trial Chamber's review power here is just as limited as it was at stage 2. Where the prosecutor's decision not to prosecute is based on a conclusion that there "is not a sufficient legal or factual basis" for prosecution or that the case is "inadmissible" for some other reason (perhaps because the state party is pursuing the crime or because the crime falls outside the Court's jurisdiction), the Pre-Trial Chamber may review only at the request of the Security Council or referring state party and may only "request the Prosecutor to reconsider that decision"—it cannot compel a prosecution.[62] If the prosecutor's decision is based solely on the "interests of justice" exception, however, the Pre-Trial Chamber may review "on its own initiative" and reverse the decision.[63]

In sum, the prosecutor has very broad—but not unlimited—discretion to delay prosecution and even to entirely decline to pursue certain allegations. Absent a referral by a state party or the Security Council, the prosecutor has unreviewable discretion to determine whether a "situation" requires a "preliminary examination." After a referral, where the prosecutor's decision not to proceed is based on either (1) the lack of a legal or factual basis to prove a crime or (2) her judgment that the case is inadmissible as a consequence of complementarity or insufficient gravity, then the Pre-Trial Chamber can review the decision only at the request of the referring state party or the Security Council. More important, the Pre-Trial Chamber cannot reverse the prosecutor's decision.

Finally, the nature of the prosecutor's judgments about the adequacy of evidence admits substantial discretion and leaves room for the prosecutor to delay investigation or prosecution where delay serves the interests of peace. In assessing the prosecutor's discretion, there are many mixed questions of law and fact relating to the adequacy of proof. Consider, for example, whether Mullah Omar could be convicted of having committed war crimes or crimes against humanity. Suicide bombings targeting civilians might qualify as both war crimes and crimes against humanity. But a crime against humanity would require that the suicide attacks be "committed as part of a widespread or systematic attack directed against a civilian population."[64] This requires "a course of conduct involving the multiple commission" of such acts "pursuant to or in furtherance of . . . organizational policy to commit such attack."[65] Is there proof that the perpetrators were members of the Taliban? Since the Taliban is not a state, could it be proven that it used suicide bombings as part of an "organizational policy"? Similar questions would arise for prosecution of a war crime under the Rome Treaty.[66] Even when an offense falls within the definitions of crimes under the Rome Statute, an additional jurisdictional requirement still exists: the crime must be of "sufficient gravity" to be admissible under article 17.[67]

To understand the complexity of these judgments, consider again the introductory hypothetical. Under the Rome Statute, the prosecutor must decide whether (1) the Taliban acts in question would constitute a crime under the Rome Statute; and (2) the Afghan case would be "admissible" under the jurisdictional requirements of article 17.[68] The ICC can convict a defendant only if the prosecutor proves beyond a reasonable doubt that a particular accused is criminally responsible for acts defined as crimes under the Rome Statute.[69] In the hypothetical, neither the Security Council nor Afghanistan has referred the case to the prosecutor. In deciding whether to investigate, the prosecutor would know that (1) she cannot be legally compelled to declare Afghanistan a "situation" and conduct a preliminary examination; (2) even if she proceeded *proprio motu,* there would be no review of her decision not to initiate an investigation unless that decision was based on the "interests of justice" exception; and (3) even if she began an investigation, her decision not to prosecute would not be subject to reversal by the Pre-Trial Chamber unless it was based solely on the interests of justice exception. If the prosecutor fears that taking action against Mullah Omar might well jeopardize the peace process, she has substantial ability to delay prosecution.

Indeed, this cautious wait-and-see approach is exactly how Moreno Ocampo and Bensouda have approached Afghanistan. The Office of the Prosecutor has been conducting a "preliminary examination" of Afghanistan since 2007 and sent a request for information to the Afghan government in 2008.[70] Under the guise of research and fact-finding, the prosecutor has effectively stalled any ICC action in Afghanistan, presumably pending the resolution of the war. I believe this use of the prosecutor's discretion is both wise and permitted by the Rome Statute. A formal investigation or prosecution at this time would not only be practically very difficult (particularly regarding gathering evidence and apprehending suspects like Mullah Omar, who is still on the run) but might also threaten to derail any future peace processes. If the ICC indicts Mullah Omar and his cohorts, they might choose to fight to the end rather than face criminal prosecution. This could prolong the war by deterring Taliban leaders from coming forward to engage in a peace deal.

The prosecutor has taken a similar approach to Palestine's 2009 request that the ICC investigate Israel's actions in Gaza. The prosecutor took more than three years to determine whether Palestine might properly bring an action before the ICC. In April 2012, the prosecutor decided that Palestine is not a "state" within the meaning of the Rome Statute, and thus the ICC lacked jurisdiction to hear the case.[71] The prosecutor argued that the General Assembly, not the prosecutor's office, should decide whether an entity is a "state" and that because the General Assembly has designated Palestine only as an "observer" rather than a "nonmember state," the ICC lacked jurisdiction.[72] The prosecutor emphasized that although Palestine had submitted an application for admission to the U.N. in September 2011, the Security Council and General Assembly have yet to act on the application.[73] While the question of Palestine's rights under the Rome Statute may be a challenging legal issue, it certainly could have been answered in fewer than three years. The prosecutor's delay, like his final decision denying jurisdiction, was a shrewd political act: permitting a Palestinian action against Israel would throw a monkey wrench into the difficult Israeli-Palestinian peace process. The prosecutor effectively decided that the ICC would sit this dispute out, letting political actors decide the case.[74]

Complementarity as a Tool to Consider the Interests of Peace

Article 17 of the Rome Statute, relating to "complementarity," also gives the prosecutor substantial latitude in managing the tension between the pursuit of peace and the pursuit of justice. As was true for article 53, political disagreements led the drafters of the Rome Statute to leave the precise scope of this provision somewhat vague.[75] The prosecutor's narrow reading of the interests of justice provision has been matched by a relatively expansive view of complementarity. This is wise. I believe that complementarity is a more effective provision than the interests of justice for managing the tension between peace and justice, particularly when one considers the impact on out-of-court negotiations in the prosecutor's shadow.

Article 17's complementarity provision states that the prosecutor may not investigate or prosecute crimes if a state party with jurisdiction has made a genuine investigation or prosecution of the crimes.[76] A state can meet the requirements of complementarity even if it does not prosecute crimes, as long as that decision not to pursue the crimes does not result from "the unwillingness or inability of the State genuinely to prosecute."[77] In Rome, there was a debate over whether a *criminal* investigation was necessary to satisfy complementarity, or whether an alternative justice mechanism like a South African–style truth and reconciliation commission (TRC) might suffice. Even delegations strongly committed to criminal prosecutions were hesitant to lay down "an iron rule for all time mandating prosecution as the only acceptable response in all situations."[78] The South African delegation argued that the statute should explicitly provide that TRCs satisfy complementarity.[79] The statute does not resolve this problem, but article 17 is susceptible to a reading that permits the prosecutor to defer prosecution in the face of a wide range of domestic "investigations," including TRCs.[80]

Moreno Ocampo indicated that he would take a broad view of complementarity, arguing in his 2007 policy paper that "truth seeking, reparations programs, institutional reform and traditional justice mechanisms in the pursuit of a broader justice" may all satisfy article 17.[81] He subsequently refused to foreclose the possibility that national proceedings not strictly prosecutorial in nature might satisfy complementarity.[82] Moreno Ocampo's prosecution strategy recognized that part of his job was to help state parties "better identify the steps required to meet national obligations to investigate and prosecute serious crimes."[83]

The prosecutor's reading of article 17 is not only sound statutory interpretation; it is smart policy. Creating a robust exception on the basis of complementarity creates incentives for states to more precisely tailor justice mechanisms to local needs. By proactively using complementarity, the prosecutor may encourage war-torn countries to take greater ownership of the peace process and pursue justice wherever possible.[84] The purpose of complementarity was to preclude the prosecutor from meddling with domestic investigations and prosecutions. But by using complementarity as an offensive tool and by implicitly threatening to investigate if the state with jurisdiction does not, the prosecutor can help create the space for more active and effective domestic investigations. These domestic investigations are also more likely to be in tune with local understandings of the best way to pursue justice.

By cabining the interests of justice, the policy paper has made it even more important that the prosecutor avail herself of the substantial wiggle room that complementarity affords. Thus, to return to the Afghanistan hypothetical, the prosecutor should encourage Afghans to take ownership of the justice process and investigate the crimes, even if this investigation does not culminate in a traditional criminal trial.

Moreno Ocampo's preliminary examinations in Guinea and Kenya illustrate what this proactive complementarity might look like. The prosecutor visited those countries and issued statements and press releases to pressure those countries to investigate crimes that might otherwise fall within the Court's jurisdiction.[85] Of course, for proactive complementarity to work, bold statements must be coupled with a willingness to take action and actually investigate or prosecute where domestic states are unwilling to do so. Otherwise, war criminals will easily see past the rhetoric and be undeterred by the threat of criminal prosecution. But an effective policy of complementarity necessarily provides time and space for states to pursue justice in ways that do not threaten peace.

Some Guidelines for the Prosecutor

The prosecutor faces an abiding tension between peace and justice, but this tension is manageable. The prosecutor, as a political actor responsible for a nascent legal institution, may wisely and diplomatically manage the inescapable tension between the pursuit of justice and the pursuit of peace. I suggest four guidelines to help the prosecutor navigate this task.

The Prosecutor Should Never Acknowledge the Validity of Unconditional Blanket National Amnesty Programs Negotiated as Part of a Peace Process

The Rome Statute does not explicitly address the amnesty question, probably because the framers could not agree on the issue one way or the other.[86] Different provisions of the statute point in conflicting directions.[87]

The preamble appears to rule out the possibility of amnesty, declaring that "the most serious crimes of concern to the international community as a whole must not go unpunished and that their effective prosecution must be ensured."[88] Meanwhile, article 17 complementarity requires the prosecutor to act where a "state is unwilling or unable genuinely to carry out the investigation or prosecution."[89] As discussed earlier, however, complementarity can be satisfied even if there is no criminal prosecution as long as the investigations are legitimate.

Explicitly acknowledging the validity of an unconditional blanket amnesty would hurt the prosecutor's goal of deterrence. Blanket amnesty undermines the prosecutor's efforts to create international legal norms against genocide, war crimes, and crimes against humanity. It also tells warlords that they may bargain for immunity and thus gain impunity, eliminating the ICC's deterrent force. If blanket amnesty from *criminal* prosecution is granted, the prosecutor should insist the parties to engage in some form of alternative justice, like a noncriminal TRC.

In the case of the Afghanistan hypothetical, the prosecutor should not acknowledge the validity of any absolute national amnesty program that provides blanket amnesty to every individual. This does not mean that the prosecutor must insist that every wrongdoer be prosecuted or that the prosecutions must be criminal in nature. However, if the prosecutor turns away completely from the atrocities, she would abdicate her institutional role and send an encouraging message to future warlords that they, too, may escape paying for their crimes. Because the overarching goal of the Rome Statute is to deter "the most serious crimes of international concern" and put an "end to impunity for perpetrators of these crimes,"[90] the prosecutor can hardly suggest a broad interpretation that would provide discretion for her to approve a broad grant of amnesty or be drawn into explicitly bargaining with someone like Mullah Omar.

The Prosecutor Should Not Be Party to a Bargain Where a Particular Leader Escapes All Punishment by Laying Down His Arms or Giving Up Power

Just as the prosecutor should not approve unconditional blanket amnesties, her office should not directly participate in any bargain with a particular leader who seeks to lay down his arms in exchange for immunity. Many of the same arguments against blanket amnesties pertain to individual cases. Thus the prosecutor should not sit at the table with Mullah Omar and negotiate about who will be investigated and what those investigations should look like. This does not mean that the prosecutor should necessarily choose to prosecute these crimes, but there is a critical difference between delaying prosecution and waiting for domestic institutions to act, on the one hand, and explicitly guaranteeing immunity on the other hand. There is a difference between granting impunity—which may be seen as a politically charged decision—and acknowledging that ICC prosecution is not always and everywhere appropriate, which is a practical legal decision. By refraining from entering these negotiations, the prosecutor ensures that she is seen as a legal rather than a political actor.

The Prosecutor Should Use Timing, Including the Delay of Investigation or Prosecution, to Take into Account Considerations of Peace and Reconciliation

The Rome Statute does not force the prosecutor to commence her investigations or prosecutions within any particular time period. On the contrary, the prosecutor has ample space to delay bringing an indictment or commencing a trial.[91] I am not suggesting that the prosecutor should permanently stay her hand under circumstances where the process of reconciliation turns out to be a sham and the concerns of victims are forever ignored. But delay can be a powerful tool, enabling the prosecutor to stall investigations and thus allow domestic justice mechanisms time to address the situation and satisfy complementarity. Rather than rushing to indict, the prosecutor should wait patiently to see how the situation develops on the ground. This would be the wise approach in Afghanistan.

Along these lines, there should be a strong presumption against bringing indictments *during* a civil war. Wars are terrible events that beget awful atrocities, and in the midst of a war, the priority must be placed on removing the tyrant and ending the war as soon as possible. Often, this requires granting a dictator exile in exchange for abdicating power. Indictments eliminate the full range of negotiated options for dealing with tyrants, including not simply foreign exile but also deals that would have the leader remain in the country and even retain some power during a transition to a more democratic regime. As distasteful as it is, the better part of wisdom often requires diplomats to bargain with devilish tyrants. An indictment while a war is still going on can interfere with diplomatic negotiations that might save lives.

Libya represents an example of this. The international criminal prosecutor brought an indictment against Muammar Gaddafi and two top deputies in the midst of the civil war. The rebels, aided by NATO support, eventually ousted Gaddafi. But his indictment in the middle of a civil war was probably a mistake because it precluded diplomatic options that might have ended the bloodshed earlier and hampered the West's ability to offer Gaddafi exile in order to end the carnage.

The indictment occurred after the Security Council unanimously referred the Libya situation to the prosecutor. Gaddafi had few friends in the international community, and the prosecutor no doubt wanted to be responsive to the Security Council. This has been the sole instance to date when the Security Council referred a case to the prosecutor. Now, however, it seems apparent that the prosecutor acted in haste. In less than three months, the prosecutor investigated and persuaded the Court to issue arrest warrants alleging crimes against humanity for Muammar Gaddafi; his son, Saif; and the Libyan head of intelligence. It is entirely possible that the speed of the process did not allow for an investigation of the possible war crimes committed by Gaddafi's opponents or even satisfy article 54's requirement that the prosecutor "investigate incriminating and exonerating circumstances equally."[92]

Human rights champions applauded the prosecutor's actions because they believed that those actions underscored that dictators could now be held legally accountable under the Rome Treaty, and the indictments bolstered the rebels' morale. But the indictments may have cut off certain routes to a negotiated solution and an earlier end to the conflict. As the International Crisis Group warned, to insist that Gaddafi "both leave the country *and* face trial in the International Criminal Court is virtually to ensure that he will stay in Libya to the bitter end and go down fighting."[93] In fact, as the war dragged on, news reports suggested that diplomats from Great Britain and France—as well as some Libyan rebel leaders—sought (unsuccessfully) to interest Gaddafi in a negotiated deal whereby he gave up power in exchange for immunity. As it turned out, the issuance of the arrest warrants might not have made any difference because Gaddafi may have been unwilling to accept a negotiated diplomatic deal under any circumstances. But I believe the prosecutor should not have proceeded so hastily with his investigation and should have deferred seeking an indictment until the civil war ended.

The Prosecutor Should Proactively Use Complementarity to Encourage the Development of Institutions of Accountability

The prosecutor has limited resources and could not possibly intervene in every instance where a crime within the Rome Statute's jurisdiction has been committed. Even if the prosecutor *could* always intervene, it is doubtful that she *should* always intervene. The pace of international criminal justice is slow, and the one-size-fits-all response of criminal prosecution is not always the best means to achieve justice.[94] And litigation is a slow, blunt instrument often ill suited for untangling the complex web of responsibility for genocide, war crimes, and crimes against humanity.[95] That is why transitional societies often choose to respond to past events by something less than full-scale criminal prosecutions. It would be better for the prosecutor to encourage member states to take up for themselves the mantle of investigation and prosecution, adopting more tailored local solutions while permitting the prosecutor to save her resources for cases where the state is unwilling or unable to prosecute. Indeed, Moreno Ocampo has suggested that he would like to see a world where ICC prosecutions are unnecessary because matters are fully addressed by the sovereign states.[96]

These domestic accountability mechanisms need not be criminal in nature.[97] Alternative justice mechanisms such as TRCs are consistent with the statute's text and with the framers' intent and may also be more effective at helping a war-torn country move past atrocities it has suffered. Certain contexts may call for less aggressive solutions that permit a society to come to terms with and make a break with the past without meting out formal criminal punishment.[98] Often, much of the benefit comes not from sending people to jail but from having them publicly admit the truth.[99] The key question is whether the state has taken steps to discover "the truth about victims and attribute individual responsibility to perpetrators."[100]

The prosecutor should proactively use complementarity to insist on a baseline of domestic investigation and prosecution.[101] This approach has several virtues. It permits the prosecutor to discuss with government officials of state parties the various ways they might be responsive to victims and provide a degree of accountability without actually requiring her to sit down at the negotiating table and thus appear to be a political actor with whom parties may bargain. Instead, the parties will bargain in the shadow of the law that she has cast. She can then monitor the domestic institutions over time to ascertain whether the investigations are in fact genuine. She can always initiate an investigation or prosecution if she is unsatisfied with the domestic actions and if she believes doing so will not unduly interfere with the peace.

Conclusion

The prosecutor faces a paradox of sorts. On the one hand, the exercise of discretion is inevitable. The prosecutor lives in a world of limited resources, and she must pick and choose which cases are worth her time and money.[102] Her budget is not large enough to investigate and prosecute every crime within the Court's jurisdiction.[103] And investigations cannot be entered into lightly. Article 54's requirement that the prosecutor "investigate incriminating and exonerating circumstances equally"[104] entails that "the cost involved in the investigation is enormous."[105] Furthermore, the article 53 admissibility inquiry, which requires the prosecutor to determine whether complementarity and gravity are satisfied, demands that the exercise of discretion. The complementarity inquiry requires a judgment as to the genuineness and sufficiency of domestic prosecutions. The gravity criterion demands that the prosecutor determine whether the crimes committed are serious enough to merit investigation and prosecution. These are standards, not rules, and they demand interpretation.

Conversely, the explicit acknowledgment that the consideration of peacemaking efforts will be taken into account in the exercise of discretion threatens to undermine the prosecutor's goal of establishing the ICC's legitimacy. Much of the Court's influence will come not from its prosecution in discrete cases but from its ability to deter future crimes. The prosecutor claims that his goal is to enlarge the shadow of the International Criminal Court—to influence the behavior of a large number of actors through his conduct in a small number of investigations and prosecutions. By ending impunity and refusing to engage in political negotiation and bargaining with war criminals, he will deter the would-be war criminals of the future from committing their acts.

The pursuit of international criminal justice through judicial means has both benefits and costs. On the one hand, actions by the prosecutor punish criminals and aim to deter heinous conduct during wars and violent conflict. On the other hand, by initiating an investigation or bringing criminal charges, a prosecutor may inhibit and constrain delicate diplomatic efforts aimed at ending a bloody violence through negotiation. Recent events in Libya suggest as much. Moreover, in some circumstances, postwar reconciliation may be better fostered by means other than the pursuit of criminal sanctions through a formal judicial process. The experience in South Africa with "truth and reconciliation" demonstrates the possible value of alternative, noncriminal justice mechanisms.

In deciding whether to initiate action in a specific case at particular time, the prosecutor has the discretion to consider both potential costs and benefits. The prosecutor's chief policy goal is to deter the war crimes of tomorrow by ending impunity for those crimes today. The prosecutor rightly recognizes that to achieve this goal, she must engender a commitment to the rule of law. Nonetheless, the law hardly requires the prosecutor to ignore the impact of her possible actions on the pursuit of peace and reconciliation. As I have shown, there is substantial discretion built into the Rome Statute, principally through article 17 complementarity and the prosecutor's ability to delay prosecution. Where wisdom suggests that the costs in terms of peace and reconciliation outweigh the benefits of immediate investigation and prosecution, the prosecutor has ample room to legitimately decline to pursue a crime. Through proactive complementarity and wise timing, the prosecutor can more productively engage with transitional states, and more effectively cast a long shadow for the ICC.

In suggesting that wisdom requires that the prosecutor ignore the more extreme rhetoric found in the policy paper—the rhetoric suggesting that peacemaking is never relevant to the exercise of prosecutorial discretion under the Rome Statute—I might be accused of endorsing a degree of hypocrisy: allowing the prosecutor to say one thing but do another. But as Rochefoucauld once said, "Hypocrisy is the homage vice pays to virtue."[106]

NOTES

My research assistant, William Marra, JD 2012 Harvard Law School, was my collaborator in the creation of this chapter. His efforts were indispensable and invaluable. Although the policy conclusions are entirely my responsibility, I regret that he did not accept my invitation to be listed as a junior coauthor. I am also grateful to Professors Fionnuala D. Ni Aolain, Gabriella Blum, Philip Heymann, Chibli Mallat, and Alex Whiting, all of whom provided helpful comments on earlier drafts. An earlier version of this chapter appeared in 20 *Harvard Negotiation Law Review* 101 (2013) and is included here with permission.

1. *See* Rome Statute of the International Criminal Court, 2187 U.N.T.S. 90 (July 17, 1998) (hereinafter Rome Statute). There is substantial evidence that the Taliban committed war crimes and crimes against humanity during the conflict. *See Afghanistan: Taliban Should Stop Using Children as Suicide Bombers*, HUMAN RIGHTS WATCH (Aug. 31, 2011), http://www.hrw.org/news/2011/08/31/afghanistan-taliban-should-stop-using-children-suicide-bombers; *Afghanistan: Taliban Should Be Prosecuted for War Crimes*, HUMAN RIGHTS WATCH (Aug. 10, 2010), http://www.hrw.org/news/2011/08/31/afghani stan-taliban-should-stop-using-children-suicide-bombers.

2. Darryl Robinson, *Serving the Interests of Justice: Amnesties, Truth Commissions, & the International Criminal Court*, 14 EUR. J. INT'L. L. 481, 495 (2003) (quoting Mahnoush H. Arsanjani, *The International Criminal Court & National Amnesty Laws*, in 93 PROCEEDINGS OF THE 101ST ANNUAL MEETING [ASIL] 65 [1999]).

3. ALEXANDER HAMILTON, THE FEDERALIST NO. 74 (Clinton Rossiter ed., 1961). In the words of David Scheffer, the former U.S. ambassador at large for war crimes issues, "One must understand, amnesty is always an option on the table in [peace] negotiations" (Michael P. Scharf, *The Letter of the Law: The Scope of the International Legal Ob-*

ligation to Prosecute Human Rights Crimes, 59 LAW & CONTEMP. PROBS. 41, 60 [1996] [quoting Scheffer, Remarks at International Law Weekend (Nov. 2, 1996)]). *See also* José Zalaquett, *Balancing Ethical Imperatives & Political Constraints: The Dilemma of New Democracies Confronting Past Human Rights Violations,* 43 HASTINGS L.J. 1425, 1429 (1991–92) ("Political leaders cannot afford to be moved only by their convictions, oblivious to real-life constraints."). Amnesties have been used with success in the past, including in conjunction with the South African Truth and Reconciliation Commission of the 1990s, during the 1995 Dayton Accords for peace in Bosnia and Herzegovina, and at the conclusion of the American Civil War to reintegrate Confederate soldiers back into American society. *See* Michael P. Scharf, *The Amnesty Exception to the Jurisdiction of the International Criminal Court,* 32 CORNELL INT'L L.J. 507, 508–9 (1999) (hereinafter Scharf, *Amnesty Exception*).

4. Office of the Prosecutor, ICC, *Policy Paper on the Interests of Justice,* at 1 (Sept. 1, 2007), http://www.icc-cpi.int/NR/rdonlyres/772C95C9-F54D-4321-BF09-73422B B235 28/143640/ICCOTPInterestsOfJustice.pdf (hereinafter *Interests of Justice*).

5. *Id.* at 4.

6. *Id.* at 9 ("The broader matter of international peace and security is not the responsibility of the Prosecutor; it falls within the mandate of other institutions.").

7. *Id.* at 1, 8.

8. In an October 2012 speech in Pretoria, South Africa, Bensouda stated,

> I should stress here that the "interests of justice" [of article 53] must not be confused with the interests of peace and security, which falls within the mandate of other institutions, notably the UN Security Council and the African Union. The Court and the Office of the Prosecutor itself are not involved in political considerations. We have to respect our legal limits. The prospect of peace negotiations is therefore not a factor that forms part of the Office's determination on the interests of justice.

Fatou Bensouda, Prosecutor, ICC, *Reconciling the Independent Role of the ICC Prosecutor with Conflict Resolution Initiatives* (Oct. 10, 2012), http://www.issafrica.org/uploads/10Oct2012ICCKeyNoteAddress.pdf.

9. Situations come before the prosecutor in one of three ways: a state party to the Rome Statute requests under article 14 that the prosecutor investigate the situation, the Security Council lodges a similar request under article 13(b), or the prosecutor initiates an investigation *proprio motu* (of her own initiative) under article 15. *See* Rome Statute art. 13(b), 14–15.

10. First, the Court's jurisdiction is limited to "the most serious crimes of concern to the international community as a whole," including genocide, war crimes, and crimes against humanity. *See id.* art. 5(1). Second, there is a temporal aspect to jurisdiction: the ICC has jurisdiction only over crimes committed after the Rome Statute entered into force in July 2002. *See id.* art. 11. Third, the Court has authority only over states that submit to the jurisdiction of the Court. *See id.* art. 12.

11. All three jurisdictional criteria are likely to be satisfied in Afghanistan: sufficient evidence probably exists to give a "reasonable belief" that serious crimes have been committed; Afghanistan is a party to the Rome Statute; and many alleged crimes postdate 2002. Thus the Court would likely have jurisdiction over the Afghan situation.

12. WILLIAM A. SCHABAS, AN INTRODUCTION TO THE INTERNATIONAL CRIMINAL COURT 15 (2001).

13. Jack Goldsmith, *The Self-Defeating International Criminal Court*, 70 U. CHI. L. REV. 89, 90 (2003).

14. As Professor Goldsmith points out, this is a substantially weaker check than the requirement of prior Security Council *approval* sought by the United States. As adopted, the Rome Statute "reverses the burden of Security Council inertia by permitting an ICC case to go forward as long as a single permanent member supports prosecution and thus vetoes any delay." *Id.* at 90–91.

15. *See* William W. Burke-White, *Proactive Complementarity: The International Criminal Court & National Courts in the Rome System of International Justice*, 49 HARV. INT'L L.J. 53, 57, 66 (2008).

16. Rome Statute art. 53(1)(c).

17. *See id.* art. 53(2).

18. Brian D. Lepard, *How Should the ICC Prosecutor Exercise His or Her Discretion?: The Role of Fundamental Ethical Principles*, 43 J. MARSHALL L. REV. 553, 566 (2009–10) ("If a prosecution is likely to stall settlement efforts and thereby result in many more future civilian deaths, then 'justice' may not be served in this larger sense, even if it is served by reference to a narrow concept of criminal justice focusing only on the gravity of the particular past crime being charged.").

19. For a discussion of the drafting of the "interests of justice" and complementarity provisions of the Rome Statute, *see, e.g.,* William A. Schabas, *Prosecutorial Discretion v. Judicial Activism at the International Criminal Court*, 6 J. INT'L CRIM. JUST. 731, 749 (2008); Daniel D. Ntanda Nsereko, *Prosecutorial Discretion before National Courts & International Tribunals*, 3 J. INT'L. CRIM. JUST. 124, 138 (2005); Robinson, *supra* note 2, at 483; Mahnoush H. Arsanjani, *The Rome Statute of the International Criminal Court*, 93 AM. J. INT'L L. 22, 38 (1999); Scharf, *Amnesty Exception, supra* note 3, at 521–22.

20. Nsereko, *supra* note 19, at 138; Robinson, *supra* note 2, at 483 (noting that some delegations were hesitant to lay down "an iron rule for all time mandating prosecution as the *only* acceptable response in all situations").

21. Robinson, *supra* note 2, at 483.

22. *Id.* ("[T]he very purpose of the ICC was to ensure the investigation and punishment of serious international crimes, and to prompt states to overcome the considerations of expedience and *realpolitik* that had so often led them to trade away justice in the past.").

23. Schabas, *supra* note 19, at 749.

24. *Id.* at 521–22 (1999) (quoting Philippe Kirsch, chair of the Rome Diplomatic Conference).

25. *Interests of Justice, supra* note 4, at 1.

26. *See id.* The prosecutor's views appear to have changed over time. In 2003, the prosecutor had indicated a willingness to consider "various national and international efforts to achieve peace and security" under the "interests of justice" inquiry. Henry Lovat, *Delineating the Interests of Justice*, 35 DENV. J. INT'L L. & POL'Y 275, 277 (2007) (quoting Office of the Prosecutor, ICC, *Second Report of the Prosecutor of the International Criminal Court, Mr. Luis Moreno Ocampo, to the Security Council Pursuant to UNSC 1593* (Dec. 13, 2005), at 6, http://www.icc-cpi.int/NR/rdonlyres/2CFC1123-B4DF-4FEB-BEF4-52E0CAC8AA79/0/LMO_UNSC_ReportB_En.pdf). But by 2007, with the publication of the policy paper on the "interests of justice," the prosecutor's

views had shifted away from those hinted at in the 2005 report, and the prosecutor explicitly rejected the view that the interests of peace might be considered. *See id.* The view that peace might not be considered is captured not only in the 2007 policy paper but also in *2009 Regulations of the Office of the Prosecutor*, which do not state that the prosecutor may consider the interests of peace when deciding when to prosecute. *See* Office of the Prosecutor, ICC, *Regulations of the Office of the Prosecutor* (Apr. 23, 2009), http://www.icc-cpi.int/NR/rdonlyres/FFF97111-ECD6-40B5-9CDA-792BCBE1E695/280253/ICCBD050109ENG.pdf.

27. *Interests of Justice, supra* note 4, at 1.

28. *Id.* at 4.

29. *Id.* at 3.

30. *Id.* at 5.

31. *Id.*

32. *Id.* at 7.

33. *Id.*

34. *Id.* In the 2007 policy paper, the prosecutor emphasizes that the ICC's actions should be consistent with the pursuit of justice at the local level. The paper indicates that a wide range of domestic justice mechanisms may satisfy complementarity, including, "domestic prosecutions, truth seeking, reparations programs, institutional reform and traditional justice mechanisms in the pursuit of a broader justice." The list of processes that may satisfy complementarity will change over time, as advances are made in the "development of theory and practice in designing comprehensive strategies to combat impunity." *Id.* at 7–8. I discuss complementarity later in this paper.

35. *Id.* at 8.

36. *Id.* at 9.

37. *See* HUMAN RIGHTS WATCH, POLICY PAPER: THE MEANING OF "THE INTERESTS OF JUSTICE" IN ARTICLE 53 OF THE ROME STATUTE 4 (2005) (noting that "neither the language of the Rome Statute nor actual language in the *travaux préparatoires*" reflects any definitional agreement on the meaning of "interests of justice," including whether or not the prosecutor may "consider the existence of a national amnesty or truth commission process, or ongoing peace negotiations as factors to be evaluated").

38. *Id.* at 4–5.

39. Schabas, *supra* note 19, at 749 ("In attempting to codify how the discretion created by Article 53 should be exercised, the Prosecutor, with the encouragement of certain states and NGOs, is indirectly amending the ICC Statute.").

40. *See* THOMAS C. SHELLING, THE STRATEGY OF CONFLICT (1960).

41. Of course, the aspirational statement that "justice will be done," uncoupled with action, is unlikely to deter would-be war criminals. The prosecutor's rhetoric must be coupled with the willingness and political ability to pursue these crimes.

42. Robert H. Mnookin & Lewis Kornhauser, *Bargaining in the Shadow of the Law: The Case of Divorce*, 88 YALE L.J. 950, 968 (1979).

43. Luis Moreno Ocampo, Prosecutor, ICC, *Keynote Address at the Council on Foreign Relations* 9–10 (Feb. 4, 2010), www.cfr.org/courts-and-tribunals/prepared-remarks-luis-moreno-ocampo-prosecutor-icc/p21375.

44. *Id.* at 9–13.

45. The Pre-Trial Chamber, a judicial body, exercises oversight of the prosecutor's deci-

sions. *See* Rome Statute art. 53(3)(b). As I will show later in the chapter, the prosecutor's decisions with respect to timing and complementarity are less constrained by judicial review.

46. Robert H. Jackson, *The Federal Prosecutor,* 31 J. CRIM L. & CRIMINOLOGY 3, 5 (1940).

47. *Interests of Justice, supra* note 4, at 7.

48. *See* Goldsmith, *supra* note 13, at 92.

49. *See* Carlos S. Nino, *The Duty to Punish Past Abuses of Human Rights Put into Context: The Case of Argentina,* 100 YALE L.J. 2619, 2620 (1990–91).

50. *See* Eric Blumenson, *The Challenge of a Global Standard of Justice: Peace, Pluralism, & Punishment at the International Criminal Court,* 44 COLUM. J. TRANSNAT'L L. 801, 825–26 (2005–6).

51. *See* Burke-White, *supra* note 15, at 54; MARTHA MINOW, BETWEEN VENGEANCE & FORGIVENESS (1999).

52. ICC, *Programme Budget for 2012,* at 24, ICC Doc. ICC-ASP/10/Res.4 (Dec. 21 2011), http://www.icc-cpi.int/iccdocs/asp_docs/ASP10/Resolutions/ICC-ASP-10-Res.4-ENG.pdf.

53. *See* Burke-White, *supra* note 15, at 66. Additionally, the Rome Statute requires that the prosecutor investigate incriminating and exonerating circumstances equally. Rome Statute art. 54(1)(a). This provision of the statute ensures that "the cost involved in the investigation is enormous." Nsereko, *supra* note 19, at 125 n.2.

54. ICC, *Proposed Programme Budget for 2010 of the International Criminal Court,* at 31, ICC Doc. ICC-ASP/8/10 (July 17, 2009), http://www.icc-cpi.int/iccdocs/asp_docs/ASP8/ICC-ASP-8-10.Proposed%20Programme%20Budget%20for%202010.ADVANCE.17Jul1630.pdf.

55. Jean Galbraith, *The Pace of International Criminal Justice,* 31 MICH. J. INT'L L. 79, 140 (2009–10). Thus, the Rome Statute requires a pretrial hearing to confirm criminal charges (article 61), while article 82 provides broad permission for interlocutory appeals. *See* Rome Statute arts. 61, 82. All this has earned the ICC the derisive moniker of the "slowest institution of its kind" since the birth of international criminal justice at Nuremberg. *See* Schabas, *supra* note 19, at 758.

56. *See* Rome Statute art. 13.

57. *See id.* art. 15.

58. *See id.* art. 15(3).

59. *See id.* art. 53.

60. *See id.* art. 53(3)(a).

61. *See id.* art. 53(3)(b).

62. *See id.* art. 53(3).

63. *See id.*

64. *See id.* art. 7(1).

65. *See id.* art. 7(2)(a).

66. "Willful killing," *see* Rome Statute art. 8(2)(a)(i), is a war crime only if it is "part of a plan or policy or part of a large-scale commission of such crimes." *See id.* art. 8(1). For example, the conflict in Afghanistan may not be "of an international character." See *id.* art. 8. While "violence to life and person" including "murder of all kinds" may be a war crime (*see id.* art. 8[2][c][i]), the Rome Treaty does not apply to "situations to of internal disturbances and tensions, such riots, *isolated and sporadic acts of violence* or other acts of a similar nature" (*see id.* art. 8[2][d]; emphasis added).

67. *Id.* art. 17.

68. The prosecutor must also decide whether the "interests of justice" exception would not apply and whether, under the complementarity doctrine, there should be no deference to the State that would have jurisdiction. I address these two additional issues in the next section.

69. *See* Rome Statute art. 66.

70. *See* U.N. General Assembly, *Rep. of the International Criminal Court to the United Nations,* ¶66, U.N. Doc. A/65/313 (Aug. 19, 2010), http://www.icc-cpi.int/NR/rdon lyres/EA7DF985-4549-40EF-A0DC-814BE440655C/282599/ICC6RepEng.pdf.

71. Office of the Prosecutor, ICC, *Situation in Palestine,* at 1–2 (Apr. 3, 2012), http://www.icc-cpi.int/NR/rdonlyres/C6162BBF-FEB9-4FAF-AFA9-836106D2694A/284387/SituationinPalestine030412ENG.pdf.

72. *See id.*

73. *See id.* at 2.

74. In this regard, the prosecutor's decision may be analogized to the political question doctrine sometimes employed by U.S. courts to avoid deciding sensitive political issues. *See* Baker v. Carr, 369 U.S. 186, 209 (1962).

75. Indeed, the chair of the Rome Diplomatic Conference has characterized the interests of justice provision as encompassing "creative ambiguity." *See* Scharf, *Amnesty Exception, supra* note 3, at 521–22 (quoting Philippe Kirsch).

76. *See* Rome Statute art. 17(1)(a).

77. *See id.* art. 17(1)(b).

78. Robinson, *supra* note 2, at 483.

79. *See id.* at 499.

80. Article 17 never specifies that the "investigation" must be a *criminal* investigation. *See* Rome Statute art. 17. Thus, as long as there is a minimum level of investigation and inquiry, TRCs and similar alternative justice mechanisms should satisfy article 17. *See* Blumenson, *supra* note 50, at 871 ("Such institutions as the South African TRC, with its amnesties conditioned on confession, should also be recognized as a human rights advance, and in certain circumstances a necessary and morally acceptable option for the ICC."); Carsten Stahn, *Complementarity, Amnesties, & Alternative Forms of Justice: Some Interpretative Guidelines for the International Criminal Court,* 3 J. INT'L CRIM. JUST. 695, 711 (2005).

81. *Interests of Justice, supra* note 4, at 8.

82. Office of the Prosecutor, ICC, *Policy Paper on Preliminary Examinations (draft),* ¶¶52–66 (Oct. 4, 2010), http://www.icc-cpi.int/NR/rdonlyres/9FF1EAA1-41C4-4A30-A202-174B18DA923C/282515/OTP_Draftpolicypaperonpreliminaryexaminations04101.pdf.

83. *See* Office of the Prosecutor, ICC, *Prosecutorial Strategy 2009–2012,* ¶38 (Feb. 1, 2010), http://www.icc-cpi.int/NR/rdonlyres/66A8DCDC-3650-4514-AA62-D229D1128F65/281506/OTPProsecutorialStrategy20092013.pdf.

84. As discussed earlier, decisions not to prosecute on the basis of complementarity have another advantage: they typically are not subject to judicial review by the Pre-Trial Chamber. Decisions not to act under the "interests of justice" exceptions always are.

85. HUMAN RIGHTS WATCH, COURSE CORRECTION: RECOMMENDATIONS TO THE ICC PROSECUTOR FOR A MORE EFFECTIVE APPROACH TO "SITUATIONS UNDER ANALYSIS" 7–8 n.14 (2011).

86. There is an extensive literature on the extent to which under the Rome Statute an amnesty may be recognized or taken into account. *See, e.g.,* John Dugard, *Dealing with Crimes of a Past Regime: Is Amnesty Still an Option?*, 12 LEIDEN J. INT'L L. 1001, 1013–15 (1999) (suggesting that the Rome Statute left the issue ambiguous and was a compromise package that should be interpreted to recognize that the prosecutor has the discretion to recognize an amnesty in limited circumstances). Dugard believes the unsettled nature of the present state of international law is desirable because it would allow "prosecutions to proceed where they will not impede peace, but at the same time permit societies to 'trade' amnesty for peace where there is no alternative." *Id.* at 1015. He would not permit unconditional amnesties, especially for "atrocious crimes," but would allow Truth and Reconciliation Commissions for those crimes. *Id.*

87. The drafting of the Rome Statute has been called "schizophrenic," perhaps because different subcommittees drafted different parts. *See* Scharf, *Amnesty Exception, supra* note 3, at 522.

88. Rome Statute pmbl.

89. *See id.* art. 17(1)(a).

90. *See id.* art. 1, 17.

91. Galbraith, *supra* note 55, at 140.

92. *See* Rome Statute art. 54(1)(a).

93. INTERNATIONAL CRISIS GROUP, MIDDLE EAST/NORTH AFRICA REPORT NO. 107, POPULAR PROTEST IN NORTH AFRICA & THE MIDDLE EAST (V): MAKING SENSE OF LIBYA 1 (2011).

94. Galbraith, *supra* note 55, at 139.

95. MINOW, *supra* note 51, at 87 (1998).

96. Moreno-Ocampo Keynote Address, *supra* note 43, at 9–13.

97. One commentator has argued that the Geneva Convention or the Genocide Convention may require criminal prosecution and that they thereby limit the prosecutor's ability to accept blanket amnesty or even noncriminal prosecutions. *See* Scharf, *Amnesty Exception, supra* note 3, at 523–24.

98. *See* Minow, *supra* note 51, at 2–3.

99. CHANDRA LEKHA SRIRAM, CONFRONTING PAST HUMAN RIGHTS VIOLATIONS: JUSTICE VS. PEACE IN TIMES OF TRANSITION 9 (2004).

100. *See* Scharf, *Amnesty Exception, supra* note 3, at 526.

101. *See* Burke-White, *supra* note 15, at 57.

102. *See* MINOW, *supra* note 51 (noting that resource constraints are particularly acute in the context of international criminal prosecutions).

103. *See* Burke-White, *supra* note 15, at 66.

104. *See* Rome Statute art. 54(1)(a).

105. *See* Nsereko, *supra* note 19, at 125 n.2.

106. *See* FRANÇOIS DUC DE LA ROCHEFOUCAULD, REFLECTIONS; OR, SENTENCES & MORAL MAXIMS, at Maxim 218 (1871), http://www.gutenberg.org/files/9105/9105-h/9105-h.htm.

The Evolution of the Office of the Prosecutor at the International Criminal Court

Insights from Institutional Theory

Jens Meierhenrich

Among many underresearched topics pertaining to the International Criminal Court (ICC), the question of institutional development has arguably received the least attention. Few scholars have taken the ICC seriously as an evolving international organization comprised of numerous distinct yet interrelated bureaucracies. In an attempt to move beyond snapshot descriptions of the ICC—and to complement the important doctrinal and jurisprudential literature—this chapter explores the origins and effects of institutional change in the Office of the Prosecutor (OTP) during the first decade of its operation.[1] Among other things, it makes a case for shifting our attention from explaining moments of institutional choice to understanding processes of institutional development.[2]

By identifying some of the mechanisms that have generated operational opportunities as well as constraints, I chart the institutional development of one of the ICC's most influential bureaucracies. In retrospect, what is interesting about this development is the cumulative effect of ongoing but subtle changes in its institutional makeup. In one striking example, consider the transformation of the OTP from its inception in June 2003, when it was led by Luis Moreno Ocampo, to its present form under the leadership since June 2012 of ICC prosecutor Fatou Bensouda.

With this account of the OTP's institutional emergence and evolution, I speak to the larger theoretical question of gradual institutional change, for as James Mahoney and Kathleen Thelen have pointed out, "[a]lthough less dramatic than abrupt and wholesale transformations, . . . slow and piecemeal changes can be equally consequential for patterning human behavior and for shaping substantive political outcomes."[3] The long and winding road of institutional development in the OTP has given rise to virtuous as well as pathological dynamics in the investigation and prosecution of international crimes. Or, to use the language of political science, the downstream effects of institutional development in the early stages of the OTP have substantially increased the costs of institutional adaptation in more recent years. Over the next decade, Bensouda will have to contend with these costs. Unfortunately, most predictions for her ten-year term in office have focused only on the substantive challenges of prosecuting international crimes. Missing from these predictions is an appreciation of the institutional challenges that she will face and that will structure the menu of options available to her for solving substantive problems. This chapter provides such an appreciation.

This chapter opens by discussing insights from institutional theory relevant to the study of the ICC in general and the OTP in particular. Next, the chapter applies this theoretical framework to interrogate certain aspects of the OTP's institutional development between 2003 and 2012. This application both explores the dynamics of institutional emergence (or birth dynamics) and inquires into the dynamics of institutional evolution (or growth dynamics). The first period lasted roughly from 2003 until early 2005 and was characterized by what one staff member called "a very ad hoc mode of operation."[4] The second period, which began in approximately 2005 and continues today, began to exhibit "a standardized mode of operation."[5] Both ways of doing things have had profound effects on the OTP's institutional culture, which in turn has had considerable consequences for the prosecution of international crimes.[6] To illustrate these effects and consequences, I build an analytic narrative around four key moments in the OTP's institutional development. My analysis contributes a sense of the long-run consequences of institutional development at the ICC, with particular reference to the OTP. The chapter concludes with a consideration of the implications of my analysis for both the theory and practice of international law.

Institutional Theory

In an attempt to identify institutional effects, I disaggregate the process of the OTP's institutional development into two major phases, institutional emergence and institutional evolution. To be sure, in empirical terms, the transition between these phases is difficult to pinpoint with any degree of certainty. Yet for analytic purposes, it is nevertheless useful to distinguish between birth dynamics and growth dynamics of organizations such as the OTP if only to emphasize that institutions are living organisms.

Indeed, as organizational theorists point out, a shift "to process-based thinking most differentiates interpretive theorizing from positivistic thinking, which is predicated on static notions of outcomes and entities."[7] This latter emphasis has interfered with progress in the study of the OTP. In the past decade, the focus on outcomes—from the indictment or non-indictment of alleged perpetrators to the inclusion or exclusion of certain charges in indictments—has largely distracted from the everyday forms of prosecution at the ICC. This is understandable but unfortunate—understandable given the stakes involved, unfortunate because it paints only an incomplete picture of the determinants of prosecutorial behavior at the ICC.[8] To gain a better understanding of the choices that prosecutors make, I focus on a number of critical junctures in the OTP's institutional development.

Generally speaking, the study of critical junctures is concerned with the nature and consequences of "brief phases of institutional flux," as Giovanni Capoccia and Daniel Kelemen note.[9] In these contexts, "the unit of analysis is typically some institutional setting in which actors' decisions are constrained during phases of equilibrium and are free during phases of change."[10] Figure 1 gives a schematic illustration of the logic of path dependent explanation.

The OTP is an ideal setting for this type of analysis because its life cycle during 2002–12 was marked by phases in which the choices of prosecutorial staff were relatively unconstrained, subject only to oversight by the Assembly of States Parties, and other phases during which the institutional constraints under which the OTP's investigators, prosecutors, and diplomats acted were considerable. The OTP is therefore a most interesting "action arena," to quote a term coined by the late Nobel laureate Elinor Ostrom, a noted scholar of institutional dynamics.

The underlying assumption of research on critical junctures is that during such periods of institutional disequilibrium, "the range of plausible choices open to powerful political actors expands substantially and the consequences of their decisions for the outcome of interest are potentially much more momentous."[11] In keeping with methodological practice in political science, I focus on critical junctures that "have a duration that is short relative to the path-dependent process that it initiates."[12] For the purpose of this chapter, I single out four such junctures, identified in table 1.

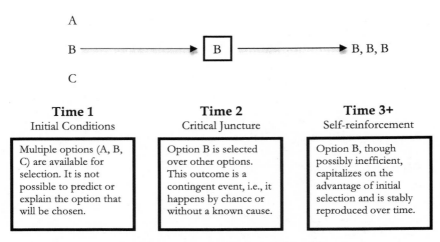

Fig. 1. The Logic of Path Dependent Explanation. (Adapted from James Mahoney, *Path Dependence in Historical Sociology* 29 THEORY & SOC. 507, 514 [2000].)

I focus, respectively, on (1) the establishment of the Jurisdiction, Complementarity, and Cooperation Division (JCCD); (2) the introduction of Joint Teams; (3) the creation of the Executive Committee (ExCom); and (4) the drafting of the confidential Operational Manual of the OTP. Although on the face of it, each of these institutional choices carries the whiff of the mundane, the impact on the prosecution of international crimes of the institutional designs to which they have given rise is arguably more causally significant than the incessantly invoked politics of international law. This is so because the everyday lives of prosecutors—save that of the prosecutor who stands at the helm—are first and foremost about everyday procedures. These procedures open or foreclose opportunities for shaping the prosecution of international crimes. As John Zysman once put it in a different context, "The definition of interests and objectives is created in institutional contexts and is not separable from them."[13] The same goes for what Avner Greif and David Laitin have called

TABLE 1. Critical Junctures in the Institutional Development of the OTP, 2003–2012

Critical Juncture	Objective
The Invention of the JCCD	Elevation of diplomacy
The Introduction of Joint Teams	Integration of expertise
The Creation of ExCom	Centralization of authority
The Drafting of an Operational Manual	Standardization of practices

"endogenous institutional change"—that is, forms of institutional development that cannot be attributed to changes in parameters exogenous to the institution under study but that have to be located inside the institutional environment.[14]

In an effort to contribute empirical insights not only to our understanding of the OTP but also to the larger debate about endogenous institutional change, I demonstrate, against the background of a fuller history of institutional development in the OTP, how each of the four aforementioned junctures set in motion path dependent dynamics that led to a routinization of certain behavioral practices, both virtuous and pathological. Paul Pierson recently described the general logic of the argument to come:

> As actors adapt to institutional arrangements, the status quo gains additional support, making it stable under a broader range of circumstances than was initially the case. An important implication of this claim is that effective challenges to the institutional status quo will often require substantial time to emerge. Developments unfavorable to institutional reproduction must reach a critical threshold level that makes reform possible.[15]

Important aspects of the institutional development of the OTP can be profitably explained by recourse to these insights from institutional theory. In what follows, I explain why some of the institutional choices and designs involving the OTP proved extremely "sticky" and how this fact of institutional resilience not only increased the transaction costs of the prosecution of international crimes but also affected the institutional culture. The point is to show how the nature and effects of institutional development were largely the result of structured contingency—and thus not always foreseeable. What emerges is the picture of an OTP populated by a whole host of mostly well-meaning staff, many with conflicting visions of the appropriateness of certain institutional practices, who become embroiled in a bureaucracy not entirely of their own making—often for the better but sometimes for the worse.

"A Very Ad Hoc Mode of Operation": The Institutional Emergence of the OTP

Between 2003 and 2012, the OTP underwent a number of far-reaching institutional transformations, all of which had a profound effect on the everyday life of international prosecution at the ICC. In what follows, I analyze how the most important of these transformations unfolded and why they mattered.

The OTP's institutional history begins in the mid-1990s. It was deeply embedded in the larger discussion about the principle of complementarity, which arose as a way to curtail the powers of a future ICC prosecutor. David Scheffer, the former U.S. Ambassador-at-Large for War Crimes Issues, recalls that in the spring of 1995, he "began to stress the importance of complementarity in the work of the court. That meant that the court should defer to national investigations and prosecutions of suspected war criminals and only when the nation that claimed jurisdiction proved unwilling or incapable of undertaking that responsibility would the court step in to pick up the case and seek or retain custody of the suspect."[16]

The question of institutional checks and balances was also a hotly contested issue in the context of the 1998 United Nations Conference of the Plenipotentiaries on the Establishment of an International Criminal Court. The majority of diplomatic interventions in the run-up to and throughout the Rome Conference concerned the independence and power of the prosecutor. At stake were the ground rules of the prosecutorial game. On July 1, 2002, after these rules were in place, the Preparatory Commission for the ICC (not to be confused with the Preparatory Committee on the Establishment of an International Criminal Court, or Prep-Com) established the Advance Team of Experts. Its mandate was the creation from scratch of a set of institutions that could enact the metarules established in Rome. Here we turn from questions of institutional choice to institutional design. The work of the Advance Team is important as far as the OTP is concerned primarily because key planks of the institutional design that it proposed were immediately discarded by the prosecutor. But let us start in Rome.

Initial Conditions

The ground rules laid at the Rome Conference served as critical parameters for all subsequent institutional choices about the OTP. Based on their experiences with the International Criminal Tribunals for the Former Yugoslavia (ICTY) and for Rwanda (ICTR), many states were reluctant to invest the prosecutor of the ICC with unbridled capabilities. As Allison Marsten Danner writes, "The question of whether or not to authorize the prosecutor to initiate investigations absent a prior complaint by a state or the Security Council became one of the most contentious issues in the negotiations over the ICC. Both supporters and opponents of a prosecutor with *proprio motu* powers grounded their arguments on fears of politicizing the court."[17]

Although space constraints force me to sidestep the extensively covered debate over of the nature and function of the prosecutor's *proprio motu* powers and to focus instead on other institutional dimensions of the OTP that have received short shrift in the existing literature, a brief overview of the contentious politics of Rome is in order. This background sketch is necessary for understanding more fully the *initial conditions* (see figure 1) in which the prosecutor and his staff found themselves several years later, when they formed preferences about institutional strategies for the investigation and prosecution of international crimes.

Briefly stated, the debate at Rome over the OTP's institutional architecture centered on a single compound question: "Who controls the prosecutor, and how?" The International Law Commission (ILC) in its treaty draft of 1994, which it transmitted for consideration to the United Nations General Assembly, had proposed a radical solution: do not give the prosecutor any independent powers (initially called ex officio powers but now more commonly discussed as *proprio motu* powers) to initiate an investigation of international crimes. The ILC reasoned from the assumption that a permanent international criminal court would be "a facility available to States parties to its statute, and in certain cases to the Security Council."[18] Even though one commission member suggested "that the Prosecutor should be authorized to initiate an investigation in the absence of a complaint if it appears that a crime apparently within the jurisdiction of the court would otherwise not be duly investigated," the majority in the ILC felt that a more progressive institutional design was not advisable "at the present stage of development of the international legal system."[19]

After the U.N. General Assembly had considered the ILC draft and commentary, it created the aforementioned PrepCom, which met between 1996 and 1998 and produced a revised draft statute for the ICC. During this period, the mood began to change, and fears of a "'lone ranger running wild' around the world with excessive powers" subsided somewhat.[20] But the Rome Conference was nevertheless divided on what kind of institutional safeguards were necessary and sufficient to hold in check a future prosecutor. After much bargaining, a compromise formula was found. It tied the exercise of the prosecutor's *proprio motu* powers to judicial oversight by the Pre-Trial Chamber. This institutional choice became enshrined in article 15 of the Rome Statute of the ICC.

Of greater significance for the institutional development of the OTP was article 42(2) of the Rome Statute, which grants the prosecutor "full authority over the management and administration of the Office, including the staff, facilities and other resources thereof." This seemingly mundane provision goes a long way toward enshrining a modicum of organizational independence inside the ICC. Unlike the OTPs at the ICTY and ICTR, which depended on the registry for the administration of matters of staffing and recruitment, the OTP at the ICC is entirely self-governing. This configuration is not insignificant, given that some observers saw the ICTY Registry as retarding the functioning of the OTP through its oversight in the administration of human resources.[21]

Although the institutional structure conceived in Italy is not as inhibiting as some delegations had intended, it nevertheless put in place considerable institutional constraints on the development of the OTP, a topic to which I return later in the chapter. This is an opportune moment at which to leave behind the international dimensions of the OTP's institutional development. Rather more interesting for our purposes is the question of what kind of organizational decisions were contemplated (and made) within the broad institutional parameters that the international community imposed on the prosecutor. For as Jan Wouters and his coauthors put it, "The Rome Statute understandably remains, as far as the working conditions at the Prosecutor's Office are concerned, at the level of general principles."[22] This brings us to the internal dimensions of institutional development. Whereas the Rome Conference defined the rules of the game for the OTP, it remained for the incoming prosecutorial staff to further refine these rules and to imbue them with social meaning. In other words, what was drawn up in Rome had to be adapted to the everyday demands of the prosecution of international crimes in the Hague.

Multiple Options

The history of the OTP as an existing institution begins a year prior to the arrival of the prosecutor, in August 2002. At that time, the ICC's Advance Team of Experts took up residence in the Hague to cobble together from scratch a functioning bureaucracy in time for the arrival of the judges and prosecutor (who had not yet been elected) in the following year. The matters to be addressed were manifold and mundane—and of far-reaching significance. The work of the Advance Team merits a closer look because it throws into sharp relief the gradual emergence of contending visions of institutional design. Despite important continuities between the thinking of the Advance Team and that of the prosecutor, notable differences quickly emerged when Luis Moreno Ocampo took over the reins in the summer of 2003. But first, let us explore the thinking about institutional design as it existed in the Advance Team.

The Preparatory Commission established the Advance Team on July 1, 2002. Headed by Samuel Muller, the group consisted of specialists in legal, administrative, and related matters. The seven or eight "independent, mid-level experts," as PrepCom called them, were meant "to provide guidance and assistance to the Court during its initial stages."[23] This included advice on tasks that ranged from the drafting of personnel contracts and the creation of an accounting system to the preparation of a computerized case management system and obtaining custody of documents that constitute potential evidence in future proceedings before the ICC, among many other matters that confronted the experts who were ultimately hired. A few months later, in his report to the first session of the ICC Assembly of States Parties (ASP), Philippe Kirsch, chair of PrepCom, however, was forced to concede that the creation of the Advance Team had been more difficult than anticipated.[24]

In this preparatory period, the institutional future of the OTP was imagined first and foremost by Klaus Rackwitz and Morten Bergsmo. Rackwitz, who subsequently became the OTP's senior administrative manager and only recently left for a senior management position at Euro-Just, made probably the greatest contribution to the administration of international prosecutions at the ICC, notably in the context of data management and human resources. The Advance Team contracted with Bergsmo, formerly of the ICTY, to serve as a senior legal adviser, a position in which he was preoccupied with the investigative and prosecutorial challenges of the future OTP. As Phakiso Mochochoko, one of the Advance Team members and since February 2011 the head of the JCCD, remarked, "Bergsmo was . . . looking at everything having to do with the OTP."[25] Within the Advance Team, he was "generally taking care of the OTP interest in the discussions that we were having."[26] To this end, he and his colleagues were "consulting with more than 125 criminal justice experts and visiting national prosecution institutions with experience in large, complex cases, like the Serious Fraud Office (UK) and the *Generalbundesanwalt beim Bundesgerichtshof* [the Office of the Federal Prosecutor at the Federal Court of Justice] (Germany)."[27] Let us take a closer look at the institutional blueprint for the OTP that emerged from this preparatory work.

A first sketch for the institutional design of the OTP appeared as an annex to the ICC's first budget and was unveiled in September 2002, coinciding with the ASP's first session. Bergsmo and the Advance Team proposed a bureaucracy comprised of ten divisions, units, and sections to be run by a projected fifty-one staff members.[28] An Immediate Office of the Prosecutor (IOTP), assisted by an Administrative Unit, was intended to oversee the two OTP's major divisions, the Prosecution Division (PD) and the Investigation Division (ID). The former was further divided into a Prosecution Section, a Legal Advisory and Policy Section, and an Appeals Section, while the latter comprised an Information and Evidence Section, an Investigation Section, and an Analysis Section.[29] Two items are noteworthy: the fact that the blueprint based one deputy prosecutor inside the IOTP and the fact that the Legal Advisory and Policy Section was located inside the PD. According to official documentation, the PrepCom delegates "assumed that, in the first financial period of the Court, the Prosecutor would need only one Deputy Prosecutor to assist him/her on matters such as recruitment, investigation and prosecution policies, structure of the Office, etc."[30] The institutional role of the deputy prosecutor(s) is interesting because institutional practice and institutional redesign subsequently led to a de facto marginalization of these positions in the hierarchy of the OTP. Although akin to an U.N. assistant secretary-general in terms of pay scale (compared to the position of prosecutor, which is assessed at the level of U.N. undersecretary-general), the deputy prosecutors in the OTP primarily served as department heads.[31]

The Advance Team's mandate came to an end on October 31, 2002, shortly after the Division of Common Services took over the administration of the barely existing ICC. Although Bergsmo stayed on for a short while as senior manager of the OTP, where he headed the Legal Advisory and Policy Section, he left the ICC in October 2003. His departure came in the wake of the first major institutional choice affecting the OTP's institutional design.

The Invention of the JCCD

Something to which Bergsmo's organizational design gave short shrift were the international dimensions of the OTP. Moreno Ocampo championed this issue more than any other not only when he was first elected to the fledgling international court but also throughout his tenure. Unlike some of his critics, he recognized that the prosecution of international crimes was as much about mastering the intricacies of international relations as it was about mastering the minutiae of international law. As one observer noted, "Despite the increasing autonomy granted to the prosecutor over the course of the negotiating history of the Rome Statute, the Court remains heavily dependent on state-cooperation in order to investigate its cases, arrest its suspects, and imprison the individuals it convicts."[32]

While state cooperation posed a similar challenge to the efficacy of both the ICTY and ICTR, the issue was exacerbated within the ICC in light of the OTP's dependence on international cooperation.[33] To his credit, Moreno Ocampo recognized this challenge early on and took steps to create the institutional foundations for meeting it. For this reason, says Moreno Ocampo, "it was so important to have a diplomat with me—to learn how to do it."[34] The diplomat in question was Sylvia Fernández de Gurmendi, formerly a leading representative at the Rome Conference and presently an ICC judge. Moreno Ocampo put Fernández de Gurmendi, a fellow Argentine, in charge of the IOTP. In addition to her role as *chef de cabinet,* Fernández de Gurmendi headed the newly created External Relations and Complementarity Unit inside the IOTP.

The unit was slated to house one senior external relations adviser (P-5), two external relations advisers (P-4 and P-3 respectively), and two external relations assistants (GS-OL). This amendment to Bergsmo's institutional design was formalized in a June 2003 administrative instruction.[35] The External Relations and Complementarity Unit was the forerunner of the JCCD. As already intimated, this particular institutional design feature of the OTP was the expression of an operational strategy that deemed the international relations of prosecution to be of equal significance to the international law of prosecution. In some respects, the creation of the JCCD may also have resulted from institutional learning. Although it is not clear whether Moreno Ocampo was fully aware of this, he was not the first prosecutor to be partially dependent on the international cooperation of states. Richard Goldstone's memoir of his time as the first chief prosecutor at the ICTY and ICTR is brimming with expressions of frustration over the vagaries of international diplomacy.

Recalling a particularly difficult meeting in which former U.N. secretary-general Boutros Boutros-Ghali questioned the wisdom of Goldstone's international travels on behalf of the OTP, Goldstone writes that the U.N. chief "was not impressed with my explanation that we needed the cooperation of the governments involved to proceed successfully with our investigations. Also, in order to ensure that cooperation, I had no option but to make personal contact with the relevant government ministers and senior administration officials. I was astounded when he told me that if I needed to speak to political leaders I should request them to come and see me."[36]

Given the reduced powers of the ICC prosecutor relative to those enjoyed by Goldstone at the ICTY and ICTR, as well as the ICC's much larger geographic playing field, the invention of the JCCD was an inspired institutional choice. Moreover, this is why a consideration of the initial conditions—that is, the institutional significance of the Rome Conference—is so important. By inserting the complementarity plank into the international criminal law regime, the international conference created operational challenges that had not previously existed on the same scale. It introduced significant uncertainty into the practice of international criminal law. As one analyst recently put it, "Early on, the OTP was swamped with analysing multiple situations of potential jurisdiction, assessing national proceedings under the complementarity regime, and seeking cooperation from states and organizations (due to the ICC's lack of an enforcement arm)."[37] This complexity is further evidenced by the fact that international lawyers needed more than a decade to produce a comprehensive assessment of the theory and practice of the complementarity regime.[38] OTP staff had considerably less time to come to terms with the meaning of the institutional architecture pieced together in Rome.

Even though the OTP has been rightly criticized—and at one point sanctioned by Trial Chamber I—for its occasional grandstanding on the diplomatic stage, it is important not to underestimate the innovation of the institutional choice in question. Unfortunately for the OTP's institutional culture, the prosecutor was not always successful in persuading all of his staff of the need to integrate law and diplomacy in building the ICC. The same was true for observers on the outside looking on. As Benjamin N. Schiff writes regarding the reception of contending institutional designs, "Critics of Bergsmo's proposal saw it as too rigid; critics of the Moreno Ocampo OTP say it's too political."[39]

Over the ICC's first decade, the JCCD became further differentiated. It presently consists of three constitutive units—the International Cooperation Section (ICS), the Situation Analysis Section (SAS), and the International Relations Task Force (IRTF). ICS is charged with taking the lead in fostering the kinds of cooperative relations necessary for advancing investigative and prosecutorial activities. The duties of the SAS, by contrast, are less operational and more intellectual in nature. Among other tasks, it is responsible for the legal analysis of any and all jurisdictional matters and questions of admissibility. It maintains a close relationship with the Crime Pattern Analysis (CPA) unit in the Investigation Division. Yet whereas the CPA chiefly employs social science methodology, the SAS prioritizes legal methodology. Finally, the IRTF is the most forward-looking of the JCCD sections. Its mandate is the cultivation and advancement of diplomatic relations with all of the OTP's interlocutors—most notably, the ASP, U.N., European Union, African Union, and states parties, but also other governments that might be willing to share intelligence or otherwise assist. Over the years, the OTP has entered into a number of tailor-made arrangements: "Examples include the arrangement of modalities for the conduct of operations in states where the Office is carrying out investigative activities, such as Uganda and the D[emocratic] R[epublic of] C[ongo]. Other agreements have related to the provision of classified information. . . . The conclusion of arrangements, particularly for the provision of classified information, often requires extensive negotiations in order to provide the necessary assurances to information providers, as well as to ensure that the information is supplied in a manner that can be of optimal use to the Office."[40] Outreach to nongovernmental organizations and related actors is also part of the IRTF remit, and the prosecutor's periodic reports to the U.N. Security Council and other bodies originate there as well.

The creation of the JCCD marked a critical juncture in the institutional development of the OTP for two reasons. First, the establishment of the JCCD occurred at a moment when the range of plausible choices available to the prosecutor was substantial; second, the decision to elevate the role of diplomacy in the OTP had far-reaching consequences. Although the OTP has undeniably been struggling to achieve cooperation, notably in Africa and at the Security Council, it stands to reason that these outcomes are overdetermined and therefore may not necessarily reflect poorly on the performance of the JCCD. By creating the institutional foundations for a new class of international prosecutor—the diplomat—Moreno Ocampo arguably prepared the OTP well for the entirely novel demands of the new complementarity regime in international criminal law. Yet by prioritizing the international relations of prosecution over the international law of prosecution, Moreno Ocampo also selected an institutional option that made it progressively more difficult—both within the OTP and without—to stave off criticism related to his legal expertise.

The upgrading of the JCCD in the internal hierarchy of the OTP and the concomitant relative downgrading—inadvertent or otherwise—of lawyers in other units and divisions appears to have had the unintended effect of creating a disgruntled subset of staff in the Prosecution Division. (In many respects, this outcome, too, was overdetermined because inadequate role definition in other areas of the OTP's everyday life contributed to frustration.) Although Moreno Ocampo's prior and diverse experience in Argentina had given him a deeply rooted grasp of the nature and importance of investigative practices and he possessed an innate predilection for bringing charges against representative defendants, he had little patience for the minutiae of international law. For example, in response to the question of whether he felt that at the time of his arrival in the Hague in 2003, he had a sufficient grasp of international criminal law and procedure, he responded in a manner that belittled the complexity of the adjudication of international crimes: "I had normal knowledge and knew the level of crimes. You can read the documents and books about crimes against humanity, about genocide. It's not so difficult, is it?"[41] For Moreno Ocampo, the real predicament during his first six months in office lay elsewhere: "I saw two big challenges: keeping international support and being able to conduct good investigations."[42] As far as the investigation of international crimes was concerned, Moreno Ocampo's arrival in the OTP led to another early innovation with long-run consequences—the introduction of Joint Teams.

The Introduction of Joint Teams for Investigations and Trials

Simply put, the introduction of Joint Teams meant that the investigation and prosecution of each and every situation would draw on the integrated expertise of staff from different OTP units and, by implication, from different professional backgrounds. In September 2003, the term itself had not been invented. In its "Paper on Some Policy Issues before the Office of the Prosecutor," the first in a series of public statements on its work, the OTP spoke of "the existence of a variable number of investigation teams, the size and composition of which will fluctuate" as a prospective "third principle" that would guide its operations.[43]

The adoption in 2009 of the Regulations of the Office of the Prosecutor eventually codified the Joint Team innovation, several years after its emergence. Regulation 32(2), for example, provides that "each joint team shall be composed from the three Divisions in order to ensure a coordinated approach throughout the investigation."[44] Regulation 32(3) stipulates that the exact composition and size of each Joint Team "shall depend on the needs and stage of the investigation."[45] Evidence of the institutional centrality of the Joint Teams can be gleaned from the OTP's 2006 three-year report, which considered them to be "the core operational units of the office."[46] The idea behind the approach, at least as conceived in 2003, was to "provide flexibility in the management of investigations."[47] The expectation at the time was that it would "enable the Office to expand its capacity as needed, and subsequently shrink it back to the core permanent staff level within reasonable time."[48] In June 2004, the first interdivisional team was formed for the purpose of investigating alleged international crimes in the DRC, an action triggered by the DRC's self-referral. In 2006, the OTP provided a first account: "The Office assembled a joint team to carry out this investigation, combining staff members from different disciplines and belonging to each of the Office's three Divisions. Members of the joint team for the DRC investigation have been deployed to Ituri since July 2004 and have conducted more than 70 missions inside and outside the DRC, interviewing almost 200 persons."[49] In practice, however, reliance on Joint Teams produced a series of unintended consequences. Among various other problems, the collaboration between lawyers and former police investigators of varying ages, different genders, and numerous jurisdictional backgrounds proved trying.

Separately, in July 2004, a Joint Team for the investigation of international crimes in Uganda formally commenced its work. Within ten months, the fifteen-member team had, according to OTP records, "conducted over 50 missions to the field and collected sufficient information to successfully apply for five warrants of arrest against the top L[ord's] R[esistance] A[rmy] commanders."[50] Joint Teams were also established for the other situations that were beginning to reach the office. Each of the Joint Teams initially worked separately, as if in an institutional vacuum. Subsequently, however, staff members were moved across teams in response to operational needs. The rotation of investigators and lawyers and diplomats set in motion a process of gradual institutional change as the result of which informal ways of doing things began to converge and stabilize.

As the first investigations were nearing the trial stage, the OTP also introduced the idea of "Trial Teams." According to Regulation 32(5), "Upon confirmation of the charges [in a given case], an interdivisional Trial Team is formed to carry out prosecutions."[51] The principal organizational difference between the two kinds of teams is their authority structure. Whereas Joint Teams rely on a collective leadership model—that is, a troika representing all of the OTP's three divisions—Trial Teams are run by lawyers from the Prosecution Division. Informally, there is an expectation in the higher echelons of the OTP that joint and Trial Teams develop cooperative relationships. Perhaps unsurprisingly, a host of institutional and interpersonal challenges have interfered with the efficacy of both Joint Teams and Trial Teams.

The Joint Teams did not emerge fully formed, however. As one OTP staff member put it, "The joint team structure exists quite concretely now, but back [in 2004], things were much more ad hoc."[52] As a result, the transaction costs of establishing clear lines of authority were substantial.

Professional, doctrinal, gender, and other cleavages vitiated against the emergence of efficient procedures. In one sense, then, the challenges that plagued the ad hoc Joint Team arrangements mirrored the issues facing the OTP at large. As one respondent recalled, "We started with the absence of an institutional culture. Everyone either fell back on their previous jurisdiction's legal culture or on whatever they thought was the right thing to do in the context."[53] This informality was inevitable because the miniscule OTP staff was forced to hit the ground running. Unlike the ICC Chambers, where the workload was extremely light in the first few years, the OTP from the beginning faced a deluge of communications from a whole host of actors. In addition to finding a way of administering these interactions with the outside world, the legal and nonlegal staff had to find a way of commencing with the examination and investigation of international crimes.

"A Standardized Mode of Operation": The Institutional Evolution of the OTP

This part of the chapter turns from critical junctures in the institutional emergence of the OTP to those that left a mark on its institutional evolution. Arguably more important for the OTP's institutional development than the arrival of Moreno Ocampo was the arrival of Situations. The rapidly increasing workload, especially in the wake of the Darfur referral by the U.N. Security Council, necessitated a greater centralization of OTP norms and institutions. At the level of institutional choice, the invention of ExCom has perhaps had the most far-reaching impact on the everyday lives of the OTP's three hundred investigators, prosecutors, and diplomats.

The Creation of ExCom

In one of the first public mentions of ExCom, the OTP stated in September 2006 that ExCom provided "strategic oversight." Comprised of the prosecutor and the heads of ID, JD, and JCCD, the new unit "defines the Office policies and supervises the operations of the project-driven joint teams."[54] In the spring of 2009, the management committee of the OTP finally received its legal foundation. As codified in Regulations 4(1) and 4(2) of the Regulations of the Office of the Prosecutor, ExCom "shall provide advice to the Prosecutor, be responsible for the development and adoption of the strategies, policies and budget of the Office, provide strategic guidance on all the activities of the Office and coordinate them."[55] However, this eminently reasonable language hides the dynamics of contention that have accompanied ExCom's institutional practices.

As a starting point, one critical aspect of ExCom is how its nature and composition have changed over the years—often for the better, sometimes for the worse. Consequently, as an institution, ExCom has facilitated both productive and pathological outcomes. In productive terms, it has substantially reduced transaction costs in the administration of international prosecution. Particularly in the latest incarnation of ExCom—which includes not only the three division heads but also the OTP's relatively new investigation coordinator and prosecution coordinator—has ensured a more streamlined response to the myriad challenges facing its staff. However, several years passed before an institutional design—and matching institutional culture—were devised that did not alienate lower-level staff. The effort was not helped by the Orwellian acronym ExCom, which initially did little to inspire confidence on the part of many staff members. Various OTP staff members noted in interviews that they and their colleagues did "not dare" to speak up when summoned with their Joint Teams to present their work to ExCom, at least not during the "dark ages."[56]

A second institutional feature that warrants discussion is the adoption, in the latter part of the first prosecutor's tenure, of three-year employment contracts for individuals serving in the OTP. In the early years of the OTP, it was an institutional norm that low- and mid-level investigators and lawyers received short-term contracts ranging in duration from three months to six months, later eight months, and eventually one year. Why would this human resource matter be at all significant? In practice, the uncertainty associated with short-term contracts often gave rise to a wide variety of professional anxieties. The existence of such anxieties, in turn, created disincentives for frankness when it came to the deliberation of operational choices inside the bureaucracy. According to some of those involved, this dynamic played itself out in the context of ExCom's expanding reach into the OTP's everyday life. As a result, many lower-level staff came to feel alienated from their work.[57] The upshot of this alienation was that over time, the prosecutor grew to be insulated from his staff, a development that stood in sharp contrast to the decentralized way of doing things that prevailed in the first few years of the OTP. By nature a team worker, the prosecutor initially cultivated a flattened hierarchy that suited his natural style. The very small size of the OTP invited such informality. Unfortunately, it created expectations of access and participation on the part of many staff members that were bound to be disappointed in the long run.

In its 2006 *Report on Prosecutorial Strategy,* the OTP therefore declared that it "aims to stabilize its structural design, keeping the flexibility needed to address different situations around the world but ensuring consistency."[58] Moreno Ocampo, as one observer suggested, created ExCom with the principal purpose of centralizing control as much as possible.[59] Some believe it was for the same reason that the prosecutor never filled the vacant post of deputy prosecutor (investigations) after Belgian lawyer Serge Brammertz, currently the ICTY chief prosecutor, left the ICC in mid-2007. A plausible argument can be made that this was an institutional response to the unintended consequences of early informality, but this is merely one of several competing explanations. An equally plausible argument is that the public humiliation that the OTP experienced in the wake of its missteps in the Lubanga investigation, during which it refused to disclose potentially confidential exculpatory evidence as well as relied on questionable intermediaries in the DRC, persuaded Moreno Ocampo not to reappoint.

Be that as it may, Moreno Ocampo was aided in the centralization of authority by his second *chef de cabinet,* Beatrice Le Fraper du Hellen, who also succeeded Fernández de Gurmendi as head of the JCCD. By all accounts a divisive figure, Le Fraper du Hellen played a major role in the transformation of the OTP from an institution with a relatively flat hierarchy to one where ExCom ranks supreme. According to a staff member, "Management is one of the most underdeveloped areas of the OTP, with poor results obtained in internal surveys."[60] Yet it would be wrong to condemn outright the centralization of authority in the OTP. That said, institutional choice was not only unavoidable but necessary given the practical imperative to grow the OTP quickly into a more sizable bureaucracy that could cope with the increasing demands placed on it and do so efficiently. As one staff member aptly stated, "When you have a common understanding [of the work to be done], it is much easier to decentralize control. Here you don't have any dominant culture, and, as a result, in order to make sure that everybody is on the same page, you have to have a much more centralized structure."[61]

The difficulty of establishing a common way of doing things was exacerbated by the OTP's rapid expansion. From 2003 through 2006, the OTP grew "five-fold the first year, more than double[d] the second and still increas[ed] by 26% in the third year."[62] In June 2003, the total number of full-time staff in the OTP was eleven, including the prosecutor. Three years later, "there were 81 professionals including the Chief Prosecutor, and 43 support staff."[63] (See table 2.) In many ways, then, this rapid transformation and growth necessitated a switch from relative informality to relative formality in the management of the OTP. As the three-year report conceded, "The rapid expansion of Court activities, exponential growth of the Office and the immense energy required to maintain the pace of the Office present challenges to maintaining Office consistency, team unity and training."[64]

The creation of ExCom marks a critical juncture in the development of the ICC because by imposing a more structured hierarchy that reduced the access concomitant with informality, it disappointed the expectations of many OTP staff, thereby increasing transaction costs. A seemingly minor yet telling example of these changes is that staff access to the prosecutor no longer remained automatic and instead became subject to prior appointment. What would be an entirely normal situation in any other executive office created adjustment problems in the OTP. This new, more formal organizational setup was perhaps most difficult for those investigators and lawyers who came from the ad hoc tribunals. As one current ICC and former ICTY staff member explained,

> For lawyers who are used to working in a decentralized structure where they have a lot of autonomy, a lot of control, it is hard to adapt to a structure that is very centralized. I'm sure you hear people complaining about micromanagement, but that is a necessary development for a lot of different reasons.[65]

The respondent offered three reasons that help explain the ICC's greater need for centralization:

> One is because you don't have this shared culture; two, this is a permanent institution and so you are making decisions today that will affect the institution for years and years and years, whereas with the

TABLE 2. Staff Growth in the Office of the Prosecutor, 2003–2006

Year	Professional Staff	Support Staff	Total
2003	5	6	11
2004	27	16	43
2005	66	31	97
2006	81	43	124

Source: International Criminal Court, Office of the Prosecutor, *Report on the Activities Performed during the First Three Years (June 2003–June 2006)*, at ¶73 (Sept. 12, 2006). All figures were calculated in the month of June in the year in question.

ICTY, at least you had a sense of [it being] a contained project. And then the third thing is, since you have so many different situations that raise a lot of different issues in different forms, it is much harder [at the ICC than at the ICTY] to coordinate across situations to make sure that we are taking a unified approach and that we are consistent. . . . That is another reason for having centralized control.[66]

The former staffer then identified a fourth, quite distinct reason: "The ICTY is much more decentralized, and here it is very tightly managed. It is managed from the top. Of course the other reason for [greater centralization] is the personality of the prosecutor. He is quite open about it. He likes to be involved in cases, and he has that need to control cases."[67] This portrayal is analytically interesting because it points to interaction effects between structural and individual variables in the centralization of authority. By all accounts, the prosecutor spent a lot of time thinking about questions of institutional design. As someone who was party to such deliberations put it, "In the context of revising the Operational Manual . . . we had a lot of discussions about this."[68]

Here is one final account of how the creation of ExCom marks a critical juncture in the institutional development of the OTP:

Establishing the Joint Team model and ExCom . . . being in control, that was a hard won victory for the prosecutor. [It] took a lot of work to get people to get used to the fact that ExCom was running the show. He is very reluctant to move away from that because he has seen the other extreme, which is everyone running in their own direction. Each senior lawyer or each senior investigator trying to run the show like they know best. The prosecutor wants to avoid going back, falling back to that, moving toward that.[69]

Significantly, however, this conclusion was not shared by everyone at the OTP. Even aside from the senior lawyers and the senior investigators who left the OTP—often after bitter substantive disagreements with the prosecutor, some of which were publicly aired—some staff members feel alienated from the OTP's work and remain less invested in the contours of prosecutorial strategy.

Transparency and inclusiveness were not highly valued at early ExCom meetings. As one party noted, "The ExCom meetings used to be very secret. . . . Nobody could go in. It was just the heads of the Divisions and Luis [Moreno Ocampo] and Danielle [Hayaux du Tilly, personal assistant to the prosecutor]. It was very cocooned."[70] This difficult period notwith-standing, even demoralized staff members acknowledge that in the last few years of Moreno Ocampo's tenure, the prosecutor again became more approachable. "Now it is even interesting to go to ExCom. . . . Before you didn't even want to go to the 12th floor [the location of the prosecutor's office]. You wanted to avoid it."[71] This change may arguably have resulted in part from a small but consequential tweak to ExCom's institutional de-sign: its gradual enlargement from five to nine members. Some respon-dents initially referred to the latest incarnation as "ExCom Plus." More recently, however, the enlarged institutional design, which first emerged sometime around late 2010 or early 2011, slowly became the norm. Some staff members believe that its emergence was inadvertent rather than de-liberate. "I think part of [the emergence of ExCom Plus] was because [the prosecutor] traveled so much."[72] The implication is that the need for pro-fessional representation occasioned the drafting of additional members into ExCom meetings. This de facto institution, then, evolved into a de jure institution, which became enshrined in the Operational Manual.

My field research suggests that the regular inclusion of the investigation and prosecution coordinators, two newly created OTP positions, as well as the head of the Legal Advisory Section (LAS), improved the communica-tion between division heads and their staff. The modified institutional de-sign approximated a middle ground between the excessive decentralization of the early days (when informality reigned) and the excessive centraliza-tion (when formality ruled) that followed on its heels.[73] Prior to these changes, however, ExCom achieved relatively few advances in terms of en-hancing the OTP's efficacy or efficiency. In fact, for some, ExCom was ini-tially not much more than an Orwellian acronym. Seen from that perspec-tive, the hidden forms of resistance initially produced by ExCom did little to streamline the OTP, instead modifying an abstract institutional design that did not make sense to many staff members. As sociologist Arthur Stinchcombe writes, "To be communicable, an abstraction has to be trans-missible to and interpretable by the people who have to do the activity be-ing governed."[74]At least initially, OTP leaders were far more adept at com-municating with the world at large than with their own staff.

The Drafting of an Operational Manual

Indicative of the fact that the OTP was finally on the road to a more con-sidered and consistent way of doing things, is the entry into force, in April 2009, of the Regulations of the Office of the Prosecutor, a requirement mandated by rule 9 of the Rules of Procedure and Evidence, as adopted by the ASP in September 2002.[75] For this respondent, the creation of the Operational Manual marks the "evolution from a very ad hoc mode of operation into a standardized mode of operation."[76]

The seven-year delay is not entirely surprising given that the OTP experienced numerous transformations during this period as its staff came to terms with the unique challenges inherent in a permanent court operating in a less than accommodating international system. According to official documents, "The Office spent the first three years developing and shaping its policies and regulations."[77] Two defining features of the OTP's early years of institutional emergence—its ad hoc evolution and its tendency to muddle through challenges—worked against the publication of regulations for the long run. This is not to say that the OTP did not try. In fact, one of the most remarkable aspects of the institutional development of the OTP at the ICC was an early interest in the standardization of behavior.

One of the most unusual innovations coming out of the OTP relates to the production of policy papers. According to Regulation 14(2) of the Regulations of the Office of the Prosecutor, the occasional publication of such papers is meant to "reflect the key principles and criteria of the Prosecutorial Strategy."[78] As table 3 shows, the OTP published four policy papers between 2003 and 2012, one of them only in draft form. In addition, the OTP has issued two reports. The first of these, dated September 2003, sets out the principal "policy issues" that the prosecutor faced when he took office. The second, from December 2011, concerns the topic of preliminary examinations, which are the early stage analyses of goings-on in settings that may subsequently form the basis of a formal investigation. What does the decision to publish policy papers have to do with the question of institutional development? As it turns out, quite a lot: the release of policy papers introduced a modicum of transparency, which in turn raised external expectations of the OTP's accountability.

In addition to the four published policy papers, most of which were

TABLE 3. Reports and Policy Papers by the Office of the Prosecutor, 2003–2012

Title	Date
Paper on Some Policy Issues before the Office of the Prosecutor	September 2003
Report on Prosecutorial Strategy	September 2006
Policy Paper on the Interest of Justice	September 2007
Policy Paper on Victims' Participation	April 2010
Draft Policy Paper on Preliminary Examinations	October 2010
Report on Preliminary Examinations	December 2011

circulated in draft form to relevant interlocutors outside of the ICC, notably nongovernmental organizations, the OTP has been working on additional framework papers. For example, the OTP has draft policy papers on case selection, positive complementarity, sexual and gender crimes, the protection of witnesses, and evidentiary review and disclosure. The OTP has also issued a September 2006 report on prosecutorial strategy and a December 2011 report on preliminary examinations. Taken together, these publications offer ample evidence of what William Schabas has described as "an impressive and unprecedented degree of transparency."[79]

This reflexive and forward-looking approach to the making of prosecutorial strategy indeed merits respect. It represents a marked departure from the reactive manner in which most of the OTPs at the nonpermanent international courts and tribunals have functioned. As Schabas writes,

> Rare indeed are examples of attempts by the prosecutors of the ad hoc tribunals for the former Yugoslavia, Rwanda, Sierra Leone and Lebanon to explain or justify their policies and their exercise of discretion. By contrast, the Prosecutor of the International Criminal Court has held public consultations and issued position papers and similar documents in order to explain his choices and determinations.[80]

The decision to champion transparency may be interpreted as a form of institutional self-binding in the sense that it put pressure on the OTP to abide by its own norms and procedures. At the same time, the commitment to transparency can be interpreted as a strategy to preempt future criticism. It could also be argued, however, that at least in the context of preliminary examinations, the prosecutor had no choice but to offer a glimpse into the OTP's workings. In that rather special context, article 15(6) of the Rome Statute requires the prosecutor to "inform those who provided the information" in the event that the prosecutor concludes that no reasonable basis for a preliminary examination exists. It would be wrong, however, to construe from this provision any wider obligation to keep the international community abreast of the OTP's thinking and doing. According to Schabas, Moreno Ocampo "has interpreted the provision liberally, issuing detailed public documents with respect to his decision not to initiate investigations concerning Iraq and Venezuela, as well as general comments as to why certain situations fall outside the jurisdiction of the Court."[81]

This is not to say that the deliberative process involved in the drafting of the OTP reports and policy papers has necessarily led or will lead in the future to improved outcomes in the prosecution of international crimes at the ICC. Creatively thinking about the requisites of sustainable prosecution is certainly not enough. As one senior OTP practitioner puts it, "The policies about important issues in the office are interesting, but they don't really bind the office very much. For the most part, they simply outline factors to be considered and how the decision making is structured, but as policies they leave considerable discretion in the office."[82] Having said that, the prosecutor and the staff members involved must be credited for their attempt to institutionalize a worthwhile exercise in reflection.

Unlike the policy papers, the Operation Manual was intended entirely for internal rather than external consumption. It was a tool for improving the OTP's institutional practices. It was an attempt at nudging into existence an institutional culture replete with an institutional memory. The need for such a tool became apparent when the various Joint Teams in Uganda, the DRC, and Darfur "started developing different practices for the same thing."[83] The need to get investigations under way meant that learning by doing carried the day. "Each of these teams was facing challenges that we didn't have a template for. We had the prior practice of the ICTY and ICTR [to drawn on], but . . . we did not have any institutional knowledge [of our own]."[84] This resulted in very idiosyncratic ways of doing things. "Whenever there was an [operational] challenge—how to make a filing, how to investigate a situation, how to deal with a particular legal provision—we [were] coming up with nonstandardized practices in each team."[85] The rising transaction costs of operating in this manner were an important factor in the institutional decision to create the Operational Manual. Recalls one practitioner, "Each team had a different way of doing things. While maybe sustainable in the early years, it is not sustainable when you have maybe six teams [working simultaneously] and when you have to function as an institution with a large [law] practice. I think [this realization] gave rise to the idea of regulations, the [notion of the] Operational Manual, the decision [to craft] standard operating procedures."[86]

The lack of an institutional culture troubled many OTP staff at all levels of the bureaucracy during the ICC's first decade. As one lawyer asked, "What is the culture of this office? What is the identity of this office? We have many identities, and we do our work together, but we don't have a common culture. . . . You need someone who is very clear about what the culture of the office is, which I think we miss in a way."[87] How did the OTP staff deal with the institutional uncertainty?

Although the drafting of the Operational Manual was directed first and foremost at the reduction of transaction costs, it also had a constitutive effect. In hindsight, the Operational Manual appears to have laid the foundations for an *emergent* institutional culture. Intended or otherwise, the codification of good practices and deliberations regarding better practices reduced uncertainty on the part of many OTP staff, especially in the lower ranks. While some staff members inevitably resented the standardization of their responsibilities and duties, the everyday life of the OTP became, on the whole, more predictable. More important than the final product, however, were the practices of deliberation and consultation that accompanied the drafting process.

Given the centrality of the drafting process, let us take a closer look at how the Operational Manual came about. Moreno Ocampo first requested a compilation of protocols and standard operating procedures (SOP) in 2005. Yet, as the SOP were not yet uniform and easily accessible to all staff, ExCom, in August 2006, established an SOP working group with an eye toward creating a database of documents for everyday use. On March 16, 2007, ExCom then established the Standing Committee on Regulations. Seven months later, on October 31, ExCom had the LAS compile and review all internal OTP documents with the goal of producing the Operational Manual.[88] According to the OTP's 2006 three-year report, it had "formulated over 130 draft policies, guidelines and standard operation procedures" related to more than eleven major aspects of its work.[89] After sifting through these documents, LAS produced a first draft of a manual on January 31, 2008. In the fall of 2008, after several rounds of additions and revisions, ExCom, decided to appoint an interdivisional committee to take over the drafting process with assistance from LAS. This interdivisional committee presented iterative drafts in November and December 2009. On February 12, 2010, after approval by ExCom, a draft of the Operational Manual was circulated to all OTP staff members. Finally in September 2011, the OTP published—for internal use only—the current Operational Manual.[90] With fourteen chapters and a total of 185 pages, the manual covers OTP activities such as public information and outreach, screening and handling information, evidence review and disclosure, and the protection of and support for witnesses and others persons at risk.[91]

According to the 2006 three-year report, the OTP pursued "institution-building and policy and protocol development with the same rigor with which it has pursued its investigative and prosecutorial activities."[92] Yet the former activities have received virtually no attention in the burgeoning literature on the prosecution of international crimes at the ICC. This is unfortunate because advances in the study of institutions over the past twenty years have shown in no uncertain terms that institutional and organizational ways of doing things—sometimes referred to as the rules of the game in positive political theory—have a substantial structuring effect on social performance. Although the bulk of scholarship has focused on economic and political performance, there is no reason to assume that legal performance is not be subject to the enabling and constraining effects of particular institutional environments.

Conclusion

On June 16, 2012, Gambia's Bensouda took office as the second ICC prosecutor. She inherited not only an OTP rich in talent and experience but also an institutional structure that had a more than random effect on the choices OTP investigators and prosecutors made in the preceding decade. (For additional information on the precise shape of this institutional structure, see figure 2.) Given her previous service as the ICC deputy prosecutor, Bensouda is familiar with the opportunities and challenges of a decade's worth of institutional development. After all, she had a hand in many of the moments of institutional choice, design, and change over the preceding decade. Yet if our understanding of institutional development in other bureaucracies offers any guidance, Bensouda will face sunk costs as she sets about streamlining the OTP's institutional landscape.

My evolutionary account shows how early decisions about institutional design in the OTP have affected later ones. Although space constraints have meant that I have largely bracketed the question of how the OTP's institutional development affected investigative, prosecutorial, and political decisions by Moreno Ocampo and his staff, this work has laid the foundation for such research. "Exploring the sources and consequences of path dependence," writes Pierson, "helps us understand the powerful inertia or 'stickiness' that characterizes many aspects of political development—for instance, the enduring consequences that often stem from the emergence of particular institutional arrangements."[93]

The four critical junctures in the institutional development of the OTP have had a far greater impact on its activities in the period under investigation than is commonly assumed. For what makes junctures "critical" is the fact that "they place institutional arrangements on paths or trajectories, which are then very difficult to alter."[94] Future research is required—preferably on the ground, not from hundreds or thousands of miles

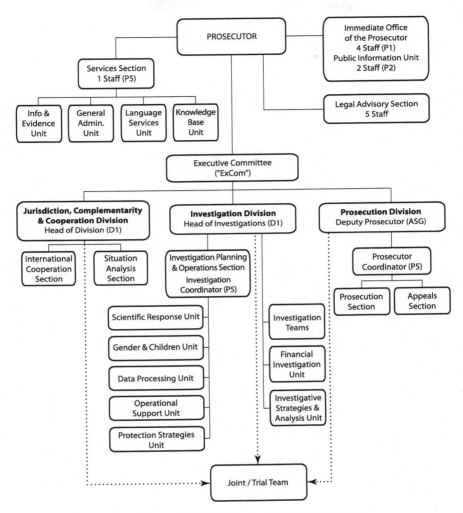

Fig. 2. The Organizational Structure of the OTP in 2012

away—on the *specific* paths or trajectories down which the OTP traveled during the first decade of its operation. I have sketched in the organizational background against which any such analysis should proceed. It remains for scholars interested in the everyday lives of international courts to populate the foreground in my institutional portrait, preferably with a thickly described account of agents, preferences, strategies, and outcomes in the context of the specific proceedings that are finding their way to the ICC.

NOTES

1. The chapter draws on more than one hundred hours of interviews with former and current OTP staff members. Only a small portion of the collected data are reflected in the analysis. A comprehensive, book-length account—and one that speaks more directly to theoretical debates in anthropology, political science, and sociology—is in the works under the title, THE EVERYDAY LIFE OF INTERNATIONAL LAW: AN ETHNOGRAPHY OF THE INTERNATIONAL CRIMINAL COURT. I gratefully acknowledge financial support for this larger project from the British Academy, the Leverhulme Trust, the Suntory and Toyota International Centres for Economics and Related Disciplines (STICERD) at the London School of Economics and Political Science, and the Institute for Advanced Study, Princeton, where I wrote this chapter while in residence as the Louise and John Steffens Founders' Circle Member. I presented earlier versions at Harvard Law School and in the Program in Law and Public Affairs at Princeton University.

2. On the importance of this analytic shift, see PAUL PIERSON, POLITICS IN TIME: HISTORY, INSTITUTIONS, & SOCIAL ANALYSIS 133 (2004).

3. *See* James Mahoney & Kathleen Thelen, *A Theory of Gradual Institutional Change,* in EXPLAINING INSTITUTIONAL CHANGE: AMBIGUITY, AGENCY, & POWER 1 (James Mahoney & Kathleen Thelen eds., 2010).

4. *See* Interview with OTP Staff Member, the Hague, Neth. (July 31, 2012).

5. *Id.*

6. *See* JENS MEIERHENRICH, THE EVERYDAY LIFE OF INTERNATIONAL LAW: AN ETHNOGRAPHY OF THE INTERNATIONAL CRIMINAL COURT (in progress).

7. *See* Mary Jo Hatch & Dvora Yanow, *Organization Theory as an Interpretive Science,* in THE OXFORD HANDBOOK OF ORGANIZATION THEORY: META-THEORETICAL PERSPECTIVES 74 (Haridimos Tsoukas & Christian Knudsen eds., 2003).

8. For the sake of convenience, I use the term *prosecutors,* unless stated otherwise, to refer to all staff employed in the OTP regardless of whether they are investigators, prosecutors (conventionally understood), or diplomats.

9. *See* Giovanni Capoccia & Daniel Kelemen, *The Study of Critical Junctures: Theory, Narrative, & Counterfactuals in Historical Institutionalism,* 59 WORLD POL. 341, 341 (2007).

10. *Id.* at 349.

11. *Id.* at 343.

12. *Id.* at 351.

13. *See* John Zysman, *How Institutions Create Historically Rooted Trajectories of Growth,* 3 INDUST. & CORP. CHANGE 243, 244 (1994).

14. *See* Avner Greif & David D. Laitin, *A Theory of Endogenous Institutional Change,* 98 AM. POL. SCI. REV. 633 (2004).

15. *See* PIERSON, *supra* note 2, at 164.

16. *See* DAVID SCHEFFER, ALL THE MISSING SOULS: A PERSONAL HISTORY OF THE WAR CRIMES TRIBUNALS 175 (2012).

17. *See* Allison Marsten Danner, *Enhancing the Legitimacy & Accountability of Pros-*

ecutorial Discretion at the International Criminal Court, 97 AM. J. INT'L L. 510, 513 (2003).

18. *See* Rep. of the Int'l Law Comm'n, 46th Sess., May 2–July 24, 1994, at 45, UN Doc. A/49/10; GAOR, 49th Sess., Supp. No. 10 (1994), http://legal.un.org/ilc/documentation/english/A_49_10.pdf.

19. *Id.* at 46.

20. *See* Silvia A. Fernández de Gurmendi, *The Role of the International Prosecutor,* in THE INTERNATIONAL CRIMINAL COURT: THE MAKING OF THE ROME STATUTE 181 (Roy S. Lee ed. 1999).

21. *See* John R. W. D. Jones, *The Office of the Prosecutor,* in THE ROME STATUTE OF THE INTERNATIONAL CRIMINAL COURT: A COMMENTARY, VOLUME I 273 (Antonio Cassese, Paula Gaeta, & John R. W. D. Jones eds., 2001).

22. *See* Jan Wouters, Sten Verhoeven, & Bruno Demeyere, *The International Criminal Court's Office of the Prosecutor: Navigating between Independence & Accountability?,* 8 INT'L CRIM. L. REV. 273, 276 (2008).

23. *See* U.N. Preparatory Comm'n for the Int'l Criminal Court, *Guide to the Report of the Preparatory Commission,* July 1–12, 2002, at 15, U.N. Doc. PCNICC/2002/3 (July 25, 2002), http://legal.un.org/icc/prepcomm/report/prepreport.htm.

24. *See* ICC, Assembly of States Parties, *In First Meeting, Assembly of States Parties to Rome Statute of International Criminal Court Approves Financial, Administrative Arrangements,* U.N. Press Release L/3012 (Sept. 3, 2002), http://www.un.org/News/Press/docs/2002/L3012.doc.htm.

25. *See* Interview with Phakiso Mochochoko, head of the OTP Jurisdiction, Complementarity, and Cooperation Division, the Hague, Neth. (Sept. 19, 2011).

26. *Id.*

27. *See* ICC, Office of the Prosecutor, *Report on the Activities Performed during the First Three Years (June 2003–June 2006),* at ¶55 (Sept. 12, 2006) (hereinafter *OTP Report 2003–6*), http://www.icc-cpi.int/NR/rdonlyres/D76A5D89-FB64-47A9-9821-725747378AB2/143680/OTP_3yearreport20060914_English.pdf.

28. *See* ICC, Assembly of States Parties, First Session, Sept. 3–10, 2002, Official Records, Doc. ICC-ASP/1/3, at 304.

29. For more detailed information on the Advance Team's visions of the staffing requirements of and division of labor among the OTP's divisions, units, and sections, *see* PREPARATORY COMM'N FOR THE INT'L CRIMINAL COURT, PROCEEDINGS OF THE PREPARATORY COMMISSION AT ITS NINTH SESSION (Apr. 8–19, 2002), Addendum at ¶¶51–64, U.N. Doc. PCNICC/2002/L.1/Rev.1/Add.1 (Apr. 26, 2002), http://daccess-dds-ny.un.org/doc/UNDOC/LTD/N02/353/19/PDF/N0235319.pdf?OpenElement.

30. *Id.* at 45.

31. Serge Brammertz, currently the ICTY prosecutor, was appointed deputy prosecutor (investigations) at the ICC on Nov. 3, 2003. Fatou Bensouda, now the ICC prosecutor, was appointed deputy prosecutor (prosecutions) on Nov. 1, 2004. Brammertz went on leave from his position in the OTP in Jan. 2006 and submitted his resignation from the ICC in June 2007.

32. *See* Danner, *supra* note 17, at 527.

33. *See, e.g.,* VICTOR PESKIN, INTERNATIONAL JUSTICE IN RWANDA & THE BALKANS: VIRTUAL TRIALS & THE STRUGGLE FOR STATE COOPERATION (2009).

34. *See* Interview with Luis Moreno Ocampo, ICC Prosecutor, the Hague, Neth. (Apr.

16, 2012). Unless otherwise stated, all interviews with Moreno Ocampo referenced in this chapter were conducted jointly with Carsten Stahn and Joseph Powderly of Leiden University in preparation for a book of conversations. All other interviews are my responsibility alone.

35. *See* ICC, Office of the Prosecutor, *Administrative Instruction Concerning the Organization & Staffing of the Office of the Prosecutor* (June 2003, copy on file with the author). Another significant change related to the institutional location of the Legal Advisory and Policy Section. Whereas it was previously attached to the prosecution division, it was now incorporated into the IOTP, within arm's reach of the prosecutor.

36. *See* RICHARD J. GOLDSTONE, FOR HUMANITY: REFLECTIONS OF A WAR CRIMES INVESTIGATOR 100 (2000).

37. *See* Gregory Townsend, *Structure & Management,* in INTERNATIONAL PROSECUTORS 288 (Luc Reydams, Jan Wouters, & Cedric Ryngaert eds., 2012).

38. *See* THE INTERNATIONAL CRIMINAL COURT & COMPLEMENTARITY: FROM THEORY TO PRACTICE (Carsten Stahn & Mohamed M. El Zeidy eds., 2011).

39. *See* BENJAMIN N. SCHIFF, BUILDING THE INTERNATIONAL CRIMINAL COURT 113 (2008).

40. *See OTP Report 2003–6, supra* note 27, at ¶83.

41. *See* Interview with Luis Moreno Ocampo, *supra* note 34.

42. *Id.*

43. *See* ICC, Office of the Prosecutor, *Paper on Some Policy Issues before the Office of the Prosecutor* 9 (Sept. 2003) (hereinafter *OTP Policy Paper 2003*), http://www.icc-cpi.int/nr/rdonlyres/1fa7c4c6-de5f-42b7-8b25-60aa962ed8b6/143594/030905_policy_paper.pdf.

44. *See* ICC, *Regulations of the Office of the Prosecutor* 18 (Apr. 23, 2009) (setting forth Regulation 32[2]), http://www.icc-cpi.int/NR/rdonlyres/FFF97111-ECD6-40B5-9CDA-792BCBE1E695/280253/ICCBD050109ENG.pdf.

45. *Id.* (setting forth Regulation 32[3]).

46. *See OTP Report 2003–6, supra* note 27, at ¶67.

47. *See OTP Policy Paper 2003, supra* note 43, at 9.

48. *Id.*

49. *See OTP Report 2003–6, supra* note 27, at ¶14.

50. *Id.* at ¶27.

51. *See* ICC, *Regulations of the Office of the Prosecutor, supra* note 44, at 18 (setting forth Regulation 32[5]).

52. *See* Interview with OTP Staff Member, the Hague, Neth. (Sept. 16, 2011).

53. *Id.*

54. *See OTP Report 2003–6, supra* note 27, at ¶67.

55. *See* ICC, *Regulations of the Office of the Prosecutor, supra* note 44, at 8 (setting forth Regulation 4[2]).

56. *See* Interview with OTP Staff Member, *supra* note 52.

57. *See generally* Interviews with OTP Staff Members, the Hague, Neth. (Sept. 2011).

58. *See* ICC, Office of the Prosecutor, *Report on Prosecutorial Strategy,* at ¶11 (Sept. 14, 2006), http://www.icc-cpi.int/NR/rdonlyres/D673DD8C-D427-4547-BC69-2D363E07274B/143708/ProsecutorialStrategy20060914_English.pdf.

59. *See* Interview with Anonymous, the Hague, Neth. (Sept. 22, 2011).

60. As quoted in Townsend, *supra* note 37, at 293.

61. *See* Interview with OTP Staff Member, the Hague, Neth. (Sept. 26, 2011).

62. *See OTP Report 2003–6, supra* note 27, at ¶73.

63. *Id.*

64. *Id.* at ¶74.

65. *See* Interview with OTP Staff Member, *supra* note 61.

66. *Id.*

67. *Id.*

68. *Id.*

69. *Id.*

70. *See* Interview with OTP Staff Member, the Hague, Neth. (Sept. 15, 2011).

71. *See id.*

72. *See id.*

73. On the virtues—and vices—of formality in law and organizations, *see* ARTHUR L. STINCHCOMBE, WHEN FORMALITY WORKS: AUTHORITY & ABSTRACTION IN LAW & ORGANIZATIONS (2001).

74. *Id.* at 20.

75. *See* ICC, R. PROC. & EVID. 9.

76. *See* Interview with OTP Staff Member, *supra* note 52.

77. *See OTP Report 2003–6, supra* note 27, at ¶54.

78. *See* ICC, *Regulations of the Office of the Prosecutor, supra* note 44, at 12 (setting forth Regulation 14[2]).

79. *See* WILLIAM SCHABAS, AN INTRODUCTION TO THE INTERNATIONAL CRIMINAL COURT 381 (4th ed. 2011).

80. *Id.* at 381–82.

81. *Id.* at 382.

82. Personal Correspondence from OTP Staff Member to author (Aug. 20, 2013) (on file with author).

83. *See* Interview with OTP Staff Member, *supra* note 52.

84. *Id.*

85. *Id.*

86. *Id.*

87. *See* Interview with OTP Staff Member, *supra* note 70.

88. ExCom had already discussed the idea on Apr. 17, 2007, but for a number of reasons the project was put on hold on June 12, 2007, and only revived in the fall.

89. *See OTP Report 2003–6, supra* note 27.

90. *See* Interview with Hans Bevers, legal adviser, OTP Legal Advisory Section, the Hague, Neth. (Sept. 20, 2011).

91. The *Operational Manual of the Office of the Prosecutor* was described to me in interviews with OTP staff members.

92. *See OTP Report 2003–6, supra* note 27, at ¶53.

93. *See* PIERSON, *supra* note 2, at 11.

94. *Id.* at 135.

Investigations and Institutional Imperatives at the International Criminal Court

Alex Whiting

Luis Moreno Ocampo, the first prosecutor of the International Criminal Court (ICC), has been widely praised for establishing a functioning prosecution office and making the institution relevant, while at the same time criticized for the quality of some of his office's investigations.[1] John Prendergast, the cofounder of the nongovernmental organization Enough, said that, "Moreno-Ocampo has helped place the issue of accountability for war crimes front and center on the international radar screen."[2] A report done by the War Crimes Research Office at American University found that the Office of the Prosecutor (OTP) "has achieved substantial successes in a short period of time, as evidenced most strikingly by the recent conviction of its first suspect and the issuance of warrants and summonses involving a wide range of charges for war crimes, crimes against humanity, and genocide against multiple suspects across seven diverse situations in fewer than ten years."[3] Finally, Barry Stevens, who directed and produced *The Prosecutor,* a film about the ICC, summed up the view of many when he wrote at the end of the first prosecutor's term that the "Court is thoroughly established in the collective mind of the world. It isn't going away. Those who would commit gross human rights violations now face a greater possibility that their actions may land them in jail. And part of that achievement is Moreno-Ocampo's. He had quite a few failures, but he did more to put the Court on the map than anyone."[4]

At the same time, some of Moreno Ocampo's investigations have been specifically criticized by judges of the Court and outside commentators, and his successor, Fatou Bensouda, has taken steps to adjust the office's investigative strategy in future cases.[5] In the two judgments handed down to date at the Court, one convicting Thomas Lubanga of child soldier crimes and the other acquitting Mathieu Ngudjolo of all crimes, the judges criticized the lack of thoroughness of the prosecution's investigations.[6] Commentators have raised concerns about the Court's overall record to date, noting that several cases have failed at the confirmation stage, a preliminary assessment of the evidence that occurs after arrest or summons but before trial.[7] The overarching concern has been that the prosecutor's cases were pushed forward on the basis of insufficient evidence, perhaps enough to have persons charged (which requires only a showing of "reasonable grounds") but not enough to confirm the charges (requiring a showing of "substantial grounds to believe") or to convict at trial (requiring "proof beyond a reasonable doubt").[8]

Much can certainly be learned from both the successes and the failures of the first prosecutor's investigations and prosecutions, and the office will find ways to improve in the coming years. But just as "one train may hide another,"[9] the criticisms of the first prosecutor's investigations neglect a more profound critique of the institution itself. With precious few investigative tools and extremely limited resources, the ICC cannot proceed as a domestic investigation would or even as other international criminal investigations have as a consequence of striking differences in institutional design, political context, and resources. In this light, Moreno Ocampo's efforts need to be assessed in relation to design of the institution of the ICC itself.

Unlike most national prosecutors and investigators, international criminal prosecutors lack both investigative tools and a reliable political constituency supporting them. They are entirely dependent on state cooperation to conduct investigations, build cases, and effectuate arrests, but this cooperation is highly contingent and often erratic. As a result, international criminal prosecutors must often galvanize support for their work from critical states, which in turn requires those prosecutors to be forward-leaning and proactive in initiating investigations and bringing cases.

International prosecutors therefore face a treacherous dynamic: they must build support for their institutions and investigations by bringing cases, which they can only do with significant international support as a consequence of their limited tools. This need to show activity and results creates a pressure to bring cases forward quickly, when there may be sufficient evidence to bring charges but before they are fully investigated. Thus, while national prosecutors with established power and legitimacy can afford to proceed cautiously and conservatively (even if in some cases other pressures cause them to do otherwise), international criminal prosecutors face institutional pressures to be to take risks and show results to justify the underlying endeavor.

The prosecutors at the ad hoc tribunals enjoyed particular advantages that allowed them to succeed despite this dynamic, as is exemplified by an examination of the International Criminal Tribunal for the Former Yugoslavia (ICTY). Although that court's prosecutors felt significant pressure to show results in the institution's early years and as a result brought cases that were not necessarily fully investigated at the time of charging, the court ultimately succeeded because of the institution's sustained focus and the support from critical actors at crucial moments (including the judges, states in the region, and influential states in the international community).

The ICC's experience has been very different. The Court's first prosecutor also sought to generate support for his investigations, but the resources allowed and the responses from other actors have not been the same. The judges have been extremely demanding both procedurally and in terms of substantive evidence, and a number of the prosecution's early cases failed. With respect to the international community, while relevant actors have generally backed the institution, specific support for the prosecution's investigations has been very uneven and often nonexistent, either because of a lack of sustained interest or because of the lack of leverage over situation countries. While many factors account for both the successes and failures at the ICC, a lack of consistent support for the Court's work has contributed to the prosecutor's inability to push a number of cases forward beyond the charging stage.

This broader perspective on the first prosecutor's investigations allows for a more nuanced assessment of these first years of the OTP and suggests that changes to the prosecution's strategy going forward may be necessary but not sufficient. The prosecutor has been praised for driving the institution forward and making it relevant, but this approach has ultimately exposed some of the fragilities of the Court. Success of future investigations will require not just a new prosecutorial strategy, but also further consideration of the ICC's institutional design and the commitment of states to the success of the international criminal justice project.

The Dependence on Cooperation for ICC Investigations

National prosecutors ordinarily have powerful investigative tools at their disposal. For example, when faced with a crime scene, prosecutors in the United States can ensure that it is promptly and thoroughly examined, searched, analyzed, and documented by investigators and forensic experts.[10] Federal prosecutors and many state prosecutors can use a grand jury to subpoena witnesses to testify under oath and can subpoena bank, financial, phone, business, or any other kinds of records. They can obtain email or other computer records. They can also ask investigators to conduct surveillance or to interview witnesses. By show of probable cause, they can apply for warrants to search locations, such as houses, offices, or cars. In some cases, they can apply to have listening devices placed on phones or other electronic communications devices. When there is sufficient evidence to proceed with arrests, they will ordinarily have confidence that those charged will in fact be arrested and brought in, and that some defendants could be persuaded to testify against others. While some of these investigative tools are particular to the U.S. system, most established national prosecutors or investigators have a similar range of powers at their disposal.

International criminal investigators and prosecutors have virtually none of these tools on their own. Crime scenes are often inaccessible until months or even years after the crimes have occurred. Investigators have no ability to compel witnesses to provide information or testify and cannot require persons or entities to surrender records or physical evidence. They do not have the authority to conduct searches or to intercept electronic communications. They do not even have the power of arrest.

As a result, international criminal investigators depend almost entirely on cooperation from states to conduct investigations and effectuate arrests. Article 93 of the Rome Statute sets forth all the different ways that states parties are required under the statute to cooperate, including facilitating witness interviews (as long as they are voluntary), collecting documents, examining physical sites, conducting searches and seizures, and any other investigative measures that are consistent with the law of the requested state.

Although the statute requires all of these forms of cooperation from states parties—article 93 says that states parties "shall" provide the requested assistance—enforcement is difficult. Pursuant to article 87(7) of the statute, if a state party fails to cooperate with a request for assistance, then the Court "may make a finding to that effect and refer the matter to the Assembly of States Parties or, where the Security Council referred the matter to the Court, to the Security Council." Thus cooperation can be enforced only through a political mechanism rather than through a legal or judicial one. But states can be quite good at constructing what former ICTY prosecutor Carla del Ponte so aptly described as "the *muro di gomma,* the wall of rubber, the rejection disguised so it won't appear as a rejection."[11] In connection with the ICC prosecutions in Kenya, the OTP complained in May 2013 that "since the beginning of the OTP's investigations in April 2010, the [government of Kenya] has constructed an outward appearance of cooperation, while failing to execute fully the OTP's most important requests."[12] Even when countries openly defy the ICC, the Assembly of States Parties (ASP) or the Security Council are not necessarily well designed to react, and many countries will be impervious to international pressure. For example, the ICC has repeatedly complained to the U.N. Security Council about Sudan's failure to cooperate with ICC investigations or execute ICC arrest warrants, but the Council has not reacted beyond words, and it is not clear what kinds of pressures could be brought to bear on Sudan to induce it to cooperate. In its most recent report to the Security Council on Sudan, the ICC prosecutor stated, "The Office takes this opportunity to recall the eight communications from the Court informing the Security Council about non-cooperation in the Darfur situation, either by the Government of the Sudan or by other States, in relation to the four suspects at large. . . . The Council has not yet responded to these communications, neither has it taken any action."[13] The prosecutor further quoted the statement of one Chamber that "the ICC has no enforcement mechanism and thus relies on the States' cooperation, without which it cannot fulfill its mandate and contribute to ending impunity."[14]

So while the OTP depends on state cooperation to advance its investigations and prosecutions, countries will generally provide genuine cooperation only when they determine that it is in their interest to do so, either because it advances national goals or because influential outside countries make cooperation a priority. The formal mechanisms provided in the Rome Statute will do little to produce cooperation if the political will to do so does not somehow also exist.[15] The question then concerns the dynamic between the work of the prosecutor and the level of cooperation that he or she receives. Can states be expected to take the lead, or can the prosecutor play a role in motivating states to provide support to the Court?

Building the ICC through Cases

Although Moreno Ocampo famously stated in his inaugural address that the ICC would be successful if it brought no cases,[16] and although some observers thought that the Court should establish itself slowly and cautiously, most people understood that the Court would have to prove its relevance quickly by bringing cases:

> The court's newly elected judges were restlessly awaiting work, and the advocacy community that had played a critical role in creating the court was eager to see it take action. The prosecutor's suggestion that the court could succeed even without launching investigations provoked a strong reaction. [Nongovernmental organization] leader William Pace bristled at the suggestion of an inactive court. Several judges also objected to the vision of a court exerting influence by its mere presence rather than its caseload. From inside and outside The Hague, there was intense pressure on the new institution to become operational.[17]

Moreno Ocampo knew that the new institution would have to start investigations and bring cases. In *The Reckoning*, one of the first movies made about the ICC, the prosecutor said,

> Six months after my beginning I received a referral from Uganda. And some people were advising me, be careful, you have to build an institution for the next two centuries. I knew I had to run. I had to show very quickly some outcome, some results.[18]

He saw that the institution would be built *through* activity, by doing cases and demonstrating that the Court could function. At the end of his term, he said, "I had a responsibility to build an institution. In 2003, when I arrived, there were two public officers in my office and eighteen judges waiting for cases. So of course after eight years, we have much more cases, much more activity. It's a normal result."[19]

Separately, he understood that only by bringing cases could the Court have an impact and deter future crimes—in his view, one of the primary goals of the institution.[20] To this end, from a very early stage, he adopted a policy of focusing on those most responsible.[21] As Moreno Ocampo told the Council on Foreign Relations in 2010, "The true relevance of the Court is its global impact."[22] This objective would be achieved by doing cases that would have effects across the world.[23] As he elaborated:

> This is the way forward. Our Court will deal with only a few cases over the years but the impact of its cases and rulings extends to at

least 110 States, which are Parties to the Rome Statute and even beyond to reach non States Parties. The shadow of the Court.[24]

The following year, the prosecutor told the ASP that one of his key policy objectives was "to maximize the Office's 'contribution to the prevention' of future crimes, to better protect victims from violence."[25] In the film *The Prosecutor,* Moreno Ocampo talked about the shadow of his first case: The "Lubanga case has impact in Ituri, but has impact in Nepal, has impact in Colombia. That is why in Colombia, they discuss child soldiers now. And that is why in Nepal they demobilized 3,000 kids. That is an impact."[26] He also noted that the cases that he brought in Kenya addressing the postelection violence of 2007–8 helped contribute to the country's peaceful elections in 2013.[27]

The prosecutor also believed that the Court had to take the *lead* in enforcing the law and that states would then adjust and follow. He understood that while states might support international criminal accountability in principle and even back the creation of institutions to investigate and prosecute international crimes, their interest in accountability would often waver in the moment, when faced with actual atrocities to investigate. In the short term, concerns about achieving stability or security or simply a desire to "move on" and forget the past would often loom large, getting in the way of a commitment to investigate and prosecute perpetrators. Samantha Power has powerfully described how international actors will tend toward inertia in the face of mass atrocity: "Despite graphic media coverage, American policymakers, journalists, and citizens are extremely slow to muster the imagination needed to reckon with evil."[28] In his speech to the ASP, the prosecutor himself recognized that "States Parties have struggled to prioritize their commitment to international justice over more immediate economic or political interests."[29] He repeatedly said during his tenure that his "duty [was] to apply the law without political considerations. Other actors have to adjust to the law."[30] And he sought to motivate: "I asked diplomats to support justice. . . . Because many diplomats didn't expect prosecutors to request that kind of assistance, some might have perceived me as making political requests or comments."[31]

In practical terms, this meant not just opening investigations but bringing cases forward.[32] Actual cases would show that the Court could function and have a broader impact, and they would induce states to support the Court if they did not want to see the cases (and the institution) fail. As Moreno Ocampo explained, "I have to build that the national states support me as a normal issue in the same way that, in Canada, the Ontario chief of police will help the federal prosecutor in a normal case. So that's it. It would be normal in Canada. And it has to be normal in the world."[33] While this particular vision is certainly ambitious if not unimaginable in the present world, it captures the essential dynamic: the institution would succeed if it could persuade states to provide support and cooperation for its investigations, and it would do so in part by bringing cases forward.

Investigations have no timetable, no necessary urgency. States will provide investigative support if motivated but will otherwise not necessarily be engaged as long as the prosecution remains in the "investigation stage." But by initiating actual cases, the prosecutor focuses potential cooperation and assistance from states on specific events and individuals and creates a new urgency. Once individuals are charged, both legal and political consequences follow, and other actors (the judges, defense counsel, and the Registry) become engaged. Arrests and summonses trigger judicial deadlines. In addition, the stakes are raised because the failure of a case can send a strong signal of impunity to the world, potentially undermining the institution itself. When the prosecutor initiated cases in Sudan, he pushed hard for arrests, arguing that impunity could lead to further bloodshed.[34] Jonathan Fanton of the MacArthur Foundation has warned that "unless the arrest warrants are enforced, the court will not succeed."[35]

In a slightly different but related context, speaking about governmental responses to mass atrocity, David Scheffer, the first U.S. war crimes ambassador, argued,

> Violent humanitarian catastrophes may require unorthodox responses, speedy and innovative policy-making, and determined efforts to focus political will on the imperative of human survival. Atrocities do not wait for well-briefed discussions in regularly scheduled meetings of high-level officials. Atrocities do not fit well within rigid guidelines for policy-making. Atrocities, or the imminent launch of such atrocities, scream out for immediate, imaginative, and bold actions tailored to the unique threat. *Timing is everything.*[36]

A similar point can be made about international criminal prosecutors. Lacking independent powers to investigate and prosecute, and dependent on international, political, and slow bureaucratic structures to support their work, international prosecutors will often feel a need to be bold and take the lead to create urgency, move forward, and break through resistance to state cooperation.

The Comparison between ICC Investigations and the Investigations of the Ad Hoc Tribunals

So how has the process of motivating support from states manifested itself at the ICC as compared to the ad hoc tribunals? As commentators and policymakers have taken stock of the ICC's first decade and the successes and failures of the first prosecutor, inevitable comparisons to the ad hoc tribunals—and particularly the ICTY and the International Criminal Tribunal for Rwanda (ICTR)—have arisen. Many observers have questioned why the ICC has been unable to mimic the successes of these ad hoc institutions. As one academic recently wrote, "Compared to the other international prosecution forums, such as the ICTY and ICTR, the docket of the ICC is quantitatively dismal. . . . The ICC could learn a few lessons from the ICTY and ICTR."[37]

Comparing the ICC to the ad hoc tribunals or the scorecards of different international criminal prosecutors is a difficult and complex undertaking that must account for institutional, historical, situational, and personality factors, among others. But one way to look at the trajectory of the ad hoc tribunals is that the early prosecutors at those institutions followed a similar path to the first prosecutor at the ICC but had quite different results. At the ICTY, for example, the early prosecutors also faced pressure to bring cases, and consequently many of the early cases initiated were either weak or involved relatively low-level individuals. Even in later years, cases were advanced with enough evidence to bring charges but without being fully investigated. But over time, the ICTY largely succeeded. Why? In part, because other factors allowed the prosecution to strengthen its cases and therefore succeed.

Although there existed a range of expectations for what the ICTY would do when it was first established, those who staffed the court in the early years quickly understood that they would need to show results to continue, particularly since the "United States and Europe did not initially give the courts the kind of national backing they needed to succeed."[38] Richard Goldstone, the first ICTY prosecutor, felt this pressure to bring cases from various quarters but in particular from the judges. As one account notes, "Goldstone knew he needed to raise the tribunal's visibility, and even the judges were urging him to issue more indictments."[39] The president of the ICTY, Antonio Cassese, was particularly eager to see the court become operational and pushed for more indictments, especially against senior leaders.[40] One commentator noted that Goldstone "and Cassese made an odd pair: the top judge with the temper of a prosecutor,

and the top prosecutor with the temper of a judge."[41] The judges even issued a public statement in February 1995, noting "their concern regarding
the substance of their programme of judicial work for 1995" and expressing "their concern for the urgency with which adequate indictments must
be made."[42] Goldstone also felt pressure from the U.N. through the budget
process. Shortly after arriving in the Hague in August 1994, Goldstone
learned that

> at least one indictment had to be issued before the November meet-
> ing in order to demonstrate that the system was working and that
> the tribunal was worthy of financial support. It must be remem-
> bered that the United Nations was already then starved for cash and
> that every dollar voted for the tribunal was one dollar less for other
> important agencies. For that reason we issued our first indictment,
> against Dragan Nikolić.[43]

The early prosecutors also understood that activity was critical to obtaining cooperation from states for the court's investigations. As long as
the ICTY was simply investigating, its existence and mission remained
diffuse and abstract, and states could pursue other priorities while ordinary bureaucratic practices kept cooperation on a slow track.[44] Many factors of course led countries to support the ICTY during critical years, but
the initiation of actual cases undoubtedly both intensified pressure on
countries to cooperate—particularly if those countries had an interest in
the institution succeeding—and focused that cooperation on evidence
pertaining to specific suspects. As one commentator on the ICTY wrote,
"Goldstone could also put pressure on the West simply by issuing more
indictments. On February 13 [1995], he indicted twenty-one Bosnian Serbs
for running the Omarska concentration camp in 1992."[45] The second ICTY
prosecutor, Louise Arbour, made the point in the opposite way when she
told U.S. authorities in January 1997, shortly after she assumed her post,
that the "more people think the tribunal is in jeopardy, the harder it will
be to get cooperation."[46]

Unsurprisingly, therefore, the ICTY initially brought some cases that
were very thinly investigated. As one early commentator assessed, "In addition to this remarkable growth in substantive international criminal law,
a broader prosecutorial strategy has increased the chances that cases
would be based on weak evidence."[47] Some of the cases relied on only a
few witnesses, and some observers thought that the evidence was insufficient to prove responsibility at trial.[48] By the time Goldstone left the ICTY,

a number of line prosecutors were concerned about the cases that had been charged and even hoped that some suspects would not be surrendered.[49] The second prosecutor dismissed a number of her predecessor's indictments.[50]

Even in later years, many cases that were charged had to be more thoroughly investigated after the suspects were brought to The Hague. As a result, indictments were often amended several times after arrest or surrender and sometimes even after trials started. The prosecution also sought leave to add witnesses and documents to its evidence as trials progressed. Because the trials were lengthy and the judges wanted access to all available evidence, these motions were ordinarily granted, and the defense received additional time to respond to the prosecution's new evidence.[51] In the Milošević case, for example, one of the signature cases of the ICTY, the Prosecution continued to gather incriminating evidence during the trial.[52] Only in the last phase of the ICTY, when the U.N. Security Council began to pressure the court to wind up its proceedings, did the judges begin to take more control over the cases and apply the rules more rigorously.[53]

If the ICTY started with thinly investigated cases, how did it succeed? Both the judges and ultimately the international community supported the tribunal in ways that were critical to its success. In the first years of the ICTY, nobody knew what it would become or if it could succeed. The judges, who were in fact pushing the prosecution to be more proactive, were generally indulgent with respect to requests for more time or to amend charges and add evidence.[54] While complaints arose, primarily from the defense and some commentators, that the pretrial phase and trials were too long and that the prosecution was given too much latitude to adjust its case theory during the trial, the prosecution was, for the most part, allowed to continue investigating and developing its cases after arrest.

Even more critical to the Court's success has been its institutional design, the political will of central players, and historical circumstances. The ICTY, with roughly the same budget as the ICC today, was permitted to focus on just one set of interrelated conflicts in the former Yugoslavia for a sustained period of time. This focus, which will never be matched by the ICC, permitted the institution to establish itself and build its body of evidence, knowledge, and expertise. Although people complained about the early prosecutions of "small fish"—low-level actors—those cases helped the institution gain its footing and helped the prosecution build cases against more senior actors.

Further, the court received critical support from influential actors at an important moment in the institution. Starting in 2001, the United States and the European Union conditioned aid and ascension to the EU on demonstrated support for the ICTY.[55] This pressure was transformative. All of the most high-level accused (including Milošević, Karadžić, Mladić, and Gotovina) were surrendered after conditionality was instituted and the ICTY gained access to critical documents and records and witnesses from both Serbia and Croatia.[56] Simply put, the court would not have had its successes without the strong backing of powerful and influential countries. This international commitment was mirrored by political transformations in both Serbia and Croatia, which saw leaders come to power who prioritized moving beyond the war, rebuilding their countries, and reengaging with the other countries in the region and the international community.[57] Further, the presence of North Atlantic Treaty Organization forces in Bosnia and later in Kosovo gave the tribunal yet another tool to gain further arrests, searches, and access to evidence.[58]

In sum, therefore, although the prosecution at the ICTY was initially pushed to bring forward cases that were not fully investigated, the circumstances of the ICTY—notably, the willingness of its judges to permit the time necessary for factual development and of powerful states to leverage their global presence in support of the ICTY—allowed the prosecution to succeed over time. As the institution grew and became more established, the judges became more exacting and rigorous in their enforcement of procedure, but by that time, the prosecution had established itself.

Constraints Challenging ICC Investigations

So what, then, has been the experience at the ICC? In short, the circumstances to date have been very different. First, the institution is not designed to focus on one conflict for an extended period of time, allowing for the development of a body of evidence and expertise. The Court must engage several situations at once—as of August 2014, it was investigating in eight different countries—and it must reestablish itself each time it begins investigating a new conflict. Despite an increase in activity, the ASP has kept budget increases to a minimum.[59] Since the Court can only ever take on a few cases from each conflict, it lacks the ability to build cases from the bottom up and develop evidence over time.

Second, the judges at the ICC have been far more exacting in terms of procedure and evidence. In a way, the ICC is a victim of the ICTY's success. The procedure set forth in the Rome Statute and in the ICC's Rules of Procedure and Evidence is already more demanding on the prosecution than was the case at the ICTY.[60] For example, unlike the ICTY, which had only indictments and trials, the ICC rules require a third proceeding, confirmation hearings, between arrest and trial. Further, the ICC Statute explicitly requires the OTP to investigate both incriminating and exonerating information (though most prosecutors would do so even without such a mandate).[61] More striking, however, has been the rigorous application of the rules and the high expectations of the judges. At least two of the Pre-Trial Chambers have held that the prosecution must complete its investigation *before* the confirmation hearing is held and can conduct further investigation afterward only if it can show extraordinary circumstances (for example, that the evidence was not available before the confirmation hearing).[62] In other words, the judges expect the prosecution to be fully trial-ready much earlier in the process than was ever required at the ICTY, and the judges have been much more reluctant to allow the prosecution to continue its investigations after confirmation and during trial. In addition, the Appeals Chamber has held that while the confirmation hearing is a preliminary proceeding at which the prosecution may rely entirely on written witness statements and even statement summaries, the judges should also assess credibility and weigh contradictions that might arise in the evidence.[63] The prosecution has cogently argued that it is impossible to evaluate contradictions in witness evidence without hearing the witnesses themselves, but to date the judges have been unpersuaded and have insisted on their approach. This development is another signal to the OTP that it must satisfy a high standard of review early in the proceedings.

Further, the judges have shown in the first two judgments that they will be extremely exacting in the evaluation of the evidence, perhaps even more than is required by the applicable standard of proof. In both cases, the judges set aside considerable parts of the prosecution's evidence, finding that it lacked sufficient credibility leading to an acquittal in one case.[64] One Pre-Trial Chamber set forth the kind of evidence it expected even at the confirmation hearing stage:

> As a general matter, it is preferable for the Chamber to have as much forensic and other material evidence as possible. Such evidence should be duly authenticated and have clear and unbroken chains of custody. Whenever testimonial evidence is offered, it should, to the extent possible, be based on the first-hand and personal observations of the witness. Although there is no general rule against hearsay evidence before this Court, it goes without saying that hearsay statements in the prosecutor's documentary evidence

will usually have less probative value. Reliance upon such evidence should thus be avoided wherever possible.[65]

While such a "preference" for better evidence might seem unexceptional and unobjectionable, the tone of the decision plainly indicates that evidence that falls short of these expectations is unlikely to be sufficient for a successful prosecution.

In addition, the ICC has often lacked the support of other influential actors who were critical to the success of the ICTY. In the case of self-referrals—for example, the situations in Uganda, the Democratic Republic of Congo, and Côte d'Ivoire—the OTP unquestionably has benefited (at least to some extent) from the support of the referring nation's central government. Similarly, there is no doubt that the states parties have often backed the *idea* of the ICC and have at times supported its efforts, whether by assisting with collecting evidence or arresting suspects.[66] At critical times, however, the ICC has not received the basic support it requires to be effective. Whether as a consequence of competing priorities or the inability of influential international actors to exert pressure, this lack of support has allowed certain states and governments to avoid producing evidence or arresting suspects.

Two persuasive examples of this pattern can be found in the situations of Sudan and Libya. Both were referred to the ICC by the U.N. Security Council, a phenomenon that would appear to indicate considerable support for investigations in those countries. In Sudan, the ICC has charged four government officials, including President Omar al-Bashir, with crimes against humanity and genocide, but the international community has exerted little concerted effort to insist on enforcement of the warrants or the provision of additional evidence.[67] This failure to support the ICC cases reflects a focus on other priorities—such as achieving peace and security in the region—and supportive countries' lack of leverage over the Sudanese government.

In Libya, the Security Council acted to refer the case to the ICC within weeks of the beginning of the brutal government crackdown on the February 2011 uprising.[68] The ICC investigation initially had strong support.[69] But the North Atlantic Treaty Organization's military operations in Libya soon began to stall, and support for an interventionist approach began to diminish.[70] After the ICC brought charges against Muammar Gaddafi; his son, Saif; and Gaddafi's security chief, Abdullah al-Senussi, the international community showed little interest in the cases.[71] Before the government fell, one of the prime movers behind the ICC referral, France, even reportedly considered negotiating a settlement with the Gaddafi regime.[72] When the government fell a few months later, the international community turned completely away from an interest in accountability and focused on rebuilding the country, economic opportunities, and security.[73]

A third example is evident in Kenya, where the prosecutor acted pursuant to his *proprio motu* powers to open an investigation and ultimately brought charges against six prominent Kenyans. Although the Kenyan government claims to have cooperated with the ICC investigation, the OTP has complained about the lack of real support, and two of the accused ultimately ran and were elected president and vice president of the country, in part on an anti-ICC platform.[74] Outside countries that might have influence in Kenya have provided little concerted support beyond formal statements. The ICC's cases in Sudan and in Kenya have deepened the emerging rift between the Court and many African countries, and countries outside of Africa have prioritized economic and security concerns and have not significantly pressured Kenya to cooperate with the Court. In addition, the OTP has faced staggering witness security problems in its Kenya case (as well as in its other cases) that have not been adequately addressed by the Victims and Witnesses Unit within the Registrar or by states parties providing assistance to the Court.[75] In the Sudan, Libya, and Kenya, the ICC has had difficulty advancing its cases, and in Kenya in particular, the cases are failing.[76]

In sum, the OTP has faced challenges from within the Court and outside the institution that far surpassed those faced by the ICTY. As Mirjan Damaška has written, "The [ICC] will often experience more problems in securing outside assistance and thus face greater difficulties in processing crimes of unusual complexity than preexisting international criminal courts, while it is pursuing goals more demanding than did its predecessors."[77] At the ICTY, the prosecution had the space to build its cases and the institution over time. Similar circumstances will often not exist at the ICC.

Conclusion

Comparing the early years of the ICC to the ICTY is not about assigning responsibility or blame for the difficulties that some of the first cases have encountered. Whatever lessons are to be learned about the first investigations, clearly they include a need for the prosecution to bring stronger, better-supported cases.

But the comparison adds nuance to an assessment of the first prosecutor's term and situates the investigative challenges faced by the ICC within a broader institutional context. The prosecutor drove the Court forward to a place of relevance and even prominence. To borrow David Scheffer's words, he took "immediate, imaginative, and bold actions" to force the issue, to keep attention on accountability, to bring evidence to light, to push cases forward. He tested the limits of the judicial processes but often received rigid and formalistic responses from the judges. He tried to lead, but others in the international community did not always follow. Imagine if in the early years he had pursued a more cautious, conservative course within the constraints imposed on him, he might have succeeded in investigating and charging one case, maybe two, during his nine-year term. It is hard to imagine that the Security Council would turn to such an institution in Sudan and Libya or that commentators would today describe it as being "on the map." Instead, critics would be deploring the institution's failure and the missed opportunities.

In charting a course for the future, it is easy to mythologize the successes of the ad hoc tribunals and assume that they resulted solely from a strategy or approach that can be replicated at the ICC. The situation is much more complicated. The ad hoc tribunals succeeded because the stars aligned: dynamic prosecutors drove the institutions and received critical support along the way. The ICC is a very different institution that must contend with completely new challenges and will often be operating in less hospitable political and historical contexts than those faced by the ad hoc tribunals. Caution by the prosecutor at the ICC even today may lead to quiescence and ultimately irrelevance if no other world force drives hard toward accountability.

The struggles of the early ICC cases must raise questions about the prosecution's practices but should also lead us to think about the institution itself and what it requires to succeed. As one scholar notes,

> International criminal courts, still struggling to justify themselves, cannot afford to disregard the attainability of the goals they profess to pursue. The gap between promise and achievement may disappoint their audiences and disillusion their friends, while providing argumentative ammunition to their enemies. For these courts, as for all fledgling institutions, the viability of professed goals is a close cousin of legitimacy.[78]

In the case of the ICC, success may require more than adjustments to the prosecution's strategy. For example, states parties should consider whether to further fortify the OTP's budget and whether more could be done to support witness security measures, such as providing greater opportunities for witness relocation. Further, could the OTP receive additional powers? As Antonio Cassese has written, "States shy away from taking the only audacious step capable of making international criminal courts fully autonomous and effective: that is, authorizing once and for all that international investigators, police officers and court marshals be allowed freely to enter the territory of sovereign states and there execute international judicial orders to gather evidence, interview witnesses and arrest suspects or indictees."[79] Such a dramatic development remains unimaginable, but are more modest steps possible? Could more be done to compel state cooperation, and could the Court receive certain investigation and prosecution tools, even if not all those possessed by national prosecutors? As we continually assess what is required for the ICC's success, it will not be enough simply to decide that the OTP will do better investigations. In the next phases of the institution, we will need seriously to engage the larger questions of institutional design and support for the institution.

NOTES

My thanks to Martha Minow, Luis Moreno Ocampo, Philip Heymann, Menno Goedman, Darryl Robinson and James Stewart for their comments and suggestions. My particular thanks to Samuel Birnbaum for his extensive research assistance, ideas, and comments on this chapter. The ideas expressed are mine alone.

1. *See, e.g.,* Karen L. Corrie, *International Criminal Law,* 46 INT'L LAW. 145, 151–52 (2012) ("While often a lightning rod for criticism, Moreno-Ocampo has successfully established a well-functioning structure for the OTP, and pushed it to be efficient and proactive."); Kirsten Ainley, *The International Criminal Court on Trial,* 24 CAMBRIDGE REV. INT'L AFF. 309, 318 (2011) ("The prosecutor . . . at the ICC [has] shown real courage in [his] initial actions.").

2. *See* Laura Heaton, *Historic Day for ICC as Ocampo Passes the Mantle of Chief Prosecutor to Bensouda,* ENOUGH PROJECT (June 15, 2012), http://www.enoughproject. org/blogs/historic-day-icc-ocampo-passes-mantle-chief-prosecutor-bensouda.

3. *See* WAR CRIMES RESEARCH OFFICE, INVESTIGATIVE MANAGEMENT, STRATEGIES, & TECHNIQUES OF THE INTERNATIONAL CRIMINAL COURT'S OFFICE OF THE PROSECUTOR 1 (2012), http://www.wcl.american.edu/warcrimes/icc/documents/ICCReport16.pdf.

4. *See* Barry Stevens, *Prosecutor & the International Criminal Court—An Update,* TVO DOCSTUDIO (July 9, 2013), http://docstudio.tvo.org/blog/doc-studio-blog/prosecutor-and-international-criminal-court-update. *See also* David Bosco, *Brave Thinkers 2011: Luis Moreno-Ocampo,* THE ATLANTIC (Oct. 4, 2011), http://www.theatlantic.com/magazine/archive/2011/11/luis-moreno-ocampo/308697/ ("Moreno-Ocampo has put a fragile new institution on the map. When his term ends next year, he will hand over an office that still faces formidable challenges. But being relevant will not be one of them.").

5. The new strategy is set forth in the prosecutor's strategic plan for 2012–15, which can be accessed on the ICC website. *See* ICC, Office of the Prosecutor, *Strategic Plan: June 2012–2015* (Oct. 11, 2013), http://www.icc-cpi.int/en_menus/icc/structure%20 of%20the%20court/office%20of%20the%20prosecutor/policies%20and%20strategies/ Documents/OTP-Strategic-Plan-2012–2015.pdf.

6. *See* Prosecutor v. Thomas Lubanga Dyilo, Case No. ICC-01/04-01/06, Judgment Pursuant to Article 74 of the Statute, ¶¶178–484 (Mar. 14, 2012); Prosecutor v. Mathieu Ngudjolo, Case No. ICC-01/04-02/12, Judgment Pursuant to Article 74 of the Statute, ¶¶115–23 (Dec. 18, 2012). *See also* Caroline Buisman, *Delegating Investigations: Lessons to Be Learned from the Lubanga Judgment,* 11 NW. U. J. INT'L HUM. RTS. 30 (2013) (analyzing the intermediary findings in the Lubanga judgment).

7. *See* ESLAM AL-FATATRY ET AL., HENRY M. JACKSON SCHOOL OF INTERNATIONAL STUDIES, THE INTERNATIONAL CRIMINAL COURT: CONFRONTING CHALLENGES ON THE PATH TO JUSTICE 55–67 (2013), (evaluating results and criticisms of all investigations); WAR CRIMES RESEARCH OFFICE, *supra* note 3, at 1 (noting that cases or charges have failed both at confirmation and thereafter).

8. These criticisms are often overstated, and many of the case "failures" have been controversial. Moreover, the cases have often been affected by circumstances outside the control of the prosecution, in particular by the intimidation or bribery of key witnesses.

9. I am indebted to David Sklansky for this very useful metaphor. *See* David Sklansky, *One Train May Hide Another: Katz, Stonewall, & the Secret Subtext of Criminal Procedure,* 41 U.C. DAVIS L. REV. 875 (2008).

10. I rely on the experience of the United States as an example because it is one I am most familiar with. Previously, I served as a U.S. federal prosecutor for ten years.

11. *See* CARLA DEL PONTE & CHUCK SUDETIC, MADAME PROSECUTOR: CONFRONTATIONS WITH HUMANITY'S WORST CRIMINALS & THE CULTURE OF IMPUNITY 3 (2008).

12. *See* Prosecutor v. Uhuru Muigai Kenyatta, Case No. ICC-01/09-02/11, Public Redacted Version of the 8 May 2013 Prosecution Response to the "Government of Kenya's Submissions on the Status of Cooperation with the International Criminal Court, or, in the Alternative, Application for Leave to File Observations pursuant to Rule 103(1) of the Rules of Procedure and Evidence," at ¶4 (May 10, 2013), http://www.icc-cpi.int/ iccdocs/doc/doc1591193.pdf.

13. *See* ICC, Office of the Prosecutor, *Eighteenth Report of the Prosecutor of the International Criminal Court to the U.N. Security Council Pursuant to UNSCR 1593* (2005), at ¶¶53–54 (Dec. 11, 2013), http://www.icc-cpi.int/iccdocs/otp/OTP-18ReportUNSCDa furDecember2013.pdf.

14. *See id.* at ¶54. *See also* True-Frost, in this volume, for further elucidation on the Security Council's limited ability to support the Court.

15. *See* Amal Alamuddin, *Collection of Evidence,* in PRINCIPLES OF EVIDENCE IN INTERNATIONAL CRIMINAL JUSTICE 243 (K. Khan et al. eds., 2010) (stating that all international tribunals "share an Achilles heel, however, which is that states may not live up to their cooperation obligations, thereby potentially thwarting a prosecutor's investigation.").

16. *See* Luis Moreno Ocampo, Prosecutor, ICC, *Statement to the Assembly of States Parties* (Apr. 22, 2003), http://www.iccnow.org/documents/MorenoOcampo22A-pr03eng.pdf.

17. *See* DAVID BOSCO, ROUGH JUSTICE: THE INTERNATIONAL CRIMINAL COURT IN A WORLD OF POWER POLITICS 90 (2014).

18. *See* THE RECKONING: THE BATTLE FOR THE INTERNATIONAL CRIMINAL COURT (Skylight 2009), http://skylight.is/films/the-reckoning/. *The Reckoning,* directed by Pamela Yates and produced by Paco de Onis (2009).

19. Luis Moreno Ocampo, Interview by Till Papenfuss (Jan. 25, 2002), http://www.theglobalobservatory.org/interviews/197-interview-with-luis-moreno-ocampo-chief-prosecutor-of-the-international-criminal-court.html.

20. *See* Nick Grono, *The Deterrent Effect of the ICC on the Commission of International Crimes by Government Leaders,* CRISIS GROUP (Oct. 5, 2012) ("The ICC's first decade has seen broad claims made about the Court's ability to deter the commission of international crimes by government leaders. . . . Over the longer term prosecutions can act to dissuade future generations of leaders from the commission of such crimes."), http://www.crisisgroup.org/en/publication-type/speeches/2012/grono-the-deterrent-effect-of-the-icc.aspx.

21. *See* ICC, Office of the Prosecutor, *Paper on Some Policy Issues before the Office of the Prosecutor* (Sept. 2003), http://www.icc-cpi.int/nr/rdonlyres/1fa7c4c6-de5f-42b7-8b25-60aa962ed8b6/143594/030905_policy_paper.pdf.

22. *See* Luis Moreno Ocampo, Prosecutor, ICC, *Keynote Address to the Council on Foreign Relations* 9 (Feb. 4, 2010), http://www.cfr.org/courts-and-tribunals/prepared-remarks-luis-moreno-ocampo-prosecutor-icc/p21375.

23. *Id.*

24. *Id.*

25. *See* Luis Moreno Ocampo, Prosecutor, ICC, *Address to the Tenth Session of the Assembly of States Parties* 5 (Dec. 12, 2011), http://www.icc-cpi.int/iccdocs/asp_docs/ASP10/Statements/ASP10-ST-ProsecutorLMO-ENG.pdf.

26. *See* THE PROSECUTOR (White Pine Pictures 2011), http://www.whitepinepictures.com/all-titles/ijd-the-prosecutor/.

27. *See* Mike Corder, *Ex-Prosecutor: Int'l Cases Changed Kenya,* ASSOCIATED PRESS (Mar. 14, 2013), http://bigstory.ap.org/article/former-prosecutor-icc-cases-changed-kenya.

28. *See* SAMANTHA POWER, A PROBLEM FROM HELL: AMERICA & THE AGE OF GENOCIDE (2002).

29. *See* Moreno Ocampo, *supra* note 25, at 6.

30. *See* Moreno Ocampo, *supra* note 22, at 5–6; *see also* Moreno Ocampo, *supra* note 25, at 5–6 ("The fear of a frivolous Prosecutor, abusing the powers granted by the Statute was replaced by the challenges created by a serious institution. The States Parties of the Rome Statute have to adjust to these new challenges.").

31. *See* BOSCO, *supra* note 17, at 143 (quoting interview with Moreno Ocampo).

32. That is not to say that he sought to move on all possible situations. David Bosco persuasively argues that Moreno Ocampo was cautious about where he focused his investigations but that once he opened an inquiry, he was aggressive about bringing cases. *See id.* at 163 ("The prosecutor's approach suggested a sharp differentiation between the court's strategic positioning and its tactical operations. Once the prosecutor had been clearly accorded jurisdiction, he was willing to defy major-power pressure regarding who he investigated and when he sought indictments, as the Bashir indictment demonstrated.").

33. *See* THE PROSECUTOR, *supra* note 26.

34. *See* BOSCO, *supra* note 17, at 137.

35. *Id.*

36. *See, e.g.,* DAVID SCHEFFER, ALL THE MISSING SOULS: A PERSONAL HISTORY OF THE WAR CRIMES TRIBUNALS 68 (2012).

37. *See* Joseph M. Isanga, *The International Criminal Court Ten Years Later: Appraisal & Prospects,* 21 CARDOZO J. INT. & COMP. L. 235, 320 (2013). *See also* Stevens, *supra* note 4 ("How well did the Prosecutor and the ICC do? Well, at the end of Luis Moreno-Ocampo's nine year term, only two trials had been completed. Compared to the tribunal for the former Yugoslavia, which convicted 64, and the Rwandan tribunal [29 guilty verdicts] this is a low number.").

38. *See* POWER, *supra* note 28, at 492.

39. *See* JONATHAN GARY BASS, STAY THE HAND OF VENGEANCE: THE POLITICS OF WAR CRIMES TRIBUNALS 223 (2000); RICHARD J. GOLDSTONE, FOR HUMANITY: REFLECTIONS OF A WAR CRIMES INVESTIGATOR 89 (2000) ("When I arrived in The Hague, the judges, as I have already mentioned, were frustrated and angry at the fact that they had no work to do.").

40. *See* Julian Davis Mortenson, *This Very Human Institution: A Biography of the Yugoslavia Tribunal,* 13 COLUM. J. EUR. L. 471, 476–77 (2007) (book review).

41. *See* BASS, *supra* note 39, at 219.

42. *See* Mortenson, *supra* note 40, at 478 (quoting reviewed book that quotes ICTY Press Release, CC/PIO/003-E [Feb. 1, 1995]).

43. *See* GOLDSTONE, *supra* note 39, at 105.

44. *See, e.g.,* SCHEFFER, *supra* note 36, at 38–39, 126, 142, 153, 156 (describing instances of competing priorities of war crimes prosecutions and bureaucratic hurdles to cooperation).

45. *See* BASS, *supra* note 39, at 227.

46. *See* SCHEFFER, *supra* note 36, at 143.

47. *See* Jenia Iontcheva Turner, *Defense Perspectives on Law & Politics in International Criminal Trials,* 48 VA. J. INT'L L. 529, 588 (2008).

48. *See* BASS, *supra* note 39, at 223.

49. *Id.* at 260–61.

50. *Id.* at 223.

51. *See* RICHARD MAY & MARIEKE WIERDE, INTERNATIONAL CRIMINAL EVIDENCE 97 (2001) (emphasizing need to avoid rules that would have the result that "much potentially probative evidence would go unheard in a jurisdiction where any evidence is scarce and difficult to obtain"); Christopher Gosnell, *The Changing Context of Evidential Rules, in* PRINCIPLES OF EVIDENCE IN INTERNATIONAL CRIMINAL JUSTICE 225–26 (K. Khan et al. eds., 2010) (reviewing jurisprudence allowing liberal admission of evidence in trials); KARIM KHAN & RODNEY DIXON, ARCHBOLD INTERNATIONAL CRIMINAL COURTS: PRACTICE, PROCEDURE, & EVIDENCE 555–58 (2009) (detailing rules and decisions at ad hoc tribunals allowing prosecution to add evidence during trial).

52. *See* GIDEON BOAS, THE MILOŠEVIĆ TRIAL: LESSONS FOR THE CONDUCT OF COMPLEX INTERNATIONAL CRIMINAL PROCEEDINGS 133, 136 (2007); CHRIS STEPHEN, JUDGEMENT DAY: THE TRIAL OF SLOBODAN MILOŠEVIĆ 193, 195 (2004).

53. *See* Gosnell, *supra* note 51, at 224–26.

54. *See id. See also* Patricia Wald, *Reflections on Judging: At Home & Abroad,* 7 U. PA. J. CONST. L. 219, 233 (2004) (noting permissive approach of judges at ICTY in the early years).

55. *See* Alex Whiting, *Justice Delayed Can Be Justice Delivered*, 50 HARV. INT'L L. J. 323, 343–45 (2009) (reviewing history of conditionality and its effect on cooperation).

56. *Id.*

57. *See* Mirjan Damaška, *The International Criminal Court between Aspiration & Achievement*, 14 UCLA J. INT'L L. & FOREIGN AFF. 19, 20 (2009) (noting that the ICTY's success was largely "the result of internal political changes in successor states and successful outside pressures on them").

58. *See* SCHEFFER, *supra* note 36, at 142–49. While NATO forces provided some support, NATO countries were also reluctant to risk the lives of soldiers in support of arrests of ICTY fugitives. *Id. See also* BASS, *supra* note 39, at 226.

59. *Compare* Assembly of States Parties to the International Criminal Court, ICC-ASP/11/10, Proposed Programme Budget for 2013 of the International Criminal Court, ¶2 (Aug. 16, 2012), http://www.icc-cpi.int/iccdocs/asp_docs/ASP11/ICC-ASP-11-10-ENG.pdf (proposing a total 2013 budget for the ICC of €118.75 million), *with* Assembly of States Parties of the International Criminal Court, ICC-ASP/10/10, Proposed Programme Budget for 2012 of the International Criminal Court, ¶2 (July 21, 2011), http://www.icc-cpi.int/iccdocs/asp_docs/ASP10/ICC-ASP-10-10-ENG.pdf (proposing a total 2012 budget for the ICC of €117.73 million).

60. *See* Damaška, *supra* note 57, at 24–25 (arguing that the procedures at the ICC are more complex than at other international tribunals).

61. *See* Rome Statute of the International Criminal Court, art. 54, July 17, 1998, 2187 U.N.T.S. 90.

62. *See* Prosecutor v. Laurent Gbagbo, Case No. ICC-02/11-01/11, Decision Adjourning the Hearing on the Confirmation of Charges Pursuant to Article 61(7)(c)(i) of the Rome Statute, ¶25 (June 3, 2013), http://www.icc-cpi.int/iccdocs/doc/doc1599831.pdf; Prosecutor v. Francis Kirimi Muthaura and Uhuru Muigai Kenyatta, Case No. ICC-01/09-02/11-614, Decision Requesting Observations on the "Prosecution's Request to Amend the Final Updated Document Containing the Charges Pursuant to Article 61(9) of the Statute" (Jan. 29, 2013), http://www.icc-cpi.int/iccdocs/doc/doc1546087.pdf.

63. *See* Prosecutor v. Callixte Mbarushimana, Case No. ICC-01/04-01/10-514, Judgment on the Appeal of the Prosecutor against the Decision of Pre-Trial Chamber I of 16 December 2011 entitled "Decision on the Confirmation of Charges," ¶44 n.89 (May 30, 2012), http://www.icc-cpi.int/iccdocs/doc/doc1420080.pdf.

64. *See* Prosecutor v. Thomas Lubanga Dyilo, Case No. ICC-01/04-01/06, Judgment Pursuant to Article 74 of the Statute (Mar. 14, 2012), http://www.icc-cpi.int/iccdocs/doc/doc1379838.pdf; Prosecutor v. Mathieu Ngudjolo, Case No. ICC-01/04-02/12, Judgment Pursuant to Article 74 of the Statute (Dec. 18, 2012), http://www.icc-cpi.int/iccdocs/doc/doc1579080.pdf; Buisman, *supra* note 6.

65. *See* Prosecutor v. Laurent Gbagbo, Case No. ICC-02/11-01/11, Decision Adjourning the Hearing on the Confirmation of Charges Pursuant to Article 61(7)(c)(i) of the Rome Statute, ¶¶27–28 (June 3, 2013), http://www.icc-cpi.int/iccdocs/doc/doc1599831.pdf.

66. For example, Jean-Pierre Bemba was arrested by Belgian authorities and Callixte Mbarushimana by French police.

67. *See* Fatou Bensouda, Prosecutor, ICC, *Statement to the United Nations Security Council on the Situation in Darfur, the Sudan, Pursuant to UNSCR 1593 (2005)*, at ¶7 (Dec. 13, 2012), http://www.icc-cpi.int/iccdocs/PIDS/statements/UNSC1212/UN

SCDarfurSpeechEng.pdf (describing the Sudan government's lack of cooperation in the ICC's investigation).

68. S.C. Res. 1970, U.N. Doc. S/RES/1970 (Feb. 26, 2011).

69. *See* ICC, Office of the Prosecutor, *First Report of the Prosecutor of the Int'l Criminal Court to the UN Security Council Pursuant to UNSCR 1970* (2011), at ¶28 (May 4, 2011), http://www.icc-cpi.int/NR/rdonlyres/A077E5F8-29B6-4A78-9EAB-A179A1057 38E/0/UNSCLibyaReportEng04052011.pdf (characterizing the support of states parties for the Libya investigation as "excellent").

70. *See* BOSCO, *supra* note 17, at 169 ("Some US officials, in particular, had become concerned about the pace of the ICC investigation and the possibility that it might interfere with diplomatic efforts.").

71. *See* ICC, Office of the Prosecutor, *Fifth Report of the Prosecutor of the Int'l Criminal Court to the U.N. Security Council Pursuant to UNSCR 1970* (2011), at ¶8 (May 8, 2013), http://www.icc-cpi.int/iccdocs/otp/UNSC-report-Libya-May2013-Eng.pdf (noting that some requests to states for cooperation in the Libya investigation have not been fulfilled and urging state parties to cooperate fully with the investigation). *See also* Patricia M. Wald, *Apprehending War Criminals: Does International Cooperation Work?*, 27 AM. U. INT'L L. REV. 229, 251–52 (2012).

72. *See* Ruth Sherlock & Richard Spencer, *Libya: France Risks NATO Split over Call for Gaddafi Talks*, THE TELEGRAPH (Jul. 11, 2011), http://www.telegraph.co.uk/news/world-news/africaandindianocean/libya/8630778/Libya-France-risks-Nato-split-over-call-for-Gaddafi-talks.html.

73. *See* Mark Kersten, *Between Justice & Politics: The International Criminal Court's Intervention in Libya*, at 22 (2012) (describing loss of interest by international community in pursuing justice in Libya), http://www.academia.edu/1558775/Between_Justice_and_Politics_The_International_Criminal_Courts_Intervention_in_Libya#.

74. *See* Prosecutor v. Uhuru Muigai Kenyatta, Case No. ICC-01/09-02/11, Public Redacted Version of the 8 May 2013 Prosecution Response to the "Government of Kenya's Submissions on the Status of Cooperation with the International Criminal Court, or, in the Alternative, Application for Leave to File Observations Pursuant to Rule 103(1) of the Rules of Procedure and Evidence," at ¶4 (May 10, 2013), http://www.icc-cpi.int/iccdocs/doc/doc1591193.pdf.

75. *See* Catrina Stewart, *ICC on Trial along with Kenya's Elite amid Claims of Bribery & Intimidation*, THE GUARDIAN (Oct. 1, 2013), http://www.theguardian.com/world/2013/oct/01/icc-trial-kenya-kenyatta-ruto; INT'L BAR ASSOCIATION, WITNESSES BEFORE THE INTERNATIONAL CRIMINAL COURT 27–33 (2013) (detailing problems in Victims and Witnesses Unit at ICC).

76. The cases against two of the six accused were dismissed at the confirmation stage. An additional case was later dropped by the prosecution. The prosecution has just sought to postpone another case. The trial is proceeding against two of the accused. The prosecution has complained about lack of cooperation and the loss of many witnesses as the result of bribery and intimidation.

77. *See* Damaška, *supra* note 57, at 27.

78. *Id.* at 20.

79. *See* Antonio Cassese, *Reflections on International Criminal Justice*, 9 J. INT'L CRIM. JUST. 271, 273 (2011).

The Prosecutor's Interactions with
Other International Actors

The Relationship between the Office of the Prosecutor and the Judicial Organ

Conflict and Opportunity

Julie Rose O'Sullivan

The Statute of the International Criminal Court (the Statute)[1] gives the ICC's judicial organ a variety of powers designed to check the operation of the Office of the Prosecutor (OTP) at all stages from investigation to appeal. Some of the powers discussed in this chapter are the Pre-Trial Chambers' power to issue arrest warrants (ICC article 58) and their authority to confirm any charges the prosecutor seeks to levy against potential defendants (ICC article 61). The Trial Chamber is also invested with a great deal of discretion in the conduct of the trial. Most pertinent for present purposes, it can determine how witnesses may be prepared, what evidence will be admitted, and the extent of victims' participation. This discretion is augmented by the power of the Trial Chamber to ask for evidence and directly question witnesses. And, of course, the Trial Chamber also renders the final verdict and sentence, subject only to review by the Appeals Chamber.

These, and other, judicial checks on prosecutorial power were built into the institution in part to reassure potential states parties that the prosecutor could not run amok in pursuit of his[2] agenda. They thus are a means of legitimating the functioning of the institution as a whole. This chapter explores the fallout from the statute's contemplation that chambers will check the prosecutor in the conduct of his powers—the ensuing contests between the OTP and the Pre-Trial and Trial Chambers over the appropriate scope of the Chambers' supervisory powers—and posits that these contests may have the unanticipated effect of strengthening the legitimacy of the prosecution function as well as the institution as a whole.

Bureaucratic theory predicts that a bureaucratic unit, such as the judicial organ, will seek autonomy to the extent possible, meaning that it will seek to contain the interference of other bureaucratic units in its decision making.[3] This theory certainly has proved true over the ten years of the ICC's operation, as the ICC's Pre-Trial and Trial Chambers have consistently read their powers broadly to maximize their power, often at the expense of the OTP. Indeed, these judges have, consciously or not, tried to move the ICC from a hybrid system in which the common law adversarial model predominates toward one that has a much more civil law flavor—with a concomitant movement toward a more active and central role for the judicial organ than was originally contemplated.

To explore this thesis, this chapter examines instances in which the OTP and often the defense have been at odds with the judicial organ over the proper allocation of power under the statute as well as the numerous instances in which Pre-Trial and Trial Chambers have made decisions that illustrate their civil law bias. When these seemingly isolated contests are evaluated together, one sees that Pre-Trial and Trial Chambers consistently act to gather to themselves as much control as possible over everything from the content of the charges to the conduct of trials.

The pretrial and trial judges' aggrandizement of power created a dilemma for prosecutor Luis Moreno Ocampo. On one hand, he recognized that he could only be as successful as the institution of which he was a part and that if he attacked the judicial organ, the legitimacy of the entire enterprise would be imperiled. On the other, the legitimacy of the ICC project as a whole also depends on the preservation of the independence and institutional integrity of the OTP. In response to this dilemma, Moreno Ocampo pursued a two-pronged strategy designed to safeguard the powers of his office while enhancing the credibility of the work of the Court as a whole.

First, at the pretrial, trial, and appellate levels, the prosecutor fought judicial attempts to aggrandize the Chambers' power or to undermine his role in the adversary process. A close look at the full range of litigated issues shows that a significant contest between the judicial and prosecutorial organs was ongoing in the Court's day-to-day business during the first prosecutor's tenure. Moreno Ocampo's attempts to defend the prerogatives of his office generated tension between the OTP and at least some in the ICC's judicial organ. This tension occasionally erupted into public view in spectacular fashion, as when, on two different occasions, Trial Chamber I effectively dismissed (in ICC terms, *stayed*) the OTP's first trial in *Prosecutor v. Thomas Lubanga Dyilo (Lubanga)* and ordered the defendant released from custody.[4]

At the same time, the prosecutor exercised a great deal of restraint in his public comments.[5] Moreno Ocampo never publicly criticized any ruling of any chamber of the Court. And the language employed in the prosecutor's filings, even in highly charged matters, was consistently respectful and temperate—indeed, more measured than the language employed by some of the judges in their opinions.[6]

The prosecutor's decision to vindicate the powers of his office in court, rather than in the court of public opinion, has meant that he absorbed more than his fair share of criticism. Many commentators appear to have adopted the habit of accepting whatever the judicial organ of the ICC does as correct and just. Perhaps as a consequence, the existing literature contains little if any systematic critique of the output of the judicial organ but a great deal of critical analysis of the prosecutorial function. Thus, if ICC judges rule against the prosecutor, there is little inquiry into the wisdom or competency of the judicial organ—even when the decisions in question are highly contestable if not clearly wrong.

The prosecutor's dual strategy, though it appeared to open him up to more criticism than may be warranted, should ultimately enhance the credibility of both the institution and the OTP. First, the prosecutor's decision to maintain a public silence, particularly where he believed Chambers to have acted wrongly, represented a self-conscious choice to take his lumps—even if undeserved—to enhance the legitimacy of the ICC as a whole. It also ought to increase respect for the OTP's professionalism. Further, although it is difficult to draw causal connections between the OTP's restraint and the output of the Appeals Chamber, the prosecutor's respectful approach may have eased the ICC Appeals Chamber's challenge in serving as a dispassionate referee between the OTP and the Pre-Trial and Trial Chambers. The Appeals Chamber appears to have adopted for itself the role of ensuring that the statute's balance of power is carefully calibrated—a role that would certainly be significantly complicated were the OTP to wage public war with the lower chambers.

As of this writing, only two of the ICC's trials have yet come to judgment,[7] and, although appeals have been filed, the Appeals Chamber has yet to issue rulings in either *Prosecutor v. Lubanga* or *Prosecutor v. Mathieu Ngudjolo Chui (Ngudjolo)*. Accordingly, the corpus of Appeals Chamber decisions consist of interlocutory appeals. Interlocutory appeals on issues relating to pretrial release, jurisdiction, or admissibility may be taken as of right,[8] but the Pre-Trial or Trial Chamber whose decision is impugned must grant the aggrieved party leave to secure appellate review of any other type of interlocutory issue.[9] Because these Chambers have not been particularly generous in granting leaves to appeal,[10] final judgments cannot yet be drawn regarding the Appeals Chamber's orientation. That said, it is striking that when the OTP has succeeded in securing review by the Appeals Chamber of fundamental questions regarding the allocation of power between the OTP and Pre-Trial and Trial Chambers, the OTP has prevailed more frequently than it has lost. Even where the OTP has seemingly lost at least a portion of the legal battle on appeal, as in the two *Lubanga* stay appeals, it won the war in that the substantive results in both cases were significantly more favorable to the OTP than the lower court ordered and the stays were ultimately lifted.

The OTP's successes are extraordinary given the contextual factors that make appellate reversals particularly difficult to achieve in the ICC. Thus, when assessing the Appeals Chamber's rulings, one should consider the close proximity in which all the ICC judges operate and their egalitarian self-conception. The Appeals Chamber judges are elected from the same lists as the judges in the Pre-Trial and Trial Chambers, and there is thus "no structural rationale for considering the Appeals Chamber superior in any sense other than its position on the hierarchy."[11] Accordingly, the Appeals Chamber approaches its task "in the spirit of reviewing a decision of a peer chamber rather than an inferior chamber."[12] In this context, one would expect to see very few reversals of Trial and Pre-Trial Chambers rulings. Yet when the Appeals Chamber has had the opportunity to weigh in, the OTP has often seen its positions—and power—vindicated.

Similarly, the more combative aspect of the prosecution's strategy—fighting for the OTP's prerogatives in court—appears to be working. As noted, when the OTP's positions can be argued on appeal, they prevail more often than not. Even when the OTP is unsuccessful, however, the tension between the OTP and the "lower" chambers may have its own value. Indeed, far from hurting the ICC, the public contests over the proper allocation of power between the OTP and the judicial organ ought to enhance its legitimacy. They certainly expose the Pre-Trial and Trial Chambers' fierce independence and desire to exercise their checking powers to the fullest. And these chambers are charged with the daily fare of overseeing certain of the OTP's investigation, charging, and trial practices. In short, the contests discussed in this chapter amply demonstrate that the OTP and the judicial organ are fully independent and often in conflict. Far from being a kangaroo court where verdicts of "guilty" can be counted upon, the Court is an entity where the prosecution is viewed with a skeptical and sometimes even jaundiced eye. The record proves this to be true: thus, the OTP has secured one guilty verdict in *Lubanga*, but Trial Chamber II acquitted Ngudjolo after a lengthy trial. (As of this writing, no verdicts have yet come down in the trials of Jean-Pierre Bemba Gombo and Germain Katanga.) In addition, although the Pre-Trial Chambers have confirmed charges against nine defendants, Chambers have refused to confirm charges tendered by the OTP in four cases (Callixte Mbarushimana, Bahir Idriss Abu Garda, Henry Kosgey, and Mohammed Hussein Ali).

Although its battles may be hard-fought, the OTP—not just the Court as a whole—should ultimately benefit from these contests. Any augmentation of the Court's perceived impartiality has the power to enhance the credibility of each prosecutorial victory, particularly where the Chambers are acting zealously to contain the prosecutor's powers. Thus, the OTP's requirements for judicial sanction of prosecutorial decision making obviously lend gravity and the imprimatur of judicial objectivity to the exercise of prosecutorial discretion in the investigation, arrest, and charging of international criminals. Where a particular prosecution is controversial—for example, the case of President Omar al-Bashir of Sudan—judicial decisions to issue arrest warrants and confirm charges lend the credibility of the entire institution to the imperative of apprehending the defendant. There is one reason the ICC's credibility might be damaged as a result of the otherwise healthy tension between the OTP and Chambers is if the Pre-Trial and Trial Chambers continue to resolve virtually every issue that arguably implicates the scope of power under the statute in the favor of Chambers at the expense of the OTP and the Registry. In such circumstances, they will eventually evoke calls for a check on the judicial organ and harm the credibility of the ICC more generally.[13]

The Record of the Judicial Organ

Victim Participation in Investigations and Trials

The Appeals Chamber has published two major decisions concerning the extent of victim participation in OTP investigations and in ICC trials. In the first, the OTP's and defense's position that victims ought not participate in OTP investigations prevailed over a Pre-Trial Chamber decision to the contrary. This was clearly a victory for the OTP in that it is difficult to know how one could conduct sensitive investigations during ongoing armed conflict involving vulnerable witnesses—for example, under the gaze of victim representatives who may have mixed feelings about the wisdom of a prosecution. In the second, the OTP's and defense's position that victim participation at trial ought to be restricted to that contemplated by the text of the statute—providing "views and concerns"—was rejected and the Pre-Trial Chamber's more generous reading affirmed. Although this issue arguably threatened the defense's interests more obviously than the OTP's, the result may well mean that the prosecutor's ability to put on short, clean, well-organized cases is seriously impaired. It certainly means that though the most obvious winners here were the victims, the institutional victor in this case, both in reasoning and in result, was the judicial organ.

In the first victims' rights case (concerning the situation in the Democratic Republic of Congo [DRC]), Pre-Trial Chamber I ruled that it could accord victim status to persons wishing to participate in the prosecutor's investigation of the situation in the DRC. "Victim status" would "confer upon victims participatory rights, entitling them to express their views and concerns generally in respect of the prosecutor's investigation into the situation."[14] Presumably, victim participation would inject the Pre-Trial Chamber into the investigation as well, given that the Chamber passes on victim qualifications and would presumably provide the venue in which victims' views and concerns would be expressed. The prosecutor and the Office of the Public Counsel for the Defence took the position that participation by victims can only be granted under ICC article 68(3), which requires that "proceedings" be extant. The prosecutor argued that victims may bring to the notice of the OTP any matter affecting the investigation into a situation, but granting victims general participatory rights during investigations would "impact adversely on the fairness and impartiality of the proceedings by acknowledging to victims a right and a role outside the remit of the Statue and the Rules."[15] The Appeals Chamber reversed the Pre-Trial Chamber, concluding that article 68(3) does indeed confine victim participation to judicial "proceedings" and that an investigation is not such a proceeding.[16]

The prosecutor and the defense were once again on the same side in the litigation concerning the permissible extent of victim participation at trial in *Prosecutor v. Lubanga;* in this common cause, however, they were unsuccessful. In *Lubanga,* Trial Chamber I ruled that victims have the right to "lead" (that is, introduce) evidence pertaining to the guilt or innocence of the accused and to challenge the admissibility or relevance of evidence subject to the following requirements: "(i) a discrete application, (ii) notice to the parties; (iii) demonstration of personal interests that are affected by the specific proceedings; (iv) compliance with disclosure obligations and protection orders; (v) determination of appropriateness and

(vi) consistency with the rights of the accused and a fair trial."[17] The Trial Chamber in this instance granted the defense's and prosecutor's application for leave to appeal.[18]

The Appeals Chamber majority, over a dissent by Judge Pikis, endorsed the Trial Chamber's reading of the statute. The text at issue—ICC article 68(3)—states that

> where the personal interests of the victims are affected, the Court shall permit their *views and concerns* to be presented and considered at stages of the proceedings determined to be appropriate by the Court and in a manner which is not prejudicial to or inconsistent with the rights of the accused or a fair and impartial trial.[19]

The parties and the dissent first made the obvious plain-language argument: "'views and concerns' does not constitute the submission of evidence."[20] The Appeals Chamber rejected this textual argument, concluding instead that to "give effect to the spirit and intention of article 68(3) of the Statute in the context of trial proceedings it must be interpreted so as to make participation by victims meaningful."[21] The Appeals Chamber's willingness in this case to look beyond text and to add powers to the plain language of the statute is aberrational; in general, the Chamber's interpretive approach has been cautious and heavily text-driven.[22] It is difficult to account for this interpretive turnabout, but it may relate to the issue of judicial power that lurked behind the question of the appropriate scope of victim participation.

The Appeals Chamber "underscore[d]" that the right to lead evidence or challenge others' submission of evidence lies "primarily with the parties" at trial.[23] It went on, however, to rule that the parties' rights in this regard are not exclusive. In so doing, it seemed to be concerned primarily with vindicating the prerogatives of the judicial organ rather than the questions of fairness raised by the defense. The defense and the Appeals Chamber dissent[24] argued that "authorising victims to submit evidence or to express their opinion on the evidence would mean forcing the defendant to confront more than one accuser, which would violate the principle of equality of arms, one of the necessary elements of a fair trial."[25] The majority opinion did not respond to these charges in terms. Rather, the Appeals Chamber majority leaned heavily on ICC article 69(3), which provides, inter alia, that the "Court shall have the authority to request the submission of all evidence that it considers necessary for the determination of the truth."[26] The Chamber concluded that the "fact that the onus lies on the Prosecutor cannot be read to exclude the statutory powers of the court, as it is the court that 'must be convinced of the guilt of the accused beyond reasonable doubt.'"[27]

Finally, the Appeals Chamber emphasized the central role of and discretion afforded to the Trial Chamber in determining on a case-by-case basis whether permitting victims to lead or challenge evidence would be consistent with the rights of the accused and a fair trial.[28] In subsequent decisions, Trial Chambers have read broadly the scope of this authority, giving victims' rights akin to those of parties. Thus, the Chambers have ruled that victims may make opening and closing statements.[29] To help victims' legal representatives prepare for trial, the OTP must provide victims with the prosecution's witness list and summary of evidence.[30] And victims may choose to testify against the accused rather than simply providing their views and comments through their representatives, although Trial Chambers have exerted tight control over victim testimony, and pressures to expedite trials may result in fewer victim witnesses in the future.[31]

The Appeals Chamber opinion obviously represents a notable shift in that the participation of victims in the course of trial is virtually unheard of in common law adversarial proceedings. More important, it represents a sweeping assertion of judicial power over the content and construction of the trial record at the expense of those normally invested with this responsibility in adversarial proceedings—that is, the defense and the prosecution. Now, at the discretion of the judges, the defense may face hundreds of accusers, a phenomenon that must have a seriously detrimental impact on the defense's ability effectively to prepare for trial. Given the numbers of victims granted leave to participate in ICC proceedings— more than three thousand victims in the *Prosecutor v. Bemba* case alone— the Trial Chambers' unfettered power to decree the nature and extent of any victim's participation may prove to have just as outsized a negative impact on the prosecutor's ability to organize and present a coherent case in an efficient way. In short, one could argue that the OTP is no longer the master of its case; the Trial Chamber is.

The Lubanga Stays

The OTP and Trial Chamber I clashed over two issues in *Prosecutor v. Lubanga* that threatened to derail the ICC's first trial. The first contest concerned the OTP's use of a statutory provision, ICC article 54(3)(e), for gathering confidential information in a way that threatened to impair its ability to meet its disclosure obligations to the defense. The second concerned the OTP's attempts to avoid turning over to the name of a protected person to the defense until measures designed to keep him safe were in place. In both cases, the Pre-Trial Chamber permanently "stayed" the case—effectively dismissing the prosecution—and ordered the defendant released. In both cases, the Appeals Chamber, while siding with the Trial Chamber on the issues of judicial prerogatives presented, issued decisions that in effect gave the OTP much of what it wanted, including a ruling that the Trial Court's stay was an inappropriate remedy in the second matter.

The first dispute concerned ICC article 54(3)(e), which specifies the powers and duties of the OTP and authorizes the prosecutor to agree "not to disclose, at any stage of the proceedings, documents or information that the Prosecutor obtains on the condition of confidentiality and solely for the purpose of generating new evidence, unless the provider of the information consents."[32] Rule 82 of the ICC's Rules of Procedure and Evidence (RPE) further provides that where the prosecutor has possession or control of material or information that is protected under article 54(3)(e), the "Prosecutor may not subsequently introduce such material or information into evidence without the prior consent of the provider of the material or information and adequate prior disclosure to the accused."[33]

The U.N., nongovernmental organizations (NGOs), and states have provided the OTP with information about past crimes under assurances of confidentiality pursuant to article 54(3)(e). These confidentiality guarantees serve a number of purposes, some compelling. Thus, for example, aid agencies and other NGOs attempting to address humanitarian crises in war-torn states wish to avoid charges that they are taking sides. Some states desire confidentiality because they want to avoid not only potential political ramifications but also the possibility that their intelligence sources will be compromised. The difficulty is that the OTP apparently relied heavily on such materials at the beginning of its operation for evidence as well as the purpose provided in article 54(e)(3)—that is, as a lead or springboard to other sources of evidence—because of the great difficulty it encountered in investigating in war zones and the enormous pressure it was under to bring cases quickly. Accordingly, the prosecutor accepted the materials deemed confidential, reviewed them, and then asked the information providers under RPE Rule 82 to waive confidentiality so that the prosecutor could use the information as evidence at trial.[34] It was the OTP's position that article 54(3)(e) did not limit confidentiality agreements to information obtained solely for the purpose of generating new evidence because Rule 82 anticipates that materials obtained under article 54(3)(e) may later be introduced as evidence with provider consent.

The prosecutor's practice created a conflict between his duty to abide by his confidentiality assurances under article 54(3)(e) and his concurrent duties to provide exculpatory materials to the defense under ICC article 67 and other disclosures under RPE Rule 77. Despite the prosecutor's attempts to have the information providers waive confidentiality and thus permit disclosure of potentially exculpatory and discovery materials, some providers initially refused to do so—at least as of June 2008. The prosecutor asserted that he was unable not only to turn over these confidential documents to the defense but also to permit the Trial Chamber to view them by virtue of an agreement between the ICC and the United Nations and others regarding such evidence.[35] That the Trial Chamber viewed this as an affront is clear throughout its opinion, as is its continual emphasis on the primary responsibility of Chambers, not the OTP, to ensure full disclosure is made.[36]

The OTP asserted that it had made disclosure of sufficient "similar materials" to permit a fair trial, but the Trial Chamber disagreed, suspending proceedings—essentially dismissing the prosecution—after the prosecutor refused to give it access to documents obtained under article 54(3)(e). The Chamber ruled that Lubanga's right to a fair trial was irreparably damaged by the OTP's refusal.[37] On July 2, 2008, the Trial Chamber ordered Lubanga's release and granted the prosecutor's application for leave to appeal; Lubanga's release was also stayed pending the Appeals Chamber's decision.[38]

The Appeals Chamber affirmed the Trial Chamber's judgment, but the decision also gave the prosecutor much of what he wanted. Thus, the Appeals Chamber ruled that the prosecutor could rely on article 54(3)(e) only for "a specific purpose, namely as a springboard to new evidence."[39] At the same time, however, the Chamber agreed with the OTP that article 54(3)(e) materials could be used at trial under Rule 82.[40] And it held that reliance on article 54(3)(e) did not need to be "exceptional"—as the Trial Chamber had indicated—and indeed declined to "limit the number of documents that could be obtained on the condition of confidentiality, or otherwise to restrict inappropriately the use of the provision."[41] In short, the Trial Chamber may have won the judgment, but the prosecutor seems to have won the war regarding his use of article 54(3)(e) in all but one respect: the role of the judiciary in policing the OTP's disclosure obligations with respect to these confidential materials.

Although the Appeals Chamber—unlike the Trial Chamber—was

sympathetic to the practical concerns that drove the prosecutor to use article 54(3)(e),[42] it determined that the prosecutor had erred in receiving material on the condition of confidentiality that might lead to breaches of the prosecutor's disclosure obligations and in agreeing to shield these materials from review by the judicial organ. The Appeals Chamber spent much of its energies on the latter point:

> Whenever the Prosecutor relies on article 54(3)(e) of the Statute he must bear in mind his obligations under the Statute and apply that provision in a manner that will allow the Court to resolve the potential tension between the confidentiality to which the Prosecutor has agreed and the requirements of a fair trial. . . . [T]he final assessment as to whether material in the possession or control of the Prosecutor has to be disclosed under that provision will have to be carried out by the Trial Chamber.[43]

The Appeals Chamber reiterated throughout its concern that in accepting large amounts of confidential material under agreements that barred *in camera* review by the judicial organ, the prosecutor "effectively prevented the Chambers from assessing whether a fair trial could be held in spite of the non-disclosure to the defense of certain documents."[44] Finally, the Appeals Chamber upheld the power of the Trial Chamber to issue what the Appeals Chamber chose to characterize as a "conditional" stay as a remedy for the prejudice to the defense caused by the prosecutor's inability, due to article 54(3)(e), to make full disclosure.[45]

After this judgment was delivered, the parties and the Trial Chamber resolved the disclosure difficulties created by the prosecutor's article 54(3)(e) agreements, and the trial commenced in January 2009.[46] The trial proceeded for about a year and a half before the Trial Chamber again effectively dismissed the case and ordered the release of the defendant because of the prosecutor's alleged noncompliance with a Trial Court order requiring the prosecutor to immediately disclose to the defense the name of a nonwitness "intermediary," over the prosecution's objection that such disclosure would endanger the life of the nonwitness and that the protective measures previously ordered by the Victim's and Witnesses Unit (VWU) and the Chamber were not yet operationalized.[47]

"Intermediaries" are persons working in conflict zones who are used by the OTP and others, such as victim representatives, to gain information and identify witnesses and handle logistical tasks (such as arranging transport of witnesses to interview locations) to avoid visible interactions between the witnesses and OTP that would expose the witnesses to potential reprisals. Use of intermediaries may be necessary for a variety of reasons. Intermediaries can locate victims and witnesses scattered throughout the region in internally displaced persons camps. In many cases where the conflict is ongoing and security is scarce, direct approaches by the OTP may endanger the victims and witnesses; intermediaries can operate with lower visibility and, with knowledge of prevailing local conditions, greater safety. Finally, intermediaries may share the language and culture of the victims and witnesses and thus can facilitate effective communication and promote mutual trust. In seeking to help the OTP, however, intermediaries may put their own lives and those of their families at risk.

The defense in *Lubanga* and other cases have alleged that some of these intermediaries have sought to influence the testimony of the victims and indeed may have persuaded witnesses to lie to the court about their experiences. Accordingly, the defense sought the identity of certain intermediaries. ICC article 81(4) authorizes protective measures for "persons at risk on account of the activities of the court" beyond victims and witnesses, and Chambers have used this authority to require that protective measures be put in place prior to disclosure of intermediaries' identities.[48] At their most extreme, these protective measures may compel the intermediaries and their families to move to another country, leaving behind their livelihoods, relatives, friends, and homes—a process that can be lengthy as well as wrenching.

In some cases where disclosure of intermediaries' identities was ordered, at least some evidence suggested that the intermediaries may have improperly influenced witnesses' testimony.[49] The greatest controversy, however, surrounded the disclosure of the identity of Intermediary 143, for whom the prosecutor contended that there was no basis for believing such allegations credible.[50] In May 2010, Trial Chamber I had ordered the OTP to disclose the identity of Intermediary 143 to the defense, but after consulting with the VWU, the Chamber ordered that such disclosure should occur only "once the necessary protective measures [were] implemented."[51] The Trial Chamber then declined to grant the prosecution's application for a leave to appeal the disclosure order; in this decision, the Trial Chamber reiterated that disclosure would occur only after necessary protective measures for Intermediary 143 were implemented.[52]

The prosecutor, of course, is not authorized to implement protective measures and indeed has no control over such matters, which are by statute entrusted to the VWU, a division of the Registry. Various delays ensued regarding implementation of the protective measures designed to protect Intermediary 143 and his family. On July 6, Trial Chamber I was informed that there was an additional delay and that the protective measures could not be fully implemented until July 16. At that point in the trial, defense counsel was questioning a witness and argued that doing so effectively required the disclosure of 143's identity. Concerned about a trial delay, the Chamber, without prior consultation with the VWU, ordered the prosecution "immediately" to disclose the identity of the intermediary— under the restriction that his identity would "only" be shared with the defense team, a defense resource person on the ground in the DRC, and the accused himself.[53] The prosecution, having introduced reams of evidence that Mr. Lubanga was capable of committing international crimes far worse than obstruction of justice, did not agree that the Chamber's "restrictions" afforded adequate protection because, inter alia, the defendants' telephone calls from prison were neither restricted nor, in the usual course, monitored. At the conclusion of the day's hearing on July 6, the prosecution notified the Chamber that it intended to file for leave to appeal and required the full five days provided by the Rome Statute framework to file its application. The Chamber instead "stayed its order overnight, to give time for reflection."[54]

At the beginning of the hearing on July 7, 2010, Trial Chamber I reiterated its order of the preceding day, stating that it did not "consider that there is any potential increased risk to 143 and, [did] not consider it necessary to suspend that order pending any application that may be made by the Prosecutor for leave to appeal."[55] The Chamber then gave the OTP half an hour to disclose the name of the intermediary.[56] When Moreno Ocampo sought reconsideration of the order, arguing his belief that there was a real risk that Intermediary 143 might be killed if his identity was known without protective measures in place, the Chamber restated that it was satisfied that there was no danger to the intermediary and ordered disclosure of the identity by the end of the day.[57]

On July 8, the prosecution again attempted to persuade the Chamber to reconsider, convinced that such immediate disclosure could endanger the life of the intermediary and his family. The OTP asked that the order be stayed for the limited time necessary to work with the VWU to put in place emergency protections. Moreno Ocampo recognized his responsibility to comply with Court orders but begged the Chamber to consider the dilemma he faced by virtue of his statutory obligation to ensure witness safety.

The Trial Chamber I chose to treat the prosecutor's requests for reconsideration as an "unequivocal refusal to implement the repeated orders of this Chamber to disclose the identity of 143."[58] The Chamber further asserted that the prosecutor appeared to argue that the OTP "claims a separate authority which can defeat the orders of the Court, and which thereby involves a profound, unacceptable and unjustified intrusion into the role of the judiciary."[59] Instead of exploring obvious remedial options, such as striking the testimony of any witnesses who had come to the attention of the OTP through the offices of Intermediary 143, the Trial Chamber instead chose to employ the most drastic remedy within its powers: staying (that is, dismissing) the case and ordering the defendant's release.[60] The Chamber also provided Moreno Ocampo and deputy prosecutor Fatou Bensouda with the warning that must precede a contempt sanction under ICC article 71. It did, however, at last grant the prosecutor leave to appeal.[61]

Trial Chamber I also stayed the implementation of the protective orders it had previously required for Intermediary 143's safety.[62] In the meanwhile, however, Trial Chamber II, which was dealing with many of the same issues in another case arising out of the DRC, *Prosecutor v. Katanga,* had ordered protective measures be implemented before the identity of Intermediary 143 could be exposed to the defense in that case.[63] On September 13, 2010, the Registry notified the *Lubanga* Trial Chamber that the protective measures had been implemented for Intermediary 143. On the same date, the prosecutor attempted to comply with the Chamber's July 7 order by offering to supply the defense with Intermediary 143's identity.[64]

On September 14, the prosecution asked Trial Chamber I to partially lift its stay in *Lubanga* so that provisional evidence could be taken during the pendency of the stay (and appeal). The OTP argued that "this proposed measure would enhance the rights of the accused, by contributing to an earlier conclusion of these proceedings than otherwise will be the case; it would be to the advantage of the parties and the victims; and the pending witnesses would similarly benefit from this measure because of the 'continuing stress [of] the indefinite postponement of their testimony.'"[65] The Trial Chamber refused to accept this invitation. It contended that while the prosecutor had addressed the particular matter at issue in its stay decision— the OTP's refusal to disclose 143's identity—it had not cured the larger issue of what the Trial Chamber saw as Moreno Ocampo's continued assertion of a "right not to implement the Chamber's orders if he is of the view that they conflict with his interpretation of his other obligations."[66]

Finally, on October 8, 2010, the Appeals Chamber issued the unsurprising ruling that the OTP has to follow the orders of the judicial organ of the Court—a proposition that the OTP did not contest despite the dire conclusions of the Trial Chambers.[67] Once again, the Appeals Chamber privileged the prerogatives of the judicial organ, ruling that "even if there is a conflict between the orders of a Chamber and the Prosecutor's perception of his duties, the Prosecutor is obliged to comply with the orders of the Chamber."[68] In this case, as before, however, the Trial Chamber won the battle and lost the war. Thus, the Appeals Chamber reversed the Trial Chamber's remedy as excessive, holding that

> sanctions under article 71 of the Statute ["Sanctions for Misconduct before the Court," meaning contempt] are the proper mechanism for a Trial Chamber to maintain control of proceedings when faced with the deliberate refusal of a party to comply with its orders. Before ordering a stay of proceedings because of a party's refusal to comply with its orders, a Trial Chamber should, to the extent possible, impose sanctions and give such sanctions reasonable time to bring about compliance.[69]

The Appeals Chamber also reversed the Trial Chamber's decision to release Lubanga.[70] The trial proceedings thus resumed, and no further sanctions were imposed on the OTP.

The Trial Chamber ultimately held that "given the pattern of unreliability as regards the [four] witnesses introduced by Intermediary 143 and called to give evidence during trial . . . the Chamber accepts that there is a real risk that he played a role in the markedly flawed evidence that these witnesses provided to the OTP and to the Court."[71] Thus, "although other potential explanations exist," the Court concluded, "the real possibility that Intermediary 143 corrupted the evidence of these four witnesses cannot be safely discounted."[72] Trial Chamber I concluded, however, that it was able to reach a fair judgment based on the testimony of the many other witnesses heard and other evidence introduced.

The first *Lubanga* stay contest underscores the extent to which the judicial organ is determined to have the final say on all matters as to which it has arguable competence. For example, in the United States, the prosecution is generally regarded as having primarily responsibility for determining the appropriate scope of its disclosure obligations, at least in the first instance. The court may be called on to resolve discovery disputes, but in general it is assumed that the court should not play an active role in supervising the prosecution in this regard. Clearly, the judicial organ of the ICC views its role as much more expansive. The second contest unequivocally mandates judicial supremacy in decisions regarding potential witnesses' safety, even where the statute gives the prosecutor an equal duty of protection. Both decisions illustrate the extraordinary—and at least as to the second case, excessive—lengths to which the Trial Chamber will go in guarding what it perceives as its prerogatives.

Article 58: Arrest Warrant Standard

Under article 57 of the ICC Statute, the prosecutor generally must seek the assistance of the Pre-Trial Chamber for the issuance of such orders and warrants as may be required for purposes of the investigation.[73] The Pre-Trial Chambers have interpreted their authority very broadly, particularly with respect to the issuance of arrest warrants under article 58. Indeed, their scrutiny has been so strict that on at least three occasions that we know of, the Appeals Chamber has ruled that Pre-Trial Chambers have applied an overly stringent standard of review in evaluating the prosecutor's requests for arrest warrants—and, on remand, the warrants have been issued.

First, in the *Situation in the DRC,* the Pre-Trial Chamber denied a request for a warrant for the arrest of Bosco Ntaganda based on its determination that the case was inadmissible for lack of "gravity."[74] The prosecutor was able to make an appeal as of right because the arrest warrant decision was ultimately founded on a ruling regarding admissibility.[75] The Appeals Chamber ruled that the Pre-Trial Chamber applied too stringent a standard in two respects: a determination of admissibility is not a prerequisite for the issuance of an arrest warrant under article 58, and the Pre-Trial Chamber erred as a matter of law in its interpretation of "sufficient gravity" for admissibility purposes under article 17(1)(d).[76]

With respect to the first error, the Appeals Chamber noted that article 58(1) of the statute "stipulates only two substantive prerequisites for the issuance of a warrant of arrest: firstly, the Pre-Trial Chamber must be satisfied that there 'are reasonable grounds to believe that the person has committed a crime within the jurisdiction of the Court' . . . ; secondly, the arrest of the person must appear necessary for at least one of the three reasons enumerated in article 58(1)(b) of the statute."[77] The Appeals Chamber ruled that this statutory list is exhaustive and may not be supplemented by the Pre-Trial Chamber.[78]

More significant was the Appeals Chamber's reasoning in finding a second error. The Pre-Trial Chamber had articulated a three-part test for gravity that required, in summary, that the conduct alleged either be systematic or large-scale and cause social alarm and that it include only the most senior leaders suspected of being most responsible for the identified crimes.[79] Had the Appeals Chamber endorsed the Pre-Trial Chamber's analysis, the prosecutor's discretion in choosing cases and charging defendants would have been severely limited. Instead, the Appeals Chamber definitively rejected the proposed criteria identified by the Pre-Trial Chamber and remanded for reconsideration the arrest warrant application.[80] That application was, in due course, approved.[81]

The second case in which the Appeals Chamber held that the Pre-Trial Chamber had applied too stringent a standard in denying an arrest warrant involved the prosecution of President Omar al-Bashir of Sudan. The prosecutor had filed a request for an arrest warrant against President al-Bashir charging genocide, crimes against humanity, and war crimes. The Pre-Trial Chamber issued an arrest warrant on the charges of crimes against humanity and war crimes but rejected the application for the crime of genocide.[82] The Trial Chamber gave the prosecutor leave to appeal,[83] and the Appeals Chamber determined that the Pre-Trial Chamber had applied an overly restrictive standard of review in rejecting the genocide charge.

The Pre-Trial Chamber had determined that it could not confirm a genocide charge unless the "materials provided by the Prosecution . . . show that the only reasonable conclusion to be drawn therefrom is the existence of reasonable grounds to believe in the existence of a [genocidal intent, that is, a] specific intent to destroy in whole or in part" the identified groups.[84] The Appeals Chamber found this determination in error because it essentially required proof beyond a reasonable doubt of genocidal intent at the arrest warrant stage, when only the lowest evidentiary threshold—that of "reasonable grounds to believe"—is required by the ICC Statute.[85] Accordingly, the Appeals Chamber remanded the question to the Pre-Trial Chamber for reconsideration under the correct standard,[86] and the Pre-Trial Chamber subsequently issued an arrest warrant charging President al-Bashir with genocide.[87]

The Appeals Chamber, in short, has, to the best of our knowledge, faced three questions regarding the appropriate scope of the Pre-Trial Chamber's review of arrest warrant applications and in all three instances has ruled that the Chambers exceeded their authority.

Article 61 Confirmation

One of the most important checks on the power of the prosecutor can be found in ICC article 61, which requires that the ICC Pre-Trial Chamber "confirm" the charges on which the prosecutor intends to seek trial in an adversary process. In American criminal proceedings, the power to determine the charges is confined to the prosecutor, subject only to the testing of the grand jury or examining magistrate to see whether the probable cause standard has been satisfied. Indeed, even were a grand jury to return a true bill on amended or additional charges, its altered indictment would not be effective; the prosecution is at all times the master of the content of the charging document.

In the course of confirmation proceedings, the ICC Pre-Trial Chambers have taken an interpretative approach that is much more in line with civil law charging decisions, even though that approach is contrary to the express terms of the ICC Statute. Thus, in two significant confirmation decisions, two different Pre-Trial Chambers determined to arrogate to themselves the charging authority granted to the prosecutor by statute. In *Lubanga*, Pre-Trial Chamber I assumed authority beyond that expressly authorized by the statute to recharacterize the charges the prosecution sought, while in *Bemba*, Pre-Trial Chamber II asserted a power to deny confirmation on grounds beyond those authorized on the face of the statute. In both instances, the Chambers denied the prosecutor leave to appeal—essentially forcing him to trial on charges he did not believe legally appropriate (*Lubanga*) or to forgo the charges he concluded were necessary to reveal the true scope of the defendant's criminality (*Bemba*).

The article 61 confirmation procedure differs from the system used in the ad hoc tribunals, "where, more simply, the confirmation of indictment takes place in an ex parte hearing before a single judge, without any involvement of the Defence and is based only on the Prosecutor's allegations."[88] In the ICC, the prosecutor is required at a confirmation hearing before the ICC Pre-Trial Chamber to support each charge "with sufficient evidence to establish substantial grounds to believe that the person committed the crime charged."[89] This standard of proof lies between the lesser standard needed to obtain an arrest warrant and the higher standard employed to secure a conviction. Although the accused may object to the charges, challenge the prosecutor's evidence, and present evidence,[90] the fact that this is supposed to be a screening mechanism rather than a full-blown trial is demonstrated by the provision allowing the prosecutor to "rely on documentary or summary evidence" and excusing him from calling the witnesses expected to testify at the trial.[91] In reality, Pre-Trial Chambers have, in the course of confirmation proceedings, demanded extensive disclosure and evidentiary submissions by the prosecution; conducted trial-like hearings that have, on occasion, extended for weeks;[92] and issued confirmation decisions that run into the hundreds of pages.[93]

These decisions have all the elements of a final judgment with a different standard of proof; they include rulings on myriad legal issues ranging from admissibility to the elements of crimes, very extensive findings of fact, and just as extensive discussions detailing the application of the law to the facts.

To evaluate the *Lubanga* and *Bemba* confirmation decisions, close attention must be given to the language of ICC article 61(7), which sets forth the Pre-Trial Chamber's powers in responding to the prosecutor's application. That article gives the Pre-Trial Chamber three options at the conclusion of the prosecutor's (and if it so chooses, the defense's) case:

1. Confirm those charges in relation to which it has determined that there is *sufficient evidence*, and commit the person to a Trial Chamber for trial on the charges as confirmed;
2. Decline to confirm those charges in relation to which it has determined that there is *insufficient evidence*;
3. Adjourn the hearing and *request the prosecutor to consider*
   a. Providing further evidence or conducting further investigation with respect to a particular charge; or
   b. *Amending a charge* because the evidence submitted appears to establish a different crime within the jurisdiction of the Court.[94]

Notably, then, article 61 provides approval for a declination of charges only in cases of evidentiary insufficiency and requires that the Pre-Trial Chamber ask the prosecutor amend charges where that may be appropriate, rather than permitting Chambers to amend the requested charges *sua sponte*.[95]

Despite the plain language of the Statute, Pre-Trial Chamber I in *Lubanga* determined that it had the power, *sua sponte,* to amend the charges brought by the prosecution, over the prosecution's objection. The prosecutor had sought to levy three war crimes charges—conscripting and enlisting children under age fifteen into an armed group and using such children to participate actively in hostilities—in the context of an armed conflict not of an international character pursuant to articles 8(2)(e)(vii) and 25(3)(a) of the statute.[96] In confirming the charges against Thomas Lubanga Dyilo, however, the Pre-Trial Chamber determined that there were substantial grounds to believe that the armed conflict identified for purposes of the war crimes charges was international rather noninternational[97] in scope during a portion of the charged conduct—an important distinction in the laws of war and one that changes the charges and the proof required. Thus, the Pre-Trial Chamber confirmed six charges: conscripting, enlisting, and using child soldiers in an international armed conflict from September 2002 to June 2, 2003, and conscripting, enlisting, and using child soldiers in a noninternational armed conflict from June 2, 2003, to August 13, 2003.[98]

The prosecutor sought leave to appeal, arguing that

the clear language of the Statute . . . only allows the Chambers to adjourn the proceedings and request the Prosecution to consider amending a charge, if the Chamber is of the view that the evidence submitted appears to establish a different crime. As a result, the Prosecution is forced to proceed with a crime that it had already determined, after careful examination of the evidence in its possession, should not be charged, and to devote time and resources to supplement that evidence, if possible, in order to adequately substantiate that crime at trial.[99]

Pre-Trial Chamber I denied the prosecutor's—and the defense's—request for leave to appeal its confirmation decision and directed them to seek relief from the Trial Chamber.[100] The Appeals Chamber rejected the defense's attempt to appeal the confirmation decision as a decision on detention, which can be appealed as of right under the ICC Statute.[101] The Trial Chamber also spurned the parties' attempt to seek review of the Pre-Trial Chamber's confirmation decision. It determined that it had no authority to change the charges confirmed by the Pre-Trial Chamber, noting that the "power to frame the charges lies at the heart of the Pre-Trial Chambers functions" and ruling that the Pre-Trial Chamber remains in control of the charges until trial begins.[102]

The prosecutor's legal judgment regarding the facts ultimately was vindicated at judgment. Thus, after trial, Trial Chamber I concluded that the Pre-Trial Chamber was wrong and that the OTP charge had correctly identified the situation in the DRC. Thus, the Chamber chose to modify the legal characterization of the facts to reflect this determination, pursuant to Regulation 55 (discussed further within),[103] and convict Lubanga of conscripting, enlisting, and using child soldiers in a noninternational armed conflict under article 8(2)(e)(vii).[104]

In a later case, *Prosecutor v. Bemba*, the contest between Pre-Trial Chambers and the OTP regarding charging prerogatives took a different cast but again revealed the Pre-Trial Chamber's determination to extend its power beyond that granted by statute—as well as its disinclination to have this critical determination reviewed by the Appeals Chamber. In *Bemba*, Pre-Trial Chamber II confirmed five charges against the defendant but declined to confirm three charges on two bases, one of which—cumulative charging—is material for our purposes.[105] To summarize, the Pre-Trial Chamber declined to confirm charges of torture as a crime against humanity and outrages against personal dignity as a war crime on the ground that they were founded on the same conduct—rapes—that also served as the factual basis of the confirmed charges of rape as a crime against humanity and rape as a war crime. The Chamber concluded that this "cumulative charging for one and the same criminal conduct is detrimental to the rights of the Defence since it places undue burden on the Defence."[106]

The rules regarding cumulative charging are different in civil and common law systems. As the Appeals Chamber of the International Criminal Tribunal for the Former Yugoslavia (ICTY) explained in adopting the more relaxed common law pleading rules,

> Cumulative charging is to be allowed in light of the fact that, prior to the presentation of all of the evidence, it is not possible to determine to a certainty which of the charges brought against an accused will be proven. The Trial Chamber is better poised, after the parties' presentation of the evidence, to evaluate which of the charges may be retained, based upon the sufficiency of the evidence. In addition, cumulative charging constitutes the usual practice of both this Tribunal and the I[nternational] C[riminal] T[ribunal for] R[wanda].[107]

Civil law systems are generally stricter in their pleading rules and often "preclud[e] cumulative charging or charging in the alternative as part of prosecutorial strategy."[108] Obviously, neither approach is necessarily right or wrong, and neither approach is endorsed in the ICC Statute. The Pre-Trial Chamber chose to pursue the more restrictive civil law approach and disregard ICTY practice—although it cited no authority for doing so other than its own conviction regarding what fairness to the defense (alone) required.

The prosecutor sought leave to appeal, arguing that the Pre-Trial Chamber "is not entitled to choose the counts that it believes best reflect the harm suffered by victims and the criminality engaged in by the Accused, and to reject others as cumulative." The prosecutor asserted, based on the plain language of article 61(7), that "when charges are supported by evidence, the choice of counts to prosecute at trial is a right granted to the Prosecutor, not to the Pre-Trial Chamber."[109] The Pre-Trial Chamber determined, however, that the "mere formality" of the lack of statutory authority for its course should not control:

> The Chamber's role cannot be that of merely accepting whatever charge is presented to it. To restrict the competences of the Pre-Trial Chamber to a literal understanding of article 61(7) of the Statute, to merely confirm or decline to confirm the charges, does not correspond to the inherent powers of any judicial body vested with the task to conduct fair and expeditious proceedings while at the same time paying due regard to the rights of the Defence. . . . Thus, the Chamber is not convinced by the Prosecutor's argument that the Statute would not authorise the Chamber to decline a charge because it considers the charge unduly burdensome to the Defence. . . . The duty of the Prosecutor is to present the facts that he has investigated and to provide his view on their legal characterisation in the document containing the charges. But it is for the judges of the Pre-Trial Chamber to apply the law to those facts as presented by the Prosecutor and give the legal characterisation to those facts.[110]

The prosecutor argued that the elimination of these charges, and the denial of appeal, meant that the final judgment would not reflect the full range of facts and charges brought by the prosecutor.[111] The Pre-Trial Chamber took solace, however, in its reading of Regulation 55 of the Regulations of the Court, which it apparently believed permitted the Trial Chamber to "recharacterise" the Pre-Trial Chamber's application of the law to the facts in such a way as to permit the defendant to be convicted on the charges for which confirmation was denied.[112] This, as we shall see below, is a view that is not (apparently) shared by the Appeals Chamber.

In sum, two Pre-Trial Chambers have chosen both to read their authority to include amending the charges sought by the prosecution or declining confirmation on grounds not contained in the statute despite the plain language of the Statute to the contrary. In both instances, they blocked appellate review of these critical decisions; were the Appeals Chamber to employ its usual plain-language textual analysis[113] and hew to its belief that the prosecutor is, under article 61, responsible for proffering charges,[114] these decisions would not stand.

Recharacterization of Facts/Additional Charges

The judges in the *Lubanga* Trial Chamber have continued, in line with their Pre-Trial brethren, to attempt to assert judicial control over the charges for which the defendant should be answerable. The Appeals Chamber, however, rebuffed the *Lubanga* Trial Chamber's attempt to read the Regulations of the Court to essentially add charges not contained in the confirmation decision.

Article 74 of the statute describes the requirements for a judicial verdict. It provides in part that the Trial Chamber's decision "shall be based on its evaluation of the evidence and the entire proceedings. The decision shall not exceed the facts and circumstances described in the charges and any amendments to the charges." Regulation 55(1) of the Regulations of the Court provides that in rendering its decision under article 74, "the Chamber may change the legal characterisation of facts to accord with the crimes under articles 6, 7, 8, or to accord with the form of participation of the accused under articles 25 and 28, without exceeding the facts and circumstances described in the charges and any amendments to the charges." Regulation 55(2) provides that if, during the trial, the Chamber believes that the legal characterization of facts may be subject to change, the Chamber should give the parties both notice and an opportunity to be heard on any proposed change.

Victims participating in the *Lubanga* trial requested that the Trial Chamber trigger the procedure for a modification of the legal characterization of the facts under Regulation 55 of the Regulations of the Court to include five additional charges: the war crimes and crimes against humanity of sexual slavery and inhuman or cruel treatment.[115] The Trial Chamber majority accepted a tortured reading of Regulation 55 whereby recharacterizations of facts at trial (article 55[2]) could exceed the facts and circumstances in the charging instrument as long as notice and an opportunity to be heard were provided; it ruled that such recharacterizations need only be confined by the facts and circumstances of the charging document at the judgment stage (article 55[1]). Thus, the Trial Chamber served notice on the parties that it was considering legal recharacterization of the facts to include war crimes and crimes against humanity that were not charged by the prosecutor or approved at confirmation by the Pre-Trial Chamber.[116]

The Trial Chamber's decision was the subject of an extensive dissent by Judge Fulford,[117] who rejected the majority's reading of Regulation 55. Although one might imagine that such a dissent would be concerned, first and foremost, with legality issues, Judge Fulford's principal objection instead seemed to be that the Trial Chamber's proposed course impinged on the prerogatives of the Pre-Trial Chamber, insisting that "the Statute, in explicit terms, left control over framing and effecting any changes to the charges (under article 61[9] of the Statute) exclusively to the Pre-Trial Chamber."[118] He argued that whatever the Regulation intended by permitting "legal recharacterizations" (and that intent was unclear), "Regulation 55 must not constitute an amendment to the charges, an additional charge, a substitute charge or a withdrawal of a charge, because these are each governed by article 61(9)."[119]

The Trial Chamber granted the defense's and the prosecutor's applications for leave to appeal.[120] The Appeals Chamber rejected the Trial Chamber's reading of Regulation 55 and held that the legal recharacterization of facts—whether at trial or at the judgment stage—could not under that regulation go beyond the "facts and circumstances described in the charges or any amendments to the charges."[121] In particular, the Appeals Chamber defended the prosecution's prerogative (not, as Judge Fulford would have it, that of the Pre-Trial Chamber) to determine the charges, stating,

> The Appeals Chamber observes that it is the Prosecutor who, pursuant to article 54(1) of the Statute, is tasked with the investigation of crimes under the jurisdiction of the Court and who, pursuant to article 61(1) and (3) of the Statue, proffers charges against suspects. To give the Trial Chamber the power to extend *proprio motu* the scope of a trial to facts and circumstances not alleged by the Prosecutor would be contrary to the distribution of powers under the Statute.[122]

The Appeals Chamber declined to pass on an issue that it concluded was not fully raised or passed on below—that is, whether the statute and regulations of the Court permit the addition of new offenses in addition to those listed in the confirmation of charges.[123] Given the Appeals Chamber's conclusion regarding the prosecutor's primary responsibility for the scope of the charges, it seems likely that the Chambers would find it inappropriate for the Trial Chamber to add additional counts over the prosecutor's objection.[124]

In subsequent decisions, various Chambers have used Regulation 55 to recharacterize legal facts, sometimes in controversial ways. Thus, the *Lubanga* judgment reflects a recharacterization of the nature of the armed conflict. In *Prosecutor v. Bemba,* Trial Chamber III notified the parties, after hearing all the evidence in the prosecution's case, that it might modify the legal characterization of the facts confirmed against Mr. Bemba to the extent that he would be charged with the same mode of responsibility—command responsibility under article 28—but the alternative form of knowledge permitted under that article would be used (that is, that he "should have known" that forces under his effective command were committing the crimes charged).[125] And in *Prosecutor v. Katanga,* Trial Chamber II advised the parties, after the trial had concluded, that it would recharacterize Germain Katanga's mode of participation in the alleged crimes from responsibility as a principal (in the form of indirect co-perpetration) to that of an accomplice (complicity in the commission of a crime by a group of persons acting with common purpose).[126] This prompted a passionate—and compelling—dissent by Judge Van den Wyngaert, who asserted that this belated recharacterization was unfair to the defense, which had constructed its case on the mode charged and was severely prejudiced by the modification after the close of evidence. Judge Van den Wyngaert asserted that "the Majority's application of Regulation 55 can only be understood as a consequence of a fundamental misconstruction of the adversarial process":

> In inquisitorial systems, the main responsibility for fact-finding is centralized in the hands of a neutral magistrate and the evidence is largely collected in before the start of the actual trial. Thus, applying the legal recharacterisation that the Majority is proposing in that kind of system is not likely to give rise to the same concerns as the ones voiced in this [dissenting] opinion. Indeed, in such a procedural model, the entire evidence of the case is centralized in a shared dossier, the contents of which are known to the parties and participants right from the start of the proceedings. The Chamber trying the case can freely decide which evidence to call and rely upon, independently of the parties.
>
> By contrast, in adversarial proceedings, the spectrum of available evidence is more limited and, crucially, determined by what the parties actually proffer. What evidence the defence will present is a direct reaction to what the charges are. If the defence had known that a conviction [as an accomplice under the recharacterized theory] was a possibility, it may not have presented precisely those items of evidence which the Majority now bases itself on for the [decision to recharacterize the charges].[127]

Conduct of Trial

Trial Chambers have asserted significant authority in the conduct of the trials, both in attempting to limit the discretion of other actors,[128] most particularly the prosecutor, and in determining, where the statute is silent or ambiguous, to adopt civil law practices that enhance the power of the Court. For present purposes, three examples should suffice: rulings on witness proofing, the rules of evidence, and judicial participation in the calling and examination of witnesses.

Witness Proofing

One notable difference between civil law trial practice and trial preparation in many common law countries concerns what is known as witness proofing, preparation, or familiarization. "A U.S. lawyer who fails to interview witnesses carefully and prepare them for the rigors of trial, even rehearsing ('mooting') them, has done an inadequate job, verging on malpractice. Of course, lawyers may not suborn perjury or knowingly put on false testimony. But so long as a witness testifies truthfully, there are few, if any, limits on coaching the witness before trial."[129] In many civil law countries, however, witness proofing is not only forbidden, it is viewed as unethical.[130] There are many legitimate reasons for witness proofing, including, as Moreno Ocampo consistently insisted, ensuring truthful and efficient witness testimony; there are also legitimate objections to the practice, especially when it is used to improperly influence the unaided recollection of the witness.

This issue is not resolved in the statute and thus could legitimately be decided either way—although witness proofing had been common practice in the ad hoc tribunals.[131] Trial Chamber I chose to adopt a different practice, ruling that the "Trial Chamber is not convinced that either greater efficiency or the establishment of the truth will be achieved by these [witness proofing] measures. Rather, it is the opinion of the Chamber that this could lead to a distortion of the truth and may come dangerously close to constituting rehearsal of in-court testimony."[132] In particular, the Chamber determined that it would rather have "helpful spontaneity during the giving of evidence by a witness."[133] Like the Pre-Trial Chamber's ruling on the propriety of cumulative charging, this decision is not improper or inappropriate, but it is one more piece of evidence regarding the Pre-Trial and Trial Chambers' bias toward civil law methods of criminal adjudication—and toward expanding judicial power at the expense of the OTP's ability to control its case.

Evidence

A hallmark of civil trial practice is the relatively lax rules of evidence employed. Perhaps because expert fact-finders (judges) are employed instead of juries, the rules of evidence are much less technical and more permissive, leaving it to the judges at the judgment stage to decide how much weight to accord hearsay and other types of evidence that is excluded from fact-finders' view in many common law systems. What cast the rules of evidence ought to take was not expressly resolved by the Statue. Thus, for example, early on, Trial Chamber I in *Lubanga* indicated that it had not yet determined the evidentiary standards to be employed and that the status of, in particular, hearsay, was not resolved by the statute.[134]

Ultimately, Trial Chamber I adopted the view that the "statutory and regulatory framework undoubtedly establishes the unfettered authority of the Trial Chamber to rule on procedural matters and admissibility and relevance of evidence, subject always to any contrary decision of the Appeals Chamber."[135] Trial Chambers have used this asserted authority to employ a very liberal standard of admission of evidence, including extensive hearsay evidence. Thus, in *Lubanga,* Trial Chamber I concluded that the statutory framework has "clearly and deliberately avoided proscribing certain categories or types of evidence."[136] It then identified the four key factors that ought to guide its discretion (in which, it should be noted, the vindication of the Trial Chamber's right to seek evidence takes primacy over the imperative of a fair trial):

> First, pursuant to Article 69(3) of the . . . Statute, the Chamber has the authority to request the submission of any evidence that it considers necessary in order to determine the truth. Second, the Chamber is under an obligation to ensure that the trial is fair and expeditious, and that it is conducted with full respect for the rights of the accused under Article 64(2) of the Statute. Third, notwithstanding the desirability that witnesses should give evidence orally in accordance with Article 69(2) of the Statute, there is "a clear recognition that a variety of other means of introducing evidence may be appropriate." . . . Fourth, Article 64(9) of the Statute confers upon the Chamber a "wide discretion to rule on admissibility or relevance and to asses[s] any evidence, subject to the specified issues of 'fairness.'"[137]

With these principles in mind, the Chamber's "rules of evidence" boiled down to a very general three-step process for determining on a case-by-case basis the admissibility of nonoral evidence:

> First, the Chamber shall determine whether the evidence in question is, *prima facie,* relevant to the trial, in that it relates to matters that are properly to be considered by the Chamber in its investigation of the charges against the accused. Second, again on a *prima facie* basis, the Chamber must consider whether the evidence has probative value. . . . Third, where relevant, the Chamber has to weigh the probative value of the evidence against its prejudicial effect.[138]

If its wide discretion was not sufficiently clear, Trial Chamber I reiterated that "there should be no automatic reasons for either admitting or excluding a piece of evidence" and that it would not impose "artificial limits on its 'ability to consider any piece of evidence freely, subject to the requirements of fairness.'"[139]

This liberality reached its high point in *Prosecutor v. Bemba,* when a majority of Trial Chamber III, over a dissent by Judge Ozaki, simply admitted into evidence all items on the prosecution's proposed list of evidence for trial based on the Chamber's prima facie finding of admissibility, without any item-by-item evaluation.[140] The Trial Chamber majority reassured the parties, however, that it would evaluate "the probative value and appropriate weight to be given to the evidence as a whole, at the end of the case when making its final judgement."[141] The Trial Chamber granted the defendant's and the OTP's request for leave to appeal,[142] and the Appeals Chamber reversed. That Chamber determined that evidence is "submitted" only if it is "presented to the Trial Chamber by the parties on their own initiative or pursuant to a request by the Trial Chamber for the purpose of proving or disproving facts in issue," not simply by virtue of the parties including potential pieces of evidence on lists designed to fulfill disclosure obligations.[143] The Trial Chamber must determine the relevance or admissibility of the evidence and weighs its probative value against any undue prejudice it may cause, on an item-by-item basis, not wholesale.[144]

Seeking Evidence/Querying Witnesses

In a common law adversarial system, determining what evidence to introduce and when is the sole province of the parties; judges are referees, not active participants, in the formulation of the trial record. Judges may ask questions to clarify matters, but they certainly are not permitted to seek evidence, call witnesses, or (generally) to extensively examine the parties' witnesses. In this instance, the statute itself decreed that the situation should be otherwise in the ICC and that the civil law convention should control. ICC article 69(3) provides, inter alia, that the "Court shall have the authority to request the submission of all evidence that it considers necessary for the determination of the truth."[145]

On the basis of this provision, the Trial Chambers have asserted that "the right to introduce evidence during trials before the Court is not limited to parties, not least because the Court has a general right (that is not dependent on the cooperation or the consent of the parties) to request the presentation of all evidence necessary for the determination of the truth."[146] Thus, for example, Chambers can permit victims to testify as well as provide "views and comments," as contemplated in the statute.[147]

Once again, the Trial Chambers refused to accept any limits on the scope of its authority. In particular, Trial Chamber I claimed for itself extraordinarily wide latitude in questioning the parties' witnesses. The defense in *Lubanga* tried to suggest that to preserve the perception of impartiality, the judges ought to limit the scope of their questions directed at defense witnesses to the charges and to avoid leading questions. The defense also gingerly asserted that it ought to have the power to object to a particular line of judicial inquiry. Trial Chamber I rejected all three suggestions, claiming for itself plenary power to ask any and all questions on any subject and in any form without objection.[148] It noted, without any apparent irony, that one of the reasons for not permitting parties to challenge judicial questions is that "such an approach would put the Bench in the unrealistic position of ruling on its own questions, following objection and submissions."[149]

Conclusion

The above survey demonstrates that, at least in the first cases, Pre-Trial and Trial Chambers have read their powers expansively in virtually every instance in which they are able to do so—and that the prosecutor has fought these efforts at every turn, with limited success. The Pre-Trial Chamber unsuccessfully sought to inject itself, through its supervision of victim participation, into the investigation of cases, but Trial Chambers successfully claimed the power to permit victims to act as a third party during trial—opening, leading evidence, challenging the parties' evidence, testifying, and closing—subject to the ultimate discretion only of the judges themselves. The Pre-Trial and Trial Chambers successfully claimed the power to closely supervise the OTP's disclosure compliance as well as to have the final say on questions of protection of those put at risk by the ICC's activities. The Pre-Trial Chambers unsuccessfully attempted to exercise powers not granted by the statute to refuse arrest warrants based on their assessment of the gravity—and given the criteria they articulated, the worthiness—of a particular prosecution and the standard of review appropriate to particular charges. They have asserted the power not granted in the plain terms of the statute to amend the charges submitted for their review by the prosecutor and to refuse charges based on criteria nowhere found in the relevant article—and refused leave for appellate review of these decisions. Trial Chambers have even asserted, unsuccessfully, the right to add unconfirmed charges at trial that exceed the facts and circumstances charged and to apply the laxest of evidentiary procedures. And the Pre-Trial and Trial Chambers have chosen to pursue civil law rules on a variety of issues, all of which enhance their control over charging and trial and limit the prosecution's powers.

Moreno Ocampo's strategy of confining his battles with the judicial organ to the courtroom and avoiding any hint of public criticism of even the judges' more questionable rulings has served the institution well. It may also have served his purposes, given his success on review. When he was able to appeal what could be characterized as Pre-Trial and Trial Chambers power grabs, the prosecutor won more than he lost. Thus, he earned a split decision on victim participation (winning with respect to investigations but losing on the scope of victim participation at trial), won on at least some of the legal issues in the first *Lubanga* stay litigation and on the critical question of remedy in the second, swept the field on the three issues raised in the arrest warrant context, and prevailed on the limited scope of the Trial Chambers' ability to recharacterize the facts to add charges dependent on facts and circumstances beyond the charging document and on the proper procedure for the submission and acceptance of evidence.

This scorecard illustrates that the Pre-Trial and Trial Chambers are pursuing their checking function with outsized enthusiasm and indeed that the Appeals Chamber has been forced to do some checking of its own colleagues to maintain the appropriate institutional balance. The continual tug-of-war between Pre-Trial and Trial Chambers and the OTP, far from being a negative, should enhance the legitimacy of the ICC by demonstrating, beyond peradventure, that the judicial and prosecutorial organs are independent. Indeed, to the extent that these Chambers view prosecutorial discretion as suspect and attempt to closely police the OTP's exercise of its powers, they will enhance the perceived credibility of every hard-fought arrest warrant, confirmation decision, and final judgment.

NOTES

Many thanks to Sara Criscitelli for her comments and corrections; any remaining errors—as well as the editorial comments—are, obviously, my own.

1. *See* Rome Statute of the International Criminal Court, 2187 U.N.T.S. 90 (July 7, 1998) (hereinafter cited as Rome Statute or Statute).

2. Readers should be aware that this chapter was originally commenced during Luis Moreno Ocampo's tenure as prosecutor. Because, even at the time of publication, prosecutor Fatou Bensouda has been in office a short time and thus has not had time to reconsider and amend the policies and practices of the office, and because much of the litigation described within was conducted under Mr. Moreno Ocampo's direction, I have chosen to retain my focus on his work and interaction with the judicial organ.

3. *See* JAMES Q. WILSON, BUREAUCRACY: WHAT GOVERNMENT AGENCIES DO & WHY THEY DO IT 181–85 (1989). Of course, bureaucratic theory also predicts that the OTP will seek to extend its powers, but at least in contests with the judicial organ, the prosecutor's assertions of autonomy will succeed only to the extent that the judges wish to recognize them.

4. *See infra* notes 32–72 and accompanying text.

5. In one decision, Trial Chambers I took the OTP to task for what it felt were inappropriate remarks, but the remarks were not directed at the Chamber or critical of it. Rather, an OTP representative essentially publicly expressed confidence in the integrity of an OTP investigation and opined about the likely result of its efforts. In criticizing the OTP representatives in intemperate terms, the Chamber expressed its apparent belief that the OTP could not publicly reiterate its litigation positions outside of court without somehow usurping the judicial prerogatives of the Chambers. *See, e.g.*, Prosecutor v. Lubanga, Case No. ICC-01/04-01/06-2433, Decision on the Press Interview with Ms Le Fraper du Hellen, ¶¶49–53 (May 12, 2010).

6. The language used, on occasion, by Trial Chamber I is unfortunate. It had a tendency to characterize as "misconduct" OTP actions and decisions founded on principled readings of the statute with which the Chambers simply disagreed. *See, e.g.*, Prosecutor v. Lubanga, Case No. ICC-01/04-01/06-1401, Decision on the Consequences of Non-Disclosure of Exculpatory Materials Covered by Article 54(3)(e) Agreements and the Application to Stay the Prosecution of the Accused, Together with Certain Other Issues Raised at the Status Conference on 10 June 2008, ¶73 (June 13, 2008) (use of ICC art. 54[3][e] to obtain materials that may be used at trial is a "wholesale and serious abuse"). *See also supra* note 5.

7. See Prosecutor v. Ngudjolo, Case No. ICC-01/04-02/12-3, Judgment Rendered Pursuant to Article 74 of the Statute (Dec. 18, 2012); Prosecutor v. Lubanga, Case No. ICC-01/04-01/06-2842, Judgment Pursuant to Article 74 of the Statute (Mar. 14, 2012).

8. *See* Rome Statute, *supra* note 1, art. 82(1)(a)–(c).

9. *See id.* art. 82(1)(d).

10. The prosecutor took issue with the way the Pre-Trial and Trial Chambers applied the standard contained in ICC Article 82(1)(d) for evaluating requests for leave to appeal. Where there is no right to interlocutory appeal under article 82, however, the Appeals Chamber held that it cannot hear cases in which leave has not been granted, even for purposes of evaluating the appropriateness of the Chambers' application of Article 82(1)(d). *See* Situation in the Democratic Republic of Congo, Case No. ICC-01/04-168, Judgment on the Prosecutor's Application for Extraordinary Review of Pre-Trial Chamber I's 31 Mar. 2006 Decision Denying Leave to Appeal, ¶¶3, 34, 37, 39, 42 (July 13, 2006).

11. Jason Manning, *On Power, Participation, and Authority: The International Criminal Court's Initial Appellate Jurisprudence*, 38 GEO. J. INT'L. L. 803, 808 (2007).

12. *See id.* at 809.

13. In this regard, the Chambers have read the ICC's jurisdictional reach broadly in cases in which defendants have challenged the scope of ad hoc consents and self-referrals. *See, e.g.,* Prosecutor v. Gbagbo, Case No. ICC-02/11-01/11-321, Judgment on the Appeal of Mr Laurent Gbagbo against the Decision of Pre-Trial Chamber I on Jurisdiction and Stay of the Proceedings (Dec. 12, 2012); Prosecutor v. Mbarushimana, Case No. ICC-01/04-01/10-451, Decision on the "Defence Challenge to the Jurisdiction of the Court" (Oct. 26, 2011). The ICC Appeals Chamber has also endorsed the reading of article 17 that underlies "positive complementarity." Thus, inaction by a state with jurisdiction over the offense is sufficient to show that that state has waived its complementarity option and there is no need for a referring state to demonstrate that it is domestically unable or unwilling to investigate the crime. *See* Prosecutor v. Katanga, Case No. ICC-01/04-01/07-1497, Judgment on the Appeal of Mr. Germain Katanga against the Oral Decision of Trial Chamber II of 12 June 2009 on the Admissibility of the Case, ¶78 (Sept. 25, 2009). Finally, Chambers have exercised close scrutiny over states' attempts to exercise their "complementarity option." *See, e.g.,* Prosecutor v. Ruto, Case No. ICC-01/09-01/11-307, Judgment on the Appeal of the Republic of Kenya against the Decision of Pre-Trial Chamber II of 30 May 2011 entitled "Decision on the Admissibility by the Government of Kenya Challenging the Admissibility of the Case Pursuant to Article 19(2)(b) of the Statute," ¶1 (Aug. 30, 2011). These subjects need not be further discussed, however, because they do not involve a dispute with the OTP over the scope of its powers vis-à-vis those of the Chambers.

14. Situation in the DRC, Case No. ICC-01/04-556, Judgment on Victim Participation in the Investigation Stage of the Proceedings in the Appeal of the OPCD against the Decision of Pre-Trial Chamber I as of 7 Dec. 2007 and in the Appeals of the OPCD and the Prosecutor against the Decision of Pre-Trial Chamber I of 24 Dec. 2007, ¶4 (Dec. 19, 2008). *See also* Situation in Darfur, Case No. ICC-02/05-177, Judgment on Victim Participation in the Investigation Stage of the Proceedings in the Appeal of the OPCD against the Decision of Pre-Trial Chamber I as of 3 Dec. 2007 and in the Appeals of the OPCD and the Prosecutor against the Decision of Pre-Trial Chamber I of 6 Dec. 2007 (Feb. 2, 2009).

15. Situation in the DRC, Case No. ICC-01/04-556, *supra* note 14, at ¶13.

16. *Id.* at ¶45.

17. *See* Prosecutor v. Lubanga, Case No. ICC-01/04-01/06-1432, Judgment on the

Appeals of the Prosecutor and the Defence against Trial Chamber I's Decision on Victims' Participation of 18 Jan. 2008, ¶¶3–4 (July 11, 2008) (discussing the impugned Trial Chamber's decision, Prosecutor v. Lubanga, Case No. ICC-01/04-01/06-1119, Decision on Victims' Participation [Jan. 18, 2008]).

18. Prosecutor v. Lubanga, Case No. ICC-01/04-01/06-1191, Decision Granting Leave to Appeal (Feb. 26, 2008).

19. *See* Rome Statute, *supra* note 1, art. 68(3) (emphasis added).

20. Prosecutor v. Lubanga, Case No. ICC-01/04-01/06-1432, *supra* note 17, at ¶72 (quoting the Prosecutor's submission). *See also id.* at ¶15 (partly dissenting opinion of Judge G. M. Pikis) ("participation of victims is confined to the expression of their views and concerns").

21. *See id.* at ¶97.

22. *See, e.g.,* Situation in the DRC, Case No. 01/04-556, *supra* note 14, at ¶¶45–59 (plain language of statute confines participation to "proceedings"); Situation in the DRC, Case No. ICC-01/04-168, *supra* note 10, at ¶¶3, 34, 37, 39, 42 (interlocutory appeal provisions were "exhaustive" and thus could not be supplemented); Situation in the Democratic Republic of Congo, Case No. ICC-01/04-169, Judgment on the Prosecutor's Appeal against the Decision of Pre-Trial Chamber I Entitled "Decision on the Prosecutor's Application for Warrants of Arrest, Article 58," ¶¶42–45 (July 13, 2006) (article 58 arrest warrant requisites are "exhaustive" and therefore cannot be supplemented).

23. Prosecutor v. Lubanga, Case No. ICC-01/04-01/06-1432, *supra* note 17, at ¶93.

24. *See id.* at ¶14 (partially dissenting opinion of Judge G. M. Pikis).

25. *See id.* at ¶78 (quoting defense submission).

26. *See id.* at ¶¶93–99.

27. *See id.* at ¶95.

28. *See id.* at ¶¶99–104.

29. *See* Prosecutor v. Lubanga, Case No. ICC-01/04-01/06-1119, Decision on Victims' Participation, ¶117 (Jan. 18, 2008). *See also* Prosecutor v. Lubanga, Case No. ICC-01/04-01/06-1556-Corr-Anx1, Public Annex 1, Decision on the Applications by Victims to Participate in the Proceedings, ¶135 (Dec. 15, 2008).

30. Prosecutor v. Lubanga, Case No. ICC-01/04-01/06-1556-Corr-Anx1, Public Annex 1, *supra* note 29, ¶136.

31. *See* Prosecutor v. Katanga, Case No. ICC-01/04-01/07-1665-Corr, Directions for the Conduct of the Proceedings and Testimony in Accordance with Rule 140, ¶¶5, 19 (Nov. 20, 2009)

32. *See* Rome Statute, *supra* note 1, art. 54(3)(e).

33. ICC Rules of Procedure and Evidence (RPE) 82(1).

34. As the prosecutor explained to the Trial Chamber in *Lubanga,* the point of receiving these documents was "for the sake of the ongoing investigation and then to allow the Office of the Prosecutor to identify the materials it wishes to use as evidence and then seek permission." Prosecutor v. Lubanga, Case No. ICC-01/04-01/06-1401, *supra* note 6, at ¶¶26–27.

35. *See id.* at ¶¶64–66.

36. *See, e.g., id.* ¶¶44–45, 64–69, 82–88.

37. *See id.* at ¶¶42–43, 51, 60–61.

38. Prosecutor v. Lubanga, Case No. ICC-01/04-01/06-1417, Decision on the Prosecution's Application for Leave to Appeal the "Decision on the Consequences of Non-

Disclosure of Exculpatory Materials Covered by Article 54(3)(e) Agreements and Application to Stay the Prosecution of the Accused" (July 2, 2008); Prosecutor v. Lubanga, Case No. ICC-01/04-01/06-1423, Decision on the Request of the Prosecutor for Suspensive Effect of His Appeal against the "Decision on the Release of Thomas Lubanga Dyilo" (July 7, 2008).

39. Prosecutor v. Lubanga, Case No. ICC-01/04-01/06-1486, Judgment on the Appeal of the Prosecutor against the Decision of Trial Chamber I Entitled "Decision on the Consequences of Non-Disclosure of Exculpatory Materials Covered by Article 54(3)(e) Agreements and the Application to Stay the Prosecution of the Accused, Together with Certain Other Issues Raised at the Status Conference on 10 June 2008," ¶¶1, 41 (Oct. 21, 2008).

40. See id. at ¶54.

41. See id. at ¶55.

42. See id. at ¶42.

43. See id. at ¶¶44, 46. See also id. at ¶¶97–101.

44. See id. at ¶45.

45. See id. at ¶83.

46. Prosecutor v. Lubanga, Case No. ICC-01/04-01/06-1644, Reasons for Oral Decision Lifting the Stay of Proceedings (Jan. 23, 2009).

47. Prosecutor v. Lubanga, Case No. ICC-01/04-01/06-2517-Red, Redacted Decision on the Prosecution's Urgent Request for Variation of the Time-Limit to Disclose the Identity of Intermediary 143 or Alternatively to Stay Proceedings Pending Further Consultations with the VWU (July 8, 2010).

48. See Prosecutor v. Lubanga, Case No. ICC-01/04-01/06-1924, Decision Issuing Corrected and Redacted Versions of "Decision on the 'Prosecution's Request for Non-Disclosure of the Identity of Twenty-Five Individuals providing Tu Quoque Information' of 5 Dec. 2008," ¶34 (June 2, 2009).

49. See Prosecutor v. Lubanga, Case No. ICC-01/04-01/06-2434-Red2, Redacted Decision on Intermediaries, ¶¶138, 140 (May 12, 2010).

50. See id. at ¶¶43–47, 143, 150(i). See also Prosecutor v. Lubanga, Case No. ICC-01/04-01/06-2582, Judgment on the Appeal of the Prosecutor against the Decision of Trial Chamber I of 8 July 2010 Entitled "Decision on the Prosecution's Urgent Request for Variation of the Time-Limit to Disclose the Identity of Intermediary 143 or Alternatively to Stay Proceedings Pending Further Consultations with the VWU," ¶5 (Oct. 8, 2010) (noting that no specific allegations were made against Intermediary 143).

51. See Prosecutor v. Lubanga, Case No. ICC-01/04-01/06-2517-Red, supra note 47, at ¶¶143, 150(i).

52. See Prosecutor v. Lubanga, Case No. ICC-01/04-01/06-2463, Decision on the Prosecution Request for Leave to Appeal the "Decision on Intermediaries," ¶30 (June 2, 2010).

53. Prosecutor v. Lubanga, Case No. ICC-01/04-01/06-2582, supra note 50, at ¶7.

54. Prosecutor v. Lubanga, Case No. ICC-01/04-01/06-2517-Red, supra note 47, at ¶9.

55. See id. at ¶10.

56. See id. at ¶11.

57. See id. at ¶12.

58. See id. at ¶¶1–2.

59. *See id.* at ¶27.

60. *See id.* at ¶¶30–32.

61. Prosecutor v. Lubanga, Case No. ICC-01/04-01/06-T-ENG ET WT, Transcript of Hearing of 15 July 2010, at 14.

62. Prosecutor v. Lubanga, Case No. ICC-01/04-01/06-2574, Decision on the "Prosecution's Application to Take Testimony while Proceedings Are Stayed Pending Decision of the Appeals Chamber," ¶3 (Sept. 24, 2010).

63. *See id.* at ¶5.

64. *See id.* at ¶6.

65. *See id.* at ¶12.

66. *See id.* at ¶22.

67. Prosecutor v. Lubanga, Case No. ICC-01/04-01/06-2544-Red, Prosecution's Document in Support of Appeal against Trial Chamber I's Decision on 8 July 2010 to Stay the Proceedings for Abuse of Process, ¶3 (July 30, 2010). The prosecution did and does acknowledge and respect the Chamber's final authority in all matters affecting the conduct of the trial process, including questions of appropriate protective measures and what is necessary to secure a fair trial. What the prosecutor asserted was not to set itself above the Chamber with respect to protection decisions but rather to implement its statutory duty of protection. *Id. See also id.* at ¶¶3–8 (arguing that the Trial Chamber provided insufficient opportunity, as a matter of due process, before ordering prosecution disclosure).

68. Prosecutor v. Lubanga, Case No. ICC-01/04-01/06-2582, *supra* note 50, at ¶2.

69. *See id.* at ¶3.

70. Prosecutor v. Lubanga, Case No. ICC-01/04-01/06-2583, Judgment on the Appeal of the Prosecutor against the Oral Decision of Trial Chamber I of 15 July 2010 to Release Thomas Lubanga Dyillo (Oct. 8, 2010).

71. Prosecutor v. Lubanga, Case No. ICC-01/04-01/06-2842, *supra* note 7, at ¶2

72. *Id.*

73. *See, e.g.,* Rome Statute, *supra* note 1, art. 57.

74. Situation in the DRC, Case No. ICC-01/04-169, *supra* note 22, at ¶¶8–12.

75. *See id.* at ¶¶9, 18.

76. *See id.* at ¶¶1, 3. The Appeals Chamber further noted that while the Pre-Trial Chamber has the discretion to address admissibility under Article 19(1), it "should exercise such discretion only when it is appropriate in the circumstances of the case, bearing in mind the interests of the suspect." *Id.* at ¶2. In this case, the Appeals Chamber ruled, such an exercise of discretion would be erroneous. *Id.* at ¶¶2, 48.

77. *See id.* at ¶43.

78. *See id.* at ¶42.

79. *See id.* at ¶56.

80. *See id.* at ¶¶56–65, 68–82, 92.

81. *See* Prosecutor v. Ntaganda, Case No. ICC-01/04-02/06-2-Anx-tEN, Arrest Warrant, under Seal (Aug. 22, 2006).

82. Prosecutor v. Al Bashir, Case No. ICC-02/05-01/09-73, Judgment on the Appeal of the Prosecutor against the "Decision on the Prosecution's Application for a Warrant of Arrest against Omar Hassan Ahmad Al Bashir," ¶¶2–3 (Feb. 3, 2010).

83. *See id.* at ¶5.

84. *See id.* at ¶13.

85. *See id.* at ¶¶ 30–39.

86. *See id.* at ¶ 42.

87. Prosecutor v. Al Bashir, Case No. ICC-02/05-01/09-95, Second Warrant of Arrest for Omar Hassan Ahmad Al Bashir (July 12, 2010).

88. Michela Miraglia, *Admissibility of Evidence, Standard of Proof, and Nature of the Decision in the ICC Confirmation of Charges in* Lubanga, 6 J. INTL. CRIM. JUST. 489, 490 (2008).

89. Rome Statute, *supra* note 1, art. 61(5), (7).

90. *Id.* art. 61(6).

91. *Id.* art. 61(5).

92. *See, e.g.,* Prosecutor v. Lubanga, Case No. ICC-01/04-01/06-803-tEN, Decision on the Confirmation of Charges, ¶ 30 (Jan. 29, 2007) (hearing lasted from Nov. 9, 2006 to Nov. 28, 2006).

93. *See, e.g.,* Prosecutor v. Bemba, Case No. ICC-01/04-01/06-424, Decision Pursuant to Article 61(7)(a) and (b) of the Rome Statute on the Charges of the Prosecutor against Jean-Pierre Bemba Gombo (June 15, 2009)(186 pages); Prosecutor v. Katanga, Case No. 01/04-01/07-717-Corr, Decision on the Confirmation of Charges (Sept. 30, 2008) (226 pages); Prosecutor v. Lubanga, Case No. ICC-01/04-01/06-803-tEN, *supra* note 92 (157 pages).

94. *See* Rome Statute, *supra* note 1, art. 61(7) (emphases added).

95. If the Pre-Trial Chamber declines to confirm charges, the prosecution is not precluded from subsequently requesting confirmation if that request is supported by additional evidence. Rome Statute, *supra* note 1, art. 61(8).

96. *See, e.g.,* Prosecutor v. Lubanga, Case No. ICC-01/04-01/06-803-tEN, *supra* note 92, at ¶¶ 9, 200.

97. *See id.* at ¶¶ 220–21.

98. *Id.* at 156–47. For a summary of the changes, see Prosecutor v. Lubanga, Case No. ICC-01/04-01/06-1084, Decision on the Status before the Trial Chamber of the Evidence Heard by the Pre-Trial Chamber and the Decisions of the Pre-Trial Chamber in Trial Proceedings, and the Manner in Which Evidence Shall Be Submitted, ¶ 23 (Dec. 13, 2007).

99. Prosecutor v. Lubanga, Case No. ICC-01/04-01/06-806, Application for Leave to Appeal Pre-Trial Chamber I's Jan. 29, 2007 "Décision sur la confirmation des charges," ¶ 2 (Feb. 5, 2007).

100. Prosecutor v. Lubanga, Case No. ICC 01/04-01/06-915, Decision on the Prosecution and Defence Applications for Leave to Appeal the Decision on the Confirmation of Charges, ¶ 44 (May 24, 2007).

101. Prosecutor v. Lubanga, Case No. ICC-01/04-01/06-926, Decision on the Admissibility of the Appeal of Mr. Thomas Lubanga Dyilo against the Decision of the Pre-Trial Chamber I Entitled "Décision sur la confirmation des charges" of 29 Jan. 2007 (June 13, 2007).

102. Prosecutor v. Lubanga, Case No. ICC-01/04-01/06-1084, *supra* note 98, at ¶¶ 39–40.

103. Prosecutor v. Lubanga, Case No. ICC-01/04-01/06-2842, *supra* note 7, at ¶¶ 527–30.

104. *See id.* at ¶ 568.

105. Prosecutor v. Bemba, Case No. ICC-01/05-01/08-532, Decision on the Prosecu-

tor's Application for Leave to Appeal the "Decision Pursuant to Article 61(7)(a) and (b) of the Rome Statute on the Charges of the Prosecutor against Jean-Pierre Bemba Gombo," ¶4 (Sept. 18, 2009). *See also* Prosecutor v. Bemba, Case No. ICC-01/05-01/08-424, Decision Pursuant to Article 61(7)(a) and (b) of the Rome Statute on the Charges of the Prosecutor against Jean-Pierre Bemba Gombo (June 15, 2009).

106. Prosecutor v. Bemba, Case No. ICC-01/05-/01/08-532, *supra* note 105, at ¶30.

107. Prosecutor v. Delalic, Case No. IT-96-21-A, Judgment, ¶400 (Feb. 20, 2001) (the *Čelibići* case). *See also* Musema v. Prosecutor, Case No. ICTR-96-13-A, Judgment, ¶369 (Nov. 16, 2001). The ad hoc tribunals generally addressed issues arising from the improper accumulation of counts at the sentencing stage. *See, e.g., id.* at ¶360.

108. *See, e.g.,* Attila Bogdan, *Cumulative Charges, Convictions, and Sentencing at the Ad Hoc International Tribunals for the Former Yugoslavia and Rwanda*, 3 MELB. J. INTL. L. 1, 3 (2002).

109. Prosecutor v. Bemba, Case No. ICC-01/05-01/08-532, *supra* note 105, ¶36 (Sept. 18, 2009).

110. *See id.* at ¶¶52–53, 55.

111. *See id.* at ¶39.

112. *See id.* at ¶56.

113. *See supra* note 22 and accompanying text.

114. Prosecutor v. Lubanga, Case No. ICC-01/04-01/06-2205, Judgment on the Appeals of Mr. Lubanga Dyilo and the Prosecutor against the Decision of Trial Chamber I of 14 July 2009 Entitled "Decision Giving Notice to the Parties and Participants That the Legal Characterisation of the Facts May Be Subject to Change in Accordance with Regulation 55(2) of the Regulations of the Court, ¶94 (Dec. 8, 2009).

115. See Prosecutor v. Lubanga, Case No. ICC-01/04/-01/06-2093, Clarification and Further Guidance to the Parties and Participants in Relation to the "Decision Giving Notice to the Parties and Participants that the Legal Characterization of the Facts May Be Subject to Change in Accordance with Regulation 55(2) of the Regulations of the Court," ¶7 (Aug. 27, 2009); Prosecutor v. Lubanga, Case No. ICC-01/04/-01/06-2049, Decision Giving Notice to the Parties and Participants That the Legal Characterization of the Facts May Be Subject to Change in Accordance with Regulation 55(2) of the Regulations of the Court ¶1 (July 14, 2009).

116. Prosecutor v. Lubanga, Case No. ICC-01/04/-01/06-2093, *supra* note 115, at ¶11 (Aug. 27, 2009).

117. Prosecutor v. Lubanga, Case No. ICC-01/04-01/06-2069-AnxI, Second Corrigendum to "Minority Opinion on the 'Decision Giving Notice to the Parties and Participants That the Legal Characterisation of the Facts May Be Subject to Change in Accordance with Regulation 55(2) of the Regulations of the Court' of 27 July 2009, Annex I (July 31, 2009) (Fulford, J., dissenting from the majority opinion).

118. *See id.* at ¶16.

119. *See id.* at ¶¶17, 20.

120. *See* Prosecutor v. Lubanga, Case No. ICC-01/04-01/06-2107, Decision on the Prosecution and Defence Applications for Leave to Appeal the "Decision Giving Notice to the Parties and Participants That the Legal Characterisation of the Facts May Be Subject to Change in Accordance with Regulation 55(2) of the Regulations of the Court" (Sept. 3, 2009).

121. Prosecutor v. Lubanga, Case No. ICC-01/04-01/06-2205, *supra* note 114, at ¶92–94.

122. *See id.* at ¶94.

123. *See id.* at ¶¶99–100, 109–11.

124. *See also* Prosecutor v. Lubanga, Case No. ICC-01/04-01/06-2223, Decision on the Legal Representatives' Joint Submissions Concerning the Appeals Chamber's Decision on 8 Dec. 2009 on Regulation 55 of the Regulations of the Court, ¶¶27–39 (Jan. 8, 2010) (on remand, precluding consideration of additional charges because such charges would exceed the facts and circumstances alleged). If Trial Chambers cannot change the charge, the judges are apparently determined to restrict the prosecutor to the precise factual contours of the confirmation decision rather than the prosecutor's charging document. Thus, in *Prosecutor v. Katanga*, Trial Chamber II ordered the prosecution to prepare and file, well before trial, a table "setting out all his incriminating evidence and the list of witnesses he intended to call at trial." Prosecutor v. Katanga, Case No. ICC-01/04-01/07-1547-tENG, Decision on the Filing of a Summary of the Charges by the Prosecutor, ¶1 (Oct. 21, 2009). The document seems to have been the functional equivalent of a dossier in civil law practice in that the Chamber wished the Prosecutor to provide the defense with "a structured presentation of all of [his] evidence"; the resulting document and its annexes consumed 1,165 pages. *Id.* at ¶¶2, 3. The Trial Chamber then concluded that, despite this detailed document and a 226-page confirmation decision, the defense had insufficient notice. It therefore ordered the prosecution to prepare and file a summary of the charges. *Id.* at ¶12. In so doing, the Chamber demanded that the prosecutor limit himself not just to the charges approved by the Pre-Trial Chamber but also only to the detailed "facts and circumstances" and the legal characterization found by that Chamber. *Id.* at ¶19. It reasoned that

> In providing for a pre-trial phase, whose culminating point is the decision on the confirmation of the charges, rendered following an adversarial hearing, and in requiring the Trial Chamber to be bound by the facts and circumstances described in the charges as thus confirmed, and by them alone, the Statute does not allow either the Chamber, or even the Prosecutor, to add new facts in the course of the trial.

Id. at ¶22.

Thus the prosecutor was ordered to prepare a summary of charges referencing only the confirmation decision rather than his request for charges and containing a charge-by-charge summary of the facts discussed throughout the confirmation decision's incredibly detailed exposition, not just the concluding findings of the Pre-Trial Chamber. *Id.* at ¶29. In short, it appears that the Trial Chamber contemplates that trial will largely simply retrace the course of the confirmation decision, perhaps using live witnesses in lieu of summary or documentary evidence. *See also* Prosecutor v. Bemba, Case No. ICC-01/05-01/08-836, Decision on the Defence Application for Corrections to the Document Containing Charges and for the Prosecution to File a Second Amended Document Containing the Charges (July 20, 2010).

125. Prosecutor v. Bemba, Case No. ICC-01/05-01/08-2480, Decision on the Temporary Suspension of the Proceedings Pursuant to Regulation 55(2) of the Regulations of the Court and Related Procedural Deadlines, ¶1 (Dec. 13, 2012).

126. Prosecutor v. Katanga, Case No. ICC-01/04-01/07-3319, Decision on the Implementation of Regulation 55 of the Regulations of the Court and Severing the Charges against the Accused Persons, ¶¶6–7 (Nov. 21, 2012).

127. *Id.* at ¶¶55–57 (Van den Wyngaert, J., dissenting).

128. Thus, for example, the Trial Chambers chastised the registrar for failing to consult Chambers before withdrawing from public view a decision it was concerned might endanger witnesses without further redactions. Prosecutor v. Lubanga, Case No. ICC-01/04-01/06-1058, Decision on the Procedures to Be Adopted for Ex Parte Proceedings, ¶15 (Dec. 6, 2007). It also asserted the right to determine the role of a semi-autonomous office within the Registry, the OPCV, in the conduct of the proceedings, including decisions whether representation should be from the OPCV or other appointed counsel. Prosecutor v. Lubanga, Case No. ICC-01/04-01/06-1211, Decision on the Role of the Office of Public Counsel for Victims and Its Request for Access to Documents, ¶¶31–35 (Mar. 7, 2008).

129. DAVID LUBAN, JULIE O'SULLIVAN, & DAVID P. STEWART, INTERNATIONAL & TRANSNATIONAL CRIMINAL LAW 145 (2009).

130. *Id.*

131. Prosecutor v. Lubanga, Case No. ICC-01/04-01/06-1049, Decision Regarding the Practices Used to Prepare and Familiarise Witnesses for Giving Testimony at Trial, ¶43 (Nov. 30, 2007).

132. *See id.* at ¶51.

133. *See id.* at ¶52.

134. *See* Prosecutor v. Lubanga, Case No. ICC-01/04-01/06-1351, Decision Regarding the Protocol on the Practices to Be Used to Prepare Witnesses for Trial, ¶41 (May 23, 2008) (declining to require the VWU to warn witnesses against hearsay stating that such a warning "was inappropriate: exclusion of hearsay evidence is not expressly provided for in the Statute and the matter has not been the subject to [*sic*] a ruling by the Chamber").

135. Prosecutor v. Lubanga, Case No. ICC-01/04-01/06-1084, *supra* note 98, at ¶5. For a summary of these statutory and regulatory provisions, see *id.* at ¶4. *See also* Prosecutor v. Lubanga, Case No. ICC-01/04-01/06-1399, Decision on the Admissibility of Four Documents, ¶24 (June 13, 2008).

136. Prosecutor v. Lubanga, Case No. ICC-01/04-01/06-1399, *supra* note 135, at ¶24.

137. Prosecutor v. Lubanga, Case No. ICC-01/04-01/06-2664-Red, Redacted Decision on the "Troisième requête de la défense aux fins de dépôt de documents," ¶1 (Mar. 16, 2011).

138. *See id.* at ¶3.

139. *See id.* at ¶3 (quoting Prosecutor v. Lubanga, Case No. ICC-01/04-01/06-1399, *supra* note 135, ¶29).

140. Prosecutor v. Bemba, Case No. ICC-01/05-01/08-1022, Decision on the Admission into Evidence of Materials Contained in the Prosecution's List of Evidence, ¶35 (Nov. 19, 2011).

141. *See id.* at ¶9.

142. Prosecutor v. Bemba, Case No. ICC-01/05-01/08-1169, Decision on the Prosecution and Defence Applications for Leave to Appeal the "Decision on the Admission into Evidence of Materials Contained in the Prosecution's List of Evidence" (Jan. 26, 2011).

143. Prosecutor v. Bemba, Case No. ICC-01/05-01/08-1386, Judgment on the Appeals of Mr. Jean-Pierre Bemba Gombo and the Prosecutor against the Decision of Trial Chamber III Entitled "Decision on the Admission into Evidence of Materials Contained in the Prosecution's List of Evidence" (May 3, 2011).

144. *See id.* at ¶¶51–57.

145. Rome Statute, *supra* note 1, art. 69(3).

146. Prosecutor v. Lubanga, Case No. ICC-01/04-01/06-1119, *supra* note 29, at ¶108.

147. *See id. See also* Prosecutor v. Katanga, Case No. ICC-01/04-01/07-1665-Corr, *supra* note 30, at ¶¶5, 19, 43–48; Prosecutor v. Lubanga, Case No. ICC-01/04-01/06-2032-Anx, "Decision on the Request by Victims a/0225/06, a/0229/06 and a/0270/07 to Express Their Views and Concerns in Person and to Present Evidence during the Trial, ¶25–44 (June 26, 2009).

148. Prosecutor v. Lubanga, Case No. ICC-01/04-01/06–2360, Decision on Judicial Questioning, ¶¶1–5, 32–48 (Mar. 18, 2010).

149. *See id.* at ¶48.

The Elusive Pursuit of Trust
between Prosecutors and Judges

Patricia M. Wald

This propitiously timed review of the challenges and hurdles the new prosecutor at the International Criminal Court (ICC) faces is a welcome launch onto the second stage of an institution of potentially immense significance for global justice. The essays cover old problems that remain unsolved after a decade—victim participation, choices between civil and common law procedures—along with new ones that have sprung up as a consequence of unanticipated events such as the tug of war for custody of deposed Arab leaders. Some arise from Luis Moreno Ocampo's innovations—for example, the preliminary examination status, where candidates for a full-scale investigation have reposed for years, waiting for decisions about whether investigations will proceed. The area with which I am most familiar, however, is the one discussed in Professor Julie Rose O'Sullivan's provocative essay, "The Relationship between the Office of the Prosecutor and the Judicial Organ: Conflict and Opportunity." As a former judge on an ICC predecessor, the International Criminal Tribunal for the Former Yugoslavia (ICTY), I want to address the relationship from a judge's perspective: what makes it so tricky in the international arena, what worries a judge most about it, and what avenues may be open to improve it.

My reading of Professor O'Sullivan's thesis is that Moreno Ocampo's term has been characterized by frequent clashes between the Office of the Prosecutor (OTP) and the ICC judges, primarily in the pretrial and trial branches, over the scope of their respective powers under the Rome Statute. The judges have striven for the last word on virtually all aspects and stages of the proceedings, from investigations through characterization of the charges, disclosure of the identity of witnesses promised confidentiality by the prosecutor, standards for confirmation of charges and for issuance of arrest warrants, limits on the prosecutor's preparation of witnesses, and the circumstances in which the judges can question witnesses. As Professor O'Sullivan points out, the pretrial and trial judges hold the trump card in most of these disputes because of their ability under the Rules of the Court to prevent any appeal of their interlocutory decisions. But she appears relatively sanguine about the conflict, opining that in general, the prosecutor has taken his lumps and not gone public with complaints even though some judges have and that on the few occasions when the Appeals Chamber has ruled on these intramural disputes, it has usually upheld the OTP or at least eased its burden in complying with the dictates of the lower chambers. Overall, she concludes that the clashes have strengthened the OTP and enhanced the Court's credibility by demonstrating that the judges are not pushovers for the prosecutor but rather vigorously independent and protective of their own powers as well as defendants' rights. Between the lines I read sympathy for the prosecutor's plight: he is often right but cannot always get justice in his own court.

I am, however, less sanguine about the course of this all-important relationship. True, as Professor O'Sullivan notes, it is still in its adolescence; the first three trials at the ICC have been completed, and two more have begun. But may one not worry that if the clashes continue at the current level, as the number of trials grows and the issues involved intensify in quality and quantity, her optimistic appraisal might not be borne out? Many observers both inside and outside the tribunal already do not share her positive view of the effect of these disputes on the Court's credibility.[1] The disputes during the *Lubanga* trial over the prosecutor's use of intermediaries to locate and interview witnesses threatened to derail and in fact did delay the proceedings substantially at a time when the ICC's critics were focusing on its slowness in completing trials. It may be a given that prosecutors and judges will and should disagree even in the best-run courts (indeed, some commentators believe that the greater problem is that they are disposed to agree too much). Nonetheless a new prosecutor might well set as a legitimate goal the development of a higher degree of trust between the two to keep clashes to a minimum and to ensure that they truly implicate legal differences or the rights of defendants rather than the issue of power sharing. In my experience, unnecessary or too frequent prosecutor-judge clashes drain the human resources of participants already taxed by high-maintenance jobs and indeed could help to explain what until recently was a high rate of turnover among OTP employees. For that reason, it may be useful to point out the particularly vexing aspects of this extraordinarily important relationship in international courts, what judges can appropriately expect from the prosecutor, and what might be explored to keep that relationship on an even keel.

International and hybrid (part national, part international) courts have some unique features that accentuate the normal tensions between prosecutors and judges. In domestic court systems like that of the United States, that relationship has evolved over centuries: prosecutors and judges share the same legal culture and traditions; many judges are themselves former prosecutors; and the two genres speak and think in a common language. Prosecutors eschew partisan politics in choosing and prosecuting cases but are securely rooted in the executive branch and expected to implement the broader priorities and criminal philosophy of their administrations. Judges, conversely, are supposed to make their decisions independently and based on the facts and applicable law in individual cases, oblivious of any broader political or other concerns. Detailed codes of civil and criminal procedure keep both participants on their side of the line. Judges may occasionally lament in dicta prosecutorial policies such as sentencing guidelines or "going after the mules instead of the top guys" in drug cases, but they cannot and do not try to do anything about it in individual cases. Only when a prosecutor breaks the rules by, for example, withholding information that would help the defense will a judge publicly chastise the prosecutor or even dismiss the case.[2] Overall, the judges trust the prosecutor to follow familiar "rules of the road" agreed on in advance as to how the proceedings will be conducted.

The same is not necessarily so in international and hybrid courts .The building blocks of trust between prosecutor and judges are less sturdy. Prosecutors and their assistants and the judges and their aides are typically the products of different legal systems and often speak and think in different languages. They have no common reference points in a single country's legal practice or precedent. Even the style of questioning of a prosecutor from one country may seem irritatingly perverse to a judge from another country. For example, a prosecutor who asks, "Since you were at the scene of the crime at midnight, broke down the door, and had your weapon at the ready, why should we believe that you did not shoot the victim?" in a case where none of those propositions had been proved can set an American judge's teeth on edge. More critically, the meld of common law and civil modes of trial in these courts continues to be shaky and subject to frequent changes.

Although all prosecutors conduct their investigations and pretrial preparations in secret, while judges do everything in public except deliberate and draft opinions, thereby inevitably causing conscientious judges to scrutinize prosecutors' work product with care, this tension can cause more than the usual strain in the international tribunals, where virtually all prosecutions are initiated only after several years of field investigations. Prosecution witnesses have likely been interviewed years earlier by prosecutors who did not speak the witnesses' native tongues and used translators to chronicle the witnesses' statements, which are then introduced years later at trial either as direct evidence or as potential impeachment of the witnesses. At the ICTY, I saw several witnesses who claimed at trial that they did not understand what they had previously signed and now wished to repudiate their earlier statements. The possibility of misunderstanding or even intimidation, even if unintentional, undergirding such statements has to be a matter of concern for the international judge. Indeed that concern, along with the widespread ban on pretrial preparation of witnesses in civil law countries, may have motivated the decision of one ICC Pre-Trial Chamber to forbid the prosecution from "proofing" (preparing) any of its witnesses on any aspect of their testimony despite the risks to the integrity of the proceeding of putting a witness on the stand from a faraway country who does not speak the language of the judges or the prosecutors, has not been in contact with them for years, and knows nothing of trial procedure or of interim developments in the case. The ban on witness proofing can and some say has led to recanting of testimony at trial with its attendant confusion and delay.

Trials in international courts typically take longer. Milošević's trial at the ICTY lasted four years and ended with the death of both the accused and the presiding judge before the defense case had finished. Karadžić's trial began in 2009, and the prosecution did not complete its case until 2012, while Mladić's case will no doubt take several years to try despite amendments to the indictment designed to speed it up. Indeed, the judge ordered a postponement mid-trial as a consequence of "serious disclosure errors" on the prosecution's part. Long trials produce irritation on all sides and more frequent disputes among all the participants. Everyone needs to draw on a reservoir of basic trust and respect to keep things going smoothly. This is especially true when high-level accused choose to represent themselves, as all three of these leaders and many others have, in part because the tribunals are more lenient in allowing self-representation than the United States and most other countries and because that practice is not always made contingent on orderly behavior in the courtroom.

Another factor impeding the buildup of trust between prosecutor and judges is the temporary tenure of international court judges (nine years at the ICC) as compared to the life tenure of U.S. federal judges and the ten-to fifteen-year typical term of state judges. Although Moreno Ocampo served his full term, other tribunal prosecutors have come and gone more quickly. It takes time to build trust. Judges on short tenure away from their permanent careers and homes may also be motivated to ensure that their time is well spent and may thus be impatient with the prosecutor's long-term strategy or priorities. This notoriously occurred in the early days of both the ICTY (with respect to decisions about whether to prosecute immediately the top tier of leaders rather than build up cases starting with on-the-ground perpetrators) and the International Criminal Tribunal for Rwanda (with reference to the prosecution of neglected gender-specific crimes). Professor O'Sullivan relates several instances at the ICC where the judges have similarly intervened to take over what would normally be considered prosecutorial strategic decisions. The earlier international and hybrid courts also indigenously developed their own pretrial processes to provide an arena in which the judges could "manage" the number of witnesses, crime sites, length of time allotments to each side, and extent of pretrial disclosure. This development has frustrated prosecutors who believe that their mission is not just to convict the defendants but to demonstrate to the world the full extent of the atrocities perpetrated against innocent victims. Again, as O'Sullivan discusses, the Rome Statute provides the judges with much more ammunition for intervention by way of a formal pretrial process and other authorizations than the ad hoc tribunals' charters.

The defense in international trials operates on a more uneven playing field than in many domestic systems, and international judges may accordingly be even more protective of defendants' rights. For example, the court has no power to enforce its subpoenas to produce defense witnesses, as is the case in the United States; it can only request that the witnesses come voluntarily or that their governments require them to do so. Defense counsel operate away from their home bases and in my time at the ICTY had vastly inferior workspaces and equipment than did the prosecutor, who under all the tribunal charters is an integral part of the court family and is funded by the same source as the Chambers and Registrar. In most atrocity cases, public sentiment and the media are also more sympathetic to the prosecution. The judges, aware of all these factors and of their duty to ensure a fair trial, may understandably put prosecutors' feet to the fire when issues arise regarding the appropriateness of their conduct.

Finally, both the prosecutor and the judges must contend with the ever-present specter of political bias. According to one commentator, "Politics long has been seen as a source of the ICC's troubles."[3] In a last-minute rejection of the Rome Statute, the United States cited—ironically, as it turned out—the prosecutor's unilateral power to begin prosecutions without U.N. Security Council or state party referral. In practice, Moreno Ocampo dramatically limited his power under article 53 to decline to investigate an otherwise pursuable case where there are "substantial reasons to believe that an investigation would not serve the interests of justice." He limited his grounds for initiating investigations to considerations of crime prevention, security, and protection of victims, rejecting any consideration of "broader matter[s] of international peace and security,"[4] a somewhat controversial decision given the geographical scope of his jurisdiction and the frequency of referrals made while conflicts are still ongoing and diplomacy or settlements in the offing. Other tribunals have been criticized in the media and elsewhere for acting "politically" based on the heavy disproportion of cases brought against accused from one side or the other of internal conflicts. Even the ICC in the *Bemba* case did not escape the accusation of bias in going after a high official of the party opposing the government in power.[5] The persistent worry that their actions will be misinterpreted as politically motivated may well influence the relationship of prosecutor and judge in a far greater proportion of international cases than in domestic courts.

Special problems plague hybrid courts such as the Extraordinary Chambers in the Courts of Cambodia (ECCC), where there are co-prosecutors and coinvestigative judges (one Cambodian, one appointed by the U.N. from another country) and the proceedings are conducted according to the civil rather than the common law mode. Three out of five judges in both the trial and appeals chambers are Cambodian, but no decision can be made unless at least one international judge agrees. At the investigative stage, only one co-prosecutor is needed to advance the case, but if the other demurs, the coinvestigating judges must decide. Here again, the approval of only one judge is needed to forward the investigation. In general, a pattern has emerged in which the nationals and the internationals align vertically against each other at the ECCC, with dysfunctional results, rather than the more common horizontal alignment of prosecutors versus judges. The disputes have centered on matters such as the power of the coinvestigative judge to interview witnesses or call for evidence without involving either the prosecution or the defense. But pronounced disagreements have erupted between the national and international participants over whether to proceed with Cases Nos. 3 and 4 involving high-level Khmer Rouge leaders. Allegations were made that the Cambodians are reacting to strong pressure from their government to halt all proceedings involving potential trials in Cases Nos. 3 and 4. In the course of this dispute, an international coinvestigative judge publicly chastised the international prosecutor, who sought permission to proceed, and threatened to hold him in contempt. The dispute escalated to the point where the coinvestigating judge resigned and a new one had to be appointed by the U.N. In other proceedings, the majority of Cambodian trial judges have insisted that the prosecution's case be broken down into several smaller trials rather than one major one in which the full scope of the defendants' misdeeds could be showcased. At other times, the trial judges have limited the prosecution's evidence in the first of these smaller cases to crimes committed in the evacuation of Phnom Penh, excluding crimes committed in the lead-up to the evacuation, a limit the international co-prosecutor viewed as ruling out some of his strongest atrocity evidence.[6] All in all, Cambodia's experience may serve as a warning about the double trouble that prosecutor-judge relationships face in a hybrid court governed under the civil mode of trial where judges control the investigative as well as the trial stage.

What advice, then might be tendered to the new prosecutor, ICC judges, or Assembly of States Parties (ASP), the ICC's governing body in working toward a less combative relationship between judges and prosecutor?

First: Based on my experience in both domestic and international courts, seasoned judges with trial court backgrounds either as judges or advocates tend to maintain better control over the proceedings, are more secure in the courtroom, and are less likely to perceive prosecutorial threats to their authority. The ICTY had no requirement of prior trial experience for judges, and inexperienced judges accordingly could be and were assigned to preside over complex yearlong trials. The results sometimes reflected misunderstandings, procedural errors, and even verdict reversals. The Rome Statute sought to avoid that dilemma by requiring in article 36 that judges have either "established competence in criminal law and procedure, and the necessary relevant experience, whether as judge, prosecutor, advocate or in other similar capacity, in criminal proceedings" or "established competence in relevant areas of international law such as international humanitarian law and the law of human rights, and extensive experience in a professional legal capacity which is of relevance to the judicial work of the court." The Pre-Trial and Trial Chambers were to have a preponderance of judges in the first category. In practice, however, the interpretation of "necessary, relevant" experience has sometimes been interpreted by nominating states in an idiosyncratic fashion and has been dramatically off course in a few cases. Moreover, the horse-trading (largely on geographic grounds) that precedes judicial elections by the ASP has resulted in criticism of some judges' ability to manage proceedings smoothly. Veteran judges may draw on a corps of past experience in finding the right balance between their authority and the prosecutor's discretion that inexperienced judges cannot access.

A few years ago, the Coalition for the International Criminal Court convened a team of five jurists with international court experience to evaluate the twenty candidates nominated for six upcoming judicial vacancies. I was one of those jurists, and our evaluations were to be solely on the basis of whether the candidates' documented experience in criminal proceedings satisfied the Rome Statute. After considered study and deliberations, we found four lacking in sufficient practical experience to meet the statutory requirements. Our report, released before the judicial elections, may have contributed to the fact that none of the four was elected; ASP members reportedly referred to the report often in their preelection discussions. We also offered some general observations about the candidate pool, including a recommendation that the ASP consider adopting an age cutoff to discourage "out to pasture" candidates (international judging is a taxing job often requiring sitting for months on end listening to horrific testimony filtered through the translator as well as perusing tens of thousands of briefing and record pages sometimes written in virtually undecipherable prose). The ASP has now set up an official evaluation committee that will rate judicial candidates' article 36 qualifications.[7] Professor O'Sullivan's observation that Moreno Ocampo fared better when he was allowed to take his case to the Appeals Chamber raises some interesting questions, however. That chamber has no requirement that a majority of judges meet the qualifications of the first category, whereas judges in that category predominate in the Pre-Trial and Trial Chamber. That could suggest that the argument for experienced judges does not hold water as far as minimization of disputes with the prosecutor is concerned, although I would like to see further research before I surrender to that view.

Second: Rules can fulfill a very useful function in heading off conflicts that may otherwise arise in individual cases, including conflicts over the relative roles of prosecutors and judges in particular parts of the proceeding. The ICTY judges could (and did) amend their rules, often in reaction to problems that surfaced in cases. The ICC Rules of Procedure and Evidence, however, can only be revised by the ASP, meaning that the process is more cumbersome and revisions occur less frequently. The ICC itself can, however, adopt regulations for "routine functioning." Rulemaking at both levels should utilize advisory committees, which include prosecutors and defense counsel, so that advocates have an opportunity to make their case for or against proposed rule changes in a less contentious setting than the courtroom. As Professor O'Sullivan recounts, determined judges can interpret even clear rules in an extreme fashion; nonetheless, the mere presence of a relevant rule or regulation provides a point around which debate can center and puts a heavier burden of persuasion on both judges and prosecutors to sustain their side of any argument, as opposed to leaving both parties with ambiguous or no statutory guidance. The ICC judges have already resorted to drafting new rules on the use of intermediaries as a result of the confusion and delay in the *Lubanga* trial. A sustained focus on precollision rulemaking to head off disputes in anticipated areas of difference, such as the prosecutor's duty to disclose mitigating information to the defense, might be very useful. Similarly, rules may be helpful in structuring the prosecutor's public discussions with the media on aspects of investigation and trial.

Third: During my tenure at the ICTY, the court established a coordinating council of all three branches (i.e., the OTP, Registry, and judges) to meet regularly to discuss common administrative and logistical concerns. Other tribunals, including the ICC, have similar coordinating groups. It would be useful to see whether such groups could expand their concerns to include matters not strictly logistical, such as filing, discovery requirements, and witness protective procedures. Of course, such a group should not intrude on specific issues involved in ongoing individual cases. One wonders, for example, whether the witness proofing dispute could profitably have been discussed in such a setting rather than litigated to the undesirable result of split rulings by two separate ICC Chambers. Informal meetings can often provide a venue conducive to strengthening relationships and understanding the other person's motivations and point of view. In the D.C. Circuit in the United States, for example, judges held annual retreats with prosecutors and advocates to discuss recurring issues in a general fashion. Out-of-court contact between prosecutors and judges must, of course, be carefully managed to avoid giving rise to suspicions of special influence or pleading. Thus, where potential hot-button issues with substantive implications are raised, defense representatives should be present as well.[8]

Finally, both the judges and the prosecutor might aim for, in the words of one experienced veteran, a "change in the culture" of their respective offices. The new prosecutor might publicly acknowledge that trust between the prosecutor and the judges is in need of bolstering and commit herself publicly to a policy of dealing "straight up" with the judges. She might establish an internal ethics committee at the OTP to enforce ethical guidelines and courtroom etiquette. She might assure the judges that OTP employees will be as transparent as possible and follow the highest standards set down in their own rules as well as the Court's. As one former international prosecutor advises, "Trust is something that needs to develop, but etiquette and proper judicial manners accompanied by a fresh start would certainly help."[9] For their part, the ICC's judges might seek to cultivate a better understanding of the difficult conditions under which the OTP investigators and prosecutors work in hostile territories and might arrange for more briefings on local conditions and when feasible make visits to the areas involved or even conduct some proceedings there. They might use joint seminars or other public exchanges to probe the continuing problem of combining civil and common law adversary procedures—for example, the possible anomaly created by transplanting the civil law ban against witness proofing to an adversary system where there is no *juge d'instruction* in charge of the investigation and the prosecutor alone carries the burden of proof. Problems will always arise in this complex relationship, but those problems fester in an atmosphere of distrust. As the ICC enters its second decade, this is a most appropriate time for both parties to make a sincere and intelligent attempt to rework a relationship that is so essential to the Court's efficiency and credibility.[10]

NOTES

1. *See, e.g.*, e-mail from David Tolbert, Former Deputy ICTY Prosecutor, to Author (May 8, 2012) ("There clearly has been a breakdown in trust" between the prosecutor and the judges.) (on file with author); Sir Adrian Fulford, Judge, ICC, Reflections of a Trial Judge (Dec. 6, 2010) (referring to "delays engendered by recent and future noncompliance by the prosecutor with our Decisions") (on file with author).

2. *See* Brady v. Maryland, 373 U.S. 83 (1963). *See also* Brendan V. Sullivan Jr., *Where's the Punishment after Justice Dept. Misconduct?*, WASH. POST (July 5, 2012), http://articles. washingtonpost.com/2012-07-05/opinions/35487796_1_reckless-professional-misconduct-new-prosecutors-significant-exculpatory-evidence.

3. *See* Diane Marie Amann, *Politics & Prosecutors, from Katherine Fite to Fatou Bensouda*, IN PROCEEDINGS OF THE FIFTH INTERNATIONAL HUMANITARIAN LAW DIALOGS (2012), http://papers.SCVN.com/sol3/papers.cfm?abstract_id=204662.

4. *See* Office of the Prosecutor, ICC, *Policy Paper on the Interests of Justice* (Sept. 1, 2007), http://www.icc-cpi.int/NR/rdonlyres/772C95C9-F54D-4321-BF09-73422BB23 528/143640/ICCOTPInterestsOfJustice.pdf.

5. *See* Anjana Sundaram et al., *Bemba Casts Shadow on Upcoming DRC Election*, INSTITUTE FOR WAR & PEACE REPORTING, Nov. 19, 2010, http://iwpr.net/report-news/ bemba-casts-shadow-upcoming-drc-elections; Julie Flint & Alex de Waal, *Case Closed: A Prosecutor without Borders*, WORLD AFFAIRS, Mar. 22, 2009, http://www.worldaffairs-journal.org/article/case-closed-prosecutor-without-borders.

6. Prosecutor v. Noun Chea, Ieng Sary, Khieu Samphan, Ieng Thirith, Case No. 002/19-09-2007/ECCC/TC, Decision on Co-Prosecutors' Request for Reconsideration of the Terms of the Trial Chamber's Severance Order (E124/2) and Related Motions and Annexes (Extraordinary Chambers for the Courts of Cambodia Oct. 18, 2011), http:// www.eccc.gov.kh/sites/default/files/documents/courtdoc/E124_7_EN.PDF.

7. Independent Panel on ICC Judicial Elections, *Report on International Criminal Court Judicial Nominations 2011* (Oct. 26, 2011), http://www.iccindependentpanel.org/ sites/default/files/Independent%20Panel%20on%20ICC%20Judicial%20Elections%20 -%20Report%2026%20October%202011.pdf.

8. When the international vice president of the Extraordinary Chambers in the Courts of Cambodia met with the international co-prosecutor to discuss mutual problems, including managing, monitoring, staffing, budget, contacts with the U.N., and resources, she was challenged unsuccessfully by motions filed by defense attorneys asking for an investigation of "ex parte communications" and later asking to disqualify her from sitting on the ongoing trial. *See* Prosecutor v. Noun Chea, Ieng Sary, Khieu Samphan, Ieng Thirith, Case No. 002/13-09-2007-ECCC/TC, Ieng Sary's Request for Investigation Concerning *Ex Parte* Communications between the International Co-Prosecutor, Judge Cartwright, and Others (Extraordinary Chambers for the Courts of Cambodia Nov. 24, 2011) (alleging that the judge and prosecutor were "meeting on a regular basis . . . to talk about Court-related issues").

9. Tolbert, *supra* note 1.

10. In her first year in office, the new prosecutor, Fatou Bensouda, has reportedly "begun to help change the image of the OTP," making public a strategic plan for 2013–15 and soliciting feedback from other organs of the Court and civil society. The plan calls for the OTP to "assess the Court's decisions in relation to . . . prosecutorial practices to determine whether it is appropriate to change its prosecutorial strategies and standards," to evaluate "lessons learned" from the OTP's performance in court and "translating them into good practices," as well as to "contribute to the in-depth inter-organ lessons review of the judicial process in order to improve the fairness, transparency and expedition of the prosecution, including witness-proofing," and finally working "constructively with the organs of the Court with the aim of finding solutions to common problems, respecting the mandates of the other organs . . . within the context of its own independent mandate." The ASP has also set up a Working Group on Governance of the Court. Nonetheless the first year has been rocky, involving incidents of witness intimidation and bribing along with insufficient evidence, leading to acquittals and withdrawals of charges. See *OTP Weekly Briefing: Issue # 137*, OFFICE OF THE PROSECUTOR (ICC, the Hague, Netherlands) (Mar. 1–11, 2013), http://www.icc-cpi.int/iccdocs/otp/wb/OTP-Briefing-1-11-March-2013-137.pdf.

The Archipelago and the Wheel

The Universal Jurisdiction and the
International Criminal Court Regimes

Máximo Langer

The objectives of international criminal law combine traditional goals of criminal justice (retribution, advancing international social norms, and deterrence) with transitional justice goals (establishing a historical record of atrocities, providing a voice to victims, and reestablishing the rule of law).[1] Individual states exercising universal jurisdiction and the International Criminal Court (ICC) are the two permanent criminal law regimes available to advance these goals if no territorial state or other state with a relevant link to core international crimes prosecutes such crimes or pursues a legitimate noncriminal approach to the situation.[2]

Despite the unique function of these regimes in the enforcement of core international crimes—that is, crimes against humanity, genocide, and certain war crimes—the Office of the Prosecutor (OTP) of the ICC has paid limited attention to the relationship between the ICC and universal jurisdiction. This relationship, moreover, remains undertheorized in the literature surrounding international criminal law. To help fill these lacunae, this chapter proposes a theoretical framework to analyze what the relationship between these two regimes should be. The core argument in support of this framework is that, all else being equal, the ICC enjoys a greater degree of state consent and political, procedural, rational, and functional legitimacy than universal jurisdiction domestic statutes and proceedings. This higher level of legitimacy in these respects results from a variety of factors: more than 120 states have explicitly accepted the jurisdiction of the ICC over their territory and nationals; the Court has allowed for wider participation in the drafting of its constitutive instruments and is more accountable to the international community; a large number of world viewpoints participate in making its decisions; and it better communicates to the defendant and the world that core international crimes affect the community of states and all human beings. This higher level of legitimacy is sustained regardless of the conception of international law and international institutions adopted, including statism, cosmopolitan democracy, natural law, global administrative law, and cosmopolitan constitutionalism.

Once the components of this theoretical framework are established, I analyze three central issues in the relationship between these two legal regimes. First, I maintain that despite the ICC's higher level of legitimacy, universal jurisdiction still has a significant role in prosecuting core international crimes. Universal jurisdiction can advance the goals of international criminal law and finds a legal basis under customary international law, and a substantial portion of states and global civil society actors have embraced universal jurisdiction claims over core international crimes. In addition, prosecutions under universal jurisdiction generally meet international due process standards and are subject to informal accountability checks that prevent abuse.

Second, I examine the relationship between the two legal regimes in practice. Since the ICC Statute was adopted or entered into force, the number of statutes incorporating universal jurisdiction have probably increased, while the number of universal jurisdiction complaints has not (substantially) diminished. The vast majority of these universal jurisdiction complaints have concentrated on situations that have not been or are not being investigated by the ICC. Potential shortcomings in the functional legitimacy of universal jurisdiction may have been revealed through this limited role in supplementing the Court's investigations and prosecutions. This chapter identifies reasons for this lack of cooperation and suggests measures that the ICC and its prosecutor could take to encourage prosecutions under universal jurisdiction that better supplement the Court's work.

The final portion of this chapter analyzes whether the principle of complementarity—establishing that domestic prosecutions take precedence over ICC proceedings—should regulate the relationship between the Court and universal jurisdiction. Contrary to the majority of commentators, I maintain that the complementarity principle should not govern this relationship. None of the rationales underpinning this principle favor its application in this area, and the Court holds greater legitimacy than universal jurisdiction statutes and proceedings. Rather, the ICC and the OTP should adopt a weak primacy principle that acknowledges the higher degree of legitimacy displayed by the Court while remaining sufficiently flexible to accommodate those factors that in many circumstances favor prosecutions under universal jurisdiction over those by the ICC.

As a preface to this chapter's argument, I briefly review the universal jurisdiction and ICC regimes before turning to an analysis of these topics.

Two International Criminal Law Regimes

Under universal jurisdiction, any state may prosecute and try core international crimes without any territorial, personal, or national interest link to the crime in question when it was committed.[3] Instead, the jurisdictional claim is typically based on the nature of the crime. The classic crime prosecuted with universal jurisdiction is piracy. Piracy is committed on the high seas beyond states' territorial reach, and each state has an interest in unhindered maritime travel and commerce, so any state that arrests pirates may try them.[4]

The rationale for exercising universal jurisdiction over crimes against humanity, genocide, and war crimes is different from the rationale for piracy and relies on two sets of arguments that can be presented alternatively or in combination. First, these crimes are generally committed by or with the consent of state officials. A state thus waives its sovereignty over these crimes when its officials commit them or acquiesce in their commission.[5] Second, these crimes affect humanity as a whole,[6] for a variety of reasons that may be presented individually or in combination because they are committed against groups of people, are widespread, attack human diversity, show a serious failure of the state system to protect basic human rights, or dehumanize victims in particular ways. Since these crimes affect the entirety of humanity, any state may assert jurisdiction over them.[7] While states have claimed universal jurisdiction over the crime of piracy for more than two centuries, the exercise of universal jurisdiction over core international crimes is essentially a twentieth-century phenomenon that reflects a growing commitment to the protection of human rights and the humanization of armed conflict.[8]

The universal jurisdiction regime for core international crimes does not have its own institutional infrastructure. Rather, it relies on individual states' domestic institutional apparatus—police, prosecutors, defense counsel, courts, and prisons. Moreover, this regime lacks an institutional center because no state may formally claim a distinctive role. In this sense, universal jurisdiction can be conceptualized as an international archipelago of national legal institutions.

The tectonic structure of this archipelago is constituted by a set of distinct substantive, jurisdictional, and procedural rules—accompanied by theoretical justifications, including those outlined previously. These substantive rules include the international definitions of crimes against humanity, genocide, and war crimes laid down by treaties and customary international law,[9] together with general doctrines such as personal immunity.[10] The jurisdictional rules are derived from treaties, customary rules, and general principles of law that support universal jurisdiction claims. The procedural rules include the right to a fair trial.[11] States, policymakers, and scholars continue to debate whether other rules such as those concerning subsidiarity,[12] double criminality,[13] double jeopardy,[14] functional immunity,[15] and the defendants' presence on the prosecuting state's territory[16] should also regulate states' exercise of universal jurisdiction.

The Rome Statute, adopted in July 1998 and ratified by over 120 states, created the ICC and conferred it with jurisdiction over crimes against humanity, genocide, and certain war crimes.[17] The ICC has jurisdiction over ratifying states' territory (territorial principle) and nationals (active nationality principle) and states that have accepted the ICC's jurisdiction with respect to specific crimes.[18] The ICC's jurisdiction is thus based on the voluntary participation by states in the ICC regime. Under chapter VII of the United Nations Charter, the U.N. Security Council may also refer situations anywhere in the world to the ICC—including situations involving crimes committed by the nationals, or within the territory, of nonparty states.[19] In these cases, the ICC's jurisdiction derives from the U.N. Security Council's powers under chapter VII to adopt measures to maintain and restore international peace and security.[20]

Unlike the universal jurisdiction regime, the ICC has its own designated institutional apparatus, including an OTP with investigators; Pre-Trial, Trial, and Appeal Chambers; counsel to represent defendants or victims; and other administrative units.[21] The legal regime of the ICC, however, also includes the domestic legal institutions of state parties, which have their own functions to perform. The principle of complementarity integrates the ICC and ratifying states' legal institutions into a single regime by enabling the institutions of these states to take the lead in investigating and prosecuting international crimes.[22] The ICC Statute and other basic documents of the Court provide a common framework of substantive, jurisdictional, and procedural rules for state parties to follow.[23]

While universal jurisdiction represents an archipelago, the ICC regime is akin to a wheel—the hub composed of the ICC's institutions, with a unique role within the regime, and the spokes consisting of the various states' legal systems that retain primary responsibility for preventing and prosecuting core international crimes, at least when committed within their territories or by their nationals.

The Greater Structural Legitimacy of the ICC

Any sound analysis of the proper relationship between universal jurisdiction and the ICC must have its foundation in an explicit or implicit understanding of their relative legitimacy.[24] Yet, despite these legal regimes' distinct roles in prosecuting international crimes, their relative legitimacy has received scant attention from international criminal law policy makers and scholars.[25] The few commentators who have analyzed the two regimes' comparative legitimacy have mostly fallen into one of two camps.

According to one position, ICC and universal jurisdiction are equally legitimate to try core international crimes where due process standards are met.[26] However, provided that due process standards are equally satisfied, I argue that the ICC has a higher degree of legitimacy to try international crimes than does universal jurisdiction.

According to the other position, the ICC enjoys greater legitimacy, albeit for different reasons than those I advance. In general, members of this camp consider that the ICC's superior legitimacy derives from its characteristics: the Court would be less political or slanted against leaders of developing countries than prosecutions under universal jurisdiction while being more respectful of due process and more effective in bringing defendants to justice.[27] However, these criteria do not provide a solid basis for a theoretical framework determining what the relationship between the two regimes should be.

These criteria are mostly contingent as opposed to structural. In other words, how politically motivated, slanted against leaders of developing countries, respectful of due process, and effective in bringing defendants to justice these legal regimes are primarily depends on contingencies—including the identity of individual prosecutors and judges, which states bring prosecutions by exercising universal jurisdiction, and the variable extent of support obtained by the ICC or universal jurisdiction prosecutions from states. Where differences exist in the regimes' designs, such differences do not clearly indicate which regime will perform better based on these four criteria.

In addition, although it is too early in the ICC's life to reach a definitive conclusion, the existing record does not show substantial differences between the regimes with respect to these four criteria. First, even if political incentives differ under the two regimes, such considerations may equally affect prosecutorial decisions.[28] Second, universal jurisdiction trials have generally been true adjudicatory processes, while the ICC has not been free of criticism on its due process standards.[29] Third, both types of prosecutions have tended to focus on politically weak defendants, and the ICC has investigated situations only in Africa.[30] Finally, the ICC has formally charged several defendants who remain at large, including Joseph Kony, leader of the Lord's Resistance Army, and the president of Sudan, Omar al-Bashir.

However, assuming that these legal regimes cannot be clearly distinguished on these criteria, I maintain that the ICC does indeed enjoy more legitimacy than universal jurisdiction, but for reasons other than those proposed by other scholars. I contend that the ICC has greater *state consent, political, procedural, rational,* and *functional* legitimacy than universal jurisdiction statutes and proceedings. This makes the ICC more legitimate relative to universal jurisdiction under any of the principal theories of international law and institutions, including statist conceptions of the international order, different strands of cosmopolitan democracy, natural law, global administrative law, and cosmopolitan constitutionalism.

The ICC has greater legitimacy based on state consent—what I term state consent legitimacy—because it was created by a treaty that state parties voluntarily ratified, thereby explicitly accepting the Court's jurisdiction over their territory and nationals.[31] Statist conceptions of international law value consent by states as it respects state sovereignty, or people's self-determination.[32] Consent to an international organization given by the territorial or active nationality state thus legitimizes this organization's prosecution and adjudication of international crimes allegedly committed in the state's territory or by its nationals.[33] The consent of this state may also provide legitimacy to an international organization or legal regime, even according to nonstatist conceptions of the international order. For example, different strands of cosmopolitanism reject the state as the sole source of legitimacy in the international order but affirm that certain decisions are still best made at the national level.[34] Through state consent, the national level may legitimate the participation of an international organization in the decision-making process by conveying that participation is welcome.[35]

In contrast, universal jurisdiction is subject to weaker state-based consent. Treaty law contains a limited legal basis for universal jurisdiction— there is no international convention on crimes against humanity,[36] and the

Genocide Convention does not explicitly require or authorize the exercise of universal jurisdiction over this crime.[37] Only the Geneva Conventions of 1949 and Additional Protocol I provide a textual basis for exercising universal jurisdiction over a subset of war crimes—that is, over grave breaches of these conventions[38]—and some authorities seem to question even this interpretation.[39]

The most authoritative supporters of universal jurisdiction over core international crimes have therefore placed its principal legal basis in customary international law. The thrust of this argument is that customary international law does not contain a prohibition against exercising universal jurisdiction over these crimes. According to the *Lotus* principle, everything that is not forbidden is allowed by international law. It follows that universal jurisdiction is legal under customary international law.[40] However, even if this argument for universal jurisdiction's legality is accepted,[41] customary rules do not require the consent of every state to become legally valid. Thus, a state that never consented to a rule allowing universal jurisdiction may nevertheless find crimes committed in its territory or by its nationals subjected to such a prosecution.[42]

The ICC also displays greater political, procedural, rational, and functional legitimacy in comparison to universal jurisdiction statutes and proceedings. My starting point for this claim is the exchanges between Hannah Arendt and Karl Jaspers on the Eichmann case and the Holocaust. Arendt and Jaspers argued that "the crime against Jews was also a crime against mankind" and that "consequently the verdict can be handed down only by a court of justice *representing* all mankind."[43] It was for an international criminal court, not an Israeli court, to pass judgment on Adolf Eichmann.[44] I assume that the term *representation* is relevant in this context. This term must be unpacked to illuminate the ways in which the ICC affords greater representation to the community of states and all human beings and why this confers more legitimacy on the Court—issues that Arendt and Jaspers barely addressed. In addition, I assume that it is also necessary to move beyond this term, as *representation* does not fully exhaust the array of possible considerations concerning the legitimacy of international criminal institutions.

A first sense in which the ICC is more representative is that it has offered greater opportunities for the participation of and is more accountable to the community of states and global civil society than universal jurisdiction statutes and prosecutions. Under statist conceptions of the international order, the more participatory and accountable international regimes and organizations are with respect to the community of states that created them, the greater *political legitimacy* they carry.[45] In a political community constituted by equal states, each state would hold an equal political right to participate in deciding which crimes are international and the requirements that should apply to the prosecution of these crimes. In addition, states have the right to hold enforcers of these crimes accountable to ensure that they are responsive to concerns of the members of this community.[46] Under cosmopolitan democracy, the same idea would apply, with the exception that not (only) states but (also) all human beings and other entities or groups comprise the international community.[47] Finally, certain conceptions of international institutions—such as strands of global administrative law and cosmopolitan constitutionalism— emphasize that these institutions, regardless of their political origins, must meet certain procedural requirements. They must afford persons affected by the institutions' decisions the opportunity to participate in their proceedings and grant such persons the power to hold the institutions accountable.[48] By this reasoning, given that international criminal law institutions arguably affect all states and all human beings, the greater participation and accountability these institutions provide to states and human beings, the more *procedural legitimacy* they carry.[49]

The ICC regime has offered a higher level of participation for and accountability to the community of states and global civil society. First, a large section of the community of states and global civil society drafted and brought into effect the ICC Statute and other relevant ICC documents. Second, the community of states and global civil society retain both formal and informal mechanisms to hold the Court accountable. More than 160 states and numerous nongovernmental organizations (NGOs) and other members of global civil society participated in the drafting of the ICC Statute.[50] In addition, more than 120 states have ratified the ICC Statute.[51] These state parties may amend the ICC Statute, Rules of Procedure and Evidence, and Elements of Crimes. Among other powers, states parties appoint the key ICC officials, including the prosecutor and judges, remove these officials under certain circumstances, and contribute to and control the Court's budget.[52] To a certain extent, the ICC is also accountable to all U.N. member states in that the U.N. Security Council may refer situations and cases to the Court or defer them.[53]

Furthermore, the ICC is more transparent to states, media, NGOs, activist and expert networks, and other domestic and global groups and is thus accountable to a broader swath of the community of states and global civil society than are universal jurisdiction prosecutions. The Court works in both English and French and has four other official languages—Arabic,

Chinese, Russian, and Spanish.[54] This alone makes its documents and proceedings more globally accessible to a wider array of people. In addition,
the ICC's work is closely followed by a large group of media, NGOs, governments, and scholars from around the world. Experts from many countries are also available to explain to domestic constituencies how the ICC
regime works.

In contrast, prosecutors and judges in universal jurisdiction proceedings try international crimes by applying domestic statutes enacted by domestic authorities, are appointed and removed according to the domestic
regulations, and receive salaries and budgets determined by their state. In
addition, universal jurisdiction prosecutions are usually conducted in the
language of the domestic legal system by prosecutors and courts that in
most cases are less transparent than the ICC and follow procedures and
rules that are often obscure or unknown to an international audience.[55]

A second sense in which the ICC is more representative of the international community is that a larger number of world viewpoints participate
in formulating the ICC's decisions than in universal jurisdiction decisions,
thereby providing more *rational legitimacy* to the Court.[56] This type of
representativeness is important because the more relevant viewpoints participate or are considered in the process of adjudicating, the greater likelihood that the decision will be perceived as impartial or valid by the relevant community—here, the community of states and/or all human
beings.[57] This argument works independently of the various conceptions
of international law and international institutions—that is, despite variations of the relevant community under each of these conceptions.[58]

The practice of the ICC incorporates more world viewpoints on various grounds. First, ICC judges are nationals of states parties from different
geographical regions. Second, no two judges may be nationals of the same
state.[59] Third, in selecting judges, state parties must consider the need for
members of the Court to fairly and equitably represent gender and the
world's principal legal systems and geographical regions.[60] Finally, the
OTP, Chambers, and other units within the ICC also employ staff from
around the world. In contrast, universal jurisdiction prosecutions are pursued and adjudicated by officials residing within a single state.[61]

Finally, the Court both literally and metaphorically embodies and performs the community of states and all human beings better in comparison
to universal jurisdiction prosecutions. This affords the ICC greater *functional legitimacy* through communicating to the defendant and the world
that core international crimes are not ordinary domestic crimes and that
their commission affects the community of states and all human be-

ings—by itself advancing an international social norm against the commission of these crimes.[62] Once again, this argument is sustainable regardless of which conception of the international order and international crimes is applied, assuming it is accepted that a goal of international criminal law is to advance a global social norm against the commission of these crimes.

The ICC better performs and embodies the global community because state officials, individuals, and organizations from across the world have jointly participated in the drafting and ratification of the ICC Statute and other relevant instruments as well as prosecuting, defending, and adjudicating ICC cases. The nature of this performance and embodiment is readily apparent to observers: ICC policymakers, prosecutors, defense attorneys, judges, and other staff members come from all corners of the globe and present widely diverse ethnicities, appearances, languages, and accents. In contrast, while universal jurisdiction prosecutions and trials may be carried out on behalf of the international community, they tend to look and sound domestic.

My claims in this section are comparative, not absolute. I have not maintained that the ICC optimally meets state consent, political, procedural, rational, and functional requirements of legitimacy under any ideal theory of legitimacy. I contend only that the ICC displays greater legitimacy than universal jurisdiction based on these criteria and that therefore, all else being equal, the Court is more legitimate.

In addition, these four legitimacy arguments are supported by or compatible with all major theories of international law, international regimes, and international institutions. Rather than taking sides among these competing theories, I have articulated arguments that contribute to an overlapping consensus on the higher structural legitimacy of the ICC. In this sense, this chapter's framework aids analysis of the relationship between the ICC and universal jurisdiction regardless which theory is adopted.

The Value of Universal Jurisdiction after the Creation of the ICC

Having explained the ICC's higher level of legitimacy relative to universal jurisdiction, I now analyze three issues in the relationship between these two legal regimes: first, whether the ICC and universal jurisdiction are mutually exclusive; second, what role universal jurisdiction has assumed in practice vis-à-vis the ICC; and finally, which legal regime—ICC or universal jurisdiction—deserves priority if a jurisdictional conflict arises. This section addresses the first of these issues.

As previously noted, long before the creation of the ICC, Arendt and Jaspers claimed that the nature of Eichmann's crimes meant that he should have been prosecuted and punished not by Israel but by an international criminal court or some other institution representing the entirety of humanity.[63] Since the establishment of the Court, some commentators and policymakers have argued that universal jurisdiction over core international crimes should simply cease to exist now that the ICC is functioning. This argument is grounded in the relative greater legitimacy of the ICC— though for reasons different from those advanced here.[64] I maintain that universal jurisdiction continues to have a role after the creation of the ICC because although it has less legitimacy, universal jurisdiction statutes and proceedings meet a minimum threshold of functional, political, and due process requirements of legitimacy.[65]

Jurisdictional Gaps as Well as Institutional and Political Constraints of the ICC Regime

A first argument against abolishing universal jurisdiction over core international crimes is that it retains sufficient functional legitimacy because, in many cases, it remains the only available mechanism to advance the objectives of international criminal law. Substantial jurisdictional gaps in addition to institutional and political constraints within the ICC regime may, either de jure or de facto, prevent the Court from prosecuting international crimes that otherwise should be prosecuted. In such situations, if the territorial state or another state with a relevant link does not prosecute the international crimes in question—or implement a legitimate alternative noncriminal response to these crimes or mass atrocities—universal jurisdiction remains the sole permanent enforcement mechanism available to advance the goals of international criminal law.

As for the jurisdictional gaps within the ICC regime, the Court's personal jurisdiction is generally limited to alleged perpetrators who commit core international crimes in the territory of state parties or who are nationals of state parties.[66] This limitation means that there are, at present, about seventy states whose territories are beyond the ICC's jurisdiction. Although this figure may decrease, it is unlikely to reach zero or to include powerful states such as China, India, Russia, and the United States in the foreseeable future.

The sole exceptions to these jurisdictional limitations are cases referred by the U.N. Security Council to the ICC, which may include crimes committed anywhere and by anyone.[67] However, the U.N. Security Council frequently deadlocks over how to address specific situations, given that its five permanent members have varying global geopolitical interests and have veto power to block resolutions.

When the ICC does have jurisdiction over a case, institutional constraints and political incentives may prevent the court and its prosecutor from investigating and prosecuting certain crimes. The interaction between the International Criminal Tribunal for Rwanda (ICTR) and universal jurisdiction provides an example of this phenomenon in a different context. The U.N. Security Council created the ICTR and gave it jurisdiction over crimes against humanity, genocide, and war crimes committed in 1994 in the territory of Rwanda or by Rwandans in neighboring states.[68] In addition to jurisdiction over the genocide and other mass atrocities committed by extremist Hutus against Tutsis and moderate Hutus, the ICTR has had jurisdiction over any international crimes committed by the Rwandan Patriotic Front (RPF), which defeated the extremist Hutu government and remains in power today.

However, despite allegations that RPF members committed a number of international crimes, the ICTR has never brought formal charges against any of them.[69] In fact, when the Office of the Prosecutor of the ICTR commenced investigations into some of these allegations, the Rwandan government threatened to withdraw any support for ICTR investigations. Because of the prosecution's reliance on the cooperation of the Rwandan government to investigate and try cases against extremist Hutus who participated in the genocide, this threatened withdrawal created strong institutional constraints and political incentives for ICTR prosecutors not to bring charges against RPF members.[70]

Nonetheless, two prosecutions under universal jurisdiction provided alternative forums for the investigation of these allegations and endeavored to overcome institutional and political hurdles. The first was the Belgian investigation of Rwandan president Paul Kagamé, which was subsequently closed after Belgium restricted its universal jurisdiction regulations in 2003.[71] The second is the Spanish investigation of crimes against humanity, genocide, and war crimes committed by RPF members. A Spanish investigating judge collected evidence and issued an incriminating decision against more than forty individuals, detailing various allegations and supporting evidence.[72]

Universal jurisdiction prosecutions have the potential to play a similar role in cases formally under the jurisdiction of the ICC that should be prosecuted to advance the objectives of international criminal law but have not been as a consequence of the ICC's jurisdictional gaps or institutional and political constraints. The concurrent jurisdiction, or "jurisdictional redundancy," between universal jurisdiction and the ICC enables the former to fill these gaps.[73]

The Limited Capacity of the ICC and the Goals of International Criminal Law

A second reason for continuing prosecutions under universal jurisdiction is that even in those situations in which legal, institutional, and political constraints do not preclude prosecutions, the OTP can prosecute only a small group of defendants. The ICC may thus have limited ability to advance its goals.[74] In such situations, universal jurisdiction prosecutions may have functional legitimacy because they can advance these goals.

While, in general, crimes against humanity, genocide, and war crimes are committed by hundreds or thousands of perpetrators who are members of states or other organizations, the ICC has only eighteen judges total at the pretrial, trial, and appellate levels, its proceedings are expensive, and it has jurisdiction over situations occurring worldwide.[75] Even if the ICC concentrated on one situation of mass atrocity among the many potential candidates, it could prosecute only a handful of perpetrators.

To put this in perspective, compare the work of the ICC with that of the International Criminal Tribunal for the Former Yugoslavia (ICTY) and the ICTR. While the ICTY and ICTR indicted 161 and 92 individuals respectively for crimes committed in the former Yugoslavia and Rwanda (or by Rwandans in neighboring states), as of December 5, 2012, the ICC had issued arrest warrants or summons to appear against the following numbers of individuals in the situations in which it has opened investigations: Darfur, Sudan, 7; Democratic Republic of the Congo (DRC), 6; Kenya, 6; Uganda, 5; Libya, 3; Côte d'Ivoire, 2; Central African Republic, 1.[76] It is politically and practically infeasible for the ICC to greatly increase its capacity in the near future, given that states parties have been reluctant to approve increases in its annual budget—and that some have resisted any increase at all. If the Court did increase its capacity—by a factor of ten, for example—it would still be able to try only a fraction of those who commit core international crimes. These limitations have justifiably led the OTP to focus on "those who bear the greatest responsibility, such as the leaders of the State or organization allegedly responsible for those crimes."[77]

This low prosecution rate may jeopardize the Court's ability to fulfill its stated goals, which include traditional goals of punishment, such as retribution, spreading or reinforcing a social norm against the commission of core international crimes, and deterrence.[78] From the perspective of retribution, justice would in principle require that every participant in an international crime be punished. It is reasoned that even if the top leaders who order or unleash the commission of these crimes may be more blameworthy—and should thus be subjected to stricter sentences where possible—it would still be hard to justify why chain commanders and actual perpetrators should remain unpunished, absent consequentialist considerations that may be relevant in specific cases.[79]

As for inculcating social norms, it could be contended that punishing top leaders is sufficient to establish or reinforce an international social norm against the commission of core international crimes. But although punishing top leaders is important, it is inadequate for establishing all the necessary norms in light of the typical context in which these crimes take place. As Arendt indicated in her analysis of the Eichmann trial, one of the characteristics of the mass commission of international crimes is that many participants may be ordinary citizens who instead of hating the victims or having evil personalities are responding to the norms and incentives of the state or organization that sponsors or consents to the atrocities.[80] Prosecuting and punishing chain commanders and direct perpetrators is one method for reminding individuals in these positions that international law also applies to them and for fostering their critical judgment against such official or organizational policies.

As to deterrence, it is empirically unclear whether the threat of international criminal punishment affects the behavior of heads of states or organizations and other participants in crime.[81] However, if the threat of punishment did affect their behavior, deterring chain commanders and direct perpetrators in addition to top leaders would create additional disincentives and coordination problems within the state or organization that may prevent international crimes.[82]

Aside from the traditional goals of punishment, the ICC in particular and international criminal law in general may seek to promote the goals of transitional justice by providing a mechanism for victims to be heard and establishing a historical record of the atrocities.[83] Arguably punishing those most responsible is sufficient to accomplish these purposes, given that their trials would sufficiently document the international crimes sponsored by the state or organization. However, in practice, contemporary international criminal trials have faced difficulties in trying leaders for all the atrocities that took place within a certain territory or situation.

The death of Slobodan Milošević during his trial testifies to these challenges, with later international prosecutions taking note of these difficulties.[84] At the ICC, prosecutions have concentrated on only a portion of the crimes alleged against defendants.[85] While limiting the scope of trials against the most responsible is an understandable prosecutorial strategy as it restricts the complexity of cases, this strategy does not represent all of the victims or provide a complete historical record.

Universal jurisdiction prosecutions can thus support the ICC's efforts to advance both the traditional goals of criminal justice and transitional justice.

The Legality and Political Legitimacy of Universal Jurisdiction

A third reason for maintaining the universal jurisdiction regime as a supplement to the ICC is that universal jurisdiction over core international crimes has sufficient political legitimacy. This legitimacy arises from the large portion of states and global civil society actors embracing universal jurisdiction and from its legality under customary international law.[86] This line of reasoning will be sketched here, as space limitations do not permit a thorough analysis.

Without question, substantial controversy has arisen regarding the legality of universal jurisdiction over core international crimes.[87] However, most of this legal disagreement concerns the legal requirements for the enforcement of universal jurisdiction, not the legality per se of universal jurisdiction claims over these crimes. A crucial distinction must be made between prescriptive and enforcement jurisdiction.[88] In criminal law, prescriptive jurisdiction refers to a state's authority to apply its criminal law to certain types of conduct, generally through legislation. Enforcement jurisdiction refers to a state's authority to apply its criminal law to particular persons—that is, to prosecute, try, and eventually punish specific individuals for violating the state's criminal law.[89]

Traditional jurisdictional principles—territoriality, active nationality, passive personality, protectiveness, and universality—refer to prescriptive jurisdiction. For example, when a state invokes the territorial principle for certain crimes, this state is declaring that all conduct fitting into the definition of these crimes that takes place within its territory is subject to that state's punishment. If an individual leaves the state's territory after committing one of these crimes inside that territory, the territorial principle still applies—the criminal law of this state is applicable to the crime. However, the departure of this individual from the state's territory after committing the crime may undermine the state's enforcement jurisdiction—in other words, it may frustrate the prosecution, trial, and punishment of this individual for the commission of the crime. For example, if the state in question does not allow trials in absentia, it will not prosecute or punish the individual unless or until the arrest can be carried out.

Under universal jurisdiction, any state in the world may prosecute certain crimes, even without a territorial, personal, or national interest link to the crime when it was committed.[90] As a jurisdictional principle, universal jurisdiction refers to prescriptive jurisdiction. By way of example, international law permits all states to invoke universal jurisdiction regarding the crime of piracy. Any state may apply its criminal laws to conduct that fits the crime of piracy, even though the relevant conduct did not take place in its territory or on a vessel sailing under its flag, was not committed by or against its nationals, and did not affect its national interests. Where a state claims prescriptive universal jurisdiction over piracy, that state may limit its exercise of enforcement jurisdiction over acts of piracy with certain preconditions—such as the ability to arrest the defendant.

In the case of the core international crimes—crimes against humanity, genocide, and certain war crimes—legal disagreement centers on enforcement, not prescriptive, jurisdiction.[91] There are strong arguments that any state has authority under customary international law to invoke prescriptive universal jurisdiction over core international crimes for several reasons.[92]

First, these crimes are usually considered to be customary international law crimes—that is, crimes established by customary international law.[93] Though it does not necessarily follow that customary international law also allows the exercise of prescriptive universal jurisdiction over them, this position is a small logical step, especially if core international crimes are considered not simply as customary international law crimes but *ius cogens* crimes.[94]

Second, numerous states have passed legislation making their criminal law applicable to crimes against humanity, genocide, and/or certain war crimes based on prescriptive universal jurisdiction—including states that have protested the exercise of universal jurisdiction in individual cases.[95] The passing of universal jurisdiction legislation by such a large number of states may reflect state practice and *opinio juris* as well as political support for universal jurisdiction over core international crimes.[96]

Third, hundreds of individuals have been investigated and been subject to formal proceedings for at least one of these core international crimes, totally or partially on the basis of prescriptive universal jurisdiction.[97] In addition, by the end of 2009, twenty-seven individuals had been tried for these crimes, at least partially based on prescriptive universal jurisdiction under customary international law.[98] Decisions by state authorities to investigate cases, open formal proceedings, and try core international crimes based on prescriptive universal jurisdiction evidences evolving state practice and *opinio juris*. This state practice, coupled with the support and participation of global civil society in many of these complaints and proceedings, also indicates substantial political approval for the exercise of universal jurisdiction over core international crimes.

Though they do not always adequately distinguish between prescriptive and enforcement jurisdiction, many authorities agree that the exercise of prescriptive universal jurisdiction over one or more of the core international crimes is legal under customary international law.[99] The legal disagreement over universal jurisdiction has mostly concerned the special conditions required for exercising enforcement jurisdiction in universal jurisdiction cases. In this context, international judges and commentators, among other authorities, have reasoned that under customary international law, enforcement jurisdiction over core international crimes may not be exercised unless the defendant has a relevant link with the prosecuting state—such as being physically present in or becoming a citizen of the prosecuting state after committing the crime.[100]

The debate over enforcement jurisdiction as part of universal jurisdiction is beyond the scope of this chapter. Provided that the legality of prescriptive universal jurisdiction under customary international law is accepted for the reasons given here, there is no legal justification for eliminating universal jurisdiction. To the extent that customary international law is formed through state practice and *opinio juris,* universal jurisdiction also has sufficient political legitimacy—a large number of states have accepted its existence and a substantial portion of global civil society supports universal jurisdiction claims over core international crimes.

Analysis of Possible Objections

Even if the arguments I have advanced are accepted, could universal jurisdiction interfere with the work of the ICC, doing more harm than good for international criminal law? There are at a minimum three potential concerns in this respect, but I believe that the problems highlighted by these concerns have been overstated because universal jurisdiction prosecutions have generally met international due process standards and because the international community has subjected such prosecutions to informal accountability mechanisms.

The first of these concerns derives from claims by critics of international criminal law that the ICC and universal jurisdiction rely on a dangerous idealism that disregards the realities of international and domestic power structures and is likely to do more harm than good.[101] According to these critics, by ignoring the international power structure, prosecutions under these legal regimes could seriously disrupt international relations and even lead to war. By disregarding domestic power structures, these regimes may jeopardize peace agreements or states transitioning to democracy by prosecuting those who can guarantee and enforce such transitions and agreements. Under this line of reasoning, universal jurisdiction compounds the threats that the ICC already poses to international relations and to domestic transitions to peace and democracy.[102]

However, although these risks are substantial in theory, these critics have overlooked existing political safeguards that make the risks unlikely in practice. The same criticisms have been applied to the ICC. In discussing political checks and consequentialist considerations within the ICC regime, both supporters and critics of the Court have tended to concentrate on the power of the U.N. Security Council to defer investigations or prosecutions in addition to the requirement that the ICC prosecutor must consider the "interests of justice" when deciding whether to launch investigations and prosecutions.[103] Most supporters and critics, however, have tended to neglect an even more crucial safeguard—that is, the ICC does not have a monopoly on force anywhere in the world, not even in its seat, the Hague.[104] For all its investigative and coercive measures, the Court relies on the cooperation of states.[105] As a result, states' political branches have formal and informal ways to ignore or neutralize measures taken by the ICC with which those states' disagree.[106] Thus, in practice, the ICC regime provides for political and consequentialist considerations and restraints.

It could be reasoned that, even if these checks help prevent the realization of these potential dangers within the ICC regime, such dangers are more serious in the universal jurisdiction regime. First, the decentralized nature of the universal jurisdiction regime makes it harder to steer in any particular direction. Second, states exercising universal jurisdiction have a monopoly on force within their territories. However, as I have established elsewhere, both supporters and critics of universal jurisdiction overlook the roles that the executive and legislative branches of universal jurisdiction states play in regulating this decentralized regime. By analyzing the asymmetric incentives and disincentives of these political branches, I have demonstrated that in general, universal jurisdiction prosecutions focus on what I have called low-cost defendants—that is, those defendants that no state or only weak states would be willing to protect—about whom the international community has broadly agreed that they may be prosecuted and punished, and in practice universal jurisdiction trials have targeted such defendants.[107] If universal jurisdiction continues in this equilibrium, it is unlikely that these prosecutions would substantially increase the risk of a strong disruption to international relations, judicial chaos, or interference with political solutions to armed conflict and mass atrocities.

The second concern is that states' selection of low-cost defendants may in fact inadvertently harm international criminal law by undermining its rule-of-law nature—that is, the equal application of the law across all cases. Selectivity traditionally has been a challenge for international criminal law, including for the ICC.[108] As already noted, leaving aside referrals by the U.N. Security Council, the Court lacks global jurisdiction, which limits the selection of situations for investigation by the prosecutor. In addition, the ICC's limited resources permit prosecution of a mere handful of defendants, forcing the Court to be extremely selective. Furthermore, the Court's operation requires the economic, logistical, and political support of states. This provides incentives for the Court to concentrate on crimes committed in or by nationals of weak states as opposed to crimes associated with powerful states, on which the ICC depends for most of its economic and political support.

However, this selectivity of universal jurisdiction may alleviate rather than worsen the selectivity challenges faced by the ICC in particular and international criminal law more generally. First, in contrast to the ICC, the universal jurisdiction regime is truly universal. This universality provides reasons to abide by the norms of international criminal law for all individuals, including "high-cost" defendants and those whose states are not parties to the ICC.[109] Furthermore, the prosecution by the universal jurisdiction regime of defendants in situations under investigation by the ICC would alleviate rather than aggravate the selectivity challenges faced by the Court. It is likely that each legal regime will concentrate on different categories of defendants—the ICC on those of higher rank and universal jurisdiction on those of lower rank. I do not intend to suggest that universal jurisdiction is a panacea for the selectivity challenges faced by the ICC and international criminal law. Selectivity is a problem within international criminal law, a consequence of the political and practical obstacles involved in prosecuting core international crimes. My point is that universal jurisdiction is more likely to alleviate than to worsen these selectivity problems.

A third concern surrounding the continuing existence of universal jurisdiction is whether universal jurisdiction increases the politicization of international criminal law, thereby undermining the legitimacy of the whole enterprise.[110] Though the term *politicization* has multiple possible meanings,[111] here the main reservations are that prosecutions under universal jurisdiction fail to respect due process standards and are politically motivated—that is, used to harass or eliminate political or military enemies of prosecuting states. By this argument, such concerns would be more acute in universal jurisdiction prosecutions than for the ICC, because the decentralized character of the former would increase the opportunities for states to use prosecutions for political ends.

Although these concerns warrant consideration, I have shown elsewhere why they have not represented substantial or prevalent challenges for universal jurisdiction.[112] The actual exercise of universal jurisdiction over core international crimes thus far has mainly been a practice of developed Commonwealth and Western European states.[113] In other words, although many states have passed universal jurisdiction legislation covering core international crimes, actual official investigations, formal proceedings, and trials have been overwhelmingly concentrated in developed Western states. Such states typically meet international due process standards and have put in place safeguards against politically motivated uses of criminal justice procedures. Moreover, while other states could commence prosecutions by applying universal jurisdiction, those states most likely to make them political in character in the senses indicated here—authoritarian states—have incentives not to engage in universal jurisdiction prosecutions, which may highlight the state's human rights abuses and have a boomerang effect.[114]

Universal Jurisdiction's Actual Practice in Relation to the ICC

In the previous section, I provided four sets of reasons supporting the continued existence of universal jurisdiction, notwithstanding the ICC's greater structural legitimacy—that is, the higher degree of relative legitimacy of the ICC based on noncontingent factors. I reasoned that universal jurisdiction statutes and prosecutions display sufficient functional legitimacy. In terms of its functional legitimacy, universal jurisdiction could advance the goals of international criminal law by prosecuting cases in situations that the ICC has not investigated (what I term the universal jurisdiction regime's *horizontal supplementarity* to the ICC) or, in situations under investigation by the Court, by prosecuting those cases not prosecuted by the ICC because it chooses to concentrate on other cases arising from the same situation (what I term *vertical supplementarity*). This section analyzes whether the universal jurisdiction regime has fulfilled either or both of these functions.

At the statutory level, states have not generally invoked the ICC regime to justify repealing preexisting universal jurisdiction statutes. In contrast, the number of universal jurisdiction statutes has seemingly increased since the adoption of the ICC Statute in July 1998, with several states passing new universal jurisdiction legislation as part of their domestic implementation of the ICC Statute on the grounds that cooperation with the Court may require the exercise of universal jurisdiction.[115] In addition, those states that have restricted the scope of legislation on universal jurisdiction, such as Belgium and Spain, acted in response to pressure from other states, not because of the ICC regime.[116]

While a good number of yearly data on universal jurisdiction complaints is presently unavailable, particularly prior to 2002, the available data suggest that the creation of the ICC has not (substantially) diminished the total number of universal jurisdiction complaints.[117] According to a global survey I conducted for a broader project on universal jurisdiction, there have been universal jurisdiction complaints—or cases considered by authorities of their own accord, *sua sponte*—against at least 249 individuals, from the entry into force of the ICC Statute on July 1, 2002, until the end of 2009, out of a total of 1,050 universal jurisdiction complaints recorded since 1983.[118]

Turning to an examination of the roles played by the universal jurisdiction regime in relation to the ICC, this survey indicates that from the entry into force of the ICC until 2009, universal jurisdiction complaints almost exclusively concentrated on situations not under investigation by the ICC—the horizontal supplementarity function. In fact, from the more than 200 individuals against whom universal jurisdiction complaints were brought, only 2 individuals, in two different investigations partially relying on universal jurisdiction, were accused of participation in a situation under ICC investigation.[119]

These patterns in universal jurisdiction complaints and cases may be considered problematic. Considering that a foundation for the functional legitimacy of universal jurisdiction is its potential to vertically supplement the Court in advancing its objectives, the nearly absolute lack of universal jurisdiction complaints and cases in situations under investigation by the

ICC may reveal a flaw in the universal jurisdiction regime. In addition, such patterns may suggest that the ICC has been underutilizing a potentially beneficial tool for reaching its goals.

To shed light on these patterns, it could be hypothesized that as an empirical matter, universal jurisdiction cases have not focused on situations under ICC investigation precisely because the Court is handling these situations. According to this hypothesis, when an international criminal authority investigates a situation, victims, NGOs, and domestic authorities will not pursue their own investigations because an international authority already is doing so.

Although legal practitioners involved in universal jurisdiction cases that I interviewed mentioned this hypothesis,[120] the first problem is that it does not explain the pattern of universal jurisdiction cases vis-à-vis the ICTY and the ICTR. In contrast to the ICC, universal jurisdiction cases have vertically supplemented the work of the ad hoc tribunals in substantial numbers. According to this survey, there have been universal jurisdiction complaints or *sua sponte* cases involving 185 individuals from the former Yugoslavia, of whom 8 have been tried. In addition, universal jurisdiction complaints or *sua sponte* cases have arisen regarding 87 Rwandans, of whom 11 have been tried. These numbers are not negligible, considering that as of August 24, 2011, the ICTY had indicted 161 individuals and adjudicated cases against 77, with cases still pending against 35,[121] and the ICTR had indicted 92 individuals, adjudicated 65 cases, and had 11 pending cases.[122]

The second problem is that if this hypothesis is accurate, it would be expected that there are more universal jurisdiction cases in situations under investigation by the ICC than by the ICTY and ICTR, given that the ICC has indicted substantially fewer individuals than those tribunals (a maximum of seven per situation) and thus arguably has less fully addressed these situations. Yet the opposite has been true.

Explaining these case selection patterns in the universal jurisdiction regime would require a rigorous qualitative and quantitative empirical study that I cannot undertake here. Nevertheless, for future study, I suggest three tentative explanations for these varying patterns in universal jurisdiction prosecutions for the ICC and the ICTY and ICTR. These explanations may also suggest ways that the ICC could encourage the universal jurisdiction regime to prosecute cases in situations under investigation by the ICC.

First, with the possible exception of the situations in Darfur and Libya, none of the other six situations under investigation as of March 10, 2013—the Central African Republic, the DRC, Côte d'Ivoire, Kenya, Mali, and

Uganda—have generated the same level of global concern, especially in the main universal jurisdiction states in Europe and the developed Commonwealth, as did the situations in the former Yugoslavia and Rwanda. The violence in the former Yugoslavia constituted the worst mass atrocities committed in Europe since the Second World War and caused high levels of interest and concern in several European countries.[123] In the case of Rwanda, the genocide occurred while atrocities in the former Yugoslavia were still ongoing, helping to generate concern for the even more serious atrocities in an African country. In addition, Belgium and France were directly affected by the Rwandan genocide because their troops were involved, either as U.N. peacekeepers or because they were providing military training and support to the Hutu government.[124]

The level of domestic political concern that the core international crimes generate in states actively exercising universal jurisdiction may or may not reflect the actual gravity of international crimes—the relatively low level for the long-standing conflicts and commission of international crimes in the DRC suggests the latter. Nevertheless, this level of concern is significant as it may help explain which situations are more salient for NGOs and the general public in such states, thus creating incentives for these NGOs and the political branches and prosecutors of these states to present universal jurisdiction complaints and initiate universal jurisdiction prosecutions.[125]

A second basis for case selection patterns in the universal jurisdiction regime has to do with the availability or unavailability of victims, elements of proof, and potential defendants in states exercising universal jurisdiction. Victims may bring universal jurisdiction claims and evidence before domestic authorities. In addition, the work of international NGOs on universal jurisdiction cases is usually triggered by requests from victims or other NGOs originating where the alleged international crimes took place. The presence or residence of defendants in a potential prosecuting state is also important because it is a prerequisite for universal jurisdiction prosecutions in many legal systems.[126]

In this sense, the low level of organization of civil society and weak NGOs in the DRC may, in part, explain the failure of international NGOs to bring universal jurisdiction claims regarding this situation.[127] In addition, the conflicts in the former Yugoslavia and Rwanda brought waves of refugees to Europe and elsewhere in the West, unlike most situations under investigation by the ICC. The absence of defendants located in the territory of potential prosecuting states may also help explain, for example, why participants in international crimes in Darfur have not been prosecuted based on universal jurisdiction despite the international concern that these crimes have generated. Most of these participants have likely had no need to emigrate, given that the regime that allegedly has sponsored the atrocities remains in power.

Finally, the ICTY and the ICTR, together with the U.N. Security Council, have encouraged prosecutions under universal jurisdiction in a way that the ICC thus far has not. For example, the U.N. Security Council issued resolutions encouraging states to prosecute those responsible for the commission of international crimes in the former Yugoslavia and Rwanda.[128] As a consequence, a few states passed special statutes granting their courts universal jurisdiction over ICTY and ICTR crimes or used preexisting statutes to exercise universal jurisdiction.[129]

The ICTY and ICTR also worked with national jurisdictions by "downloading" and "uploading" cases from them in a way that may have encouraged the use of universal jurisdiction.[130] There have been a few universal jurisdiction cases that the ICTY and the ICTR prosecuted but later transferred to national jurisdictions for completion.[131] The ICC has made almost no use of universal jurisdiction in this manner.[132]

These tentative explanations suggest several measures that the OTP of the ICC could explore or expand to foster universal jurisdiction prosecutions where such prosecutions could further the Court's goals. For example, the OTP could try to persuade human rights NGOs and domestic constituencies of the seriousness of past or ongoing international crimes in specific locations or of the need for universal jurisdiction prosecutions in certain situations. The ICC could foster more domestic prosecutions based on territoriality, active nationality, or universal jurisdiction by providing technical support or sharing information and evidence with states.[133] Furthermore, the ICC could encourage domestic prosecutions by interpreting the complementarity principle strictly to render it more difficult for states to refer situations to the Court[134] or by calling on states to exercise universal jurisdiction over specific situations.[135]

In fact, the (further) use of these and similar tools would complement the conception of the prosecutor's role advanced in this collection of essays, according to which the ICC Statute "creates a role for the prosecutor as catalyst and negotiator, authorized and expected to build commitment to the norms and practices of international criminal justice."[136]

Nevertheless, the ICC prosecutor faces greater challenges than did the ICTY or ICTR in encouraging states to exercise universal jurisdiction in particular and to support the work of the Court in general. The U.N. Security Council created the ICTY and ICTR because its permanent members felt obliged to respond to past and ongoing mass atrocities that had already generated great public concern around the world.[137] Thus, some of the world's most powerful states committed themselves to the position that an international criminal law response to these atrocities was appropriate. As a result, powerful states and organizations, among them the European Union and the North Atlantic Treaty Alliance, have been willing and able to use their leverage to ensure that defendants are surrendered and evidence is provided to these tribunals.[138]

In contrast, the ICC responds to situations that took place after the Court's regime came into effect and that may not produce similar levels of concern. It is the first international criminal authority that is not a top-down creation by the U.N. Security Council or the main world powers. Moreover, it must compete with diplomatic approaches to mass atrocities even among those states that support the Court in principle. These variances have meant that the prosecutor virtually has to start from scratch in investigating new situations. To receive logistical and political support, the prosecutor must persuade a sufficiently large number of powerful states that the situation warrants an international response and the sustained mobilization of international resources. The prosecutor must then convince powerful states that a criminal law approach to resolving the situation (as opposed to an exclusively diplomatic approach) would do more good than harm.

This represents one of the main paradoxes of international criminal law. The ICC can be seen as the institutional culmination of the international criminal justice project, yet it faces greater difficulties to overcome before it can successfully advance that project's goals.[139] In the specific case of universal jurisdiction, the ICC requires more assistance from universal jurisdiction prosecutions than do the ICTY or ICTR, given the ICC's permanent character, global reach, and implicit challenge to the world's power structure. However, precisely these features of the ICC make it more difficult and therefore less likely for NGOs and states even to consider supplementing the Court's work through complaints and prosecutions under universal jurisdiction.

Why the ICC Principle of Complementarity Should Not Regulate the Relationship between the Two Regimes

The previous section discussed how the universal jurisdiction regime has assumed only one of two potential roles that supplement the work of the

ICC. Yet if universal jurisdiction prosecutions focused more on situations under investigation by the ICC, one of the central questions sure to arise would be which prosecution should have priority when ICC and universal jurisdiction prosecutions overlap in cases from the same situation. Based on the theoretical framework set forth in this essay, I argue in this section that a weak primacy principle should regulate the relationship between the ICC and universal jurisdiction prosecutions, given the Court's greater legitimacy and that none of the rationales for the complementarity principle apply in this context.

A Contextual and Teleological Interpretation of Article 17 of the ICC Statute

Article 17 of the ICC Statute regulates the relationship between domestic prosecutions and the ICC through the complementarity principle—holding that a case is inadmissible before the ICC if it has been or is being investigated, prosecuted or tried "by a State which has jurisdiction over it."[140] Commentators examining the relationship between prosecutions under universal jurisdiction and those by the Court support the application of this principle of complementarity to universal jurisdiction, at least when the exercise of universal jurisdiction is legal under domestic and international law. In defense of this position, such commentators have argued that the phrase "by a State which has jurisdiction over it" does not distinguish between different types of jurisdiction and thus, under a strict textualist interpretation, includes universal jurisdiction. Some commentators also claim that this interpretation of the complementarity principle would prevent the ICC docket from becoming overloaded.[141] Under this interpretation, as long as the state exercising universal jurisdiction is willing and able to prosecute in earnest, universal jurisdiction should always trump the ICC's jurisdiction.

But this reading of article 17 is questionable when the article is interpreted in its context, as article 31 of the Vienna Convention on the Law of Treaties urges.[142] Under a contextual reading of this article, one can interpret the phrase "a State with jurisdiction over the case" as limited to territorial and active nationality jurisdiction—the two types of jurisdiction established as a general rule elsewhere in the ICC Statute.[143]

More substantively, from a teleological perspective, none of the main rationales for the complementarity principle favor granting priority to universal jurisdiction prosecutions over the ICC. The first rationale for complementarity is that it respects state sovereignty.[144] This applies to crimes that either take place in the territory or are committed by the nationals of a state—uncontroversial bases of jurisdiction grounded in the idea that states have a privileged relationship with their territory and nationals.[145] This reasoning does not apply, however, if an outside state claims jurisdiction over a crime based solely on universal jurisdiction. In fact, as previously discussed, prosecutions under universal jurisdiction are less respectful of other states' sovereignty than are prosecutions by the ICC.

Another rationale for complementarity is that giving priority to states to investigate and prosecute international crimes better advances the objectives of international criminal law, including traditional goals of punishment and transitional justice goals.[146] For example, international crimes generally involve situations of serious or total collapse of the rule of law and are fed by deep political, social, or military conflicts. If domestic prosecutorial authorities and courts are able and willing to impartially investigate the crimes, they are better positioned to reestablish the domestic legal system and provide local constituencies with an authoritative account of the atrocities.

However, this reasoning applies when the prosecutorial authorities and courts of the territorial state address the international crimes, not when an outside state prosecutes them based on universal jurisdiction.[147] In fact, all else being equal, the ICC may be in a better position to advance the traditional goals of punishment, to reestablish the domestic legal system (for example, through positive complementarity),[148] and to provide a credible account of the international crimes because it displays greater relative structural legitimacy.

Another argument for complementarity based on practicality holds that states are better situated to investigate and prosecute international crimes than is the ICC.[149] The line of reasoning is that the territorial—and at times the active nationality—state can more easily gather elements of proof because witnesses and other evidence are available in the state's territory. In contrast, the OTP must investigate from a distance and rely on the cooperation of local authorities to provide evidence to the ICC and to permit the Court's investigators inside the state's territory.

However, once again, this rationale does not apply to prosecutions under universal jurisdiction, which face the same obstacles as the ICC. Indeed, such obstacles may be even more significant in universal jurisdiction prosecutions because those states that ratify the ICC Statute promise to cooperate with the ICC's investigations and the international nature of the ICC may avert potential turf wars with domestic authorities. As a consequence, a territorial state may be more likely to cooperate with the ICC than with a state exercising universal jurisdiction.[150]

A Weak Primacy Principle

There are strong reasons for the principle of complementarity not to govern the relationship between universal jurisdiction and prosecutions by the ICC. Instead, given its superior structural legitimacy—that is, a higher degree of legitimacy based on noncontingent factors—the ICC should adopt a weak primacy principle, thereby granting formal priority over universal jurisdiction prosecutions to the ICC.

Generally, the ICC should defer to universal jurisdiction prosecutions. First, the Court may otherwise discourage states from exercising universal jurisdiction over situations under ICC investigation, which could be detrimental to the Court's ability to advance its goals. Given that there have been almost no prosecutions under universal jurisdiction that support the work of the ICC, this would be especially unwise at present.

Second, adopting a weak primacy principle would acknowledge that there may be situations and cases in which prosecutions under universal jurisdiction are best placed to advance the goals of international criminal law. Previously, I conducted a detailed analysis on why, leaving aside contingent and case-specific considerations, prosecutions by the ICC hold more structural legitimacy in comparison to prosecutions under universal jurisdiction. Nevertheless, in some situations and cases, such contingent and case-specific considerations may outweigh structural reasons to provide greater legitimacy to a universal jurisdiction prosecution. For example, should the defendant, witnesses, or other evidence be available in the state exercising universal jurisdiction, giving priority to this prosecution may be justified for practical reasons. Alternatively, the state exercising universal jurisdiction may have linguistic, cultural, or political links—other than problematic (post)colonial ones—enabling the resulting trial to strongly affect the population of the state in which the atrocities took place and thus better advance international criminal law goals. Or the state exercising universal jurisdiction may be able to deliver justice in a substantially shorter time than the ICC. The prosecutor and the Court should consider such contingent and case-specific factors together with the structural advantages that the ICC provides when determining whether to defer to a domestic prosecution under universal jurisdiction.

Three principal distinctions exist between the proposed weak primacy principle of the ICC and the primacy principles of the ICTY and the ICTR.

First, this weak primacy principle would apply solely to domestic prosecutions under universal jurisdiction, not to territorial or active nationality prosecutions. Second, the weak primacy principle would be more limited than at the ICTY and ICTR by acknowledging that in many circumstances, universal jurisdiction prosecutions are better placed than an international authority to advance international criminal law goals. Finally, this weak primacy principle would not necessarily require the ICC solely to target the most senior and culpable defendants, while universal jurisdiction prosecutions target the rest—as has been the case at the ICTY and ICTR. Instead, the prosecutor and the Court would make determinations on a case-by-case basis, weighing the categories of factors as articulated in this chapter. However, despite these differences, these principles are also similar in that proceedings under universal jurisdiction would not automatically trump proceedings before an international authority.

This weak primacy principle could be implemented in two ways. First, it could be implemented informally by the OTP, which could convey to domestic authorities that may exercise universal jurisdiction any OTP's preference to prosecute a case in certain circumstances. This method would be most easily employed for those states (for example, Belgium and Germany) that, contrary to the position of the majority of commentators, give priority to ICC prosecutions over their own universal jurisdiction prosecutions.[151] Alternatively to, or in conjunction with, this informal implementation, this principle could be formally applied through adopted prosecutorial guidelines or a court decision which interprets Article 17 of the ICC Statute as not applicable to prosecutions under universal jurisdiction.

Conclusion

This chapter analyzes the relationship between prosecutions of core international crimes under universal jurisdiction and by the ICC. Prosecutions before the ICC display a higher level of state consent, political, procedural, rational, and functional legitimacy than do universal jurisdiction prosecutions. Nonetheless, universal jurisdiction prosecutions continue to play a supplementary role in the enforcement of core international crimes as a consequence of the minimum requirements of legitimacy met by universal jurisdiction, coupled with the jurisdictional gaps and institutional, political, and resource constraints of the ICC, which may limit the Court's ability to advance the goals of international criminal law.

Since the entry into force of the ICC Statute, prosecutions under universal jurisdiction have taken virtually no action in situations under investigation by the Court. This chapter explores potential reasons for such a pattern of universal jurisdiction prosecutions and suggests tools for use by the ICC to change this pattern. Simultaneously, the chapter identifies the challenges particular to the ICC regime (and not present in the ICTY and the ICTR) that must be surmounted.

Finally, this chapter articulates reasons to reject the application of the ICC's principle of complementarity in the relationship between the two regimes. A weak primacy principle would not discourage prosecutions under universal jurisdiction, which may advance the ICC's goals while recognizing the Court's higher degree of structural legitimacy.

NOTES

For their comments on earlier drafts, I thank Hans Bevers, Alejandro Chehtman, Harlan Cohen, Margaret deGuzman, Joshua Dienstag, Sharon Dolovich, Philip Heymann, David Kaye, Karen Knopp, Catharine MacKinnon, Mark Lewis, Timothy Meyer, Martha Minow, Robert Mnookin, Luis Moreno Ocampo, Julie Rose O'Sullivan, Leila Sadat, Carsten Stahn, Christopher Stone, Cora True-Frost, and Alex Whiting. I also thank the participants in the 2010–11 Third Hoffinger Criminal Justice Forum at NYU School of Law; Martha Minow's workshop, "Prosecution Policies and Strategy at the International Criminal Court" at Harvard Law School; the International Law Colloquium of the University of Georgia Law School; the Guest Lectures Series of the Office of the Prosecutor of the International Criminal Court in the Hague; the 2011 Public International Law and Theory Workshop at the Whitney R. Harris World Law Institute at Washington University School of Law; and the Lecture Series of the University of Buenos Aires School of Law, the DiTella University School of Law, and the Aix-Marseille University School of Law and Political Science. I also thank Caroline E. Burrell and very especially Brian Hutler for their research assistance, the UCLA School of Law Hugh & Hazel Darling Law Library for its research support, and Jacob Chodash, Scott H. Dewey, and Rachel Jones for editing the piece. I completed the research for this essay in the first half of 2012. Afterward, I only revised it and introduced minor updates to it.

    1. For critical analysis of the objectives of international criminal law, *see, e.g.,* MARK A. DRUMBL, ATROCITY, PUNISHMENT, & INTERNATIONAL LAW 149–80 (2007); MARK OSIEL, MASS ATROCITY, COLLECTIVE MEMORY, & THE LAW (1997); RUTI G. TEITEL, TRANSITIONAL JUSTICE (2000).

    2. Other international criminal tribunals have been created through international agreements (e.g., the International Military Tribunal at Nuremberg) or by the U.N. Security Council acting under chapter VII of the U.N. Charter (e.g., the ICTY and the ICTR). However, these tribunals only had a temporary character. On noncriminal responses to mass atrocities, *see, e.g.,* TRUTH V. JUSTICE: THE MORALITY OF TRUTH COMMISSIONS (Robert I. Rotberg & Dennis Thompson eds., 2000); Mnookin, in this volume.

3. *See, e.g.,* RESTATEMENT (THIRD) OF THE FOREIGN RELATIONS LAW OF THE UNITED STATES §§402 & cmts. c–g, 404 & cmts. a–b, 423 (1987).

4. In this sense, pirates are *hostes generis humani* (enemies of humanity). On possible justifications for the exercise of universal jurisdiction over piracy, *see, e.g.,* ROBIN GEISS & ANNA PETRIG, PIRACY & ARMED ROBBERY AT SEA 145–48 (2011).

5. *See, e.g.,* LARRY MAY, CRIMES AGAINST HUMANITY: A NORMATIVE ACCOUNT (2005); Win-Chiat Lee, *International Crimes & Universal Jurisdiction,* in INTERNATIONAL CRIMINAL LAW & PHILOSOPHY 15 (Larry May ed., 2009); Anthony Sammons, *The "Under-Theorization" of Universal Jurisdiction: Implications for Legitimacy on Trials of War Criminals by National Courts,* 21 BERKELEY J. INT'L L. 111 (2003).

6. On different ways in which a crime may affect humanity, *see, e.g.,* MAY, *supra* note 5, at 84–85.

7. For philosophical justification in this direction, or at least for the proposition that core international crimes affect humanity, *see, e.g.,* HANNAH ARENDT, EICHMANN IN JERUSALEM: A REPORT ON THE BANALITY OF EVIL 253–79 (1994); ALEJANDRO CHEHTMAN, THE PHILOSOPHICAL FOUNDATIONS OF EXTRATERRITORIAL PUNISHMENT (2010); MAY, *supra* note 5; LARRY MAY, WAR CRIMES & JUST WAR (2007); LARRY MAY, GENOCIDE: A NORMATIVE ACCOUNT (2010); Antony Duff, *Authority & Responsibility in International Criminal Law,* in THE PHILOSOPHY OF INTERNATIONAL LAW 589 (Samantha Besson & John Tasioulas eds., 2010); Lee, *supra* note 5; David Jay Luban, *A Theory of Crimes against Humanity,* 29 YALE J. INT'L L. 85 (2004); Richard Vernon, *What Is a Crime against Humanity?,* 10 J. POL. PHIL. 231 (2002).

8. *See, e.g.,* LUC REYDAMS, UNIVERSAL JURISDICTION: INTERNATIONAL & MUNICIPAL LEGAL PROTECTIONS (2004); M. Cherif Bassiouni, *The History of Universal Jurisdiction & Its Place in International Law,* in UNIVERSAL JURISDICTION: NATIONAL COURTS & THE PROSECUTION OF SERIOUS CRIMES UNDER INTERNATIONAL LAW 39 (Stephen Macedo ed., 2004).

9. *See, e.g.,* Convention on the Prevention and Punishment of the Crime of Genocide (Jan. 21, 1951), 78 U.N.T.S. 277 (hereinafter Genocide Convention); Principles of International Law Recognized in the Charter of the Nuremberg Tribunal and in the Judgment of the Tribunal, Principle VI, 1 U.N. GAOR (Part II) at 188, U.N. Doc. A/61/Add.1 (1946) (hereinafter Nuremberg Principles); Geneva Convention for the Amelioration of the Condition of the Wounded and Sick in Armed Forces on the Field, art. 50, Aug. 12, 1949, 6 U.S.T. 3114, 75 U.N.T.S. 31 (hereinafter First Geneva Convention); Geneva Convention for the Amelioration of the Condition of the Wounded, Sick, and Shipwrecked Forces at Sea, art. 51, Aug. 12, 1949, 6 U.S.T. 3217, 75 U.N.T.S. 85 (hereinafter Second Geneva Convention); Geneva Convention Relative to the Treatment of Prisoners of War, art. 130, Aug. 12, 1949, 6 U.S.T. 3316, 75 U.N.T.S. 135 (hereinafter Third Geneva Convention); Geneva Convention Relative to the Protection of Civilian Persons in Time of War, art. 147, Aug. 12, 1949, 6 U.S.T. 3516, 75 U.N.T.S. 287 (hereinafter Fourth Geneva Convention); Protocol Additional to the Geneva Conventions of 12 August 1949, and Relating to the Protection of Victims of International Armed Conflict (Protocol I), art. 85, Jun. 8, 1977, 1125 U.N.T.S. 3 (hereinafter Additional Protocol I); Convention (IV) Respecting the Laws and Customs of War on Land (Hague IV), Annex, Oct. 18, 1907, 36 Stat. 2277 (1911), T.S. No. 539; Statute of the International Tribunal for the Former Yugoslavia, S.C. Res. 808, U.N. SCOR, 48th Sess., U.N. Doc. S/Res/808

(1993); Statute of the International Tribunal for Rwanda, S.C. Res. 955, U.N. SCOR, 49th Sess., Annex, U.N. Doc. S/Res/955 (1994).

10. *See, e.g.,* Arrest Warrant of 11 April 2000 (Dem. Rep. Congo v. Belg.) 2002 I.C.J. 11 (Feb. 14) (hereinafter Congo v. Belgium).

11. *See, e.g.,* Fourth Geneva Convention, *supra* note 9, 6 U.S.T. at 3616 (setting forth art. 146); Nuremberg Principles, *supra* note 9, at Principle V; Additional Protocol I, *supra* note 9, 1125 U.N.T.S. at 37 (setting forth art. 75.4); Institute of International Law, Seventeenth Commission, *Resolution on Universal Criminal Jurisdiction with Regard to the Crime of Genocide, Crimes against Humanity, & War Crimes* (2005), http://www.idi-iil.org/idiE/resolutionsE/2005_kra_03_en.pdf.

12. On whether there is and should be a rule under international law that requires the forum state exercising universal jurisdiction to give priority to the territorial and active nationality states, *see, e.g.,* Congo v. Belgium, *supra* note 10, at 59 (joint separate opinion of Judges Buergenthal, Higgins, & Kooijmans); COUNCIL OF THE EUROPEAN UNION, AU-EU TECHNICAL AD HOC EXPERT GROUP, REPORT ON THE PRINCIPLE OF UNIVERSAL JURIS-DICTION, §14, Doc. 8672/1/09REV1, (2009) (hereinafter AU-EU EXPERT GROUP); Institute of International Law, *supra* note 11; Anthony J. Colangelo, *Double Jeopardy & Multiple Sovereigns: A Jurisdictional Theory,* 86 WASH. U. L. REV. 769, 827–35 (2009); Florian Jessberger et al., *Concurring Criminal Jurisdictions under International Law,* in COMPLEMENTARITY & THE EXERCISE OF UNIVERSAL JURISDICTION FOR CORE INTERNA-TIONAL CRIMES 233 (Morten Bergsmo ed., 2010) (hereinafter COMPLEMENTARITY & UNIVERSAL JURISDICTION); Cedrik Ryngaert, *Complementarity in Universality Cases: Legal-Systematic & Legal Policy Considerations,* in COMPLEMENTARITY & UNIVERSAL JU-RISDICTION), *id.,* at 165; Jo Stigen, *The Relationship between the Principle of Complemen-tarity & the Exercise of Universal Jurisdiction for Core International Crimes,* in COMPLE-MENTARITY & UNIVERSAL JURISDICTION, *id.,* at 133.

13. On the double criminality requirement, compare, for example, the Article 689-11, French Criminal Procedure Code, with the *Princeton Principles on Universal Jurisdic-tion,* in UNIVERSAL JURISDICTION: NATIONAL COURTS & THE PROSECUTION OF SERIOUS CRIMES UNDER INTERNATIONAL LAW (Stephen Macedo ed., 2003) (hereinafter *Princeton Principles*). While the former includes a double criminality requirement, the Princeton Principles do not.

14. On the prohibition against double jeopardy, *see, e.g., Princeton Principles, supra* note 13, including a prohibition against double jeopardy; George Fletcher, *Against Uni-versal Jurisdiction,* 1 J. INT'L CRIM. JUST. 580 (2003).

15. On whether functional immunity prevents prosecution in this type of case, *see, e.g.,* Congo v. Belgium, *supra* note 10; Regina v. Bartle and the Commission of Police for the Metropolis and Others, Ex Parte Pinochet; Regina v. Evans and Another and the Commission of Police for the Metropolis and Others, [1999] UKHL 17 (Mar. 24, 1999); Ingrid Wuerth, *Pinochet's Legacy Reassessed,* 106 AM. J. INT'L L. 731 (2012).

16. On whether the defendant must be present in the territory of or have another link with the prosecuting state, *see, e.g.,* Congo v. Belgium, *supra* note 10, at 59 (joint separate opinion of Judges Buergenthal, Higgins, & Kooijmans); *id.* at 3 (separate opinion of President Guillaume).

17. The Rome Statute includes the crime of aggression among the crimes over which the ICC has jurisdiction. *See* Rome Statute of the International Criminal Court art. 5(1),

July 17, 1998, 2187 U.N.T.S. 90 (hereinafter Rome Statute). However, the Rome Statute also provides that the ICC will not exercise jurisdiction over this crime until such time as state parties agree on its definition and conditions for the exercise of jurisdiction. *See id.* art. 5(2). At the ICC's first review conference, concluded in June 2010, state parties agreed on a definition and conditions. The actual exercise of jurisdiction by the Court, however, is subject to a decision after Jan. 1, 2017, by the same majority of state parties as is required for the adoption of an amendment to the statute.

18. *Id.* art. 12(2)–(3).

19. *Id.* art. 13(b).

20. *See* U.N. Charter art. 39, 41. On the legal power of the U.N. Security Council to create international criminal tribunals, *see, e.g.,* Prosecutor v. Tadic, Case No. IT-94-1, Decision on Defense Motion for Interlocutory Appeal on Jurisdiction, ¶¶28–30 (Int'l Crim. Trib. for the Former Yugoslavia Oct. 2, 1995).

21. Other units include the presidency, responsible for the overall administration of the Court; the Registry, responsible for the nonjudicial aspects of the Court's functioning; the Office of Public Counsel for Victims; the Office of Public Counsel for the Defence; and a trust fund for the benefit of victims of crimes and their families.

22. *See* Rome Statute, *supra* note 17, art. 17. The principle of complementarity also arguably applies to the relationship between the ICC and prosecutions by nonparty states. *See, e.g.,* CASSESE, *infra* note 141, at 352.

23. For examples of implementing legislation brought into force by states, *see* Crimes against Humanity and War Crimes Act, S.C. 2000, c. 24 (Can.); International Criminal Court Act, 2001, c. 17 (Eng.); *International Criminal Court Act 2002* (Cth) (Austl.); *ICC (Consequential Amendments) Act 2002* (Cth) (Austl.).

24. The question of the legitimacy of international law, international regimes, and international organizations has received renewed interest over the past few decades. For seminal work in contemporary scholarship on this question, *see* Thomas M. Franck, *Why a Quest for Legitimacy?,* 21 U.C. DAVIS L. REV. 535 (1988). The arguments in this section refer to normative, not sociological, legitimacy. At a minimum, the relative moral legitimacy of universal jurisdiction and the ICC are referenced. However, such arguments also have legal consequences to the extent that moral considerations inform or are part of legal interpretation.

25. For discussion of the legitimacy of the ICC in particular and international criminal law in general, *see, e.g.,* Aaron Fichtelberg, *Democratic Legitimacy & the International Criminal Court,* 4 J. INT'L CRIM. JUST. 765 (2006); Madeleine Morris, *The Democratic Dilemma of the International Criminal Court,* 5 BUFFALO CRIM. L. REV. (2002); and the works cited *supra* note 7.

26. This seems to be David Luban's position. *See, e.g.,* David Luban, *Fairness to Rightness: Jurisdiction, Legality, & the Legitimacy of International Criminal Law,* in THE PHILOSOPHY OF INTERNATIONAL LAW 569 (Samantha Besson & John Tasioulas eds., 2010); Luban, *supra* note 7.

27. *See, e.g.,* Gabriel Bottini, *Universal Jurisdiction after the Creation of the International Criminal Court,* 36 N.Y.U. J. INT'L L. & POL. 503 (2004).

28. *See* Máximo Langer, *The Diplomacy of Universal Jurisdiction: The Political Branches & the Transnational Prosecutions of International Crimes,* 105 AM. J. INT'L L. 1, 47 (2011).

29. *See id.* at 42–43. On the due process problems in the ICC in relation to disclosure

of evidence, *see, e.g.,* Alex Whiting, *Lead Evidence & Discovery before the International Criminal Court: The Lubanga Case,* 14 UCLA J. INT'L L. & FOREIGN AFF. 207 (2009).

30. *See* Langer, *supra* note 28. On politicization, due process problems, and selectivity as three of the traditional challenges faced by international criminal law, *see* MARTHA MINOW, BETWEEN VENGEANCE & FORGIVENESS 25–51 (1999).

31. The exception is the U.N. Security Council, relying on its Chapter VII powers, referring a situation to the ICC. In this case, the ICC may exercise jurisdiction over the territory and nationals of nonparty states, according to the Rome Statute. In such instances, even if states have formally given their consent to the U.N. Charter and U.N. Security Council's powers under Chapter VII, the ICC arguably does not hold greater state consent legitimacy than universal jurisdiction prosecutions. Refusing to join the U.N. is prohibitively costly for states, and most states had no influence during the establishment of the powers of the U.N. Security Council. *See, e.g.,* Mattias Kumm, *The Legitimacy of International Law: A Constitutionalist Framework of Analysis,* 15 EUR. J. INT'L L. 907, 914 (2004); DAVID L. BOSCO, FIVE TO RULE THEM ALL: THE U.N. SECURITY COUNCIL & THE MAKING OF THE MODERN WORLD (2009). However, while situations referred to the ICC by the Security Council may not have more state consent legitimacy, these situations have more political, procedural, rational, and functional legitimacy, for reasons demonstrated by the rest of this section's analysis. On the possible limits of state consent to provide legitimacy to international organizations, *see, e.g.,* Robert Howse, *The Legitimacy of the World Trade Organization,* in THE LEGITIMACY OF INTERNATIONAL ORGANIZATIONS 355, 355–56, 359–60 (Jean-Marc Coicaud & Veijo Heiskanen eds., 2001).

32. Statist conceptions include traditional conceptions of international law, those conceptions of the international order embraced by variants of international relations theory, and the ones articulated by political philosophers such as Thomas Nagel and John Rawls. *See* JOHN RAWLS, THE LAW OF PEOPLES (1999); Thomas Nagel, *The Problem of Global Justice,* 33 PHIL. & PUB. AFF. 113 (2005).

33. This would be the case even if most contemporary statist conceptions consider the commission of mass atrocities and other serious human rights violations as a limit to state sovereignty or self-determination. First, the list of core international crimes includes conduct that does not necessarily consist of the commission of such actions—for example, certain limitations on the way armed conflict may be waged. For an argument in this direction, *see* Madeleine Morris, *High Crimes & Misconceptions: The ICC & Non-Party States,* 64 LAW & CONTEMP. PROBLEMS 13 (2001). Second, when mass atrocities or other serious violations of human rights are committed, the territorial or active nationality state may legitimately choose among an array of responses to these atrocities—including, under certain conditions, responses not based in criminal law. The consent by the state to the jurisdiction of an international criminal law regime may thus provide more legitimacy to this criminal response relative to other responses.

34. *See, e.g.,* DAVID HELD, DEMOCRACY & THE GLOBAL ORDER 230 (1995); Mattias Kumm, *The Cosmopolitan Turn in Constitutionalism: On the Relationship between Constitutionalism in & beyond the State,* in RULING THE WORLD: INTERNATIONAL LAW, GLOBAL GOVERNANCE, CONSTITUTIONALISM 258, 291–95 (Jeffrey L. Dunoff & Joel P. Trachtman eds., 2009).

35. For example, assuming that, where they meet specific requirements, certain am-

nesties, such as those in South Africa, are legitimate responses to international crimes, the people of the state in which the international crimes took place are entitled to decide whether to accept such an amnesty, and this decision must be respected by the rest of the world. The express consent by the people through their state to participate in an international criminal law enforcement regime like the ICC would thus provide more state consent legitimacy to such a regime to intervene—for example, to evaluate whether the national response to specific international crimes is legitimate.

36. Attempts to create a convention on crimes against humanity are ongoing. *See, e.g.,* FORGING A CONVENTION FOR CRIMES AGAINST HUMANITY (Leila Nadya Sadat ed., 2011).

37. Genocide Convention, *supra* note 9, art. 6.

38. First Geneva Convention, *supra* note 9, art. 49; Second Geneva Convention, *supra* note 9, art. 50; Third Geneva Convention, *supra* note 9, art. 129; Fourth Geneva Convention, *supra* note 9, art. 146; Additional Protocol I, *supra* note 9, art. 85. *See also* Roger O'Keefe, *The Grave Breaches Regime & Universal Jurisdiction,* 7 J. INT'L CRIM. JUST. 811 (2009).

39. *See, e.g.,* Congo v. Belgium, *supra* note 10, at 3 (separate opinion of President Guillaume) (holding that the Geneva Conventions do not create an obligation to arrest or prosecute offenders not present in the state's territory and do not confer universal jurisdiction in absentia).

40. *See id.* at 59 (joint separate opinion of Judges Buergenthal, Higgins, & Koojmans); *id.* at 137 (dissenting opinion of Judge van Wyngert). For arguments in favor of the legality of universal jurisdiction under customary international law that do not rely on the *Lotus* principle, *see, e.g.,* Claus Kreß, *Universal Jurisdiction over International Crimes & the Institut de Droit International,* 4 J. INT'L CRIM. JUST. 561, 571–76 (2006).

41. Equally authoritative sources reject this interpretation of the *Lotus* principle and claim that there is no permissive customary international rule authorizing the exercise of universal jurisdiction, at least in its pure form. *See* Congo v. Belgium, *supra* note 10, at 3 (separate opinion of President Guillaume); *id.* at 57 (declaration of Judge Ranjeva).

42. Larry May argues that the ICC has more legitimacy than universal jurisdiction prosecutions as the latter represents a type of international vigilante justice, creating too great a risk for state sovereignty. *See* MAY, *supra* note 5, at 76. May's position is seemingly that the problem with universal jurisdiction prosecutions is that they are likely to infringe on other states' sovereignty too often. My argument here is not predictive but formal. In other words, my reasoning has not been that universal jurisdiction prosecutions are likely to infringe on state sovereignty too often. Instead, universal jurisdiction claims do not necessarily assume the consent of the territorial or active nationality state in the same manner as the default jurisdiction of the ICC. On why I do not think that universal jurisdiction prosecutions are likely to infringe too frequently on other states' sovereignty, *see* Langer, *supra* note 28.

43. *See* ARENDT, *supra* note 7, at 269–70 (attributing the quotation to Jaspers and subscribing to it). *See also* HANNAH ARENDT & KARL JASPERS, CORRESPONDENCE 1926–1969, at 413, 418–20, 424–25 (Lotte Kohler & Hans Saner eds., Robert Kimber & Rita Kimber trans., 1992) (discussing the issue before Eichmann's trial began) (emphasis added).

44. *Id.*

45. These theories may include traditional conceptions of international law as well as

a number of international relations theories such as institutionalism and interstate solidarism. *See, e.g.,* Veijo Heiskanen, *Introduction,* in THE LEGITIMACY OF INTERNATIONAL ORGANIZATIONS, *supra* note 31, at 1, 5. These theories may also include statist accounts by political philosophers such as Nagel, *supra* note 32, at 138, stating, "International institutions act not in the name of individuals, but in the name of the states or state instruments and agencies that have created them." *See also* RAWLS, *supra* note 32, at 93, stating that for well-ordered peoples to achieve their long-term aim of bringing all societies to honor the "Law of Peoples," they should establish new institutions to serve as a kind of a confederative center and public forum for their common opinion and policy toward non-well-ordered regimes.

46. Even if the community of states is not conceived as a political community, *see, e.g.,* Nagel, *supra* note 32, as long as the community of states is considered the principal on whose behalf international criminal law institutions are acting, the same principles seem to follow as moral principles based on a principal agent line of reasoning. In this case, this could be termed as *principal agent legitimacy.* However, for simplicity, I have used *political legitimacy* throughout the chapter to refer to these ideas. For a more detailed articulation of these arguments and ideas, *see* Máximo Langer, *Universal Jurisdiction as Janus-Faced: The Dual Nature of the German International Criminal Law Code,* 11 J. INT'L CRIM. JUST. 737 (2013).

47. For example, under certain cosmopolitan democracy conceptions, participation by and accountability to not only states but also other actors, such as individuals and transnational social movements, is a condition of the political legitimacy of international institutions. *See, e.g.,* Jürgen Habermas, *The Constitutionalization of International Law & the Legitimation Problems of a Constitution for World Society,* 15 CONSTELLATIONS 444 (2008); HELD, *supra* note 34.

48. *See, e.g.,* Benedict Kingsbury et al., *The Emergence of Global Administrative Law,* 68 L. & CONTEMP. PROBS. 15 (2005) (global administrative law requires that global institutions meet standards of accountability, transparency, and participation, not only for states but also for others affected by the institutions' regimes, such as groups and individuals); Kumm, *supra* note 31, at 926.

49. The idea may apply in global administrative law and cosmopolitan constitutionalism accounts, and also in natural law conceptions of international crimes and universal jurisdiction. On natural law conceptions over these issues, *see, e.g.,* Noah Feldman, *Cosmopolitan Law?,* 116 YALE L.J. 1023, 1056–69 (2007); Luban, *supra* note 7; Luban, *supra* note 26, even if Feldman and Luban do not include this idea in their accounts.

50. *See, e.g.,* M. Cherif Bassiouni, *Negotiating the Treaty of Rome on the Establishment of an International Criminal Court,* 32 CORNELL INT'L L.J. 443 (1999); John Washburn, *The Negotiation of the Rome Statute for the International Criminal Court & International Lawmaking in the 21st Century,* 11 PACE INT'L L. REV. 361 (2000).

51. *See* ICC, *The State Parties to the Rome Statute,* http://www.icc-cpi.int/EN_Menus/ASP/States%20Parties/Pages/the%20states%20parties%20to%20the%20rome%20statute.aspx.

52. *See, e.g.,* Rome Statute, *supra* note 17, arts. 36, 42, 46, 51, 112, 113–18, 121 (relating to the Assembly of States Parties' various authorities).

53. Rome Statute, *supra* note 17, art. 13(b), 16. It is in comparison to universal jurisdiction prosecutions by individual states that the U.N. Security Council is more representative of all U.N. members, even acknowledging the representativeness deficit of the

U.N. Security Council, with its five permanent members and their veto power. On the legitimacy problems of the U.N. Security Council, *see, e.g.,* David D. Caron, *The Legitimacy of the Collective Authority of the Security Council,* 87 AM. J. INT'L L. 552 (1993).

54. *See* Rome Statute, *supra* note 17, art. 50.

55. For a more detailed elaboration on the three lines of reasoning articulated in the last four paragraphs in relation to the legitimacy of universal jurisdiction, *see* Langer, *supra* note 46.

56. Alternatively, one can refer to this type of legitimacy as *democratic legitimacy* or *perspectival legitimacy* or *impartiality.* These terms may be better than *rational legitimacy* for those who find value in the inclusion of a larger number of community viewpoints in judging but do not consider this inclusion an improvement in rationality. Hannah Arendt herself, one of my sources of inspiration for this idea, may fall into this category. For reasons of ease of use, I have used *rational legitimacy* to refer to this idea throughout the chapter. However, I am not taking sides in the debate on whether including a larger number of community viewpoints in judging improve rationality.

57. Different theoretical traditions embrace variations on the idea that the more viewpoints that participate in or are considered throughout the judicial process, the more impartial or valid that process is. The cross-sectional ideal of the jury in the United States is one example. *See, e.g.,* JEFFREY ABRAMSON, WE, THE JURY (2000) (arguing that individual jurors are inevitably the bearers of the diverse perspectives and interests of their race, religion, gender, and ethnic background as well as that deliberations are considered impartial when group differences are not eliminated but rather invited, embraced, and fairly represented). Hannah Arendt seemed to have embraced a version of this idea in her work on judgment in politics. Jennifer Nedelsky has extended the application of Arendt's framework to legal judgment. As Nedelsky points out, "For . . . Arendt . . . the key idea of judgment is that it is neither about truth claims nor about mere subjective preference. . . . I cannot compel agreement, as I could logically with a truth claim. But I can persuade and claim that if the other judge is truly judging, is not being biased by private inclinations, he will agree. I thus claim that my judgment is valid for the community of judging others. The core of what makes such judgment possible is our 'common sense' shared by other judging subjects. It is this shared sense that allows us to exercise an 'enlarged mentality' by imagining judgment from the standpoints of others. . . . When we use this capacity for an enlarged mentality to free ourselves from idiosyncrasies and inclinations, then we are capable of true judgment, for which we claim validity." Jennifer Nedelsky, *Communities of Judgment & Human Rights,* 1 THEORETICAL INQUIRIES IN LAW 245, 249–50 (2000). My line of reasoning on the higher rational or perspectival legitimacy of the ICC thus shows a possible bridge or connection between Arendt's work on crimes against humanity and her work on judgment, not explored by Arendt.

58. Under statist conceptions of the international legal order and international institutions, the relevant community would be the community of states. Alternatively, in the case of cosmopolitan conceptions, the community would (also) include individuals and even other entities and groups.

59. Rome Statute, *supra* note 17, art. 36(4)(b), 36(7).

60. *Id.,* art. 36(8).

61. On challenges in truth determination and due process that the linguistic and cul-

tural gaps between the judges, on the one hand, and the witnesses and the defendant, on the other, have generated in the universal jurisdiction trial in Germany of Onesphore Rwabukombe for his participation in the genocide in Rwanda in 1994, *see* Christoph Safferling, *VStGB und Strafverfahren: Beweisaufnahme und Angeklagtenrechte*, in ZEHN JAHRE VÖLKERSTRAFGESETZBUCH: BILANZ UND PERSPEKTIVEN EINES DEUTSCHEN VÖLKERSTRAFRECHTS 185 (Florian Jessberger & Julia Geneuss eds., 2013). Crucially, a greater diversity of world viewpoints in international criminal jurisdictions does not provide a perfect antidote against these risks. On these problems at the ICTR, the Special Court for Sierra Leone, and the Special Panels in the Dili District Court in East Timor, *see* NANCY COMBS, FACT FINDING WITHOUT FACTS: THE UNCERTAIN EVIDENTIARY FOUNDATIONS OF INTERNATIONAL CRIMINAL CONVICTIONS (2010).

62. Arendt hints at or suggests this idea when she says in her analysis of the Eichmann case, "The very monstrousness of the events is 'minimized' before a tribunal that represents one nation only." *See* ARENDT, *supra* note 7, at 270.

63. *See supra* note 43.

64. *See, e.g.,* Bottini, *supra* note 27; Jann K. Kleffner, *The Impact of Complementarity on National Implementation of Substantive International Criminal Law*, 1 J. INT'L CRIM. JUST. 86, 108–9 (2003) (considering such an argument as plausible without embracing it).

65. My position in this section could be interpreted in two ways. Under the first interpretation, my argument would be that universal jurisdiction meets the requirements of a minimal theory about the moral legitimacy of universal jurisdiction. Under the second, my argument would be that universal jurisdiction is not so far from meeting the requirements of an ideal theory about the moral legitimacy of universal jurisdiction as to be considered (completely) illegitimate. Since I am not fleshing out a full theory on the legitimacy of universal jurisdiction here, a resolution does not need to be reached between these two competing interpretations—although *see* Langer, *supra* note 46, for my position that an ideal theory of universal jurisdiction should include the participation of and accountability to the international community as requirements of legitimacy for universal jurisdiction. On the distinction between ideal and minimal theories of moral legitimacy, *see, e.g.,* Richard Fallon Jr., *Legitimacy & the Constitution*, 118 HARV. L. REV. 1787, 1797–99 (2005), distinguishing between "*ideal* theories, which attempt to specify the necessary conditions for assertions of state authority to be maximally justified or to deserve unanimous respect," and "*minimal* theories of moral legitimacy [that] define a threshold above which legal regimes are sufficiently just to deserve the support of those who are subject to them in the absence of better, realistically attainable alternatives." As Fallon writes, "Ideal theories establish the standards of justification to which political regimes ought to aspire, even if all existing governments fall short. . . . [M]inimal theories specify the threshold conditions that a regime must satisfy in order to deserve any support or justify any official coercion." *Id.*

66. Rome Statute, *supra* note 17, art. 12.

67. *Id.*, art. 13(b).

68. Statute of the International Tribunal for Rwanda, *supra* note9, art. 1–4.

69. *See, e.g., Rwanda Tribunal Should Pursue Justice for RPF Crimes*, HUMAN RIGHTS WATCH (Dec. 12, 2008), http://www.hrw.org/news/2008/12/12/rwanda-tribunal-should-pursue-justice-rpf-crimes.

70. *See, e.g.,* FLORENCE HARTMANN, PAIX ET CHÂTIMENT: LES GUERRES SECRÈTES DE LA POLITIQUE ET DE LA JUSTICE INTERNATIONALES 261–72 (2007); Luc Reydams, *The ICTR Ten Years On: Back to the Nuremberg Paradigm?*, 3 J. INT'L CRIM. JUST. 977 (2005).

71. *See* Eric David, *Belgium*, in 8 Y.B. INT'L HUMANITARIAN L. 396, 400–402 (2005) (describing the role of the Court of Cassation and the Cour d'arbitrage in the dismissal of the Kagamé case).

72. Juzgado Central de Instrucción No 4, Audiencia National, *Sumario 3/2008—D. Auto.* For critical analyses of this decision, *see* Charles Chernor Jalloh, *Universal Jurisdiction, Universal Prescription?: A Preliminary Assessment of the African Union Perspective on Universal Jurisdiction,* 21 CRIM. L. FORUM 1 (2010); Commentator, *The Spanish Indictment of High-Ranking Rwandan Officials,* 6 J. INT'L CRIM. JUST. 1003 (2008). This case has remained open after the coming into effect of the new extraterritorial jurisdiction regulations in March 2014. *See* EL PAIS, March 19, 2014, *La Audiencia Nacional combate la eliminación de la justicia universal,* http://politica.elpais.com/politica/2014/03/19/actualidad/1395233699_903497.html.

73. On the possible functions of jurisdictional redundancy in the U.S. legal system, *see* Robert M. Cover, *The Uses of Jurisdictional Redundancy: Interest, Ideology, & Innovation,* 22 WM. & MARY L. REV. 639 (1981). In Cover's terminology, my argument in this subsection can be understood as a way to address the "dilemma of self-interest" by the ICC and the permanent members of the U.N. Security Council that block the referral of cases to the ICC.

74. Addressing insufficient economic and human resources can thus be another explanation or justification for jurisdiction redundancy distinct from the three identified by Cover, *supra* note 73—that is, self-interest, ideology, and innovation.

75. On the number of ICC judges, *see* Rome Statute, *supra* note 17, art. 36.

76. The list and description of arrest warrants and summons to appear is available on the ICC website: http://icc-cpi.int/EN_Menus/icc/Pages/default.aspx.

77. *See* Office of the Prosecutor, ICC, *Paper on Some Policy Issues before the Office of the Prosecutor* (Sept. 2003), http://www.icc-cpi.int/NR/rdonlyres/1FA7C4C6-DE5F-42B7-8B25-60AA962ED8B6/143594/030905_Policy_Paper.pdf.

78. *See, e.g.,* Rome Statute, *supra* note 17, pmbl.; Dierdre Golash, *The Justification of Punishment in the International Context,* in INTERNATIONAL CRIMINAL LAW & PHILOSOPHY, *supra* note 5, at 201.

79. Some of these consequentialist considerations are discussed in the subsection "Analysis of Possible Objections." Another argument against the punishment of chain commanders and actual perpetrators would be a strong defense of superior orders. However, domestic and international authorities have rejected the strong version of this defense. On the main positions regarding the superior orders defense in international criminal law, *see, e.g.,* GERHARD WERLE, PRINCIPLES OF INTERNATIONAL CRIMINAL LAW §§581–95 (2nd ed. 2009).

80. *See* ARENDT, *supra* note 7.

81. *See, e.g.,* Lee, *supra* note 5, at 11.

82. For an ICC argument in support of this idea, *see* Situation in the Democratic Republic of the Congo, Case No. ICC-01/04, Judgment on the Prosecutor's Appeal against the Decision of Pre-Trial Chamber I entitled, "Decision on the Prosecutor's Application for Warrants of Arrest, Article 58," ¶73 (July 13, 2006), http://www.icc-cpi.int/iccdocs/doc/doc183559.pdf.

83. *See generally* OSIEL, *supra* note 1; TEITEL, *supra* note 1.

84. *See* GIDEON BOAS, THE MILOŠEVIĆ TRIAL: LESSONS FOR THE CONDUCT OF COM-PLEX INTERNATIONAL PROCEEDINGS (2007). The prosecutorial strategy against Saddam Hussein before the Iraqi Special Tribunal demonstrates prosecutors' reluctance to repeat the strategy used in the Milošević trial. The prosecutors focused on specific incidents in successive trials instead of trying to prosecute in a single trial all the atrocities committed during his regime. *See, e.g.,* Michael P. Scharf, *Forward: Lessons from the Saddam Trial,* 39 CASE W. RES. J. INT'L L. 1, 10 (2006–8). On other efforts to expedite the processing time in international criminal law cases, *see* Máximo Langer, *The Rise of Managerial Judging in International Criminal Law,* 53 AM. J. COMP. L. 835 (2005); Máximo Langer & Joseph W. Doherty, *Managerial Judging Goes International but Its Promise Remains Unfulfilled: An Empirical Assessment of the ICTY Reforms,* 36 YALE J. INT'L L. 241 (2011).

85. For example, the prosecution limited its charges against Thomas Lubanga Dyilo to conscripting and using child soldiers despite accusations of his militia's role in killing, raping, and looting portions of eastern DRC. *See ICC Prosecution Defends Its Tactics,* INSTITUTE FOR WAR & PEACE REPORTING (July 7, 2006), http://iwpr.net/report-news/icc-prosecution-defends-its-tactics.

86. Debate has been renewed over the past couple of decades about what customary international law is and what its role is or should be (if any) in contemporary international law. For a review of part of this debate, *see, e.g.,* Anthea Elizabeth Roberts, *Traditional & Modern Approaches to Customary International Law: A Reconciliation,* 95 AM. J. INT'L L. 757 (2001). I cannot engage in this debate for the purpose of this chapter. This chapter adopts a traditional conception of customary international law. It is understood as evidence of a general practice accepted as law that has two elements: state practice and *opinio juris. See, e.g.,* Statute of the International Court of Justice, art. 38, June 26, 1945, 33 U.N.T.S. 993; RESTATEMENT (THIRD) OF THE FOREIGN RELATIONS LAW OF THE UNITED STATES §102(2) and cmts. b–d (1987).

87. *See supra* notes 41 and 42. Controversy has also arisen over whether universal jurisdiction over the core international crimes is a good idea from a policy perspective. I analyze these policy arguments in the subsection "Analysis of Possible Objections."

88. *See* Roger O'Keefe, *Universal Jurisdiction: Clarifying the Basic Concept,* 2 J. INT'L CRIM. JUST. 735 (2004). I rely on O'Keefe's lucid analysis of this distinction in this subsection.

89. On the distinctions among jurisdiction to prescribe, jurisdiction to adjudicate, and jurisdiction to enforce, *see, e.g.,* RESTATEMENT (THIRD) OF THE FOREIGN RELATIONS LAW OF THE UNITED STATES §401 & cmts. (1987). It is unnecessary for our purposes to distinguish between jurisdiction to adjudicate and jurisdiction to enforce. I thus include both ideas in jurisdiction to enforce.

90. *See, e.g.,* RESTATEMENT (THIRD) OF THE FOREIGN RELATIONS LAW OF THE UNITED STATES §§402 and cmts. c–g, 404 and cmts. a–b, 423 (1987).

91. On this disagreement, *see, e.g., supra* notes 40 and 41. Which war crimes constitute core international crimes will not be addressed here. However, I am not taking a position on whether under customary international law, states may claim prescriptive universal jurisdiction over war crimes in general. For the legal controversy over this issue, *see* JEAN-MARIE HENCKAERTS & LOUISE DOSWALD-BECK, CUSTOMARY INTERNATIONAL HUMANITARIAN LAW (2005); John B. Bellinger III & William J. Haynes II, *A U.S.*

Government Response to the International Committee of the Red Cross Study Customary International Humanitarian Law, 89 INT'L REV. OF THE RED CROSS 443 (2007).

92. This is the case regardless whether the *Lotus* principle applies—i.e., whether it must be proven that there is no prohibition against prescriptive universal jurisdiction over the core international crimes or there is a rule permitting it.

93. *See, e.g.,* U.N. Secretary-General, *Report of the Secretary-General Pursuant to Paragraph 2 of Security Council Resolution 808,* §§34–35, U.N. Doc. S/25704 (May 3, 1993).

94. The argument has been made that one of the consequences of the *ius cogens* character of a crime is that it is subject to universal jurisdiction. *See e.g.,* Prosecutor v. Furundzija, Case No. IT.95.17/1.T, ¶156 (Int'l Crim. Trib. for the Former Yugoslavia Dec. 10, 1998).

95. The practice by protesting states is significant. This practice suggests that their protest should be interpreted as opposition not to the idea of universal jurisdiction per se but rather to the way universal jurisdiction was exercised in these individual cases. The United States protested the exercise of universal jurisdiction against its nationals—e.g., by Belgium in 2003—while explicitly providing for universal jurisdiction for its federal courts regarding genocide, torture, and the war crime of recruitment or use of child soldiers. Rwanda also falls into this category, as it has protested the use of universal jurisdiction against some of its nationals yet has also stated that its courts have universal jurisdiction over the core international crimes and has even suggested that the 2001 Princeton Principles on Universal Jurisdiction should be incorporated. *See Report 2010, infra* note 96, at ¶¶34, 114.

96. There is no definitive worldwide survey setting out how many states have passed this type of legislation. Several surveys of domestic legislation have suggested the existence of general state practice accepted as law in this regard. As of early 2012, the Sixth (Legal) Committee of the U.N. General Assembly is examining the scope and application of the principle of universal jurisdiction. As part of that project, the U.N. General Assembly invited member states to submit information on their domestic legal rules and judicial practice on universal jurisdiction. Among the fifty-four reporting states, the U.N. secretary-general included thirty-three states as listing crimes against humanity, genocide, or war crimes as universal jurisdiction crimes according to their criminal codes or legislation. *See* U.N. Secretary-General, *The Scope & Application of the Principle of Universal Jurisdiction,* tables 1–2, U.N. Doc. A/65/181 (July 29, 2010) (hereinafter *Report 2010*). The list of states is larger. The reports by the U.N. secretary-general mention other reporting states, among them Rwanda and Switzerland, as having universal jurisdiction over core international crimes. *See, e.g., id.* at ¶¶34, 65. In a recent provisional survey, Amnesty International concludes that 145 out of 193 states have provided for universal jurisdiction over crimes against humanity, genocide, war crimes, or torture. *See* AMNESTY INTERNATIONAL, UNIVERSAL JURISDICTION: A PRELIMINARY SURVEY OF LEGISLATION AROUND THE WORLD 1 (2011). However, Amnesty International includes in its survey states that do not explicitly establish universal jurisdiction over these crimes but instead have provisions that can be interpreted by their courts as establishing universal jurisdiction—such as the *aut dedere aut judicare* provision or a general reference to treaty obligations to prosecute. In a survey of African and European states, the AU-EU Expert Group mentions thirty-six African states that provide for the exercise of

universal jurisdiction over at least one of the crimes under the ICC's jurisdiction. *See* AU-EU EXPERT GROUP, *supra* note 12, at ¶16. This report also mentions eleven European states that grant universal jurisdiction on the basis of customary international law. These reports do not always distinguish between universal jurisdiction based on treaty and customary international law. However, since only the grave breaches provisions of the Geneva Conventions of 1949 and Additional Protocol I provide a plausible textual basis for universal jurisdiction, and since many states have claimed universal jurisdiction over other core international crimes, it is fair to conclude that the list of states that have relied on customary international law to establish universal jurisdiction over the core international crimes is rather large.

97. For example, the Deschênes Commission in Canada recommended eighteen cases for prosecution and almost two hundred cases for further inquiry regarding the possible commission of war crimes by Nazis. *See* Commission of Inquiry on War Criminals, *Report, Part 1: Public*, at ¶¶62, 70, 74, 76 (1986). In Spain, Judge Baltasar Garzón issued incriminating decisions against roughly 120 people for their participation in the commission of international crimes in Argentina in the 1970s. *See* Langer, *supra* note 28, at 34.

98. I am referring here to twenty-seven trials whose charges included crimes against humanity, genocide, or war crimes different from grave breaches of the Geneva Conventions of 1949, given that there is a plausible textual treaty basis for the prosecution of grave breaches. I also do not include trials based only on torture as an independent international crime, because the Torture Convention also provides a textual basis for the exercise of universal jurisdiction. The period covered starts with the Eichmann trial in Israel in 1961.

99. *See, e.g.*, RESTATEMENT (THIRD) OF THE FOREIGN RELATIONS LAW OF THE UNITED STATES §404 and cmt. a (1987).

100. *See, e.g.*, Congo v. Belgium, *supra* note 10, at 3 (separate opinion of President Guillaume) (arguing that the current body of international criminal law precludes the exercise of pure universal jurisdiction); *id.* at 57 (declaration of Judge Ranjeva). *See also* REYDAMS, *supra* note 8.

101. *See, e.g.*, Jack Goldsmith & Stephen D. Krasner, *The Pitfalls of Idealism*, 132 DAEDALUS 47, 51–52, 55 (2003); Henry Kissinger, *The Pitfalls of Universal Jurisdiction: Risking Judicial Tyranny*, FOREIGN AFF. (July–Aug. 2001), at 86; Eugene Kontorovich, *The Inefficiency of Universal Jurisdiction*, 2008 U. ILL. L. REV. 389; Jack Snyder & Leslie Vinjamuri, *Trial & Errors*, 28 INT'L SECURITY 5 (2004).

102. A related criticism would be that by disregarding the international power structure, the ICC would do more harm than good to human rights by encouraging the United States to disengage from operations to protect human rights. *See* Jack Goldsmith, *The Self-Defeating International Criminal Court*, 70 U. CHI. L. REV. 89 (2003). Following that argument, it could be claimed that universal jurisdiction acting in combination with the ICC would do even more harm by discouraging U.S. participation in human rights operations. I cannot analyze this criticism in detail here, although two comments are in order. First, as I argue *infra* and have argued in Langer, *supra* note 28, the United States and other powerful states have had more leverage over the ICC and universal jurisdiction prosecutions than their critics have acknowledged. Second, there is no strong evidence that the ICC and universal jurisdiction have had this disengaging effect on the

United States. For a broader empirical debate on whether human rights treaties and criminal prosecutions might do more harm than good to human rights, *see, e.g.,* KATHRYN SIKKINK, THE JUSTICE CASCADE: HOW HUMAN RIGHTS PROSECUTIONS ARE CHANGING WORLD POLITICS (2011); BETH A. SIMMONS, MOBILIZING FOR HUMAN RIGHTS: INTERNATIONAL LAW IN DOMESTIC POLITICS (2009); Oona A. Hathaway, *Do Human Rights Treaties Make a Difference?,* 111 YALE L.J. 1935 (2002).

103. The Rome Statute provides that the U.N. Security Council may defer an investigation or prosecution for a renewable twelve-month period (art. 16) and directs the prosecutor to evaluate whether prosecution is in the interest of justice when determining when to take up a case under art. 53(1)(c) and (2)(c). For analyses of these provisions, *see, e.g.,* Office of the Prosecutor, ICC, *Policy Paper on Interests of Justice* (Sept. 1, 2007), http://www.icc-cpi.int/NR/rdonlyres/772C95C9-F54D-4321-BF09-73422BB23528/143640/ICCOTPInterestsOfJustice.pdf; L. Cordorelli & S. Villalpando, *Referral & Deferral by the Security Council,* in THE ROME STATUTE FOR AN INTERNATIONAL CRIMINAL COURT: A COMMENTARY 627 (Antonio Cassese et al. eds., 2002); Richard G. Goldstone & Nicole Fritz, *"In the Interests of Justice" & Independent Referral: The ICC Prosecutor's Unprecedented Power,* 13 LEIDEN J. INT'L L. 655 (2000); Mnookin, *supra* note 2.

104. *But see* Goldsmith, *supra* note 102 (criticizing the ICC and highlighting this issue).

105. *See, e.g.,* Rome Statute, *supra* note 17, art. 54(2)(a). A limited exception to this general rule is established in arts. 54(2)(b) and 57(3)(d). *See id.*

106. For good or bad, the al-Bashir case provides examples of this phenomenon to the extent that although two ICC arrest warrants have been issued against the Sudanese president, he has been able to travel to states parties of the ICC and states parties have included him in the negotiations on the situation in South Sudan.

107. *See* Langer, *supra* note 28.

108. On the selectivity problems of international criminal law, *see, e.g.,* WOLFGANG KALECK, MIT ZWEIERLEI MAβ: DER WESTEN UND DAS VÖLKERSTRAFRECHT (2012); MINOW, *supra* note 30.

109. Even if the regime concentrates on low-cost defendants, given the incentives for political branches in states exercising universal jurisdiction, the universal jurisdiction regime still provides reasons to officials who do not fit into the low-cost category to abide by the regime's norms. First, the category of a low-cost defendant is not fixed, and a high-cost defendant can turn into a low-cost defendant over time. In addition, even if the regime is unlikely to try high-cost defendants, this likelihood in most cases is not zero. Furthermore, even if the regime is unlikely to try high-cost defendants, other measures by the regime—the presentation of a complaint, initiation of formal proceedings, the issuing of an arrest warrant, or actual arrest—can create incentives for defendants to abide by norms of international criminal law and provide reasons to internalize these norms. In this respect, even a very high-cost defendant such as former U.S. president George W. Bush apparently had to cancel a trip to Switzerland based on concerns about the universal jurisdiction regime due to interrogation policies during his administration. *See Universal Jurisdiction,* WAR CRIMES PROSECUTION WATCH (vol. 5.23) (Public Int'l L. and Pol'y Group) (Feb. 14, 2011), http://publicinternationallawandpolicygroup.org/wp-content/uploads/2011/04/wcpw_vol05issue23.html.

110. On politicization as one of the traditional challenges faced by international criminal law, *see* MINOW, *supra* note 30.

111. On different possible meanings of political prosecutions and trials, *see* OTTO KIRCH-

HEIMER, POLITICAL JUSTICE (1963); JUDITH N. SHKLAR, LEGALISM: LAW, MORALS, & PO-
LITICAL TRIALS (1964); Jenia Iontcheva Turner, *Defense Perspectives on Law & Politics in
International Criminal Trials,* 48 VA. J. INT'L L. 529 (2008); Jeremy Peterson, *Note: Unpack-
ing Show Trials: Situating the Trial of Saddam Hussein,* 48 HARV. INT'L L.J. 257 (2007); Eric
A. Posner, *Political Trials in Domestic & International Law,* 55 DUKE L.J. 75 (2005).

112. *See* Langer, *supra* note 28, at 41–45.

113. *Id.*

114. *Id.*

115. *See, e.g.,* Loi 2010-930 du 9 août 2010 portant adaptation du droit pénal à
l'institution de la Cour pénale internationale, Art. 8, J.O., Aug. 10, 2010, p. 14678
(France); Völkerstrafgesetzbuch (VStGB) (Code of Crimes against International Law),
June 26, 2002, §1 (Ger.); International Criminal Court Act, 2001, c. 17 (Eng.). For a
similar conclusion based on a survey of domestic legislation on international crimes and
universal jurisdiction, *see* Beth Van Schaack & Zarko Perovic, *The Prevalence of "Pres-
ent-In" Jurisdiction,* in PROCEEDINGS OF THE 107TH ANNUAL MEETING (AMERICAN SOCI-
ETY OF INTERNATIONAL LAW) (2013).

116. *See* Langer, *supra* note 28. On the role of the pressure from China that led to the
restriction of universal jurisdiction in Spain in March 2014, *see, e.g.,* EL PAIS, June 23,
2014, *La Audiencia Nacional archiva la investigación sobre genocidio en el Tíbet,* http://
politica.elpais.com/politica/2014/06/23/actualidad/1403537543_926352.html.

117. I am relying on my own database (on file with author) on universal jurisdiction
complaints to make this statement due to the impossibility so far of locating the dates of
presentation for a good number of the pre-2002 complaints.

118. For a description of how this global survey was carried out, *see* Langer, *supra* note
28, at 7. My database starts with the Eichmann case, but I exclude this case here from the
total number of complaints because it took place more than two decades earlier than the
second case.

119. The two persons in question are Ignace Murwanashyaka, a leader of a Hutu militia of Rwanda, and his deputy, Straton Musoni, for crimes against humanity and war
crimes that took place in the DRC. A first investigation against them by German authorities was dismissed for insufficient evidence. A second set of proceedings has been
ongoing in Germany since 2009 and by the beginning of 2014 no trial verdict had been
issued yet. *See* Horand Knaup, *Germany Arrests Rwandan War Crimes Suspects,* SPIEGEL
ONLINE, Nov. 18, 2009, http://www.spiegel.de/international/world/0,1518,druck-661965
,00.html; Bundesgerichtshof (BGH) (Federal Court of Justice), June 17, 2010, BGHSt,
AK 3/10, http://juris.bundesgerichtshof.de/cgi-bin/rechtsprechung/document.py?Geri
cht=bgh&Art=en&Datum=2010-6-17&nr=52675&pos=7&anz=29&Blank=1.pdf.
Since the defendants were residing in Germany during the commission of the alleged
crimes, and the alleged crimes took place in the DRC, the cases have relied on the territorial and universal jurisdiction principles. I am grateful to Kai Ambos for discussing
this issue in detail with me.

120. Interview with anonymous member of the European Center for Constitutional
and Human Rights, New York, Mar. 24, 2011 (on file with author).

121. *See The Cases,* ICTY.org, http://www.icty.org/sections/TheCases/KeyFigures. By
"adjudicated cases," I refer to cases in which the defendant was tried or entered a guilty
plea. If cases that were referred to national jurisdictions, had the indictments withdrawn, or had defendants who died prior to trial are also included, then the ICTY had
completed proceedings against 126 defendants.

122. *See Status of Cases,* UNICTR.org, http://www.unictr.org/Cases/StatusofCases/tabid/204/Default.aspx. As with the ICTY, if concluded ICTR cases also included those cases that were referred to national jurisdictions or had the indictments withdrawn or in which the defendants died prior to trial, the ICTR had completed proceedings against seventy-two defendants.

123. *See, e.g.,* HAZAN, *infra* note 137.

124. *See, e.g.,* L. Walleyn, *Universal Jurisdiction: Lessons from the Belgian Experience,* 5 YEARBOOK OF INTERNATIONAL HUMANITARIAN LAW (H. Fischer & Avril McDonald eds., 2002); YVES BEIGBEDER, JUDGING WAR CRIMES & TORTURE: FRENCH JUSTICE & INTERNATIONAL CRIMINAL TRIBUNALS & COMMISSIONS (1940–2005), 275–302 (2006).

125. *See* Langer, *supra* note 28.

126. *See, e.g.,* Loi 2010-930 du 9 août 2010 portant adaptation du droit pénal à l'institution de la Cour pénale internationale, Art. 8, J.O., Aug. 10, 2010, p. 14678 (France); International Criminal Court Act, 2001, c. 17 (Eng.).

127. Interview with anonymous member of the Center for Constitutional Rights, New York, Apr. 5, 2011 (on file with author).

128. S.C. Res. 827, U.N. Doc. S/RES/827 (May 25, 1993); S.C. Res. 955, art. 2, U.N. SCOR, at 2, U.N. Doc. S/Res/955 (Nov. 8, 1994); S.C. Res. 978, U.N. Doc. S/RES/978 (Feb. 27, 1995).

129. For example, France passed Law No. 95-1 of Jan. 2, 1995 and Law No. 96-432 of May 22, 1996, which authorize the exercise of jurisdiction over international crimes committed in the former Yugoslavia and Rwanda.

130. I am grateful to Jonathan Weiner for bringing the "uploading/downloading" metaphor to my attention.

131. Both tribunals established completion strategies to finish their work by target dates. *See, e.g.,* S.C. Res. 1503, U.N. Doc. S/Res/1503 (Aug. 28, 2003). These strategies included transferring cases to domestic courts.

132. Two exceptions are the cases of Murwanashyaka and Musoni in Germany described *supra* note 119.

133. *See, e.g.,* Rod Rastan, *Complementarity: Contest or Collaboration?,* in COMPLEMENTARITY & UNIVERSAL JURISDICTION, *supra* note 12, at 83, 113–15. This type of sharing of information by the OTP was apparently important in facilitating the prosecution of Murwanashyaka and Musoni in Germany.

134. *See, e.g.,* William Schabas, *"Complementarity in Practice": Some Uncomplimentary Thoughts,* 19 CRIM. L. F. 5 (2009). *But see* Darryl Robinson, *The Mysterious Mysteriousness of Complementarity,* 21 CRIM. L. F. 67 (2010).

135. On tools that the OTP, the Court itself, or the Assembly of States Parties could use to encourage states to prosecute crimes under the jurisdiction of the Court, *see, e.g.,* Louis Arbour, *Will the ICC Have an Impact on Universal Jurisdiction?,* 1 J. INT'L CRIM. JUST. 585, 587 (2003); William Burke-White, *Proactive Complementarity: The International Criminal Court & National Courts in the Rome System of International Justice,* 49 HARV. INT'L L.J. 53 (2008); Pocar & Maystre, *infra* note 141, at 299–301. On how the notion of positive complementarity can give a framework for such measures, *see generally* MOHAMED M. EL ZEIDY, THE PRINCIPLE OF COMPLEMENTARITY IN INTERNATIONAL CRIMINAL LAW 298–306 (2008); Burke-White, *Proactive Complementarity, supra*; Carsten Stahn, *Complementarity: A Tale of Two Notions,* 19 CRIM. L. F. 87 (2008).

136. Minow, True-Frost, & Whiting, in this volume.

137. *See, e.g.,* PIERRE HAZAN, JUSTICE IN A TIME OF WAR: THE TRUE STORY BEHIND THE INTERNATIONAL CRIMINAL TRIBUNAL FOR THE FORMER YUGOSLAVIA (2004).

138. On the effect of these pressures, *see, e.g.,* John Hagan & Sanja Kutnjak Ivkovic, *Structural Pre-Conditionality, Smoking Gun Evidence, & Collective Command Responsibility for War Crimes in the Former Yugoslavia,* 14 UCLA J. INT'L L. & FOREIGN AFF. 149 (2009).

139. *See* Máximo Langer, *Trends & Tensions in International Criminal Procedure: A Symposium,* 14 UCLA J. INT'L L. & FOREIGN AFF. 1, 17 (2009).

140. Rome Statute, *supra* note 17, art. 17.

141. *See, e.g.,* Office of the Prosecutor, ICC, *Informal Expert Paper: The Principle of Complementarity in Practice,* §75 (2003); ANTONIO CASSESE, INTERNATIONAL CRIMINAL LAW 352 (2003); JANN K. KLEFFNER, COMPLEMENTARITY IN THE ROME STATUTE & NATIONAL CRIMINAL JURISDICTIONS 113 (2008); JO STIGEN, THE RELATIONSHIP BETWEEN THE INTERNATIONAL CRIMINAL COURT & NATIONAL JURISDICTION: THE PRINCIPLE OF COMPLEMENTARITY 190–94 (2008); Christopher K. Hall, *The Role of Universal Jurisdiction in the International Criminal Court Complementarity System,* in COMPLEMENTARITY & UNIVERSAL JURISDICTION, *supra* note 12, at 201, 209–12; Fausto Pocar and Magali Maystre, *The Principle of Complementarity: A Means towards a More Pragmatic Enforcement of the Goal Pursued by Universal Jurisdiction?,* in COMPLEMENTARITY & UNIVERSAL JURISDICTION, *supra* note 12, at 247; Cedric Ryngaert, *The International Criminal Court & Universal Jurisdiction: A Fraught Relationship?,* 12 NEW CRIM. L. REV. 498, 504–5 (2009). The minority of commentators has disagreed with this interpretation, although for reasons different from the ones I advance here. *See, e.g.,* Kai Ambos, *Prosecuting International Crimes at the National & International Level: Between Justice & Realpolitik,* in INTERNATIONAL PROSECUTION OF HUMAN RIGHTS CRIMES 55, 66 (Wolfgang Kaleck et al. eds., 2007); Federica Gioia, *State Sovereignty, Jurisdiction, & "Modern" International Law: The Principle of Complementarity in the International Criminal Court,* 19 LEIDEN J. INT'L L. 1095, 1110 (2006).

142. Article 31 of the Vienna Convention on the Law of Treaties establishes that a treaty shall be interpreted in good faith in accordance with the ordinary meaning to be given to the terms of the treaty in their context and in the light of its object and purpose. The ICC has agreed with this view. *See, e.g.,* Situation in Democratic Republic of the Congo, Case No. ICC-01/04-168, Judgment on the Prosecutor's Application for Extraordinary Review of Pre-Trial Chamber I's 31 March 2006 Decision Denying Leave to Appeal, ¶33 (July 13, 2006), http://www.icc-cpi.int/iccdocs/doc/doc183558.pdf.

143. Rome Statute, *supra* note 17, art. 12(2)–(3). As previously pointed out, the ICC also has jurisdiction over any case referred to it by the U.N. Security Council, even where the case involves the territory and nationals of a nonparty state. This type of jurisdiction can be understood as exceptional within the ICC regime.

144. *See, e.g.,* CASSESE, *supra* note 141, at 351; Markus Benzing, *The Complementarity Regime of the International Criminal Court: International Criminal Justice between State Sovereignty & the Fight against Immunity,* 7 MAX PLANCK Y.B. U.N. L. 591, 594–96 (2003); Manuela Melandri, *The Relationship between State Sovereignty & the Enforcement of International Criminal Law under the Rome Statute,* 9 INT'L CRIM. L. REV. 531, 535–37 (2009).

145. *See, e.g.,* RESTATEMENT (THIRD) OF FOREIGN RELATIONS LAW OF THE UNITED STATES §§402–3. It is beyond the scope of this article to discuss whether, under the complementarity principle, domestic prosecutions based on the passive personality principle should have priority over the ICC's jurisdiction.

146. *See, e.g.,* CASSESE, *supra* note 141, at 354.

147. *See* Jaime Malamud-Goti, *The Moral Dilemmas about Trying Pinochet in Spain,* 32 U. MIAMI INTER-AM. L. REV. 1 (2001).

148. On positive complementarity, *see supra* note 135.

149. *See, e.g.,* CASSESE, *supra* note 141, at 351; Benzing, *supra* note 144, at 598–99.

150. On the comparative advantage of ICC investigations vis-à-vis domestic ones, *see* Whiting, in this volume.

151. *See* CODE D'INSTRUCTION CRIMINELLE (C.I.CR.) art. 10 §1bis (Belg.) (the federal prosecutor may decide not to proceed with a case under universal jurisdiction if it appears the case should be put before an international tribunal); STRAFPROZESSORDNUNG (SGB) (SOCIAL CODE), 2002, §153(f) (Ger.) (the federal prosecutor may dismiss a case to give priority to an international court of justice, especially in those cases that have no territorial or nationality link with Germany).

The International Civil Servant

How the First Prosecutor Engaged the U.N. Security Council

C. Cora True-Frost

The relationship between the powerful U.N. Security Council and the first prosecutor of the International Criminal Court (ICC) was shaped in part by choices made by the prosecutor, Luis Moreno Ocampo. Moreno Ocampo, the first Prosecutor of the International Criminal Court, chose to craft himself as an international civil servant, bound to independently apply the law and to disregard politics, acting neither as an agent nor as a foe of the Council. Even in the face of Council hostility, he treated the Council as an institutional ally.

In this chapter, I examine Moreno Ocampo's decision to act as an international civil servant. Moreno Ocampo headed an office within an institution that lacks enforcement power against its member states, suspects, indictees, or other international organizations (IOs). Despite the tremendous power asymmetries in the relationship between the prosecutor and the Council, which I detail, over the first prosecutor's term, the Council and the prosecutor eventually engaged in both regular contact and a markedly less hostile relationship. Moreno Ocampo's administrative, diplomatic, and prosecutorial choices played a role in the increasing rapprochement with the Council.[1] Over his tenure—from June 16, 2003 to June 15, 2012—the Council increasingly frequently reaffirmed the ICC's role in prosecuting violations of international criminal law in twenty-six of its resolutions, and it eventually ceased its attempts to defer potential ICC prosecutions. It also referred the situations in the Sudan and Libya to the Court and refused to defer ongoing prosecutions when asked to do so by the African Union.[2]

The Council has borne the primary responsibility of maintaining international peace and security since 1947.[3] But in 2002, the Rome Statute established the autonomous ICC with the responsibility to "exercise . . . jurisdiction over persons for the most serious crimes of international concern, in a manner complementary to national criminal jurisdictions." The independent prosecutor of the ICC's mandate is to investigate, indict, and prosecute those most responsible for grave crimes.[4] In 2002, therefore, the Council's mandate substantially overlapped with that of the newly established ICC and its independent prosecutor.

The prosecutor and the Council's mandate are intermingled in the following ways.[5] Under the terms of the Rome Statute, the Council has the authority to stop a planned or pending ICC prosecution for a year. It may also refer situations to the ICC, including situations involving states not party to the Rome Statute.[6] In addition, the Council can ask the Pre-Trial Chamber of the ICC to review the prosecutor's choice not to prosecute pursuant to its referrals.[7]

Because the Council has the power to intervene in the Prosecutor's work in these ways, when Moreno Ocampo began his job in June 2003, he faced the formidable task of managing an unprecedented relationship with the powerful U.N. Security Council.[8] The Council is not legally accountable as a practical matter.[9] Its members, especially the five veto-wielding permanent members, have the unparalleled power to bind states under chapter VII of the U.N. Charter.[10] There are no provisions of the U.N. Charter allowing for permanent members' removal. But by contrast, a number of mechanisms hold the independent prosecutor accountable to the Council and the ICC.[11] Of course, the prosecutor is held accountable by international criminal law and must prove his cases beyond a reasonable doubt.[12] In addition, the Assembly of States Parties organ of the ICC has the power to remove the prosecutor,[13] and the ICC Pre-Trial Chamber possesses the authority to review the prosecutor's independent power to initiate prosecutions or to refrain from prosecuting.[14]

As a result, for Moreno Ocampo, ignoring the Council was not a possibility. He might, however, have simply considered himself the Council's agent, compelled to do its bidding and issue indictments were he ever to receive a referral from the Council. He also might have avoided examining situations that would be sensitive to the permanent members out of concern that the Council would defer his investigations.

Alternately, pursuing a more risky strategy, he could have treated the Council's interests as being opposed to the ICC's. Such an approach would have enabled him to avoid the criticism that the Court is a tool of the powerful members of the Security Council. Correspondingly, Moreno Ocampo might have used his office to challenge the Council's inaction in various situations or to shame the Council for its inconsistency. In a similar vein, he could have forced a confrontation with the Council on the issues of his discretion and authority by, for example, refusing to open investigations in situations referred to the Court by the Council. He would not have been the first international prosecutor to act aggressively toward U.N. Security Council members. ICTY Prosecutor Carla del Ponte investigated then-President Bill Clinton and the U.S. administration for command responsibility in Operation Storm, related to the General Gotovina indictments.[15]

However, he pursued a third course, carving a middle ground between these two options, aiming to guard his independence while remaining alert to the Council's power to alter the course of the ICC's trials. Engaging the Council as an institutional ally, the prosecutor fit the classic model of an international civil servant described by former U.N. secretary-general Dag Hammarskjöld in 1961. According to Hammarskjöld's account, the international civil servant is prohibited from seeking or receiving orders from any one government and is compelled to be and to remain politically impartial.[16] This model of the international civil servant is one of an ideal bureaucrat, more consistent with Hegel's theory of bureaucracy than with Weber's.[17] In this vein, against repeated allegations of bias, Moreno Ocampo emphasized that he would not be swayed by politics in exercising his discretion. He stated, "My Office evaluate[s] the crimes committed, their gravity and national proceedings. I have to apply the law. Nothing more, nothing less. The decision that ending impunity will ensure lasting peace and security was taken in Rome. I should not, and I will not take in[to] consideration, political considerations."[18]

Hammarskjöld's international civil servant wields significant administrative authority and discretion. Likewise, the first prosecutor had significant administrative authority over the Office of the Prosecutor.[19] As Professor Meierhenrich elaborates, Moreno Ocampo used his authority to issue policy papers and enhance institutional transparency, seeking both to secure broad support for his office's work and to guard its impartiality and independence.[20] In so doing, he foreclosed some discretion for his successors in the future and adopted a model of prosecution arguably influenced more by civil law, and less familiar to common law prosecutors.

While the international civil servant should be politically unbiased, he need not remain passive and neutral with respect to discharging the mandate of his office. Indeed, his duties may conflict with the interests of some member states, and his decisions may be unpopular, but he will work to successfully and impartially discharge his mandate, even when his actions produce controversy.[21] Similarly, Moreno Ocampo generated controversy, for example, when he adopted a policy interpreting the Rome Statute as requiring him to prosecute only those alleged to be most responsible for mass atrocities and to ignore political concerns regarding peace when deciding whether to discontinue investigations or prosecutions.[22] He also asserted his independence by deciding that his office had the independent right to decide whether to investigate situations referred to it by the Council.[23] Despite the controversy following these and other of his prosecutorial, administrative, and diplomatic actions, he saw these decisions as vital to his success pursuing his mandate to apply and enforce international criminal law.[24]

Although the international civil servant must be politically unbiased, he may need to encourage interaction with various parties to accomplish his mandate. Accordingly, the prosecutor treated the Council as an institutional ally while asserting his independence. Recognizing that the Council's hostility toward the Court could jeopardize the Court's success, he refrained from reacting to obstacles created by the Council, even when those obstacles, like the Council's early deferrals of Court jurisdiction, impeded the pursuit of his mandate. He also warned the Council before he used his power to issue indictments.[25] In addition, by mostly refraining from requesting specific assistance from the Council, he neither shamed Council members nor provoked a confrontation with them.[26]

This chapter begins with a section that outlines the legal and political powers of the prosecutor and the U.N. Security Council as well as the structures of each organ. The second section argues that the first prosecutor styled himself as an international civil servant—impartial and independent while also treating the Council as an institutional ally. Finally, the chapter explores some implications of this argument. Further study of the evolving relationship between the Council and the prosecutor is recommended. Although the Office of the Prosecutor and the ICC continue to face criticisms of the prosecutorial strategy and allegations of bias against Africa in particular, this analysis suggests that Moreno Ocampo's choices may have helped some Council members relinquish their open hostility to the ICC's role in international criminal law and engage the Court, even as his choices may bind his successors and the institution in the future. This preliminary examination of the role of the prosecutor in developing the relationships with the Council contributes to our understanding of the bounded capacity of international civil servants within IOs to diffuse norms. The analysis of the role of the international civil servant suggests that elite norm entrepreneurs may be able to their use normative and administrative authority to diffuse norms even when faced with hostility from entrenched and powerful interests.

The U.N. Security Council and the Office of the Prosecutor: Powers and Constraints

The prosecutor's options for building a relationship with the U.N. Security Council were shaped by the structure and the respective powers of both institutions. More specifically, the formal parameters of the relationship between the U.N. Security Council and the independent prosecutor of the ICC are set by the Rome Statute, the U.N. Charter, and the Relationship Agreement between the U.N. and the ICC.[27] While these documents shape interactions between the two, they are not the sole determinants of their interactions. The evolving relationship between the U.N. Security Council and prosecutor has also been affected by the changing politics of Security Council member states as well as Council members' perceptions of the Court's successes and failures. When the first prosecutor sought to encourage Security Council members to engage the ICC favorably, he had to work within these constraints.

The Council

As the sole organ with the capacity for collective judgment and mobilization of force in interpreting the U.N. Charter, the Council has broad discretion to determine what qualifies as "a threat to international peace and security" under article 39.[28] The Council's structure privileges five military powers by vesting in them permanent Council membership and veto power, but Council action requires a consensus of at least nine of the fifteen members.[29] Notwithstanding the collective responsibilities and powers granted to the Council under the U.N. Charter, as a practical matter, the five permanent and ten elected members of the U.N. Security Council undeniably represent their respective states' interests in the organ's pursuit of the collective goal of maintaining international peace and security. Indeed, the political interests of individual member states often prevent the Council from acting in the face of grave violations of international law,[30] prompting legal scholars and diplomats to advance legal arguments for Council reform or for alternatives to Council action.[31]

While the Council must not violate *jus cogens* norms or the terms of the U.N. Charter under international law,[32] as a practical matter, the Council is primarily accountable to General Assembly member states only through its reputation. The Council is not legally accountable since there is arguably no existing international or national institution with the power to enforce a binding legal judgment regarding its actions and omissions.[33]

Although the Council played a historic role in developing international criminal law,[34] its attention to violations of international criminal law has been uneven and unreliable. As of June 2014, three of the five veto-wielding permanent members—the United States, China, and Russia—are not Rome Statute members. Otherwise, the Rome Statute ratification status of the ten elected members on the Council varies from time to time, which of course has an impact on the Council's interactions with the ICC.

The ICC and the Prosecutor

After extensive negotiations, in July 1998, 120 states—with the support of a broad array of civil society organizations—adopted the Rome Statute, creating the ICC as a permanent court to focus sustained attention on atrocities and "to put an end to impunity for the perpetrators of these crimes and thus to contribute to the prevention of such crimes."[35] The autonomous ICC came into being on July 1, 2002.[36] It is composed of four organs, including the prosecutor's office. The Assembly of States Parties organ elects the prosecutor and judges and determines the budget for the Office of the Prosecutor.[37] The budget of the ICC is a central constraint on the prosecutor's work. The ICC relies on voluntary contributions and cooperation from states to support its investigations and enforce its indictments under international law.

The Office of the Prosecutor has the power to trigger the jurisdiction of the Court, to investigate crimes, and to prosecute.[38] In exercising that power, the prosecutor, who is the chief administrative authority of the office, must apply the law set forth in the Rome Statute.[39] The prosecutor should represent the collective interests of the states parties to the Rome Statute in prosecuting those accused of atrocities.[40] The bases for the prosecutor's jurisdiction as well as conditions for admissibility are set forth in the Rome Statute.[41] The Pre-Trial Chamber must confirm the prosecutor's charges,[42] and it has the corresponding legal authority to review the prosecutor's investigations as well as some failures to proceed with investigations.[43] The Council or a referring state may also ask the Pre-Trial Chamber to review the prosecutor's omissions.[44]

Significant logistical constraints and resource gaps limit the investigatory and enforcement capacities of the Office of the Prosecutor. Despite states' obligations under international law not to interfere with and to execute ICC arrest warrants, member state compliance has in practice been inconsistent. Unlike a domestic prosecutor, therefore, the ICC prosecutor must necessarily be concerned about how and whether the office's investigations will proceed and indictments will be enforced.[45]

The Legal and Political Relationship between the Security Council and the Prosecutor

Since politics influence—and sometimes are the chief determinant of—the Council's responses to different threats to peace and security, it is difficult for the Council to coordinate the various positions of both elected and permanent Council member states regarding referrals of situations to the ICC, deferrals from ICC jurisdiction, or any other expression of support for the ICC. The initial antagonism of the United States, China, and Russia[46] to the Court disturbed the possibility of consistent support for the Court from the Council. Although the Council eventually referred the situations in the Sudan and Libya[47] to the ICC, its related support has been famously weak. Indeed, the Council has stipulated that U.N. funding should not be used to support the ICC's work related to either of these referrals.[48] But even beyond providing financial and resource support, when the Council has referred situations to the ICC, it has not consistently called on states to ensure that ICC arrest warrants are enforced.[49] Nor has it condemned states parties to the Rome Statute or U.N. member states for inviting or receiving ICC fugitives, as happened when Sudanese president Omar al-Bashir visited Rome Statute members Malawi, Chad, Djibouti, Kenya, and Nigeria.[50] Indeed, even permanent Council member China has received al-Bashir on state visits.[51]

With responsibility for trying defendants before the Court, the prosecutor unquestionably faces challenges in managing a relationship with the Council.[52] Not only is it difficult to decide how to respond to or rely on action or inaction from the Council, but the Council can also intervene in prosecutions. Although the administrative and budgetary operations of the Office of the Prosecutor are not subject to the oversight of the Security Council, Council members watch the prosecutor's actions closely. Members are concerned with many issues, such as the pace of ICC cases and judicial decisions, but the actions of the Office of the Prosecutor are a focal point for Council members' perceptions of the Court.[53] If the Council does not agree with prosecutorial choices, the Rome Statute permits it to compel the prosecutor to defer investigations or active prosecutions for up to a year.[54] Moreover, the Council can request review of prosecutorial action, and acting under article 13 of the Rome Statute and chapter VII of the U.N. Charter, the Council can also refer situations to the ICC, including those involving nonparty states.[55]

Other more informal aspects of the relationship between the Court and the Council have evolved over time, thanks in part to administrative decisions in building the office, many of them made by Moreno Ocampo. For example, members of the Jurisdiction, Complementarity, and Cooperation Division of the Prosecutor in the ICC's New York office now regularly interact with Council members. In addition, other members of the Court, such as its president, meet with Council members from time to time.[56] The prosecutor's ability to engage the Council is bounded by these structural and practical constraints. However, by treating his role as that of an international civil servant, Moreno Ocampo's open rejection of politics and his emphasis of the role of law in his mandate have strengthened possibilities for his independent engagement with the Council.

The Prosecutor as an International Civil Servant

In this section, I use the lens of the international civil servant model to compare the Office of the Prosecutor with that of the U.N. secretary-general and to argue that Moreno Ocampo acted as an international civil servant in managing his relationship with the Security Council. Hammarskjöld famously described the international civil servant as one who is prohibited from seeking or receiving orders from any particular government, compelled to be and to remain politically unbiased, and nonetheless likely to run counter to some member states' interests in the pursuit of the execution of his mandate under international law.[57] To say that he followed the model of an international civil servant is not to say that his execution of his mandate was flawless; rather, it provides a helpful framework for understanding how Moreno Ocampo navigated the challenge of maintaining his independence and impartiality without running afoul of the powerful U.N. Security Council.

Administrative Authority and Prosecutorial Discretion

Hammarskjöld focused on the U.N. secretary-general in his account of the international civil servant. In many ways, however, the prosecutor of the

ICC is similar to the U.N. secretary-general in spite of the differences in their mandates and the structure of their offices.[58] As the chief administrative officer of the U.N., secretaries-general follow the general will of the General Assembly and the U.N. Security Council but have administrative authority for implementation. They must use their independent discretion in discharging responsibilities delegated to them by the Council and General Assembly under article 98 of the U.N. Charter.[59] They also have independent discretion in bringing matters to the attention of the Council.[60] Similarly, the prosecutor has "full administrative authority over the management and administration of the Office of the Prosecutor."[61] Under the Rome Statute, the Assembly of States Parties has delegated to prosecutors the duty to prosecute, and they are expected to use their independent discretion to investigate and prosecute. Hammarskjöld claims that the international civil servant is particularly useful when an organization needs "impartial implementation or execution of a decision that has been reached"[62] but where the means for implementation have not been agreed upon. In such cases, the international civil servant may receive a wide amount of latitude from states to make unpopular decisions.[63] In a similar fashion, the Assembly of State Parties delegates to prosecutors the authority to choose how to prosecute violations of international criminal law. The Council also delegates to the prosecutor the authority to make potentially unpopular decisions about who should be prosecuted in the situations it refers to the prosecutor. Neither secretaries-general nor prosecutors have unfettered discretion, however; they are constrained by the terms of the Charter and the Rome Statute, respectively.

Much as U.N. secretaries-general and World Trade Organization directors-general have the authority to schedule rounds, to generate reports, to foster state-to-state discussion, and to offer a venue for engaging various issues,[64] the prosecutor of the court, too, can not only wield prosecutorial powers but can also generate policies, schedule meetings, and foster state-to-state discussion to advance the Court's mission. Moreno Ocampo used his administrative authority to supplement the legal standards of the Rome Statute through published policy papers clarifying how he would implement the Statute.[65] These nonbinding policy papers purport to constrain the prosecutor's discretion in a way that fits more comfortably within a civil law system than with the model of prosecutorial discretion in common law systems. In these policy papers, for example, the prosecutor refined and defined the gravity and magnitude of crimes that the office would consider admissible.[66] He also controversially used his good offices to meet with states to help secure compliance. Indeed, one objection to the OTP's purported political impartiality might stem from the Moreno Ocampo's controversial actions in visiting particular states to shore up support for enforcement of arrest warrants, for example, by engaging nongovernmental organizations (NGOs) and Uganda, a state party.[67] The prosecutor's attempts to inculcate compliance by states parties through meetings and visits and leveraging corresponding reputational pressure need not imply political bias, however. Rather, such meetings and visits fit into the model I am describing here: Moreno Ocampo was acting as an international civil servant, using the soft power of his office to discharge his mandate even if his actions in this regard might have created controversy.

By pursuing both consistent application of the law and transparency in his decision making, the prosecutor sought to deepen his office's accountability—including its accountability for political bias—and sought to enhance the ICC's global legitimacy. Without the support of member states, both the U.N. secretary-general and the prosecutor have limited capacity for implementation. They must, therefore, interpret their mandates in ways that build credibility among their organizations' member states. U.N. secretary-general's initiatives have the potential to be supported by a Security Council chapter VII mandate, obliging states to comply. But for prosecutors, implementation concerns are arguably more pressing, since they must rely, absent heretofore nonexistent support from the Security Council, exclusively on contributions and cooperation from member states, NGOs, and IOs. Lacking the power to compel action, prosecutors' ability to investigate active conflicts, to maintain the security of witnesses and defendants, and to enforce arrest warrants can all be jeopardized by lack of state cooperation, arguably increasing the urgency for prosecutors to intervene with states parties. At this point in the Court's development, the support the prosecutors require is rarely easily won and remains far from predictable.[68]

Impartiality

The international civil servant, no matter how prominent, must not give in to specific political pressure in the pursuit of his mandate and thus must be willing to end up in conflict with major powers.[69] The prosecutor's job may seem to confound the notion of impartiality. At any rate, the sort of impartiality I am talking about here is *political* impartiality, not operational or juridical impartiality. He does have a stake in the outcome of his otherwise politically impartial decisions regarding how to run his office and whom to prosecute under law, and he does have moral judgments to make.[70] When he prosecutes, he is clearly an advocate. As a faithful servant of the Rome Statute member states, however, the prosecutor should remain politically impartial. As the administrative chief of the Office of the Prosecutor, he must impartially consider the feasibility of investigating, prosecuting, and engaging states and other IOs to secure compliance with the Court's investigations and warrants. As an officer of the law he must bring accused criminals to justice and undertake prosecutions with diligence and purpose. Accordingly, when the prosecutor received referrals from the Council, he might have viewed himself as bound to investigate such referrals from the "executive" body of the international system. But he instead advanced the argument that he must independently evaluate the evidence without being swayed by the political power of the referring authority. He articulated a policy of impartiality when faced with these referrals. In so doing, he cast the judiciary of the ICC as a counterweight to the U.N. Security Council in international law. In the absence of a robust international system of checks and balances of the legislative-executive functions of the U.N. Security Council, and where the prosecutor's actions can be affected by the Council, Moreno Ocampo may have seen it as imperative for him to make his political impartiality clear.

Hammarskjöld argued that the international civil servant must use integrity and conscience to self-police against bias and subjects about which he cannot be neutral.[71] He likened international civil servant's tools in his quest for impartiality to those of a judge. If the international civil servant self-polices, Hammarskjöld claims, he can render unbiased decisions, which he defines as decisions not influenced by the individual's personal—as opposed to institutional—loyalties.[72] When Hammarskjöld emphasizes the need for politically unbiased international civil servants, he has faith in the power of the law and judgment to resolve difficult issues. Skeptics, however, may have difficulty reconciling the fact that both the U.N. secretary-general and prosecutor are elected by member states but still maintain politically impartial positions.[73] Hammarskjöld's faith in the capacity to be politically unbiased was not born of blind optimism, however. Neither Hammarskjöld nor Moreno Ocampo would argue that politics are rendered moot by the existence of international law. Instead, they would claim that in specific situations, law and judgment can displace political bias. In January 1999, U.N. secretary-general Kofi Annan said, "Impartiality does not—and must not—mean neutrality in the face of evil. It means strict and unbiased adherence to the principles of the Charter—nothing more, and nothing less."[74] As prosecutor, Moreno Ocampo repeatedly emphasized that his mandate was to follow the rule of law and the rules set forth by the Rome Statute, not to do what was most politically expedient.[75]

Not Neutral about Accomplishing His Mandate

While it is critical for international civil servants to interpret their mandate impartially and according to an international legal framework, they are not neutral about accomplishing that mandate. Indeed, international civil servants must be willing to take unpopular positions to execute their mandate under law and must be ready to face whatever consequences may follow.[76] Despite the prosecutor's attempts to cast himself as a politically impartial international civil servant, many of his choices generated controversy. It is difficult to imagine how anyone might have executed the prosecutor's mandate without provoking controversy and allegations of bias.[77] The most persistent claim of bias pertains to the Court's exclusively African docket to date.[78] Moreno Ocampo replied to the claim that the Court was following a neocolonialist agenda and targeting Africa by saying, "There are 14 accused, all of them are Africans. There are more than 5 million African victims displaced, more than 40,000 African victims killed, thousands of African victims raped. Hundreds of thousands of African children transformed into killers and rapists. 100% of the victims are Africans. 100% of the accused are African. As Desmond Tutu said: Choose your side. Do you associate with the victims or the perpetrators? I am on the victims' side. I will not apologize for that."[79] He also addressed the concern that the Court was ignoring criminals in the developed countries: "Africans are tired of double standards. So am I. The issue is: are we going to implement one standard? Or are we going to reinforce the double standard? I am not the world Prosecutor; I am the Prosecutor of 110 states. Iraq, Sri Lanka, USA, Lebanon or Israel are not states parties."[80] If the U.N. Security Council were to decide to exercise its Article 16 power to defer proceedings in Africa, which it has not yet done, under the terms of the Rome Statute the international civil servant would be forced to comply with this decision.

Moreno Ocampo has also been accused of political bias by the opposition Movement for the Liberation of Congo for indicting Mr. Bemba for crimes allegedly committed in the Central African Republic (CAR).[81] Many other controversies arose as a consequence of his prosecutorial policies. For example, when the prosecutor defined his mandate as requiring him to pursue apolitical justice, not political peace, he was criticized for impeding peace negotiations between the Lord's Resistance Army (LRA) and Uganda. The prosecutor's related prosecutorial decisions not to withdraw the indictment against LRA leader Joseph Kony and to indict the Sudanese President al-Bashir were also criticized.[82]

In addition, for some time, the prosecutor preliminarily examined whether the Court might have jurisdiction over the acts alleged to have occurred in Iraq and Palestine (situations sensitive to some of the five permanent members) and eventually issued a reasoned decision explaining that the Court lacked sufficient basis to prosecute in those situations.[83] Both his decision to examine and to close the examinations were controversial. He opened a preliminary examination into Afghanistan in 2007, and as of July 2014, neither he nor his successor had made a determination about whether subject matter jurisdiction existed.[84] Under Hammarskjöld's model, these controversies and the allegations of bias that followed these decisions could be reframed as political responses to the prosecutor's attempt to pursue his mandate with integrity, not according to orders from specific governments, even as he remained mindful of concerns about the institutional longevity of his office and the Court.[85]

The Independent International Civil Servant Prosecutor Engages the U.N. Security Council as an Institutional Ally

Although he knew the Council had the potential to interfere with his work, Moreno Ocampo endeavored to convey to states that he was not influenced by political pressure from any source—including the U.N. Security Council—when he used his discretion to limit the degree to which he would be compelled to answer to the Council. As mentioned above, after he received the Council's first referral to the Court, he indicated that his office was not required to investigate the referred situation.[86] He explained that the triggering of investigations was not entirely up to the Council but that he was obliged to conduct an independent review of Council-referred situations to ascertain whether he should invoke the Court's jurisdiction and open an investigation.[87]

Although the prosecutor was aggressive in interpreting the Rome Statute to permit him to independently assess Council referrals, he was not directly aggressive toward Council members; for example, he did not proclaim that he was investigating heads of state of permanent U.N. Security Council members, as ICTY Prosecutor del Ponte had done. Rather, he sought to use his constrained powers to maintain his independence while still treating the Council as an institutional ally. With only a few exceptions, during his briefings to the Council, the prosecutor sought to retain his independence by mostly refraining from requesting the Council to take specific actions in support of his efforts.[88] He also warned the Council about the various arrest warrants he would issue in the case of the Sudan.[89] In addition, the prosecutor moved forward and sought indictments in the situation in Libya,[90] although he arguably might have chosen not to prosecute in the Council-referred situation there in light of the ongoing conflict and insecure situation on the ground, the Court's constrained resources, and the Council's failure to help enforce its previous referral of the Sudan to the Court. In these ways and others, he sought not to alienate the Council while pursuing his mandate independently.

After all, too much coordination between the U.N. Security Council and ICC has the potential to undermine perceptions of the prosecutor's independence and impartiality. Some states oppose the terms of the Rome Statute that permit the political U.N. Security Council to refer to the ICC situations of nonparty states.[91] Under the terms of the Rome Statute, the prosecutor could do little to address such objections, but Moreno Ocampo was arguably mindful of such concerns when he attempted to constrain his discretion with policy papers and use transparency to make clear the motivations for the OTP's various actions. Most important in this regard was his statement that he had an independent obligation to examine situations referred to the Court by the Council.[92] In addition to developing and publishing policy papers, he also published reasoned explanations for the disposition of his preliminary examinations and the communications received by the office.[93] Indeed, by developing and publishing transparent policies about how he would interpret his jurisdictional mandate,[94] the prosecutor facilitated an understanding with members of the international community and the Security Council that he would act as an impartial civil servant. His transparent prosecutorial policies likely helped allay—though they did not eliminate—Council members' concerns that his decisions about prosecuting would be politically motivated.[95] His restraint in not using his independent prosecutorial function aggressively arguably built more credibility with the Council than lack of restraint would have done despite the slow and flawed progress of the first cases.

Skeptical readers might ask whether the prosecutors could act as anything other than international civil servants in light of the structure of the Rome Statute. They might argue that prosecutors are international civil servants by necessity. But Moreno Ocampo had tremendous discretion in exercising his role. He could have exercised his discretion in a far more opaque manner—there was no rule requiring him to publish the Office of the Prosecutor's policy papers or information about communications received. When he received referrals, he might have seen the Rome Statute as compelling him to act as the Council's agent, or he might have chosen a much riskier strategy. For example, had he been more concerned with establishing the ICC's independence than with establishing a long-term institutional relationship with the Council, he might have been more confrontational, highlighting the inconsistencies in Council action or attempting to shame Council members as the ICTY Prosecutor once did.[96]

He did not, however, choose to pursue these routes. Rather, Moreno Ocampo worked to develop the infrastructure of the Office of the Prosecutor and focused on building its foundation.[97] Although some observers would dispute this assertion, he was initially cautious in prosecuting, awaiting state self-referrals and not initiating *proprio motu* prosecutions. The prosecutor's pursuit of his mandate in the mold of an impartial international civil servant helped him to engage the Council in the face of some of its members' opposition to the Court while developing policies to protect his independence.

Increased Engagement

Despite initial hostility from some Council members, the prosecutor and the Council gradually engaged more frequently. During Moreno Ocampo's tenure, the Council reaffirmed the ICC's role in prosecuting violations of international criminal law in twenty-six of its resolutions, and those reaffirmations came more frequently later in his term.[98] As the prosecutor published policy papers and began operations, the Council also invoked the Court in nonbinding thematic resolutions and offered limited logistical cooperation.[99] The Council eventually invoked the Court in binding resolutions, especially when referring the cases of Libya and Sudan.[100]

The prosecutor worked through different levels of engagement with the Council, recognizing that even unenforceable presidential statements (PRSTs) are important signs of support that might one day ripen into enforcement action. After the Council referred the situation in the Sudan to the Court, the prosecutor briefed the Council eighteen times,[101] and the Council issued eleven nonbinding PRSTs invoking the Court.[102] Through the briefings, the prosecutor familiarized the Council with the challenges the Court faced.

Over the course of the prosecutor's term, the Council also became progressively less (openly) hostile to the Court. The prosecutor never directly engaged the Council's early hostile resolutions of ICC deferral, and for many reasons, the Council eventually ceased adopting resolutions deferring potential ICC prosecutions. In PRSTs and open debates, not only in resolutions, the Council also mentioned the ICC's work.[103]

While my argument that Moreno Ocampo framed his role as being an international civil servant, and this brief review of the developments in the relationship between the Council and the Court cannot establish causation, Moreno Ocampo's approach to his office may be correlated with some of the progress in engagement between the prosecutor and the Council. At any rate, this account of the prosecutor's role as an international civil servant offers lessons for the prosecutor's successors as well as insight into theoretical approaches to understanding how international civil servants effect change within international organizations at the international level.

Implications for Practice: Lessons for Subsequent Prosecutors

This account of some of Moreno Ocampo's choices in engaging the Council has implications for his successors. While the second prosecutor's potential to elicit support in the near term will, of course, be affected by the composition of the U.N. Security Council,[104] support for enforcement of ICC indictments is unlikely in the near future. It is therefore advisable for the prosecutor to continue to engage the Council with the strong understanding that the Office of the Prosecutor does not require the Council's assistance to accomplish its mandate.

Rather than relying on the Council's enforcement support, future prosecutors should continue to call on the Assembly of States Parties and the Court to strengthen the ICC's investigatory and enforcement capacity. While challenging, securing support from a diffuse network of states for the Court's investigations and arrests is a more sound strategy than is expecting the Council to provide resources for the Court in the near term. Seeking to secure compliance and support from Rome Statute Parties, the Office of the Prosecutor may incur unavoidable short-term costs, including the negative reputational effects that result from an inability to enforce its arrest warrants. Over the long term, however, if the prosecutor succeeds, the office and the Court should benefit from its resulting independence and the strengthening of the Court's networks.[105]

While the international civil servant prosecutor should focus on forging national or regional consensuses regarding enforcement of arrest warrants,[106] she might concurrently welcome—and not reject or disparage—even inconsistent expressions of the Council's support for the ICC's work, whether through PRSTs, press statements, open debates, or (less likely) resolutions. Given the structure of the Rome Statute and the Council's referrals to the ICC, the Court benefits from positive engagement between the Council and the prosecutor. Despite the controversy and allegations of bias Council interaction may provoke among member states opposed to the unfairness of the existing Council structure, the prosecutor arguably has more to gain than to lose by engaging the Council. The prosecutor should therefore continue to engage the Council by providing progress updates through reports to Council members, including reports on noncompliance by Rome Statute members.

Notwithstanding the increased prosecutor-Council engagement generated during Moreno Ocampo's term, and even with two Council-referred situations on the Court's docket, the Council continues to move unevenly and cautiously in engaging the prosecutor. For example, it still restricts the prosecutor's access to its working groups. Following the November 2012 open debate, the president of the Council, Guatemala, attempted to invite the prosecutor to attend the working group on the international tribunals, but the broader membership of the Council disagreed.[107] Instead, the members continued the existing interactive dialogue format of the briefings with the prosecutor. Moreno Ocampo's successor, Fatou Bensouda, would be well advised to articulate a policy—if possible—under which she could participate in the Council working groups without compromising her independence in hopes that the Council will become more receptive to the idea of her involvement.

As an international civil servant, Bensouda can also exert external reputational pressure on the Council. She can encourage states parties that are Council members as well as nonstate actors (other international civil servants or NGOs) that frequently interact with the Council to develop and press for standards for U.N. Security Council referrals to the ICC, deferrals from prosecution, and execution of arrest warrants. More specifically, some states have suggested that the prosecutor might encourage Council members that are also states parties to the Rome Statute to establish a Rome Statute Caucus on the Council. Such a caucus could ensure that Council decisions and actions do not conflict with the Rome Statute, as the provisions inserted into resolutions 1593 and 1970 arguably did. It could also encourage future cooperation between the Council and the ICC on the two referrals.

The prosecutor might also seek additional support from other areas of the U.N., including, for example, from U.N. secretaries-general, who might also address the relationship between the ICC and the Council in their annual U.N. reports on the rule of law. Within the ICC, the Assembly of States Parties has not yet established an intersessional group on cooperation with the Council, though the Coalition for the International Criminal Court has repeatedly encouraged it to do so, and the prosecutor could support the establishment of such a group.[108] These suggestions for subsequent prosecutors take into account international civil servants' capacity to utilize administrative power and structure as well as informal processes in international organizations when pursuing their mandate.

The Role of International Civil Servants in International Organizations

This account of the prosecutor's work, in turn, preliminarily sheds light on the theoretical question of the role of elite norm entrepreneurs in international organizations. Previous international relations and international law scholarship has not fully accounted for international civil servants' role within IOs in guiding policy and interaction with other IOs. The classic rational actor accounts in international relations, realism and functionalism, focus on the role of states in directing IO behavior.[109] Institutionalists broaden the lens of analysis beyond states to examine how different interest groups and sometimes individuals can affect state behavior.[110] Constructivist international relations scholars contend that IOs can influence state interests and create new state preferences, but constructivists have not fully studied how norm diffusion occurs within and between IOs.[111] Further, until recently, scholars in international law have paid little attention to how the internal operations and staff of IOs might affect the diffusion of norms. Rationalist accounts in international law focus on state interests,[112] while norm-based legal scholarship focuses on the questions of how law influences state behavior.[113] Managerial theory, which is norm-based, seeks to explain why states comply or fail to comply with international law.[114] As Beth Simmons identifies, accounts of norm diffusion often focus on the effects of norms on state-based elite actors—state, judicial, or bureaucratic elites.[115] This chapter helps fill a gap in the international law and international relations literature about elite norm entrepreneurs by focusing on international civil servants.

The prosecutor's role in managing the relationship with the U.N. Security Council during Moreno Ocampo's tenure preliminarily suggests that the soft power that international civil servants wield might influence states and U.N. organs in an incremental fashion. At the very least, Council members' mimicry and social acceptance[116] of the role of the ICC as evidenced by references to the Court in resolutions and diplomatic practice increased over Moreno Ocampo's term. The prosecutor's decision to act as an international civil servant and to treat the Council as an institutional ally may well have played a role in helping to shift the Council's initial hostility to the Court to regularized engagement.

If so, this suggests that international civil servants can influence the work program and agenda of both their own and other IOs. International civil servants may use diplomacy and engagement to promote norms and to help reframe the "logic of appropriateness"[117] not only within their own IO but also in others. International civil servants do not exist without the international organizations that create them. The Rome Statute developed the opportunity for the prosecutor to engage with the Council and perhaps even to work to alter the strategic calculations of its state members as they interact within the Council organ. The prosecutor used Council briefings to try to persuade and to educate[118] Council members about the possibilities for the ICC's consistent application of international criminal law norms. Although the Council has wide latitude in choosing its actions, Council members have been constrained not only by politics but also by the Council's past practice and reputational concerns. This account thus suggests the ways that the prosecutor's administrative decisions might help develop—or stunt—a logic of appropriateness[119] at the international level that necessitates enforcement of international criminal law.

A rich literature documents the effects of legalization and institutionalization on norms.[120] In the words of Kal Raustiala and Anne-Marie Slaughter, "Institutionalization can alter the calculus of state decision-making . . . by embedding states in processes of cooperation that are mutually reinforcing."[121] Indeed, the existence of the law of the Rome Statute and the creation of the position of ICC prosecutor may mean that no matter how unconvinced individual permanent U.N. Security Council members may be that international criminal law norms should apply to them, these same Council members may gradually be more limited in their capacity to reject out of hand the ICC's role in a particular situation. At the same time, the international civil servant can use diplomacy and impartiality to play a role in expediting this process, helping to persuade the collective Council to take action and advance norms that individual members might not favor.[122] Members of the Security Council may find that they are constrained from obstructing ICC progress by their own previous resolutions and practice even as individual members may not be fully persuaded of the ICC's central role in the promotion of international criminal law.

Acting as an international civil servant, the prosecutor sought to secure an initially hostile Council's support and to show the Council that the Court will protect international criminal law norms.[123] Prosecutors can use their Rome Statute–granted administrative authority to investigate and indict as well as use other soft powers to promote greater acceptance of the ICC's work, perhaps even among initially opposed Security Council members. Accordingly, prosecutors have opportunities to incrementally affect the Council's institutional culture, including its use of soft and hard law to support the Court, which in turn might constrain members in ways they do not anticipate.

Conclusion

Even in his relationship with the powerful U.N. Security Council, Moreno Ocampo endeavored to act as an international civil servant bound to impartially apply the law. Navigating the overlap between the ICC's mandate and the mandate of the U.N. Security Council, he sought to project an image of impartiality in his selection of situations and cases. He did so in part by developing transparent policies and administrative practices, even at the cost of possibly circumscribing his and his successors' discretion. He also reserved the power to decide whether to investigate in Security Council–referred situations. At the same time, he sought to maintain a functioning relationship with the Council; he did not attempt to shame Council members, nor was he initially aggressive in using his *proprio motu* powers. Yet he did not avoid examining situations that were sensitive to Council members' interests, opening examinations in sensitive situations such as those in Afghanistan, Iraq, and Israel/Palestine. He also controversially indicted sitting heads of state, claiming that he must vigorously and independently investigate and prosecute cases to fulfill his mandate. Over his tenure, the U.N. Security Council increasingly engaged the ICC.

Analyzing the role of elite international civil servants such as the prosecutor in promoting norms contributes to understanding norm change at the international level. International civil servants may use rhetoric, administrative policies, work programs, and informal sources of law to vigorously promote their institutional mandate. This account implies that international civil servants might use their place at the table to at least incrementally shift the discourse and administrative practices of their own and other IOs. How rapidly, credibly, or reliably the international civil servant might use administrative discretion to manage controversy remain topics for further exploration.

NOTES

For their comments and suggestions on early drafts, I thank participants in the Office of the Prosecutor's Distinguished Lecturer Series at the ICC, the Syracuse University College of Law Junior Scholars Colloquium, the Cornell International Law/International Relations Workshop, and Jean Galbraith, Cymie Payne, Tara Helfman, Martha Minow, Alex Whiting, and David Zaring. For able research assistance, I thank Heba Girgis, Menno Goedman, Mikala Steenholdt, and Hannah Stewart. I thank Chris Ramsdell for administrative support on this book.

1. Other factors have also played important roles, including the number of Rome Statute member states on the Security Council at any given time; the Obama administration's receptiveness to the ICC; and exogenous shocks such as the Council's need to address certain situations arising from the Arab Spring. Under the Obama administration, the United States transferred Bosco Ntaganda to the Hague for trial before the ICC, deployed military advisers to Uganda to help search for leaders of the Lord's Resistance Army, and once again became an observer state at meetings of the Assembly of States Parties to the Rome Statute. *See* DAVID KAYE ET AL., THE COUNCIL & THE COURT: IMPROVING SECURITY COUNCIL SUPPORT OF THE INTERNATIONAL CRIMINAL COURT 10 (2013), http://councilandcourt.org/files/2013/05/The-Council-and-the-Court-FINAL.pdf.

2. Evidence of increased engagement between the Council and the prosecutor also includes the escalating number of Council resolutions invoking the ICC; the increasingly supportive content of those resolutions; the Council's implicit refusals to defer ICC jurisdiction in active cases; and the incorporation of discussion of the role of the ICC into various aspects of the Council's work agenda, including in open debates and presidential statements. *See infra* at section "The Role of International Civil Servants in International Organizations."

3. *See* U.N. Charter art. 24.

4. *See* Rome Statute of the International Criminal Court, July 17, 1998, 2187 U.N.T.S. 90 (hereinafter Rome Statute).

5. The Council arguably set the stage for this overlap and intermingling. In the wake of massive atrocities in Rwanda and Yugoslavia, the Council had created ad hoc international criminal tribunals as tools for promoting international security and peace after conflict, recognizing that serious crimes can threaten international peace and security. *See* S.C. Res. 827, U.N. Doc. S/RES/827 (May 25, 1993) (hereinafter S.C. Res. 827); S.C. Res. 955, U.N. Doc. S/RES/955 (Nov. 8, 1994) (hereinafter S.C. Res. 955).

6. *See* Rome Statute, *supra* note 4, art. 13, 16; Relationship Agreement between the United Nations and the International Criminal Court, U.N. Doc. A/58/874; GAOR, 58th Sess. (Aug. 20, 2004) (hereinafter Relationship Agreement).

7. *See* Rome Statute, *supra* note 4, art. 53(3).

8. Consistent with the theme of this book about the tenure of the first prosecutor, this chapter engages the relationship between these two organs from the perspective of the prosecutor, not from that of the Council.

9. The exact boundaries of legal review of the Council are still actively debated, but as a practical matter, options for binding, enforceable international-level legal review of Council action remain elusive. The International Court of Justice has advisory jurisdiction under article 96, and some scholars have suggested that its contentious jurisdiction

should be read to include international organizations. Statute of the International Court of Justice, art. 34(1), June 26, 1945, 3 Bevans 1179, 59 Stat. 1055, T.S. No. 993. The ad hoc tribunals also reviewed Council action and said that the Council is limited by the terms of the U.N. Charter. *See* Prosecutor v. Tadic, Case No. IT-94-1, Decision on Defence Motion for Interlocutory Appeal on Jurisdiction, ¶28 (Int'l Crim. Trib. for the Former Yugoslavia Oct. 2, 1995), http://www.icty.org/x/cases/tadic/acdec/en/51002.htm; Decision on the Conditions of Admission of a State to Membership in the United Nations, 1948 I.C.J. 57, 64 (May 28), http://www.icj-cij.org/docket/files/3/1821.pdf. In addition, national- and regional-level measures implementing Council resolutions have recently been struck down. *See, e.g.,* Cases C-584/10 P, C-593/10 P and C-595/10 P, Comm'n v. Yassin, 213 E.C.R. I-1 (undertaking substantive review of European regulations implementing Security Council resolutions and applying a strict standard of review to such regulations). *See generally* C. Cora True-Frost, *The Development of Individual Standing in International Security,* 32 CARDOZO L. REV. 1183 (2011).

10. The Council's determinations under chapter VII are binding on member states under article 25. *See* U.N. Charter art. 25.

11. At the broadest level, accountability creates a "duty to give account for one's actions to some other person or body." *See* Colin Scott, *Accountability in the Regulatory State,* 27 J.L. & SOC'Y 38, 40 (2000).

12. Such legal accountability has already led to failure to confirm a number of attempted charges and acquittal in case of Mathieu Ngudjolo Chui in the Democratic Republic of Congo. Prosecutor v. Mathieu Ngudjolo Chui, Case No. ICC-01/04-02/12, Judgment Pursuant to Article 745 of the Statute (Dec. 18, 2012), http://www.icc-cpi.int/iccdocs/doc/doc1579080.pdf.

13. Rome Statute, *supra* note 4, art. 46(2).

14. *Id., see, e.g.* art. 53(3)(b) (Pre-Trial Chamber may review prosecutor's decision not to prosecute); art. 56 (Pre-Trial Chamber may authorize specific investigations), art. 61 (Pre-Trial Chamber must confirm charges before trial).

15. *See* U.S. Concerns About International Criminal Court Being Proved Justified as Balkans Tribunal Considers Clinton Indictment, ANANDTECH FORUMS (July 2002) (hereinafter U.S. Concerns about ICC), http://forums.anandtech.com/archive/index.php/t-840819.html.

16. *See* Dag Hammarskjöld, Secretary-General of the United Nations, *The International Civil Servant in Law & in Fact, Lecture Delivered to Congregation at Oxford University* (May 30, 1961), in THE INTERNATIONAL CIVIL SERVANT IN LAW & IN FACT 331 (1961), http://www.un.org/Depts/dhl/dag/docs/internationalcivilservant.pdf. Hammarskjöld uses the word *neutrality,* but in this article, I use *impartiality* to capture the modern reappraisal of the role of the U.N. For further discussion of the impartiality/neutrality distinction, *see infra* note 57.

17. *See* Carl K. Y. Shaw, *Hegel's Theory of Modern Bureaucracy,* 86 AM. POL. SCI. REV. 381 (1992) (arguing that Hegel's ideal theory of bureaucracy can contribute to a liberal theory of democracy).

18. *See* Luis Moreno Ocampo, Prosecutor, ICC, *Address to the Assembly of States Parties* (Nov. 14, 2008), http://www.icc-cpi.int/NR/rdonlyres/50F9D0FA-33A0-48B3-942E-4CFF88CA3A27/0/ICCASPASP7StatementProsecutor.pdf.

19. *See* Rome Statute, *supra* note 4, art. 42(2).

20. *See infra* at section "The U.N. Security Council and the Office of the Prosecutor: Powers and Constraints." *See also* Meierhenrich, in this volume.

21. *See* Hammarskjöld, *supra* note 16. Controversy followed many of Moreno Ocampo's professional decisions and personal actions during his tenure. *See, e.g.,* Luis Moreno Ocampo, *Luis Moreno-Ocampo: World's Prosecutor,* TIMES MAGAZINE (May 26, 2012), http://www.thetimes.co.uk/tto/magazine/article3421499.ece. *Report: Unfinished Business—Closing Gaps in Selections of Cases,* HUMAN RIGHTS WATCH (Sept. 15, 2011), http://www.hrw.org/reports/2011/09/15/unfinished-business; Joshua Rozenberg, *Prosecutor Luis Moreno-Ocampo Is the Best Asset of Those Opposed to the International Criminal Court,* THE GUARDIAN (Apr. 21, 2011), http://www.theguardian.com/law/2011/apr/21/moreno-ocampo-international-criminal-court. This account engages only his administrative and legal choices as prosecutor of the ICC.

22. *See* International Criminal Court, Office of the Prosecutor, *Policy Paper on the Interests of Justice,* 4 (Sept. 2007), http://www.icc-cpi.int/NR/rdonlyres/772C95C9-F54D-4321-BF09-73422BB23528/143640/ICCOTPInterestsOfJustice.pdf (hereinafter Interests of Justice Policy Paper). It is beyond the scope of this chapter to engage the debate about whether peace or justice should take precedence when there is conflict between these goals. The key point here is that the prosecutor is not a diplomat acting on behalf of the interests of one state over another; he is interpreting his mandate to fit the legal interests of the ICC as a legal institution. For an argument that the prosecutor should consider peace concerns, *see* Mnookin, in this volume.

23. *See* Letter from Luis Moreno Ocampo, Prosecutor, ICC, to Judge Claude Jorda (June 1, 2005) (hereinafter Moreno-Ocampo Letter).

24. In this chapter, I do not analyze criticisms of the prosecutor's handling of specific cases; I focus instead on how the prosecutor framed the challenging relationship with the Council. For discussion of the prosecutor's relationship with judges and his staff, *see* O'Sullivan, in this volume; Wald, in this volume; Meierhenrich, in this volume.

25. *See infra* at section "The Legal and Political Relationship between the Security Council and the Prosecutor."

26. *Id.*

27. *See* Rome Statute, *supra* note 4; UN Charter; Relationship Agreement, *supra* note 6.

28. Council resolutions under article 39 are binding and require mandatory action by states under chapter VII of the Charter. *See* UN Charter art. 39.

29. *See* U.N. Charter arts. 23(1), 27.

30. One recent example of inaction is the Council's failure to intervene in the conflict in Syria. *See, e.g., Syria Crisis: U.N. Assembly Condemns Security Council,* BBC NEWS (Aug. 3, 2012), http://www.bbc.co.uk/news/world-middle-east-19106250.

31. *See generally* U.N. Secretary-General, *In Larger Freedom: Towards Development, Security, & Human Rights for All: Rep. of the Secretary-General,* U.N. Doc. A/59/2005 (Mar. 21, 2005), http://www.un.org/en/ga/search/view_doc.asp?symbol=A/59/2005 (proposing reforms to the U.N. Security Council); Ryan Goodman, *Humanitarian Intervention & Pretexts for War,* 100 AM. J. INT'L L. 107 (2006) (arguing that the international legal regime and norms could develop such that Security Council authorization is not required for states to intervene militarily to stop genocide or comparable atrocities).

32. *See* Questions of Interpretation and Application of the 1971 Montreal Convention Arising from the Aerial Incident at Lockerbie (Libya v. U.S.), 1992 I.C.J. 114, ¶42 (Apr. 14) (holding that the Security Council is bound by the U.N. Charter).

33. *See supra* note 9 (regarding lack of binding judicial review over the Council's actions).

34. As previously noted, building on the foundation laid by the Nuremberg trials, the Security Council created two ad hoc criminal tribunals, the International Criminal Tribunal for Rwanda (ICTR) and the International Criminal Tribunal for the Former Yugoslavia (ICTY), as subsidiary organs. *See* S.C. Res. 827, *supra* note 5; S.C. Res. 955, *supra* note 5.

35. *See* Rome Statute, *supra* note 4, pmbl. Through its complementarity principle, the Rome Statute framework encourages state-level prosecutions of alleged wrongdoers as well as "establish[es] an independent permanent International Criminal Court in relationship with the United Nations system, with jurisdiction over the most serious crimes of concern to the international community as a whole." *See also* MARLIES GLASIUS, THE INTERNATIONAL CRIMINAL COURT: A GLOBAL CIVIL SOCIETY ACHIEVEMENT (2005); THE LEGAL REGIME OF THE INTERNATIONAL CRIMINAL COURT (José Doria et al. eds., 2009); BENJAMIN SCHIFF, BUILDING THE INTERNATIONAL CRIMINAL COURT (2008). In addition, article 88 requires states to adopt domestic implementing legislation. *See* Rome Statute, *supra* note 4, art. 88.

36. The Relationship Agreement recognizes the ICC as an "independent permanent judicial institution [with an] independent legal personality." *See* Relationship Agreement, *supra* note 6, art. 2(1). The relationship between the U.N. Security Council and the ICC initially conceived in the International Law Commission Draft in 1994 made the ICC entirely subordinate to the U.N. Security Council and a part of the U.N. Charter. Indeed, the relationship between the two entities was hotly debated during the drafting and adoption of the Rome Treaty. *See* William Schabas, *United States Hostility to the International Criminal Court: It's All about the Security Council*, 15 EUR. J. INT'L L. 701, 701 (2004).

37. Rome Statute, *supra* note 4, art. 42(4).

38. Under the Rome Statute, the prosecutor has the independent authority to prosecute those individuals believed to be most responsible for grave atrocities that concern the international community as a whole. *See* Rome Statute, *supra* note 4, art. 5. As Scheffer and Meierhenrich describe in their chapters, the most challenging Rome Statute negotiations concerned the powers of the prosecutor. *See* Scheffer, in this volume; Meierhenrich, in this volume.

39. Art. 42(2) of the Rome Statute provides, "The Prosecutor shall have full authority over the management and administration of the Office, including the staff, facilities and other resources thereof." *See* Rome Statute, *supra* note 4, art. 42.

40. Art. 42 of the Rome Statute continues, "(1) The Office of the Prosecutor shall act independently as a separate organ of the Court. . . . A member of the Office shall not seek or act on instructions from any external source; (3) The Prosecutor and the Deputy Prosecutors shall be persons of high moral character, be highly competent in and have extensive practical experience in the prosecution or trial of criminal cases. They shall have an excellent knowledge of and be fluent in at least one of the working languages of the Court; . . . and (5) Neither the Prosecutor nor a Deputy Prosecutor shall engage in any activity which is likely to interfere with his or her prosecutorial functions or to affect confidence in his or her independence. They shall not engage in any other occupation of a professional nature." *See* Rome Statute, *supra* note 4, art. 42.

41. *See id.* arts. 5, 11–14.

42. *See id.* art. 15(3).

43. The Office of the Prosecutor may only initiate an investigation *proprio motu* with

the approval of the Pre-Trial Chamber. *See id.* art. 15(4). For a discussion of the role of the Court in reviewing prosecutorial action, *see generally* William A. Schabas, *Prosecutorial Discretion v. Judicial Activism at the International Criminal Court,* 6 J. INT'L CRIM. JUST. 731 (2008); Rome Statute, *supra* note 4, art. 53(3)(b).

44. Rome Statute, *supra* note 4, art. 53.

45. *See id.* arts. 86–102. To execute the arrest warrants resulting from the two U.N. Security Council–referred situations in Libya and the Sudan, the prosecutor requires the cooperation of states, international organizations, and nonparty states. *See infra* at section "The Legal and Political Relationship between the Security Council and the Prosecutor." *See also* Whiting, in this volume. It is beyond the scope of this chapter to engage fully the argument of a number of legal scholars that states should not interfere with the success of ICC arrest warrants for at least three reasons: (1) if they are signatories to the Rome Statute, they must not interfere with the object and purpose of the Rome Statute, and investigations and execution of arrest warrants are clearly related to that purpose; (2) if they have ratified the Rome Statute, they have a legal duty to assist with investigations and to enforce arrest warrants; and (3) even if they have not signed the Rome Statute, states should assist regarding the warrants that emerge from situations referred to the Court pursuant to binding, chapter VII U.N. Security Council referrals because as members of the United Nations, states are bound not to interfere with and even possibly to execute these indictments. *See generally* Alistair D. Edgar, *Peace, Justice, & Politics: The International Criminal Court, "New Diplomacy," & the U.N. System,* in ENHANCING GLOBAL GOVERNANCE: TOWARDS A NEW DIPLOMACY?, 137–39 (Andrew F. Cooper et al. eds., 2002). *See* Alexander K. A. Greenawalt, *Justice without Politics?: Prosecutorial Discretion & the International Criminal Court,* 39 N.Y.U. J. INT'L L. & POL. 583, 589–90 (2007).

46. *See* Lawrence Moss, *The U.N. Security Council & the International Criminal Court: Towards a More Principled Relationship,* FRIEDRICH EBERT STIFTUNG (Mar. 2012), 4; *Sudan Says China, Russia Seeking U.N. Resolution to Block ICC Indictments,* BBC MONITORING NEWSFILE (July 12, 2008).

47. *See* S.C. Res. 1593, U.N. Doc. S/RES/1593 (Mar. 31, 2005) (hereinafter S.C. Res. 1593); S.C. Res. 1970, U.N. Doc. S/RES/1970 (Feb. 26, 2011) (hereinafter S.C. Res. 1970). In the case of the unanimous referral of Libya, the Council reiterated this referral to the Court in three of four subsequent related resolutions. *See* S.C. Res. 1973, U.N. Doc. S/RES/1973 (Mar. 17, 2011) (hereinafter S.C. Res. 1973); S.C. Res. 2009, U.N. Doc. S/RES/2009 (Sept. 16, 2011) (hereinafter S.C. Res. 2009); S.C. Res. 2016, U.N. Doc. S/RES/2016 (Oct. 27, 2011) (hereinafter S.C. Res. 2016).

48. S.C. Res. 1593, *supra* note 47; S.C. Res. 1970, *supra* note 47. The United States cannot support funding for the ICC under the American Service-Members' Protection Act, 22 U.S.C. § 7425 (2012). A Swiss and Liechtensteinian nonpaper advances the argument that the Council, as a matter of international law, should not be permitted to preclude the General Assembly from funding the obligations ensuing from Security Council–referred situations as it did in S.C. Res. 1593 and S.C. Res. 1970. *See Financing of Situations Referred to the International Criminal Court by the United Nations Security Council,* UNITED NATIONS (July 15, 2011), http://www.securitycouncilreport.org/atf/cf/%7B65BFCF9B-6D27-4E9C-8CD3-CF6E4FF96FF9%7D/Financing_of_situations_referred_to_the_ICC_by_the_UNSC.pdf (calling on the United Nations to fund the Security Council's previous referrals and for the Council to avoid its practice of placing

all financial obligations resulting from its referrals on the ICC in the future). As a practical matter, the ICC did not have difficulty with funding the early investigation in the Libya situation. *See* Assembly of States Parties, *Report of the Court on Cooperation*, International Criminal Court, 10th Sess. Dec. 2011, ICC-ASP/10/40 (Nov. 18, 2011).

49. *See, e.g.*, S.C. Res. 1593, *supra* note 47.

50. *See* Gwen P. Barnes, *The International Criminal Court's Ineffective Enforcement Mechanisms: The Indictment of President Omar Al Bashir*, 34 FORDHAM INT'L L. J. 4 (2011) (citing Julian Borger, *Court Censures Commonwealth Chief as Rift Deepens over War Crimes Suspects: Sharma "Questions Duty" of States to Hand Over to ICC: Row Began over Kenya Refusal to Arrest Bashir*, GUARDIAN (Eng.), Oct. 28, 2010, 22 (reporting that al-Bashir caused an "uproar" by traveling to Chad and to Kenya, an ICC signatory); *ICC Urges U.N. Action on Bashir Visit to Djibouti*, REUTERS (May 12, 2011), http://www.reuters.com/article/2011/05/12/us-warcrimes-bashir-idUSTRE74B5NG20110512; Prosecutor v. Omar Hassan Ahmad Al Bashir, Case No. ICC-02/05-01/09-132, Decision Requesting Observations about Omar Al-Bashir's Recent Visit to the Republic of Chad (Aug. 18, 2011), http://icc-cpi.int/iccdocs/doc/doc1206768.pdf; Prosecutor v. Omar Hassan Ahmad Al Bashir, ICC-02/05-01/09-139, Decision Pursuant to Article 87(7) of the Rome Statute on the Failure by the Republic of Malawi to Comply with the Cooperation Requests Issued by the Court with Respect to the Arrest and Surrender of Omar Hassan Ahmad Al Bashir (Dec. 12, 2011), http://www.icc-cpi.int/iccdocs/doc/doc1287184.pdf; *Sudanese President Travels to Chad for Regional Summit*, SUDAN TRIBUNE (May 9, 2013), http://www.sudantribune.com/spip.php?article46519 (regarding al-Bashir's visits to Chad); *ICC Requests Nigeria to Arrest Sudan's President during Visit to Abuja*, U.N. NEWS CENTRE (July 16, 2013), http://www.un.org/apps/news/story.asp?NewsID=45419#.UixsRlMtvmE; *Sudan President Bashir's Nigeria Visit Causes Anger*, REUTERS (July 15, 2013), http://www.bbc.co.uk/news/world-africa-23313730 (regarding Al-Bashir's visit to Nigeria).

51. Other countries that have hosted al-Bashir, some many times, include Chad, Eritrea, Egypt, Kenya, Libya, Iraq, Ethiopia, Qatar, Saudi Arabia, Turkey, and South Sudan. *See, e.g.*, Amnesty International, *Press Release: U.N.: Demand al-Bashir's Surrender to the International Criminal Court*, http://www.amnesty.org/en/for-media/press-releases/un-demand-al-bashir-s-surrender-international-criminal-court-2013-09-20.

52. A recent example is the Council's failure to refer the situation in non-ICC member state Syria to the Court even in the face of calls for such a referral from General Assembly member states. *See generally U.N. Human Rights Chief Renews Call on Security Council to Refer Syria to ICC*, U.N. NEWS CENTRE (July 2, 2012), http://www.un.org/apps/news/story.asp?NewsID=42377#.UmQyCCTVHcU; Ban Ki-moon, Secretary-General, United Nations, *Remarks to Security Council Open Debate on the Protection of Civilians in Armed Conflict* (Feb. 12, 2013), http://www.un.org/sg/statements/index.asp?nid=6597 ("I welcome the debate triggered by the call of some Member States for the Council to refer the situation in Syria to the International Criminal Court"); U.N. SCOR, 68th Sess., 6906th mtg. at 15, U.N. Doc. S/PV.6906 (Jan. 23, 2013), http://www.un.org/en/ga/search/view_doc.asp?symbol=S/PV.6906 (revealing that Luxembourg, Great Britain, Korea, and France all supported the call for the situation in Syria to be referred to the ICC); *id.* at 16 (reflecting that the French ambassador to the U.N., Mr. Araud, stated, "That is why with 58 other States we have called on the Security Council to refer the situation in Syria to the International Criminal Court.").

53. *See* U.N. SCOR, 68th Sess., 6906th mtg. at 16, *supra* note 52; DAVID KAYE ET AL., THE COUNCIL & THE COURT: IMPROVING SECURITY COUNCIL SUPPORT OF THE INTERNATIONAL CRIMINAL COURT 15–16 (2013), http://councilandcourt.org/files/2013/05/The-Council-and-the-Court-FINAL.pdf. Council members' delegates have expressed the following concerns regarding the prosecutor and the Court: the number of ICC indictees that remain at large, the prosecutor's failure to charge crimes that appear to otherwise be supported by the facts (*e.g.,* omitting sexual violence charges in the *Lubanga* case), and dissatisfaction with the prosecutor's decision to charge sitting leaders such as al-Bashir.

54. *See* Rome Statute, *supra* note 4, art. 16 ("No investigation or prosecution may be commenced or proceeded with under this Statute for a period of 12 months after the Security Council, in a resolution adopted under Chapter VII of the Charter of the United Nations, has requested the Court to that effect; request may be renewed by the Council under the same conditions.").

55. Rome Statute, *supra* note 4, art. 13(b). As of Feb. 2014, the Security Council had referred situations in the Sudan and in Libya to the ICC under article 13 of the Rome Statute. The U.N. Security Council first referred the situation in the Sudan to the ICC in Mar. 2005. *See* S.C. Res. 1593, *supra* note 47 (referring situation in Sudan to ICC). The second U.N. Security Council referral was of the situation in Libya in 2011. *See* S.C. Res. 1970, *supra* note 47 (referring situation in Libya to ICC); S.C. Res. 2016, *supra* note 47; S.C. Res. 2009, *supra* note 47; S.C. Res. 1973, *supra* note 47. "These Libya resolutions recall the U.N. Security Council's decision to refer the situation in Libya to the International Criminal Court and . . . the importance of cooperation for . . . holding persons accountable."

56. *See* KAYE, *supra* note 53, at 15.

57. *See* Hammarskjöld, *supra* note 16, at 331. Hammarskjöld uses *political neutrality* instead of *impartiality,* but I modify his framework and use *impartiality* instead. *Impartiality* better accommodates current understandings of the desired quality of international civil servants. *See generally* Dominick Donald, *Neutrality, Impartiality, & U.N. Peacekeeping at the Beginning of the 21st Century,* 9 INT'L PEACEKEEPING 21 (2002) [hereinafter Donald, *Neutrality, Impartiality, & U.N. Peacekeeping*]; Dominick Donald, *Neutral Is Not Impartial: The Confusing Legacy of Traditional Peace Operations Thinking,* 29 ARMED FORCES & SOC'Y 415 (2003). The U.N. continues to grapple with the challenge presented by impartially pursuing an international mandate in, for example, its peacekeeping and refugee operations. It is a challenge very similar to the one before the prosecutor.

58. The secretary-general's mandate is to administer the U.N. Both the secretary-general and the prosecutor are elected by their respective constituencies of states parties to execute their mandates. The secretary-general of the U.N. is appointed by the General Assembly on the recommendation of the Security Council, while the ASP elects the prosecutor. However, while the ASP has the power to remove the prosecutor, there is no established procedure for removing the secretary-general. *Compare* Rome Statute, *supra* note 4, art. 46(2), *with* U.N. Charter art. 97.

59. U.N. Charter art. 98.

60. *See* U.N. Charter art. 98. The U.N. secretary-general acts as the chief administrative officer of the Secretariat in all meetings of the General Assembly, the Security Council, and the Economic and Social Council; creates an annual report; and refers "any

matter which in his opinion may threaten the maintenance of international peace and security." *See* U.N. Charter arts. 98–99; *see also* U.N. General Assembly, *Rules of Procedure of the General Assembly,* U.N. Doc. A/520/Rev.17 (2008) (establishing, pursuant to Rule 12, that the secretary-general shall issue the provisional agenda for a regular session and communicate it to the members of the United Nations and establishing, pursuant to Rule 48, that the secretary-general shall make an annual report and any necessary supplementary reports to the General Assembly).

61. *See* Rome Statute, *supra* note 4.

62. *See* Hammarskjöld, *supra* note 16, at 349.

63. *Id.*

64. The U.N. Charter and World Trade Organization Agreement create these two offices and enumerate many of their related powers and the international character of these offices. The enumerated powers of the World Trade Organization director-general position are few, and directors-general with different leadership styles have interpreted their mandates in different fashions. *See* Marrakesh Agreement Establishing the World Trade Organization, art. VI, Apr. 15, 1994, 1867 U.N.T.S. 154, 33 I.L.M. 1125; Peter Sutherland et al., *The Future of the WTO: Report by the Consultative Board to the Director-General Supachai Panitchpakdi* (2004), http://www.wto.org/english/thewto_e/10anniv_e/future_wto_e.pdf.

65. *See* ICC, Office of the Prosecutor, *Paper on Some Policy Issues before the Office of the Prosecutor* (Sept. 2003), http://www.icc-cpi.int/nr/rdonlyres/1fa7c4c6-de5f-42b7-8b25-60aa962ed8b6/143594/030905_policy_paper.pdf. For a list of other critical administrative initiatives of Moreno Ocampo's term, *see* Meierhenrich, in this volume.

66. *Id.* at 6–7.

67. *See* Risdel Kasasira, *ICC Prosecutor in Uganda Ahead of Bashir's Visit,* ALL AFRICA (July 13, 2009), http://allafrica.com/stories/200907131181.html.

68. *See generally* Whiting, in this volume.

69. *See* Inge Lønning, *Politics, Morality, & Religion: The Legacy of Dag Hammarskjöld,* in THE ETHICS OF DAG HAMMARSKJÖLD (Henning Melber ed., 2010).

70. *Id.*

71. The United Nations has struggled for some time with the difference between neutrality and impartiality. *See supra* note 57. For example, Alex de Waal argues that the U.N. High Commissioner for Refugees' policy of neutrality was detrimental. ALEX DE WAAL, FAMINE CRIMES: POLITICS & THE DISASTER RELIEF INDUSTRY IN AFRICA 192–95 (2009); SADAKA OKADA, THE TURBULENT DECADE: CONFRONTING THE REFUGEE CRISES OF THE 1990S 190, 192–96 (2005)(discussing political conflicts resulting from neutrality in Africa's Great Lakes region). Ultimately, the U.N. has drawn a distinction between neutrality and impartiality and has mostly abandoned the principle of neutrality in peacekeeping. *See* Donald, *Neutrality, Impartiality, & U.N. Peacekeeping, supra* note 57.

72. *See* Hammarskjöld, *supra* note 16, at 348. Hammarskjöld has been credited as having given the U.N. an ethical dimension and as having made the organization responsive to citizens, not just states. Lønning, *supra* note 69, at 19.

73. Hammarskjöld's definition of international civil service is capacious and includes those who serve the interests of public international institutions. In many domestic jurisdictions, whether a prosecutor or judge is elected or appointed, they, too, are viewed as civil servants. In the United States, in Italy, and in Brazil, for example, the prosecutor

is a judicial civil servant, with the same liberties and independence warranties as judges. Hammarskjöld, *supra* note 16.

74. General Assembly, *Secretary-General Reflects on Promise, Realities of His Role in World Affairs, in Address to Council on Foreign Relations,* U.N. Press Release PR SG/ SM/6865 (Jan. 19, 1999).

75. *See* Mnookin, in this volume.

76. *Id.*

77. For example, during the ICC's first trial, the prosecutor faced numerous criticisms, including criticisms regarding the limited scope of charges against Lubanga, the limited disclosure of evidence and fairness during the trial, investigations and indictments in Sudan, and the use of intermediaries. *See The Prosecutor v. Thomas Lubanga Dyilo—A Turbulent but Promising Retrospective,* THE HAGUE JUSTICE PORTAL (Nov. 17, 2011), http://www.haguejusticeportal.net/index.php?id=12989. Investigations in the Sudan were also criticized. *See* Julie Flint & Alex de Waal, *Case Closed: A Prosecutor without Borders,* WORLD AFFAIRS (Mar. 22, 2009), http://www.worldaffairsjournal.org/ article/case-closed-prosecutor-without-borders.

78. For discussion about allegations of the ICC's bias regarding Africa, see generally Stephen A. Lamony, *Is the International Criminal Court Really Picking on Africa?,* AFRICAN ARGUMENTS (Apr. 16, 2013), http://africanarguments.org/2013/04/16/is-the-international-criminal-court-really-picking-on-africa-by-stephen-a-lamony; Michael Birnbaum, *African Leaders Complain of Bias at ICC as Kenya Trials Get Underway,* WASH. POST (Dec. 5, 2013), http://www.washingtonpost.com/world/europe/african-leaders-complain-of-bias-at-icc-as-kenya-trials-are-underway/2013/12/05/0c52fc7a-56cb-11e3-bdbf-097ab2a3dc2b_story.html.

79. *Luis Moreno-Ocampo Responds to Questions from Workshop Participants,* FACING HISTORY & FACING OURSELVES (December 2009), https://www.facinghistory.org/reckoning/luis-moreno-ocampo-responds-questions-workshop-participants (Moreno Ocampo's response to participants in The Reckoning: Understanding the International Criminal Court Workshop).

80. See *id.*

81. *See* Flint & de Waal, *supra* note 77. *See, e.g.,* "The defense argued that in seeking charges against Mr. Bemba, the prosecution was abusing the judicial process for political purposes. It argued that CAR President François Bozizé had launched domestic prosecutions against his rivals, former President Ange-Félix Patassé and Mr. Bemba, for political reasons. And for these same reasons, they argued, President Bozizé's government referred these cases to the ICC. Further, Mr. Bemba's defense also argued that its client's prosecution at the ICC also suited the political interests of D[emocratic] R[epublic of] C[ongo] President Joseph Kabila because Mr. Bemba was his biggest domestic rival. The defense application noted that the Prosecutor met with President Kabila just one week before CAR referred the situation to the ICC. From this background, Mr. Bemba's attorneys argued that there was an appearance of bias on the part of the prosecution, and that the trial should therefore be put on hold. For the trial to proceed, they argued, the prosecution should have to prove beyond a reasonable doubt that this appearance of bias was false." Alpha Sesay, *A Decision to Allow the Trial to Proceed,* INTERNATIONAL JUSTICE MONITOR (Nov. 16, 2010) (citing *Public Redacted Version—Application Challenging the Admissibility of the Case Pursuant to Articles 17 & 19(2)(a) of the Rome Statute,* INTER-

NATIONAL CRIMINAL COURT, ICC-01/05-01/08-704-Red3 (Feb. 25, 2010), http://www.icc-cpi.int/iccdocs/doc/doc857699.pdf). About the indictment, Moreno Ocampo stated that Bemba "had done it before in CAR, he had done it before in the DRC. He had to be stopped. Mr. Bemba's arrest is a warning to all those who commit, who encourage, or who tolerate sexual crimes. There is a new law called the Rome Statute. Under this new law, they will be prosecuted." *Press Release, ICC Arrest Jean-Pierre Bemba—Massive Sexual Crimes in Central African Republic Will Not Go Unpunished*, ICC, ICC-OTP-20080524-PR316 (May 24, 2008).

    82. *See* SCHIFF, *supra* note 35, at 207 (citing *New Overture to Uganda's Rebels*, BBC [May 17, 2006], http://news.bbc.co.uk/2/hi/africa/4990086.stm).

    83. *See* Office of the Prosecutor: *Letter to Senders of Communication Regarding Iraq*, INTERNATIONAL CRIMINAL COURT (Feb. 9, 2006), http://www.icc-cpi.int/NR/rdonlyres/FD042F2E-678E-4EC6-8121-690BE61D0B5A/143682/OTP_letter_to_senders_re_Iraq_9_February_2007.pdf; Office of the Prosecutor, *Situation in Palestine*, INTERNATIONAL CRIMINAL COURT (Apr. 3, 2012), http://www.icc-cpi.int/NR/rdonlyres/C6162BBF-FEB9-4FAF-AFA9-836106D2694A/284387/SituationinPalestine030412ENG.pdf. While examining the situation in Palestine, Moreno Ocampo stated, "Creative lawyers can offer legal options. A group of South African lawyers supported by Max Du Plessis and John Dugard came to my Office to submit information on alleged crimes committed by a South African citizen who was working as the legal advisor of the Israeli Armed Forces during the Gaza operation. Regardless of the final assessment my Office will make on our jurisdiction in Palestine, their activity is a contribution to new ways of promoting a new system of justice." See *Luis Moreno-Ocampo Responds to Questions from Workshop Participants*, *supra* note 79.

    84. *See* Office of the Prosecutor, *Preliminary Examination of Afghanistan*, INTERNATIONAL CRIMINAL COURT, http://www.icc-cpi.int/en_menus/icc/structure%20of%20the%20court/office%20of%20the%20prosecutor/comm%20and%20ref/pe-ongoing/afghanistan/Pages/afghanistan.aspx. *But see* Daniel Schwammenthal, *Prosecuting American War Crimes*, WALL ST. J. (Nov. 26, 2009), http://online.wsj.com/article/SB10001424052748704013004574519253095440312.html (arguing that the First World should be exempt from prosecution and that it was inappropriate of the prosecutor to open a preliminary examination in Afghanistan and that he is somewhat unpredictable). The prosecutor has also recently been criticized for issuing indictments without sufficient evidence in the Kenya case. *See* Prosecutor v. Uhuru Muigai Kenyatta, Case No. ICC-01/09-02/11, Decision on Defence Application Pursuant to Article 64(4) and Related Requests, at 1 (Apr. 26, 2013) (J. Van den Wyngaert, separate opinion), http://www.icc-cpi.int/iccdocs/doc/doc1585626.pdf ("There are serious questions as to whether the Prosecution conducted a full and thorough investigation of the case against the accused prior to confirmation. . . . [T]he Prosecution offers no cogent and sufficiently specific justification for why so many witnesses in this case were only interviewed for the first time post-confirmation."). *See also* Wald, in this volume; O'Sullivan, in this volume; Meierhenrich, in this volume.

    85. Hammarskjöld, *supra* note 16, at 331.

    86. On June 1, 2005, the prosecutor wrote to the Pre-Trial Chamber that he had reviewed the situation in Darfur "to decide whether the criteria to initiate an investigation are satisfied." *See* Moreno Ocampo Letter, *supra* note 23. The prosecutor's decision to read article 53 to allow his independent decision to investigate Security Council refer-

rals has been applauded by some and criticized by others. For support for Moreno Oc-ampo's interpretation, *see, e.g.,* John L. Washburn, *On Some Aspects of Prosecutorial Discretion in the International Criminal Court,* WHITEHEAD J. OF DIPL. & INT'L REL. 145, 145–46 (2008); Chris Gallavin, *Prosecutorial Discretion within the ICC: Under the Pressure of Justice,* 17 CRIM. L.F. 43 (2006). But for criticism of the prosecutor's approach to reviewing situations referred by the Council, *see* Jens David Ohlin, *Peace, Security, & Prosecutorial Discretion,* in THE EMERGING PRACTICE OF THE INTERNATIONAL CRIMINAL COURT 185, 186 (Carsten Stahn et al. eds., 2009).

87. *See* Moreno-Ocampo Letter, *supra* note 23.

88. In Moreno Ocampo's eighteen briefings to the Council, he requested specific action in only three. *See* U.N. SCOR, 62nd Sess., 5789th mtg., U.N. Doc. S/PV.5789, at 6 (Dec. 5, 2007) ("I ask the Security Council for consistency. I ask the Security Council to send a strong and unanimous message today to the Government of the Sudan, requesting compliance with resolution 1593 [2005], requesting the execution of the arrest warrants.") (hereinafter S/PV.5789); U.N. SCOR, 63rd sess., 5905th mtg., U.N. Doc. S/PV.5905, at 5 (June 5, 2008) ("I ask the Security Council to send a strong message to the Government of the Sudan and to issue a presidential statement, requesting that it stop the crimes; requesting that it arrest Ahmad Harun and Ali Kushayb; requesting that all parties assist the Court; and requesting, simply, compliance with resolution 1593 [2005]. A presidential statement will send such a message.") (hereinafter S/PV.5905); U.N. SCOR, 65th sess., 6336th mtg., U.N. Doc. S/PV.6336, at 5 (June 11, 2010) ("This meeting and the Council's meeting on Monday offer a perfect opportunity for its members to integrate the request for the arrest of Harun and Kushayb into the general strategy relating to Darfur and the Sudan. Resolution 1593 [2005], as well as all other related Security Council resolutions, should be complied with.").

89. *See, e.g.,* U.N. SCOR, 61st sess., 5589th mtg., U.N. Doc. S/PV.5589 (Dec. 14, 2006); S/PV.5789, *supra* note 88; S/PV.5905, *supra* note 88.

90. *See* International Criminal Court, *Questions & Answers on the ICC Proceedings in the Libya Situation Following the Prosecutor's Request for Three Arrest Warrants,* at 1 (May 16, 2011), http://www.icc-cpi.int/iccdocs/PIDS/publications/LibyaQandAEng.pdf.

91. *See* Maria Smith, *The Rome Statute—A Missed Opportunity,* HARV. INT'L REV. (Feb. 25, 2013), http://hir.harvard.edu/the-rome-statute-a-missed-opportunity. One version of the objection is rooted in the concern that referring situations of nonparty states violates the principle of voluntarism in international law. Another objection is grounded in fairness concerns, worrying that the standards of the Rome Statute do not and likely never will apply to China, Russia, or the United States, as long as these permanent Council members choose not to ratify the statute.

92. Moreno Ocampo Letter, *supra* note 23.

93. *See, e.g.,* ICC, Office of the Prosecutor, *Report on Preliminary Examination Activities 2013* (Nov. 2013), http://www.icc-cpi.int/en_menus/icc/press%20and%20media/press%20releases/Documents/OTP%20Preliminary%20Examinations/OTP%20-%20Report%20%20Preliminary%20Examination%20Activities%202013.PDF.

94. *See, e.g.,* Interests of Justice Policy Paper, *supra* note 22.

95. *See* Scheffer, in this volume.

96. *See* U.S. Concerns About ICC, *supra* note 15.

97. *See* Meierhenrich, in this volume. Although Moreno Ocampo used the diplo-

matic powers associated with his office, I consider him to have been an elite civil servant, not a diplomat.

98. *See* C. Cora True-Frost, *How Institutional Design Favors U.N. Security Council Deference to the International Criminal Court* (draft on file with author).

99. For example, the Council took note of the international criminal law norms in the Rome Statute in four more nonbinding thematic resolutions: three on women, peace, and security and one on children and armed conflict. *See* S.C. Res. 1820, U.N. Doc. S/RES/1820 (June 19, 2008); S.C. Res. 1888, U.N. Doc. S/RES/1888 (Sept. 30, 2009); S.C. Res. 1960, U.N. Doc. S/RES/1960 (Dec. 16, 2010); S.C. Res. 1894, U.N. Doc. S/RES/1894 (Nov. 11, 2009). Moreover, there were resolutions in 2009 and 2010 regarding the Democratic Republic of Congo and two in 2011 regarding Côte d'Ivoire, in which the Council directed states to cooperate with or commended states for cooperating with the ICC. *See* S.C. Res. 1906, U.N. Doc. S/RES/1906 (Dec. 23, 2009); S.C. Res. 1925, U.N. Doc. S/RES/1925 (May 28, 2010); S.C. Res. 1975, U.N. Doc. S/RES/1975 (Mar. 30, 2011); S.C. Res. 2000, U.N. Doc. S/RES/2000 (July 27, 2011). The Council also provided logistical cooperation by lifting the 1572 travel ban on former Côte d'Ivoire president Laurent Gbagbo as well as other indictees. *See October 2012 Monthly Forecast*, SECURITY COUNCIL REPORT (Sept. 28, 2012), http://www.securitycouncilreport.org/monthly-forecast/2012-10/rule_of_law.php.

100. *See supra* note 47 (Security Council Resolutions referring the situations in Darfur and Libya to the ICC for examination).

101. The prosecutor briefed the Council fifteen times on the situation in the Sudan and three times on the situation in Libya. *See* True-Frost, *supra* note 98.

102. *See* S.C. Pres. Statement 2008/21, U.N. Doc. S/PRST/2008/21 (June 16, 2008); S.C. Pres. Statement 2010/11, U.N. Doc. S/PRST/2010/11 (June 29, 2010); S.C. Pres. Statement 2011/21, U.N. Doc. S/PRST/2011/21 (Nov. 14, 2011); S.C. Pres. Statement 2012/1, U.N. Doc. S/PRST/2012/1 (Jan. 19, 2012); S.C. Pres. Statement 2012/1, U.N. Doc. S/PRST/2012/3 (Jan. 23, 2012); S.C. Pres. Statement 2012/18, U.N. Doc. 2012/18 (June 29, 2012); S.C. Pres. Statement 2012/23, U.N. Doc. 2012/23 (Oct. 31, 2012); S.C. Pres. Statement 2012/28, U.N. Doc. 2012/28 (Dec. 19, 2012); S.C. Pres. Statement 2013/2, U.N. Doc. 2013/2 (Feb. 12, 2013); S.C. Pres. Statement 2013/6, U.N. Doc. 2013/6 (May 29, 2013); S.C. Pres. Statement 2013/8, U.N. Doc. 2013/8 (June 17, 2013). By Jan. 2014, the Security Council had adopted fourteen PRSTs mentioning the ICC. S.C. Pres. Statement 2013/12, U.N. Doc. 2013/12 (Aug. 6, 2013); S.C. Pres. Statement 2013/8, U.N. Doc. S/PRST/2013/8 (Nov. 25, 2013); S.C. Pres. Statement 2014/2, U.N. Doc. S/PRST/2014/2 (Jan. 23, 2014).

103. *E.g.*, Brazil held an open debate on the situation in Darfur and referred to the ICC as "an effective tool of deterrence" that "will greatly contribute to international security." U.N. SCOR, 60th sess., 5156th mtg., U.N. Doc. S/PV.5156, at 33 (Mar. 30, 2005). Guatemala's open debate on the rule of law produced several calls for the Council to improve its interaction with the ICC. *See* U.N. SCOR, 67th sess., 6849th mtg., U.N. Doc. S/PV.6849 (Resumption 1) (Oct. 17, 2012).

104. For example, the most recent bid by the African Union to defer proceedings in Kenya failed by a narrow margin that mostly—but not entirely—fell along Court membership lines. Non–Rome Statute members China, Russia, Togo, Azerbaijan, Rwanda, Morocco, and Pakistan voted in favor of the deferral, while the eight other members, seven of them Rome Statute members, voted against it. *See* Michelle Nichols, *Africa Fails*

to Get Kenya ICC Trials Deferred at United Nations, REUTERS, Nov. 15, 2013, http://www.reuters.com/article/2013/11/15/us-kenya-icc-un-idUSBRE9AE0S420131115.

105. *See generally* Patricia M. Wald, *Apprehending War Criminals: Does International Cooperation Work?*, 27 AM. U. INT'L L. REV. 229 (2012); Matthias Neuner, *The Security Council & the ICC: Assessing the First Ten Years of Coexistence*, 18 NEW ENG. J. INT'L & COMP. L. 283 (2012); Joseph M. Isanga, *The International Criminal Court Ten Years Later: Appraisal & Prospects*, 21 CARDOZO J. INT'L & COMP. L. 235 (2013).

106. In this regard, the Court might have found it encouraging that before the recent election, Kenya's highest court upheld the country's legal requirement to cooperate with the ICC. *See* Kenya Section of the International Comm'n of Jurists v. Attorney General and Others, (2011) eKLR (H.C.K.) (Kenya), http://kenyalaw.org/Downloads_Free-Cases/84203.pdf.

107. *See February 2014 Monthly Forecast*, SECURITY COUNCIL REPORT, http://www.securitycouncilreport.org/monthly-forecast/2014-02/rule_of_law_2.php?print=true.

108. *Comments & Recommendations to the 11th Session of the Assembly of States Parties*, COALITION FOR THE INT'L CRIM. COURT (Nov. 8, 2012), http://www.iccnow.org/documents/CICC_Cooperation_Team_Paper_-_ASP_11.pdf. At the sixth session, the ASP adopted sixty-six recommendations about state cooperation, which for the most part have not been followed.

109. *See, e.g.,* ROBERT O. KEOHANE, AFTER HEGEMONY: COOPERATION & DISCORD IN THE WORLD POLITICAL ECONOMY (1984); HANS MORGENTHAU, POLITICS AMONG NATIONS: THE STRUGGLE FOR POWER & PEACE (1985); KENNETH N. WALTZ, THEORY OF INTERNATIONAL POLITICS (1979).

110. *See, e.g.,* Andrew Moravcsik, *Taking Preferences Seriously: A Liberal Theory of International Politics*, 54 INT'L ORG. 2 (1997).

111. *See, e.g.,* John Gerard Ruggie, *What Makes the World Hang Together?: Neo-Utilitarianism & the Social Constructivist Challenge*, 52 INT'L ORG. 855 (1998); THOMAS RISSE & KATHRYN SIKKINK, THE POWER OF HUMAN RIGHTS: INTERNATIONAL NORMS & DOMESTIC CHANGE 1–38 (Thomas Risse et al. eds., 1999).

112. *See, e.g.,* JACK L. GOLDSMITH & ERIC A. POSNER, THE LIMITS OF INTERNATIONAL LAW (2005).

113. *See, e.g.,* Harold H. Koh, *Why Do Nations Obey International Law?*, 106 YALE L. J. 2599 (1997).

114. *See* ABRAM CHAYES & ANTONIA HANDLER CHAYES, THE NEW SOVEREIGNTY: COMPLIANCE WITH INTERNATIONAL REGULATORY AGREEMENTS (1995).

115. BETH SIMMONS, MOBILIZING FOR HUMAN RIGHTS: INTERNATIONAL LAW IN DOMESTIC POLITICS 145 (2009)(summarizing these three categories of elites). *See also* Martha Finnemore, *International Organizations as Teachers of Norms: UNESCO*, 47 INT'L ORG. 565 (1993), http://home.gwu.edu/~finnemor/articles/1993_unesco_io.pdf; Alistair Iain Johnston, *The Social Effects of International Institutions on Domestic (Foreign Policy) Actors*, in LOCATING THE PROPER AUTHORITIES: THE INTERACTION OF DOMESTIC & INTERNATIONAL INSTITUTIONS 145–56 (Daniel W. Drezner ed., 2002); Harold H. Koh, *How Is International Human Rights Law Enforced?*, 74 INDIANA L. J. 1397 (1999), http://www.repository.law.indiana.edu/cgi/viewcontent.cgi?article=2279&context=ilj.

116. It is clear that all Council members are not persuaded that the ICC should play a role in applying international criminal law, but it appears that even previous Court opponents increasingly mimic acceptance of the ICC's application of international crimi-

nal law norms. RYAN GOODMAN & DEREK JINKS, SOCIALIZING STATES: PROMOTING HUMAN RIGHTS THROUGH INTERNATIONAL LAW 4, 26, 32 (2013) (defining acculturation as "the general process by which actors adopt the beliefs and behavioral patterns of the surrounding culture [which] encompasses a number of microprocesses including mimicry, identification, and status maximization.").

117. According to James March, "The logic of appropriateness is a perspective that sees human action as driven by rules of appropriate or exemplary behavior, organized into institutions. Rules are followed because they are seen as natural, rightful, expected, and legitimate. Actors seek to fulfill the obligations encapsulated in a role, an identity, a membership in a political community or group, and the ethos, practices and expectations of its institutions. Embedded in a social collectivity, they do what they see as appropriate for themselves in a specific type of situation." James G. March & Johan P. Olsen, *The Logic of Appropriateness,* in THE OXFORD HANDBOOK OF PUBLIC POLICY (Michael Moran et al. eds., 2008).

118. The prosecutor can educate both U.N. Security Council members and members of civil society about the work of the ICC. *See generally,* Minow, in this volume. Moreno Ocampo has attempted on many occasions to educate the Council. *See, e.g.,* U.N. SCOR, 66th sess., 6528th mtg. at 2, U.N. Doc. S/PV.6528 (May 4, 2011) ("The Office must apply the norms established by the Rome Statute. It must establish the truth about crimes alleged to have been committed in Libya through an independent and impartial investigation. This is what we're doing."); U.N. SCOR, 67th sess., 6772th mtg. at 3, U.N. Doc. S/PV.6772 (May 16, 2013) (Moreno Ocampo framing the work of his office as complementary to "genuine national proceedings" and stating his office's mission to investigate and monitor Libya's national proceedings. He also reaffirmed his mandate to investigate high-level Libyan officials allegedly involved in Rome Statute crimes.); U.N. SCOR, 60th sess., 5216th mtg. at 2–4, U.N. Doc. S/PV.5216 (June 29, 2005) (Moreno Ocampo reaffirming his responsibility to conduct an investigation to comply with the Rome Statute and stating, "My Office will work expeditiously to those ends, conscious of the high evidential threshold for criminal responsibility imposed by the Rome Statute.").

119. *See* GOODMAN & JINKS *supra* note 116, at 26 (arguing that acculturation is a microprocess of social influence that emphasizes the "relationship of an actor to their social environment" and that "culture is typically understood as 'learned behavior'" that includes "'normative social influence' whereby actors are impelled to adopt appropriate attitudes and behavior.")

120. *See, e.g.,* Kal Raustiala & Anne-Marie Slaughter, *International Law, International Relations, & Compliance,* in HANDBOOK OF INTERNATIONAL RELATIONS (Walter Carlsnaes et al. eds., 2005).

121. *Id.* at 538.

122. *See id.* (arguing that epistemic communities, transnational advocacy groups, and widespread adoption of human rights norms throughout the U.N. led to the Council's incorporation of human rights norms in its mandate and demonstrating how the Council's consumption of these norms through nonbinding resolutions and PRSTs had impacts on the ground, with many of these norms eventually becoming part of binding chapter VII resolutions).

123. *See* SIMMONS, *supra* note 115.

The Impacts of the Prosecutor's Work

Widening the Impact of the International Criminal Court

The Prosecutor's Preliminary Examinations in the Larger System of International Criminal Justice

Christopher Stone

The ICC Paradox

The paradox at the heart of the Rome Statute is well known: The International Criminal Court (ICC) appears, at first glance, to provide a new source of hope to victims of grave crimes around the world—hope that the perpetrators will be brought to justice in the Hague even if national governments are unwilling to prosecute them.[1] This hope is all the more powerful because the victims in many situations are in utter despair, living under governments that could not care less about them. The victims of grave crimes have seen their children and parents raped, slaughtered, or both; their homes destroyed; and their possessions plundered. In addition, they have effectively been denied any avenue to complain, any help, or any opportunity for understanding. In Afghanistan, Colombia, Comoros, Côte d'Ivoire, the Republic of Georgia, Guinea, Honduras, Nigeria, the Palestinian Territories, and South Korea—to name the jurisdictions recently under preliminary examination by the ICC prosecutor—countless victims thirst simply to have these crimes acknowledged.[2]

Yet on close inspection, one sees that the ICC is unlikely to commence prosecutions in most of these desperate situations. No serious student of the ICC believes today that the prosecutor is likely to open full investigations in more than one or two of these preliminary examinations, if even that. Why, we must ask, having raised the hopes of victims so high, are so many preliminary examinations expected to go no further in the Hague?

There are three reasons. First, under the terms of the Rome Statute, the ICC is designed to be "complementary" to domestic justice and is required to defer to national investigations, prosecutions, and trials unless those domestic proceedings are shams.[3] This complementarity principle represents a complete reversal from the approach taken earlier by many of the same states in creating the International Criminal Tribunal for the Former Yugoslavia and the International Criminal Tribunal for Rwanda. In those two specific situations, the international tribunals conducted more than a hundred proceedings. The ICC, in contrast, proceeded against a total of fourteen individuals in the four situations in which it mounted full investigations in its first seven years.

The second reason, which aligns with the complementarity principle, is that the national governments that oversee the work of the Court have given it the resources to prosecute only a small number of people and cases, leaving most perpetrators to face justice in national proceedings. The relatively small number of full cases as well as the small number of individuals for whom arrest warrants have been issued are precisely what the states that finance the ICC have planned.

Third, even when the ICC itself issues arrest warrants for alleged perpetrators, the Court depends on national governments to execute those warrants, detain suspects, and otherwise give force to the Court's rulings. The prosecutor depends on national law enforcement and intelligence agencies to assist its investigations. The pursuit of justice in each case, therefore, continues to depend on the political decisions and cooperation of states, notwithstanding language in the Rome Statute that ostensibly commits states parties to support the ICC.

Hence the paradox. The prosecutor announces a preliminary examination of some grave crime that a national government appears unable or unwilling to address, and the hopes of thousands of victims soar; yet in nearly every case, justice will remain the responsibility of that same national government.

We can overcome this paradox only by examining the entire system of international criminal justice more deeply. If we look for justice only from the ICC sitting in the Hague, we will be perpetually disappointed. Instead, we need to see the ICC along with domestic courts as parts of a new, integrated system of international criminal justice. Despite the long-standing failings of the domestic courts in many countries, despite the cynicism they engender, despite their bias and corruption, domestic courts are where justice will need to be done, under the eye of the ICC. The ICC is designed as a minimalist court, acting only in rare situations and then only against a few of the leaders most responsible for atrocities when and if states are willing to support the prosecutor's efforts.

Once we understand the system of international justice as comprising both the ICC and domestic justice systems around the globe, a new set of strategic questions appears. Instead of asking how to bring all the world's grave crimes to trial in the Hague, we should be asking what the ICC and its prosecutor can do to enable and strengthen domestic justice. What can the ICC and its prosecutor do to make domestic justice remotely plausible to the victims of the world's gravest crimes?

These questions raise their own difficulties. There is no doubt that the ICC can legitimately encourage national governments to bring these cases in their own courts, but ICC officials debate how far the Office of the Prosecutor (OTP) and the Registry can go in assisting national justice systems while remaining within their mandates and budgets. In particular, the debate concerns how far beyond encouragement this "positive complementarity" can extend. For example, in a speech to the 2009 Consultative Conference on International Criminal Justice, the ICC registrar explained her thinking:

> In strengthening capacities in the national system—the legal and judicial system—obviously it's not really the mandate of, especially, the Registry to take specific action to do that. But indirectly we can do that.[4]

By "indirect assistance," the registrar was referring to training programs for lawyers who volunteer to take cases at the ICC but whose ordinary practices are in the criminal courts of countries with fragile systems of justice. In the same speech, the registrar referred to the Registry's participation in development dialogues in countries where multilateral and bilateral aid agencies are assisting in strengthening the domestic justice system. She insisted that the registrar's staff would not take active part in development assistance activities but that they could help inform the dialogue, drawing on the information the Registry collects for its own purposes in countries where the Court is engaged. Among the judges, however, even this indirect assistance raises questions about the Court's proper role.

A somewhat different perspective comes from the president of the Assembly of States Parties (ASP), Ambassador Christian Wenaweser. Ambassador Wenaweser recognizes that while the ICC's involvement is limited, it is incumbent on the national states that govern the ICC through the ASP to use other means—such as their international aid programs—to advance complementarity by strengthening the ability of domestic justice systems to handle grave crimes. At the same 2009 conference, he explained,

> Sometimes I get the impression that people have almost forgotten about complementarity. And we have to look at the functions that we can exercise as states. . . . [N]ot everything I'm saying is, properly speaking, a role of the ASP. Some of what I'm saying is a role that states can play outside of the ASP.[5]

Indeed, as the ASP President implied, the same wealthy countries that shaped the complementarity principle at Rome rarely, in their international aid programs, prioritize assistance to domestic justice systems in handling war crimes or crimes against humanity. In part, this results because the national governments in countries that have suffered grave crimes only rarely request assistance from international donors to handle these sensitive cases from the past, preoccupied as the police, prosecutors, and courts are with more ordinary crimes. Still, international assistance to domestic justice systems would do more to equip them to handle grave crimes if donor governments and institutions put greater emphasis on accountability mechanisms in the security sector, judicial independence, prosecutorial integrity, and witness protection.

Relative to the Registry and the ASP, the prosecutor has a freer hand and clearer mandate to assist states and oversee domestic proceedings. This authority is perhaps most important during the conduct of preliminary examinations. Viewed simplistically, a preliminary examination might be seen merely as a time to collect the facts that permit the prosecutor to decide whether to commence a full investigation. In practice, however, a preliminary examination is a complex, carefully structured stage of activity, not only for the OTP but also for the states concerned with the situation and for civil society. Today, these preliminary examinations are becoming fulcrums for overcoming the ICC paradox and making domestic justice plausible. They do so by establishing the relevance of law to domestic conflicts that have previously been matters solely of political and military power.

Through preliminary examinations, the prosecutor can forge a consensus that law—not merely politics and military might—will be part of the resolution of a past or present conflict. Such a consensus implies both that legal standards of conduct will be applied in judging the behavior of alleged perpetrators and that some form of legal process will ensure that victims have their experience acknowledged. When a preliminary examination begins, it is uncertain whether the prosecutor will attempt to bring law to bear only domestically or in the Hague as well and whether the result will confirm or reject the existence of grave crimes. Whatever the outcome in terms of investigation and prosecution, however, the preliminary examination seeks to establish a consensus on the relevance of law in these situations, and this alone is a significant advance for international justice.

The remainder of this chapter examines how both the prosecutor and civil society in situation countries can strengthen the preliminary examination phase in the system of international criminal justice, with the aim of establishing a consensus on the role of law in response to horrific conflict. The analysis draws on my conversations with the first ICC prosecutor, Luis Moreno Ocampo, and interactions with his office as well as on his draft policy on preliminary examinations. In addition, I draw on fieldwork in Kenya and the Republic of Georgia as well as on discussions with leaders of twelve domestic nongovernmental organizations (NGOs), all of which operate either in a country where one of six preliminary examinations was taking place or in Kenya, which was under preliminary examination from February 2008 to November 2009, when the prosecutor sought to open a full investigation.[6]

Preliminary Examinations

At this writing (2013), the ICC has charged alleged perpetrators in seven African countries, including most recently Kenya. Eight additional countries have the formal attention of the prosecutor through "preliminary examinations." These countries are more geographically diverse—Afghanistan, Honduras, Republic of Korea, Comoros, Colombia, Georgia, Guinea, and Nigeria.

The prosecutor has been disclosing these preinvestigative explorations almost from the inception of the Court, but preliminary examinations, as a specific category of prosecutorial activity, were only described at any length in the prosecutorial strategy for 2009 to 2012 and in a draft policy paper published in October 2010.[7] Unlike full investigations, preliminary examinations do not require the permission of the judges of the ICC or any other authority. The prosecutor can commence a preliminary examination on his own initiative, making the examination public or not at his discretion.

A preliminary examination is the process by which the prosecutor determines whether a situation "meets the legal criteria established by the Statute to warrant an investigation by the ICC."[8] The examination proceeds in a particular order in four distinct phases. In the first phase, the OTP filters out those communications it receives that are "manifestly outside the jurisdiction of the Court."[9] The start of the second phase represents the "formal commence[ment] of preliminary examination" and includes both issues of temporal, geographical, and personal jurisdiction and an analysis of the alleged crimes themselves.[10] Only if the prosecutor is satisfied on these questions does the office proceed to the third phase, which considers whether the state itself is conducting or has conducted genuine investigations and prosecutions, and—if not—whether the crimes are of sufficient gravity to warrant the exercise of jurisdiction by the ICC.[11] Situations that survive through phase 3 are deemed suitable for investigation unless the prosecutor determines in phase 4 that there are "specific circumstances which provide substantial reasons to believe it is not in the interests of justice" to proceed at that time. It would be "highly exceptional" for the prosecutor to decide not to proceed on this ground.[12] This process has no timelines or deadlines. Preliminary examinations can be concluded quickly or continued over many years.[13]

A Menu of Prosecutorial Actions for Use during Preliminary Examination

- Send letters to state officials concerning these preliminary examinations, disclosing these letters publicly or not
- Organize visits to the situation jurisdiction, and there meet—or not—with government officials, members of civil society, representatives of victims, and others with an interest in the situation
- Make oral statements or give interviews to journalists in which the prosecutor or others in the OTP may characterize the crimes or the situation
- Issue interim reports
- Take testimony at the seat of the Court in the Hague.
- Confer privately or publicly with government officials and others with an interest in the situation
- Receive public or private communications from interested parties or from domestic or international commissions organized for the purpose of inquiring into the situation giving rise to the preliminary inquiry

Beyond these legal steps, the prosecutor has wide discretion about how to conduct each preliminary examination. The prosecutor may—but need not—disclose the fact of a preliminary examination. The prosecutor may issue updates about the status of a preliminary examination and currently does so weekly regarding those that have been disclosed publicly. Beyond these disclosures, the prosecutor may take actions during the preliminary examination that advance the collection of information and keep the interested parties informed of what the OTP is doing (see "A Menu of Prosecutorial Actions for Use during Preliminary Examination").

While all of this activity can inform the legal decisions that the prosecutor must make, the activity also has a further purpose: to promote genuine domestic proceedings. As the prosecutor's draft policy paper explains,

> The Office will also consider, as a matter of policy, the extent to which its preliminary examination activities can serve to stimulate genuine national proceedings against those who appear to bear the greatest responsibility for the most serious crimes. In accordance with its positive approach to complementarity . . . the Office will seek to encourage and cooperate with efforts to conduct genuine national proceedings.[14]

By terming these "preliminary examinations," disclosing many of them publicly, and publishing updates about them weekly, the prosecutor is inviting others to leverage the OTP's attention to these situations into broader pressure for domestic action.

Some international NGOs are taking up this invitation. The International Center for Transitional Justice, for example, organized an August 2010 visit to the ICC by the president of the Criminal Appellate Division of the Colombian Supreme Court and three other Supreme Court justices. They met with Moreno Ocampo, members of his staff, and one of his consultants, former Spanish judge Baltasar Garzon. According to the OTP, they

> analyzed the challenges in the investigation of massive crimes committed in Colombia and the efforts carried out by national courts to establish the truth and ensure justice in Colombia. . . . The judges had the opportunity to clarify questions in relation to the ICC's preliminary analysis and explored new avenues of cooperation with the Office of the Prosecutor in the framework of positive complementarity.[15]

Prior to this, Moreno Ocampo had made multiple visits to Colombia since 2007, meeting with judges, prosecutors, other government officials, and members of civil society.

The OTP has at times made public statements in the course of these preliminary examinations that not only encourage domestic action but also offer commentary and insist that justice be pursued in a particular manner. In the case of Guinea, the prosecutor is examining allegations that government troops killed scores of civilians while repressing an anti-government rally in a stadium in Conakry in September 2009. In announcing the preliminary examination, the deputy prosecutor, Fatou Bensouda, termed the military action "appalling and unacceptable" and added,

> From the information we have received, from the pictures I have seen, women were abused or otherwise brutalised on the pitch of Conakry's stadium, apparently by men in uniform. . . . It must never happen again. Those responsible must be held accountable.[16]

The deputy prosecutor led an ICC team of lawyers to Guinea in February 2010 to pursue the preliminary examination.[17] She made several public appearances in which she assessed the extent and seriousness of the crimes. As she prepared to leave, she described the crimes as "atrocious," telling reporters,

> As the deputy prosecutor of the ICC, I end this visit with the feeling that crimes of the order of crimes against humanity were committed. . . . [M]en in uniform attacked civilians, they killed and wounded. . . . In full daylight they mistreated, violated and submitted women to unprecedented sexual violence.[18]

During that visit, Guinea's prime minister conceded that the country's justice system was not presently capable of trying those responsible:

> The judiciary is a problem in Guinea, the way it is organised, the training of the magistrates and some of their behavior presents problems between the Guinean authorities and their internal and external partners. . . . If we are honest, there are difficulties to overcome so that Guinea is up to the job of properly judging those responsible for what happened on 28 September.[19]

The Colombia and Guinea examinations show vividly how the ICC's inquiries into grave crimes can simultaneously provoke conversations about weaknesses that may plague the domestic criminal justice system and catalyze the political will for reform.

The Role of Domestic Civil Society

Domestic NGOs are taking up the opportunity presented by these preliminary examinations in three broad ways. First, some are campaigning for the perpetrators of the grave crimes being examined by the ICC prosecutor to be charged either domestically or in the Hague. Second, some are going further, urging reforms to their domestic justice systems that will allow them to deal with cases that previously have been hidden behind a wall of impunity. The focus here is generally on political crimes and crimes committed by members of powerful elites but beyond the situations being examined by the ICC. Third, some NGOs go further still, working for reforms to the domestic justice system that would strengthen the protection of rights and the administration of justice in all cases: ordinary as well as political crimes.

This is a learning process. The role of the ICC is unfamiliar to most domestic NGOs when a preliminary examination is first announced, and the reaction of national governments can vary widely from open cooperation to hostile denunciation. Each domestic NGO has a unique relationship with the national government, political elites, and ordinary citizens, and each carefully manages its reputation in these and other circles. As a result, each NGO in each country pursues its own strategy, adjusting frequently as it learns, as others react, and as the situation changes. At the same time, NGOs can coordinate their efforts, taking advantage of their different strengths.

Responding to Postelection Violence in Kenya

In the violence that followed Kenya's December 2007 presidential election, more than a thousand died, thousands more were raped, and tens of thousands were internally displaced. Moreover, the people of Kenya as a whole were unsettled to learn that severe political and ethnic violence could shake what is otherwise a relatively stable country. Weeks before Moreno Ocampo announced a preliminary examination, Kenyan NGOs active on issues of justice and human rights formed a coalition, Kenyans for Peace with Truth and Justice, for the dual purpose of supporting victims on all sides of the violence and correcting the portrayal of the violence in both domestic and international media. In contrast to the efforts of various factions to present the violence as one-sided, the coalition sought to convey the full range of violent acts and actors and soon gained international credibility for the balanced picture it presented of these atrocities.

The prosecutor's preliminary examination began in February 2011 as one of several international interventions in Kenya, and the NGOs were not familiar with the ICC's distinctive procedures and role. The Office of the U.N. High Commissioner of Human Rights began a mission to Kenya just as the prosecutor announced his examination, and the African Union had also deployed Kofi Annan, former U.N. secretary-general and chair of the organization's Panel of Eminent African Personalities, to negotiate between the governing and opposition parties.

Over the next twenty-one months, however, the NGO coalition evolved into experts on the ICC's procedures and authority. Working from opposite poles in the political structure, the coalition and the OTP exerted pressure on the national government to act responsibly in relation to the postelection violence and more generally to repair the deficiencies in the criminal justice system. A domestic commission of inquiry headed by Appellate Court judge Philip Waki and soon known simply as the Waki Commission became the prime vehicle for that pressure, revealing how the existence of the ICC and its preliminary examinations can transform the role played such domestic commissions of inquiry. Now, instead of merely calling on the government to hold perpetrators responsible, these inquiries can—and did in Kenya—hold out the prospect of turning names over to the prosecutor if domestic authorities did not take effective action to hold perpetrators responsible (see table 1).

The NGO coalition's strategy evolved through three phases during the period of the preliminary examination. Over the first nine months, the NGOs focused on victim and witness support, promotion of a balanced public narrative about the violence in both domestic and international media, and interaction with the Waki Commission. Specifically in relation to the commission, the NGOs provided background material on human rights abuses over time, identified provinces where the commission might focus inquiries and shared statements the NGOs had collected from witnesses in these provinces, made introductions for the commission among victim communities, and provided emotional, medical, and other support to the victims who testified before the commission.

TABLE 1. Timeline for the 21-Month Preliminary Examination of Post-Election Violence in Kenya

27 December 2007	Presidential election held. On 29 December, the Electoral Commission announces the results from half of Kenya's constituencies, showing opposition leader Raila Odinga leading 56% to 44%. The next day, the Electoral Commission's Chair announces that Mwai Kibaki has won the election. Violence erupts within hours.
5 February 2008	The ICC Prosecutor issues a statement that his office is considering all information available on alleged crimes committed in Kenya, opening the preliminary examination.
28 February 2008	President Mwai Kibaki and opposition leader Raila Odinga sign a power-sharing agreement brokered by Kofi Annan, providing for a Truth, Justice & Reconciliation Commission, a Commission of Inquiry into the Post-Election Violence, and more.
9 May 2008	Power-Sharing Cabinet convenes for the first time.
23 May 2008	Commission of Inquiry into the Post-Election Violence ("Waki Commission") is created.
15 August 2008	Kenyan National Human Rights Commission issues its report on the post-election violence, naming 200 it believes responsible.
15 October 2008	Waki Commission issues its findings and recommends creation of a Special Tribunal with Kenyan and international judges. The Commission delivers documents and a sealed envelope with the names of those it believes were responsible to Kofi Annan, chair of the AU Panel of Eminent African Personalities.
11 February 2009	ICC Prosecutor confirms that his preliminary examination continues, noting that the Kenyan Parliament is currently debating the bill to create a Special Tribunal as recommended by the Waki Commission. The bill is defeated the next day.
3 July 2009	ICC Prosecutor meets in the Hague with the Kenyan Minister of Land, Minister of Justice, and the Attorney General. The Kenyan representatives agree to provide all relevant information.
15 July 2009	Kofi Annan sends documents and envelope that he received in October from the Waki Commission to the ICC Prosecutor.
30 July 2009	Prime Minister Odinga announces that the government will not establish a Special Tribunal into the post-election violence, but instead will rely on the ordinary courts.
17 September 2009	ICC Prosecutor meets with leaders of Kenyan NGOs.
5 November 2009	ICC Prosecutor announces that he will submit a request to the Court for permission to open a full investigation. He submits the formal request on 25 November.
31 March 2010	ICC Judges authorize the Prosecutor to conduct a full investigation.

After the Waki Commission issued its October 2008 report calling for the creation of a special tribunal with both domestic and international judges to hear the cases of postelection violence, the NGO coalition worked to support that recommendation despite the sense among the NGO leaders that their constituents and the majority of the population were deeply skeptical about the possibility of domestic justice. With NGO support, legislation was advanced in Parliament to create a special tribunal to hear these cases, but the legislation failed in February 2009, and the government announced in July that it had abandoned efforts to revive the idea.

With that, the NGO strategy entered a third phase, encouraging the prosecutor to bring prosecutions in the ICC and supporting witnesses and victims in their dealings with the ICC prosecutor and later the Registry. The effort to encourage the prosecutor to bring cases in the Hague included an extraordinary international mission during which representatives of civil society traveled to the Hague and to various capitals to build international support for the Kenyan cases at the ICC. The NGOs also maintained close communication with the African Union and its Panel of Eminent African Personalities. Indeed, the NGO leaders traveled to Addis Ababa, the seat of the African Union, and other neighboring capitals to build regional pressure for a full inquiry into the violence. All the while, the NGOs continued to support witnesses and victims within Kenya who had presented evidence to the commission of inquiry even though they might have little interaction with the ICC. By November 2009, the prosecutor had decided to seek permission from the ICC judges to open a full investigation, and that permission was granted in March 2010.

The Kenya story captures many tactics that NGOs are using in other preliminary examinations, from documentation and victim support to advocacy for domestic legislation and liaison with international actors and foreign governments. Generalizing from this story, we can construct a large menu of activities that domestic NGOs can employ in these situations. I group the tactics into four broad categories: advocacy, documentation, direct assistance to victims, and interaction with larger structures.

We have, then, two separate menus for preliminary examinations, one for the prosecutor, and another for domestic NGOs. In some cases, international organizations—U.N. groups, regional bodies, or individual foreign governments—are also active. In every preliminary examination, however, the prosecutor influences from outside the domestic system, while domestic NGOs operate from within that system. Viewed in this light, the first preliminary examinations have served as opportunities to test how these two forces—the prosecutor and the domestic NGOs—relate to each other and how the choices they make combine to advance justice or not.

The Kenya example is and will remain atypical because it resulted in a full investigation. More commonly, the hopes for justice will be vindicated or dashed in the preliminary examination stage itself. We turn, therefore, to the question of how the prosecutor and domestic NGOs have tried to use preliminary examinations—in Côte d'Ivoire, Guinea, and Palestine—to leverage justice and accountability without the ICC moving to a full investigation.

Preventing Violence in Côte d'Ivoire and Guinea

The danger of massive violence in Côte d'Ivoire was high in early December 2010 when both incumbent president Laurent Gbagbo and his challenger, Alassane Ouattara, a former prime minister and opposition leader, insisted that they had won the presidential election. Gbagbo refused to yield power, while the United Nations, the African Union, the European Union, and more of the international community lined up behind Ouat-

TABLE 2. A Menu of Tactics for Domestic NGOs in Countries Under Preliminary Examination

Advocacy	Build NGO coalitions
	Shape the domestic and international about the violence and patterns
	Propose and support legislation
	Urge greater attention to accountability as part of justice sector reform
	Conduct diplomatic missions to relevant national capitals
Documentation	Get and give training on documentation of grave crimes
	Create a public record of the crimes
	Create memorials and other forms of collective memory
	Support witnesses and victims in their own efforts
Direct Assistance to Victims	File claims for compensation
	Pursue litigation to establish truth and obtain compensation
	Train and support victims to represent themselves
	Provide protection for witnesses who assist any inquiries
Interaction with Larger Structures	Support and assist commissions of inquiry
	Join international NGO networks
	Consult with regional bodies (e.g., the African Union, the OAS)
	Consult governments and civil society in neighboring countries
	Establish regular communication with the ICC

tara, arguing that he had won the runoff election by nine percentage points. Over the next month, a series of traumas occurred: security forces loyal to President Gbagbo shot and killed demonstrators supporting Ouattara; armed supporters of both candidates violently clashed; and soldiers fired on a U.N. patrol. Gbagbo ordered U.N. and French peacekeepers out of the country and closed the country to foreign journalists. The United States reportedly offered the incumbent president a chance to retire to the United States if he stepped down, but he first refused, leading many to fear that the violence would grow. Ultimately Mr. Gbago was arrested and transferred to the ICC in The Hague and Mr. Ouattara assumed the presidency.

While Côte d'Ivoire is not a party to the Rome Statute, in 2003 the government submitted a declaration accepting the exercise of jurisdiction by the ICC over crimes committed since 2002, when a civil war divided the country between north and south. In October 2006, a U.N. report recommended that politicians who continued to obstruct the peace process, often through killings and sexual violence, should face prosecution at the ICC. In the following month, the prosecutor made public his preliminary examination.

After announcing its preliminary examination, the OTP took several steps to help prevent further violence in Côte d'Ivoire. In July 2009, OTP representatives visited the capital, Abidjan, meeting both with government and civil society representatives. On the eve of the October 2010 elections, following consultations with domestic NGOs, Moreno Ocampo gave an interview on French television in which he pointedly used the example of Kenya—and his investigation of postelection violence there—to send a warning to politicians in Côte d'Ivoire: "I'm sure they know we're watching what they are doing."[20] When Ouattara became president, he sent multiple letters to the OTP confirming his acceptance of ICC jurisdiction and requesting OTP investigations within the state. Gbagbo has since been arrested, and the case against him for the violent events taking place after the disputed presidential elections is pending.[21]

At much the same time as the preliminary examination was under way in Côte d'Ivoire, a similar sequence of events played out in Guinea. There, the prosecutor had undertaken a preliminary examination of killings and rapes by soldiers confronting an opposition demonstration prior to elections scheduled to take place during the same week of October as the election in Côte d'Ivoire. In the same interview with French television, Moreno Ocampo signaled to leaders in Guinea that postelection violence could lead to criminal prosecutions for culpable politicians.

In both Côte d'Ivoire and Guinea, the prosecutor followed up the pre-election televised warning with additional steps designed to prevent violence and underscore the relevance of law. For example, on the day after the television interview aired, the deputy prosecutor, Bensouda, telephoned the Guinean justice and foreign ministers in Conakry and at their request followed the conversations with a letter reminding them that electoral violence might fall under ICC jurisdiction if it amounted to committing crimes against humanity or even genocide. The next day, the justice minister gave a press conference during which he repeated precisely this phrase, adding that political leaders could be held directly or indirectly criminally responsible. The deputy prosecutor Bensouda and other staff then visited Conakry in early November, immediately following the second round of voting, both to follow up on discussions of the investigation of the original violence of September 2009 and to help deter further violence.

In Côte d'Ivoire, on the same day that the top election official declared that the opposition leader had won the presidency, the deputy prosecutor made a public statement urging restraint and the domestic investigation of past crimes:

> I encourage the political leaders to call on their supporters and fellow citizens to show restraint and avoid unrest. I invite the Ivorian authorities to investigate criminal incidents that have already occurred and to do everything possible to deter future ones. All reported acts of violence will be closely scrutinized by the Office.[22]

As violence broke out in mid-December, Moreno Ocampo again spoke publicly, warning that postelection killings would be prosecuted:

> If they start to kill people then it's a crime and we will pursue them. . . . No-one can commit crime in Ivory Coast because of elections. . . . The reality is that some people in Ivory Coast are planning attacks and we know that. And I want to tell them clearly, if you do that . . . you will be prosecuted. That's a clear message.[23]

NGOs leveraged these comments in their domestic and international advocacy. Domestic NGOs in Côte d'Ivoire, for example, formed a coalition in response to the disputed elections and growing violence. They issued a joint statement calling for the prevention of violence, accountability for any security forces that engaged in violence, free and responsible journalism, and the protection of civilians. The NGOs ended their statement by reiterating the warnings issued by the ICC prosecutor and deputy prosecutor:

> Our organizations further remind that the Office of the Prosecutor of the International Criminal Court has urged supporters of both opponents and security forces to refrain from violence and has indicated that, "All reported acts of violence will be closely scrutinized by the Office."[24]

The ICC ultimately opened an investigation into the postelection violence in Côte d'Ivoire and has brought arrest warrants against Gbagbo; his wife Simone Gbabgo; and a member of Gbagbo's inner circle, Charles Blé Goudé. The ICC's investigation is continuing and additional arrest warrants could issue.

Overcoming the Resistance to Law in the Palestinian Territories

The three-week Gaza War of 2008–9, labeled in Israel Operation Cast Lead, resulted in between eleven hundred and fourteen hundred Palestinian deaths and thirteen Israeli deaths.[25] The OTP's preliminary examination was especially difficult not only because the politics of the Israeli-Palestinian conflict are so contentious but also because the Palestinian Authority's January 2009 acceptance of the ICC's jurisdiction and invitation to the OTP to investigate alleged crimes[26] committed during Operation Cast Lead is the first instance of such a declaration from an entity not universally recognized as a state. Technically, therefore, the prosecutor's preliminary examination first had to determine whether the Palestinian Territories could invoke the ICC's jurisdiction. Irrespective of how the question was ultimately answered (negatively), however, the existence of the examination itself kept open the question of the relevance of law to these alleged crimes.[27]

One NGO, the Palestinian Center for Human Rights, has been investigating and documenting human rights violations related to Operation Cast Lead, providing free legal assistance to individual victims and groups and publishing reports.[28] Perhaps most significantly, it submits claims for compensation on behalf of civilian victims, though the obstacles to such litigation are growing.[29] Another NGO, Al-Haq, has acted as a consultant to the Palestinian Authority's independent commission on the violations associated with Operation Cast Lead and advocates for greater transparency and independence in the investigation of war crimes and judicial review of the decisions of the Israeli military authorities.

None of these efforts have produced or are likely to produce any accountability under the law for what the Goldstone Report[30] termed attacks on civilian populations during Operation Cast Lead that "amounted to reprisals and collective punishment and constitute war crimes."[31] The NGOs that employ these tactics are clear about what they are doing: insisting on pursuing the forms of law even if merely to illustrate that law has no force in this conflict as yet.

The Goldstone Report, like the Waki Commission in Kenya, despaired of the failure to date of domestic justice institutions on both sides of the conflict to thoroughly investigate and prosecute the kinds of crimes that had likely been committed. Nonetheless, the Goldstone Report recommended domestic, not international, remedies. While the Waki Commission called for the creation of a special tribunal because it did not think the existing courts capable of conducting the necessary proceedings, the Goldstone Report concluded that "both Israel and the Gaza Authorities have the ability to conduct open and transparent investigations and launch appropriate prosecutions if they decide to do so."[32] The Goldstone Commission therefore recommended that the domestic systems be strongly encouraged to act. Still, just as the Waki Commission asked Annan to hand the evidence over to the ICC if Parliament did not establish the special tribunal, the Goldstone Report added that if no good-faith investigations by Israel or the authorities in Gaza were undertaken within six months, the Security Council should refer the matter to the ICC prosecutor.

It was not a surprise when the Goldstone Report was not followed by either an independent investigation or a referral. But in November 2012, the General Assembly granted Palestine nonmember observer state status, which may allow it now to refer cases to the ICC. Although the Rome Statute has not, to date, been found to apply to the conflict in the Palestinian Territories, even here we can see the complementary steps of the ICC prosecutor, domestic NGOs, and other international actors moving, however tentatively, toward a consensus that law should apply in the future. If the day comes when those who commit grave crimes in this part of the Middle East are accountable to law, it will have been through this tragically slow, macabre dance. Now that Palestine has been granted nonmember observer status in the U.N. General Assembly, the answer to the question of whether the OTP will accept Palestine's request to conduct a preliminary examination may change.[33]

Ordinary Crimes

In some cases, this NGO advocacy extends to pressing for reforms that would strengthen domestic justice in cases of ordinary crimes as well as grave ones. The Human Rights Center of Georgia, for example, is drawing connections between the failure of the domestic system in cases of grave crimes and its shortcomings in dealing with ordinary crimes. A comprehensive reform of the domestic justice system was carried out over the last several years, successfully reforming the civil justice system but leaving the criminal justice system subject to political control. The result, according to the center, is extremely high rates of detention and conviction in ordinary cases as well as neglect of victim rights in political cases:

> Miscarriages of justice remain a source of concern in "ordinary" cases as well. Equality of arms and a right to adversarial trial, as well as the obligation of the court to . . . deliver a reasoned judgment [is] widely ignored. Court hearings often constitute a mere formality. . . . [I]n an absolute majority of cases judges fully follow the motion of the prosecutor while rejecting arguments and evidence of the defense lawyers without even providing an explanation for that.[34]

The center points to excessive use of pretrial detention, very low rates of acquittal, and a tripling of the prison population in recent years as signs of the lack of judicial independence from the executive. And to underscore the point, the Human Rights Center castigates the practice of plea bargaining in Georgia, in which prosecutors fully discharge defendants in exchange for large cash payments: "a system of legalized racketeering by the state, the real motive behind which seems to be fundraising rather than [the] execution of justice."[35]

The result is not merely a lack of justice but a lack of public trust and confidence in the judiciary itself. A particularly high-profile murder case in 2006 and 2007 brought the routine violation of legal procedure to public attention as journalists documented and broadcast court proceedings that repeatedly violated the law, but Parliament responded simply by imposing a blanket ban on photo-video and film recording on the court premises and in courtrooms. These actions, according to observers, only strengthened existing mistrust.[36]

Similarly, in Côte d'Ivoire, judicial and detention practices are marked by corruption, arbitrariness, and abuse. Arrests occur without authority and without conforming to legal procedures; security concerns produce arrests and detentions apparently solely for purposes of extortion; conditions of incarceration are overcrowded and harsh, and individuals with wealth may purchase extra cell space, food, and services.[37] In response, the Ligue Ivoirienne des Droits de l'Homme conducts public education campaigns about the rights of citizens to a better administration of justice and works with other organizations to improve the administration of justice in the country.[38]

The Promise of Justice

The experience of NGOs during preliminary examinations is often frustrating, as the resistance of political elites to any legal accountability stiffens. In Kenya, the power-sharing government was first unable to get the special tribunal legislation through Parliament and eventually abandoned the idea entirely, a fate that is hardly surprising since some of these same parliamentarians could have been held responsible in any legal proceedings.[39] Indeed, in almost every situation, NGOs depend largely on shaming the government into taking some minimal action to provide justice to the victims of grave crimes. The past few years have shown that the ICC's preliminary examinations will often enhance the NGOs' efforts as well as potentially capture and direct the attention of a powerful international audience toward domestic injustices. Nonetheless, the NGOs' use of shame as a tactic remains difficult, as governments typically react only slowly, if at all.

As the OTP and domestic NGOs continue to work in their own spheres to fulfill the promises of justice implicitly and explicitly made in announcing preliminary examinations, the system of international criminal justice needs ways to define success in these cases short of prosecution in the Hague. It must be possible to end most preliminary examinations successfully without commencing a full investigation at the ICC. If not, future prosecutors will stop making public these examinations, and the power of preliminary examinations will be diminished. So what does success plausibly look like, short of prosecution in the Hague?

The answer suggested in these early experiences is clear: success lies in a consensus on the relevance if not yet the rule of law. This might take the form of genuine domestic investigations and prosecutions or such other forms as independent judicial commissions of inquiry to proceedings before regional tribunals. The articulation of legal norms in itself in these proceedings can be a real success, meaningful to victims and to society as whole.

NOTES

1. I use the term *grave crimes* as a shorthand for the three crimes over which the ICC has jurisdiction: genocide, war crimes, and crimes against humanity.

2. I am grateful to the participants in Widening the Window for Justice, a seminar organized by the Hauser Center for Nonprofit Organizations at the Bellagio, Italy, Conference Center of the Rockefeller Foundation and supported by the Ford Foundation. Many of the descriptions of the crimes, of the victims, and of the strategies local NGOs are pursuing and have pursued in these countries under preliminary examination are drawn from the discussions there. As of Dec. 1, 2013, the OTP is conducting preliminary examinations in eight situations: Afghanistan, Honduras, Republic of Korea, Comoros, Colombia, Georgia, Guinea, and Nigeria. http://www.icc-cpi.int/en_menus/icc/structure%20of%20the%20court/office%20of%20the%20prosecutor/comm%20and%20ref/Pages/communications%20and%20referrals.aspx.

3. Rome Statute of the International Criminal Court, July 17, 1998, 2187 U.N.T.S. 90, pmbl. (entered into force July, 1, 2002) (hereinafter Rome Statute).

4. Justice Sylvana Arbia, Registrar, ICC, *Remarks at the Consultative Conference on International Criminal Justice* (Sept. 2009) (transcript on file with author).

5. Ambassador Christian Wenaweser, President of the Assembly of States Parties, ICC, *Remarks at the Consultative Conference on International Criminal Justice* (Sept. 2009) (transcript on file with author).

6. On Mar. 31, 2011, in a majority decision, Pre-Trial Chamber II held that there was a reasonable basis to proceed with an investigation and that the situation appeared to fall within the jurisdiction of the Court. Preliminary examinations were formally completed at that time and the situation proceeded to the investigation stage.

7. The OTP made its preliminary examination public in the case of Colombia in 2006, Afghanistan in 2007, Kenya and Georgia in 2008, Côte d'Ivoire and the Palestinian Territories in 2009, and Guinea in 2010.

8. Office of the Prosecutor, ICC, *Policy Paper on Preliminary Examinations (Draft)* ¶2 (Oct. 4, 2010), http://www.icc-cpi.int/NR/rdonlyres/9FF1EAA1-41C4-4A30-A202-174B18DA923C/282515/OTP_Draftpolicypaperonpreliminaryexaminations04101.pdf.

9. *See id.* at ¶86(a).

10. *See id.* at ¶86(b).

11. *See id.* at ¶¶51–72, 86(c).

12. *See id.* at ¶¶73–75, 86(d).

13. *See id.* at ¶¶14, 84.

14. *See id.* at ¶17.

15. Office of the Prosecutor ICC, *OTP Weekly Briefing: Issue No. 53* (Aug. 31, 2010–Sept. 6, 2010), at 1.

16. *ICC Investigates Guinea "Abuses,"* BBC NEWS (Oct. 15, 2009), http://news.bbc.co.uk/2/hi/8308420.stm.

17. On an Apr. 5, 2012, visit to Guinea, the OTP issued a press release. This trip marked Bensouda's third visit to the state and OTP's sixth. Fatou Bensouda, Deputy

Prosecutor of the International Criminal Court, *Press Statement* (Apr. 5, 2012), http://www.icc-cpi.int/NR/rdonlyres/8BEEEB8C-D22E-48F6-AFB9-E4B72B92E3CF/0/StatementFatouBensoudaConakry050412Eng.pdf.

18. *ICC: Guinea Killings "Crime against Humanity,"* BBC NEWS (Feb. 19, 2010), http://news.bbc.co.uk/2/hi/africa/8525568.stm.

19. *Guinea PM Says Judiciary Incapable of Judging Killers,* BBC NEWS (Feb. 19, 2010), http://news.bbc.co.uk/2/hi/africa/8523601.stm.

20. *The Interview: Luis Moreno-Ocampo,* FRANCE 24 (Oct. 22, 2010), http://www.france24.com/en/20101019-moreno-ocamp-icc-kenya-sudan-war-crimes.

21. Office of the Prosecutor, *Côte D'Ivoire: ICC Prosecutor Ready to Request Judges for Authorization to Open an Investigation* (June 22, 2011), http://www.icc-cpi.int/en_menus/icc/structure%20of%20the%20court/office%20of%20the%20prosecutor/reports%20and%20statements/statement/Pages/cote%20d%E2%80%99ivoire_%20icc%20prosecutor%20ready%20to%20request%20judges%20for%20authorization%20to%20op.aspx.

22. International Criminal Court, *Statement by the Deputy Prosecutor of the ICC on the Situation in Côte d'Ivoire,* (Dec. 2, 2010), http://jurist.org/paperchase/ICC%20Ivory%20Coast%20Statement.pdf.

23. *Ocampo Now Turns His Guns on Ivory Coast,* CAPITAL NEWS, Dec. 16, 2010, http://www.capitalfm.co.ke/news/Kenyanews/Ocampo-now-turns-his-guns-on-Ivory-Coast-10897.html.

24. *See* Int'l Fed'n for Human Rights, *Ivory Coast: African Civil Society & International NGOs Call for the Protection of Civilians & Respect of the Population's Fundamental Rights,* (Dec. 20, 2010), http://www.fidh.org/Ivory-Coast-African-civil-society.

25. Jim Zanotti, *Israel & Hamas: Conflict in Gaza* (2008–9), CONGRESSIONAL RESEARCH SERVICE, Report 7-5700, at 8 (Feb. 19, 2009) (reporting that Israel suffered thirteen fatalities, while the Palestinians incurred greater casualties—fourteen hundred dead and roughly fifty-four hundred wounded).

26. International Criminal Court, *Situation in Palestine,* ¶1 (Apr. 3, 2012), http://www.icc-cpi.int/NR/rdonlyres/C6162BBF-FEB9-4FAF-AFA9-836106D2694A/284387/SituationinPalestine030412ENG.pdf.

27. The OTP issued its decision not to proceed with the Palestinian case because of a lack of jurisdiction on Apr. 3, 2012. International Criminal Court, *Office of the Prosecutor Preliminary Examinations: Completed Decision Not to Proceed—Palestine,* http://www.icc-cpi.int/en_menus/icc/structure%20of%20the%20court/office%20of%20the%20prosecutor/comm%20and%20ref/pe-cdnp/palestine/Pages/palestine.aspx; International Criminal Court, *Situation in Palestine* (Apr. 3, 2012), http://www.icc-cpi.int/NR/rdonlyres/C6162BBF-FEB9-4FAF-AFA9-836106D2694A/284387/SituationinPalestine030412ENG.pdf.

28. *See generally* the Palestinian Centre for Human Rights website at http://www.pchrgaza.org/portal/en/.

29. *See* Palestinian Centre for Human Rights, *About PCHR,* http://www.pchrgaza.org/portal/en/index.php?option=com_content&view=article&id=3027&Itemid=182.

30. The United Nations Fact Finding Mission on the Gaza Conflict, which produced the Goldstone Report, was established in Apr. 2009 by the U.N. Human Rights Council during the Gaza War as an independent international fact-finding mission to investigate alleged violations of international human rights law and international humanitarian law

in the Palestinian Territories, particularly the Gaza Strip, in connection with the Gaza War. United Nations Human Rights Council, *Report of the Human Rights Council on Its 9th Special Session,* A/HRC/S-9/2 (Feb. 27, 2009), http://www.refworld.org/docid/49997aebd.html.

31. Justice Richard Goldstone, Head, U.N. Fact Finding Mission on Gaza Conflict, *Statement on Behalf of the Members of the United Nations Fact Finding Mission on the Gaza Conflict before the Human Rights Council,* at 4 (Sept. 29, 2009), http://www2.ohchr.org/english/bodies/hrcouncil/specialsession/9/factfindingmission.htm.

32. *See id.* at 5.

33. For an interesting discussion, *see* http://jurist.org/forum/2013/01/linda-keller-icc-palestine-part1.php.

34. Paper prepared for the Bellagio Conference, 14 (on file with author).

35. *See id.* at 16.

36. *See id.*

37. *U.S. Department of State Human Rights Report: Cote d'Ivoire 2012,* pp. 6–8, http://ppja.org/countries/cote-divoire/us-department-of-state-human-rights-report-cote-di-voire-2012/view; Amnesty International, *Cote d'Ivoire: The Victors' Law. The Human Rights Situation Two Years After the Post-Electoral Crisis* 19–26 (2013), http://www.amnesty.org/en/library/asset/AFR31/001/2013/en/e5b7a774-3898-4254-8985-6755a67a0c14/afr310012013en.pdf.

38. Ligue Ivoirienne des Droits de L'Homme, Nos Activities, http://www.lidho.org/activite.html.

39. Human Rights Watch, *Kenya: Swiftly Enact Special Tribunal. International Criminal Court Should Be a Last Resort for Justice,* March 25, 2009, http://www.hrw.org/news/2009/03/24/kenya-swiftly-enact-special-tribunal; Katherine Iliopoulos, *Kenyan Officials May Face an Indictment, Crimes of War* (2011), http://www.crimesofwar.org/commentary/kenyan-officials-may-face-icc-indictment/.

"Managing Violence"[1]

Can the International Criminal Court Prevent Sexual Violence in Conflict?

Jessica Lynn Corsi

In the Central African Republic (CAR), rebel leaders are doing something that could impress even the most cynical of international lawyers: they are meeting in makeshift outdoor classrooms to learn about the Rome Statute and international law. The year is 2007 and bursts of civil conflict[2] marked by sexual violence[3] persist in the CAR. Far beyond the reaches of newspapers and the Internet, rebel fighters are tuning their scratchy transistor radios to the BBC to follow the actions of the International Criminal Court (ICC) and its first prosecutor, Luis Moreno Ocampo.[4] In particular, these rebels are interested in the ICC prosecutor's recently launched investigation into previous incidences of sexual violence in the CAR.[5] At least one rebel force in the CAR seeks and receives instruction on the Rome Statute's prohibitions on sexual violence in an effort to rebrand itself as legitimate, law-abiding combatants impervious to ICC prosecution. Is this progress?

A series of legal developments have combined to create a situation in which international criminal law and the prosecutors who apply it have unprecedented power to influence how fighting forces[6] think about sexual violence in conflict. To advance this argument, this chapter details the important ways in which the Rome Statute's criminalization of sexual violence is exceptional and analyzes why these changes are a foundational step for advancing compliance with these new rules. Next, it explores how Moreno Ocampo's actions ushered in a new era of how international criminal law responds to sexual and gender violence,[7] asserting that the commitment evidenced in the first prosecutor's (admittedly late) focus on sexual violence crimes has the potential to reshape expectations. Both the instruction of fighting forces on legal restrictions in conflict and the doctrine of command responsibility are indispensable steps for influencing fighting force behavior.

Sexual violence committed by armed forces is a common and gruesome feature of conflict. The Rome Statute of the ICC advanced international criminal law by responding to these crimes in an unprecedented fashion— for example, by including sexual violence in an enumerated list of war crimes and crimes against humanity,[8] codifying "gender" as a chargeable element of the crime of persecution,[9] and establishing prosecutorial obligations to take special note of gender when conducting investigations and prosecutions.[10] These articles of the Rome Statute are to date the most detailed and explicit international criminal provisions regarding sexual violence. This chapter examines the steps Moreno Ocampo and his team eventually took to fulfil the potential of the Rome Statute to respond to sexual violence. In the words of the then prosecutor-elect and now prosecutor Fatou Bensouda, who succeeded Moreno Ocampo as prosecutor, "We can and we will transform the public response to sexual crimes worldwide, in and outside recognized zones of conflict."[11] Reviewing the first prosecutor's strategy of charging gender crimes whenever applicable, the chapter argues that this strategy and the resultant centrality of gender crimes in almost all ICC prosecutions to date promote the legitimacy of the criminalization of sexual violence under international law. This legitimacy,[12] together with command responsibility, a mode of liability facilitating the prosecution of atrocities in conflict, increases the likelihood that combatants and those who lead them will comply with the Rome Statute's prohibitions on sexual violence. To examine Prosecutor Bensouda's assertion that "the law will help to change behaviour,"[13] this chapter employs a case study of a particular rebel group in the CAR as an example of a nonstate fighting force requesting instruction in international law. In doing so, it links the promises of the Rome Statute regarding international criminal law's response to sexual violence and the actions of Moreno Ocampo and his team to one example that might indicate that active prosecutions at the ICC can influence fighting force behavior.

Sexual Violence in Conflict: A Persistent and Widespread Problem

Sexual violence has defined the conflict in the CAR. However, the CAR is not an isolated example: armed forces the world over commit acts of rape and sexual violence at alarming levels in conflicts of various natures.[14] State military, guerrillas, and paramilitaries have used rape as a weapon of civil war in Colombia for more than fifty years.[15] Tens of thousands of women, girls, men, and boys have been raped in the Democratic Republic of Congo (DRC), where conflict has raged for more than twenty years, engendering what United Nations experts call a culture of daily violence of "genocidal proportions."[16] Former Iraqi prisoners held at the now infamous Abu Ghraib prison accused American soldiers of forced sexual acts and threats of rape.[17] Unfortunately, these incidents represent just a few of many more instances.

While the character of sexual violence in conflict is as varied as the geography of conflict itself—including mass rape enacted either by policy or through license,[18] the sexual humiliation and assault of prisoners,[19] and "bad apple" soldiers organizing the gang rape and murder of civilians[20]—no form of sexual violence can ever be justified as a legal part of conflict. In sharp contrast to other violence in warfare—such as targeting, shooting, and killing the designated enemy in compliance with the rules for applying lethal force—there is no legal basis for committing sexual violence in conflict. The law of armed conflict strictly prohibits rapes as a tactic, weapon, or outcome of conflict.[21] And yet despite the widespread and persistent nature of these crimes, prosecuting sexual violence as a crime under international law is a late-twentieth-century development. In this sense, the Rome Statute, the actions of the ICC prosecutor, and the trial judgments emerging from the ICC represent an unprecedented international legal condemnation of sexual violence in conflict.

The Rome Statute's Potential to Punish and Prevent Sexual Violence

The Rome Statute's clear and detailed articulation of sexual violence as a crime under international law ushers in a new era of international legal response to these atrocities. The status of the Rome Statute, which was adopted on July 17, 1998, and entered into force on July 1, 2002,[22] as a duly negotiated treaty and its detailed definitions of sexual violence and gender crimes build on and go substantially beyond previous international law. In doing so, it offers the strongest international legal foundation for punishing and preventing these crimes that the world has yet seen.

The International Criminal Tribunal for the Former Yugoslavia (ICTY), established in 1993, and the International Criminal Tribunal for

Rwanda (ICTR), established in 1994, were the first international criminal tribunals to have subject matter jurisdiction over rape as an international crime.[23] Like the Rome Statute, their statutes began a new era in which crimes of sexual violence were tried as crimes against humanity, genocide, and war crimes. Yet distinct from the status of the crimes in the Rome Statute, it was not clear at the founding of these two tribunals whether and to what extent sexual violence existed as a crime under international law. Both the ICTY and the ICTR acknowledged in their judgments that "no definition of rape can be found in international law,"[24] and they pioneered groundbreaking international law jurisprudence on sexual violence.[25] At the same time, the report of the U.N. secretary-general that established these tribunals[26] and later the judgments of these tribunals[27] asserted that rape definitively existed as a crime under customary international law prior to the founding of these courts.[28] Thus it seems that the birth of the modern prosecution of crimes of sexual violence under international law presented a tension between grounding crimes in previously existing international law and developing international crimes through judicial decisions.

The novelty of the crime of sexual violence articulated in the judgments of the ICTY and the ICTR presents problems of legality and legitimacy. Because the tribunals had to invent the definition of rape under international law through their written judgments, legal scholars have argued that such a "highly remarkable" number of definitions of sexual violence emerged[29] that these judgments violated the principle of *nullum crimen sine lege*.[30] But for the Rome Statute, the status of sexual violence under international criminal law might have remained disputed. The entry into force of the Rome Statute solidified the status of crimes of sexual violence under international law. Because the Rome Statute is a treaty with 122 states parties, it provides further evidence that the changes to the international law of sexual violence rendered at the ICTY and the ICTR have assumed the status of customary international law.[31] In contrast, the ICTY and the ICTR were created not by treaty but rather by the United Nations Security Council.[32] Legal theorists express a preference for treaty as a source of international law and in particular prefer a treaty-based international criminal law system as the most legitimate foundation for depriving persons of liberty. As one writes,

Constitutionally, the preferable way of handling *any* lawmaking text may be the standard method of a diplomatic conference followed by a treaty that is subject to ratification (or not) by governments. This approach is evidently preferable where the text in question is, for example, the statute for an international criminal court, which imposes itself on individuals and requires due process of law; or, more generally, where the text must be embodied in domestic law to have its effect.[33]

Thus, the multilateral treaty process by which the Rome Statute came to be international law imbues it with a legitimacy that surpasses that of the U.N. Security Council–created statutes of the ICTY and ICTR. This added strength in turn bolsters the impact of the Rome Statute's criminalization of sexual violence by removing doubt regarding the existence of these crimes in advance of ICC trials, something the ICTY and ICTR statutes were not able to do.

This multilateral negotiation process afforded the Rome Statute another hallmark of legitimacy: textual determinacy. The level of specificity with which the Rome Statute defines crimes of sexual violence is unprecedented in international law. The texts of the Nuremberg and Tokyo Charters did not mention rape or other forms of sexual or gender-based violence. The statutes of the ICTY and the ICTR included rape as a crime against humanity and in the case of the ICTR as a violation of article 3 common to the Geneva Conventions and of Additional Protocol II, but these statutes did not provide a substantive definition of rape or enumerate related crimes of sexual violence such as sexual slavery. In contrast, the Rome Statute articulates specific acts such as "forced pregnancy"[34] and sets out broader categories such as "any other form of sexual violence of comparable gravity,"[35] thereby allowing for charges within the category of sexual violence for acts not expressly enumerated. Further, the Elements of Crimes[36] substantially define the listed acts of sexual violence. By detailing these crimes in advance of prosecution charges and trials, the Rome Statute and Elements of Crimes eliminate the risk of violating *nullum crimen sine lege*. Accordingly, this achieves what jurist Thomas Franck sets out as a hallmark of legitimate, compliance-inducing international law:

> Perhaps the most self-evident of all characteristics making for legitimacy is textual determinacy. What is meant by this is the ability of the text to convey a clear message, to appear transparent in the sense that one can see through the language to the meaning. Obviously, rules with a readily ascertainable meaning have a better chance than those that do not to regulate the conduct of those to whom the rule is addressed or exert a compliance pull on their policymaking pro-

cess. Those addressed will know precisely what is expected of them, which is a necessary first step towards compliance.[37]

The specificity with which the Rome Statute defines sexual and gender crimes is meaningful. Drawing on the social meaning of the law to express values and norms, Margaret M. deGuzman argues that "the strongest justification for a special focus on sex crimes at international courts lies in the need to express the undervalued norms prohibiting such crimes."[38] The precision with which the Rome Statute codifies crimes of sexual violence expresses the status of these crimes as normatively and legally condemned, and the clarity of this legal expression has the potential to create a shift in how those who would commit these crimes approach these acts.

The Link between Law and Preventing Sexual Violence in Conflict

This chapter's central thesis asserts links between the threat of international criminal prosecution and deterrence of sexual violence. To make that link, the causes of mass violence, sexual violence, and violence against women more broadly must be addressed. International criminal law is a system that can influence behavior and act as a counterweight to the forces that drive violence, including sexual violence. The legitimacy described previously and the prosecutor's role in investigating and prosecuting (discussed in the next section) detail the contours of international criminal law and the ICC within it as a power system. Particularly when taken up by commanders in position of hierarchical power over combatants, international law's prohibitions on sexual violence in conflict can come to form part of the organizational culture and power system of the combat unit, acting as a powerful influence on combatant behavior. Because the forces that drive violence involve features such as authority and deindividuation, dehumanization, and moral disengagement rather than formal military structures, these theories apply even in situations where civilian leaders exercise control over civilians turned combatants, such as when civilian political leaders organized and ordered civilians to commit mass sexual violence in Rwanda in 1994.[39]

Social science offers insight into how mass groups of people can come to inflict gruesome sexual violence on others, including their former neighbors and friends. While criminal law is often focused on locating individual responsibility and punishing single persons or small groups of persons, the large-scale violence that takes place during conflict and/or crimes against humanity or genocide, including sexual violence, cannot be attributed to the "unusual" and "criminal" disposition of one individual. Rather, social science focuses on the systems and conducts situational inquiry. "People and situations are usually in a sense of dynamic interaction."[40] Consequently, it is important that law recognize that "systems, not just dispositions and situations must be taken into account in order to understand complex behavior patterns."[41]

Social psychologist Philip Zimbardo argues that various situational factors and instructions via power systems can cause ordinarily good people to do horrific things, including perpetrating appalling sexual violence.[42] His work assesses mass rapes, killing squads, torture, and other horrific abuses as well as more generally how people can be made to lie, cheat, steal, or otherwise conform to immoral behavior in any number of situations. His theory has many layers and is based not only on his own empirical experiments, decades of his expertise in psychology, and his service as an expert witness in Abu Ghraib torture trials but also on a thorough review of empirical psychology literature on such phenomena as conformity, moral flexibility, anonymity, and violence. His work also "puts the system on trial," investigating "command complicity" and how elites in power construct systems and situations that produce horrific violence by driving masses of other humans to commit such acts. This chapter engages these theories to ask how international criminal law—more specifically, the threat of prosecution and instructing combatants in international criminal law—can counterbalance the forces that drive violence.

To summarize Zimbardo's work, almost all human beings are capable of complying with explicit or implicit instructions—for example, via words, symbols, images, and inaction as well as action—to perpetrate brutal violence on others. This compliance is based on human nature and even the structure of the human brain: human beings have a very strong inclination to conform, a burning desire to be in the "in" rather than "out" group, and a forceful proclivity to follow the orders of those in power, even if those orders mean brutalizing other human beings and even in situations where obeying orders threatens one's own life.[43] At the same time, humans have a tendency to overestimate their individuality and their ability to resist such orders and to underestimate the power of others, situations, and systems on human behavior and standards of morality.[44] This "in group/out group" trigger to violence comports with Ruth Seinfert's analysis of sexual violence in conflict, in which she describes combatants as using rape to send a message, man to man, that the men in one group are vulnerable or conquered because they are not able to protect "their" women from rape.[45] When told that the other group is bad and must be conquered, sexual violence can become a tool for doing so and is chosen because it aligns with peacetime concepts of dominance, hierarchy, and control.

The flip side of needing to feel included and having an inclination to conform is how the dehumanization of people or groups allows previously peaceful people to commit horrible violence: "humanity" is as much a status as a way of being.[46] Public health studies on preventing sexual violence frequently site inequality between men and women and cultural, societal, and religious beliefs that women are inferior—less human than men—as causal factors for such violence.[47] "Combatants recognize that they can easily dehumanize women in wartime, thus encouraging mass rape and sexual slavery, because the necessary animosity against women previously existed."[48] As discussed in the next section, the prosecutor's office has deliberately and carefully used its power—whether in giving interviews, making speeches, issuing press releases, opening investigations, or prosecuting—to send a message that violence against women and girls will not be tolerated. These messages and their accompanying activities serve as counterweights to prevailing societal, cultural, and organizational attitudes that dehumanize females and in doing so facilitate sexual violence against them.

Human nature can be manipulated and mobilized to spur brutal atrocities. Certain features common to militaries, nonstate armed groups, and even civilians mobilized into violence squads during extreme situations help facilitate this violence. Key factors include anonymity and deindividuation, which exponentially increase the likelihood that a person will follow orders and inflict brutal violence on others.[49] Camaraderie among fighting forces, uniforms, a shared identity as one group against others— all of these things are common features in regular and irregular fighting forces, and all of them make these forces much easier to control and turn violent. Something as simple as having fighters change their external appearance—a ritual of warfare since the beginning of time—provides the anonymity needed to transform ordinarily compassionate and respectful people into violent monsters.[50] However, a changed appearance is not necessary as long as a person feels anonymous; if the person is one among many, feels ignored or overlooked, or operates without threat of punishment, it is enough to flip the switch and unleash violent behavior.[51] Combat and hierarchical combat structures provide such situational anonymity. In contrast, visible prosecutions at the ICC shine a light on this behavior, shattering the myth that it will remain hidden and unpunished. Prosecutions at the ICC also offer accountability when those in power over combatants fail to restrain them or to investigate or punish reports of illegal violence. Failure of the power structure to intervene enhances the likelihood that those perpetrating the violence will continue to do so.[52] Prosecutions at the ICC connect directly to this cause of violence. This link depends on those committing the acts viewing themselves as accountable to the ICC. The case study presented in this chapter is an example of a nonstate fighting force that felt just this connection and was influenced by it.

International criminal law interacts with combatants when it is translated through the organizational hierarchy of combat units. The importance of the command structure of a combat unit must be addressed head-on; the hierarchy of control that is central to waging conflict is a powerful tool. "Systems create hierarchies of dominance with influence and communications going down—rarely up—the line."[53] The relationship between command structure and violence is mirrored by the ICC's reliance on command responsibility as a mode of liability, linking power over combatants, mass violence, and leaders' individual responsibility. The principle of command, or superior, responsibility, articulated in article 28 of the Rome Statute,[54] provides an important link between the limited number of prosecutions that can happen at the ICC and the instruction of fighting forces. The case brought by Moreno Ocampo against Jean-Pierre Bemba for crimes committed in the CAR exemplifies the connection between prosecution of sexual violence in conflict and the role of commanders in instructing soldiers in prohibitions against these acts. During proceedings, the court linked the duty of a commander to prevent crimes to the practice of instructing troops in legal prohibitions.[55] Putting a commander on trial for failing to prevent mass rapes conforms exactly to Zimbardo's research detailing how inaction in command structures creates the necessary environment and thus promotes violence perpetrated by lower ranks.[56]

Moreover, evidence suggesting the strong likelihood that soldiers obey the orders of their superiors supports both the need to instruct soldiers in prohibitions on sexual violence and the utility of defining sexual violence as a war crime and crime against humanity under the Rome Statute. After evaluating a range of disciplines, including history, law, psychology, and organizational theory, Martha Minow concluded,

On the basis of varied sources of social science research, we can predict that soldiers will follow orders whether legal or illegal, that soldiers will conform to expectations of superiors and peers, and that soldiers will be unlikely to resist a commander or peer group authorizing or engaging in atrocities.[57]

Minow goes on to hypothesize that instructing military personnel in the law holds "real prospects for preventing atrocities by soldiers [by] changing organizational design and resources surrounding the soldier, including specifying new obligations for those in command."[58] In the same vein, a Red Cross study mirrored social psychology in emphasizing that an individual in a combat unit is not morally autonomous. This conclusion led the authors of the study to stress the importance of pressing commands to refrain from illegal violence as law: "Efforts to disseminate IHL [international humanitarian law] must be made in a legal and political matter rather than a moral one, and focus more on norms than on their underlying values, because the idea that the combatant is morally autonomous is mistaken." The study also stressed that instruction in the law was a prerequisite to compliance with the law: "Greater respect of IHL is possible only if bearers of weapons are properly trained, if they are under strict orders as to the conduct to adopt and if effective sanctions are applied in the event they fail to obey such orders."[59]

Similarly, prosecutions at the ICC under the Rome Statute have the power to influence the internal organizational culture of fighting forces and governments. Organizational theory suggests that the moral and normative space within fighting forces will be changed by instruction in legal prohibitions:

> The significance of this body of scholarship lies in the suggestion that organizational culture can actually be affected by external forces, including laws, norms, values, and aspirational targets. Consequently, articulating (and defining) international law norms, for example, may have a real impact on institutions even absent mechanisms of enforcement. This literature also suggests that training regimens can have lasting effects on institutional culture by changing the normative space within the institution.[60]

An institution's acceptance of itself as bound by a norm of international law is an example of "real impact on institutions." For example, as the case study later in this chapter reveals, the rebel leader in the CAR made instruction in international law a prerequisite for promotion. Such a policy could be interpreted as a step toward internalizing this norm and letting it shape the culture of the rebel force. The nature of combat forces as separate from and morally distinct from the general population underscores the necessity of training combatants to comply with legal standards: "Because military units are traditionally isolated from other citizens, transforming the military to reflect human rights standards requires education and training from within the system."[61]

Further adding to this concept, public health approaches to primary prevention of sexual violence also focus on social and community relationships and attitudes and influences.[62] The World Health Organization's "ecological model of violence," which draws on yet goes beyond many other assessments of causality and risk for violence, locates relational, community, and societal drivers of violence in addition to the traditional focus on the individual committing violence.[63] This model prompts those interested in prevention to address "the norms, beliefs and social and economic systems that create the conditions for intimate partner and sexual violence to occur."[64] Applying this model to the goal of preventing sexual violence perpetrated by nonstate armed groups, UNICEF and United Nations Office for the Coordination of Humanitarian Affairs (OCHA) propose that

> the individual level will be organized to describe the personal history risk factors of individual members of the non-state armed group. At the relationship level, it is the group dynamics and interactions between the members of the group that are examined. The community level describes the physical environment in which the group lives and operates (particularly in reference to the scarcity of resources) as well as their interactions with local communities. Finally, the societal level includes the larger dynamics that perpetuate the perceived need for armed resistance, such as the absence of law and order.[65]

This framework is useful in evaluating the case study of the rebel group in the CAR. More generally, the public health approach to preventing sexual violence aligns with the previously examined social science research that argues that messages from authority and even peers to commit violence is a causal driver of this violence and that the human tendency to conform means that the opposite message to refrain from violence is equally likely to be obeyed.

In addition, prosecutions at the ICC and instructing combatants regarding the Rome Statute's prohibitions on sexual violence relate to both "direct prevention" and "structural prevention" models found in the conflict management approach to preventing sexual violence. As one advocacy organization has explained,

> Direct prevention refers to short-term actions taken to prevent the imminent escalation of a conflict or the use of violence. This involves direct engagement with warring parties through dialogue, confidence-building measures, sanctions, coercive diplomacy, special envoys, and preventive deployment of, for example, peacekeeping troops to prevent potential perpetrators from gaining access to affected populations.
>
> Structural prevention entails long-term interventions that aim to transform key socioeconomic, political and institutional factors that, if left unaddressed, could lead to violence. This encompasses a broad range of factors, including but not limited to: addressing inequality, exclusion and marginalization; developing social capital and social cohesion; promoting livelihoods, local development and economic opportunities; and promoting legitimate and equitable political, justice and security institutions.[66]

The Role of the ICC Prosecutor in Punishing and Preventing Sexual Violence

The actions of the ICC prosecutor support the expressive function of the Rome Statute and the idea that "those addressed will know precisely what is expected of them." Punishment, an essential ingredient to ending impunity, is linked to prevention; the preamble of the Rome Statute declares that it is "determined to put an end to impunity for the perpetrators of these crimes and thus to contribute to the prevention of such crimes." A focus on sexual violence and gender crimes, prompted by the text of the Rome Statute, became a hallmark of Moreno Ocampo's approach, as set forth in a 2006 report on prosecutorial strategy:

> The Office will endeavour to do a selection of cases that represent the entire criminality and modes of victimization. The Office will pay particular attention to methods of investigations of crimes committed against children, sexual and gender-based crimes.[67]

His office, often through Bensouda, who was serving as deputy prosecutor at the time, specified its focus on sexual violence in public forums. In one such public speech, Prosecutor Bensouda declared, "Regarding our investigations, we have an obligation and a duty to focus our attention on sexual and gender violence."[68]

These declarations reflected the centrality of sexual violence crimes in prosecutions at the ICC. A substantial portion of the cases brought at the ICC by Moreno Ocampo addressed sexual violence and gender crimes: eleven of the sixteen cases, or almost 70 percent, charged sexual violence. The number of cases before the ICC presents a small data set, but sixteen cases is a significant enough number to conclude that Moreno Ocampo's strategy did indeed prioritize responding to crimes of sexual violence.

While his office's first case, brought against Thomas Lubanga Dyilo of the DRC, did not explicitly charge sexual violence crimes, the "evidence in this case showed how Mr. Lubanga instrumentalised sexual violations to subject child soldiers of both sexes to his will."[69] When, during an interview, a journalist pointed out that "some argue your case against Thomas Lubanga should have gone way beyond the recruitment of child soldiers," Moreno Ocampo responded,

> I think [recruiting] child soldiers is a very serious crime. Many of them can never recover. It's an awful experience, a terrible experience. Girls were systematically raped and beaten, forced to kill, forced to be raped, it's a horrific experience.[70]

After this first case, Moreno Ocampo's office began to bring explicit charges of sexual violence. In 2005, he charged Joseph Kony of the Lord's Resistance Army of Uganda with sexual enslavement as a crime against humanity, rape as a crime against humanity, and rape as a war crime.[71] In his second case, regarding the DRC and brought in 2007, he charged Germain Katanga and Mathieu Ngudjolo Chui with sexual slavery and rape as crimes against humanity and war crimes.[72] In 2010 and also regarding the DRC, he charged rape as a war crime and a crime against humanity against Callixte Mbarushimana,[73] although those charges were dismissed at the pretrial stage. On May 14, 2012, the prosecutor applied for a second warrant of arrest for Bosco Ntaganda, the amended version of which included charges of rape and sexual slavery as war crimes and crimes against humanity.[74] This warrant was issued on July 13, 2012,[75] and Bosco surrendered on March 22, 2013.[76] With a warrant of arrest issued for Sylvestre

Mudacumura, alleged supreme commander of the Forces Démocratiques pour la Libération du Rwanda, on July 13, 2012, charging rape, four out of five of the DRC cases have explicitly charged crimes of sexual violence, and the one that did not charge sexual violence presented sexual and gender crimes as a component of its case.

Three of the five cases in the situation in Darfur presented counts of sexual violence. In 2007, the prosecutor opened two cases regarding the conflict in Darfur, charging Ahmad Muhammad Harun, the former minister of state for the interior of the government of Sudan,[77] and Ali Muhammad Ali Abd-Al-Rahman (Ali Kushayb), the alleged leader of the Janjaweed militia, with rape as a war crime.[78] In 2008, he charged Sudanese president Omar Hassan Ahmad al-Bashir with rape as a crime against humanity,[79] presenting evidence that showed "that the crimes of rape and sexual violence committed in Darfur are an 'integral part' of his attempt to destroy the Fur, Masalit and Zaghawa groups, and should be charged as genocide under the Rome Statute."[80] On March 1, 2012, an arrest warrant was issued for Abdel Raheem Muhammad Hussein, the current minister of national defense for the Sudan, former minister of the interior, and former special representative of the Sudanese president in Darfur, alleging rape as a war crime and as a crime against humanity.[81] In 2011, Moreno Ocampo charged Laurent Gbagbo, the former president of Côte d'Ivoire, with rape and sexual violence as crimes against humanity alleged to have been committed "during the post-election violence [in Côte d'Ivoire] from 28 November 2010 onwards."[82] That same year, he charged rape as a crime against humanity in one of the two cases brought regarding the situation in Kenya. These charges were confirmed for Francis Kirimi Muthaura and Uhuru Muigai Kenyatta, but Pre-Trial Chamber II declined to confirm charges against Mohammed Hussein Ali.[83] Thus far, every situation excluding Libya has included a charge of sexual violence, and there is still the possibility that if evidence warrants it, the new prosecutor will charge crimes of sexual violence regarding this situation.

Perhaps the most significant sexual violence case before the ICC to date is the case against Jean-Pierre Bemba Gombo of the CAR, which has not yet concluded. The case against Bemba stands out among sexual violence jurisprudence because of the scale of the sexual violence crimes alleged and because this case prioritizes charges of sexual violence over other crimes charged. The prosecutor's case against Congolese political leader Bemba focused on the extensive number of rapes committed in the CAR during 2002–3.[84] Moreno Ocampo spoke of the significance of prosecuting crimes of sexual violence in response to a journalist's question about why he chose to charge Bemba for crimes committed in the CAR when Bemba's main operation was in Congo:

> In the Bemba case, the number of rapes outnumbered the number of killings by far. They were looking for the boss of the neighborhood and when they found him, he was raped publicly to humiliate him. Of course there are allegations of Bemba committing other crimes. My business is to investigate massive crimes, I cannot present all the crimes committed in the courtroom because then the case would never finish.[85]

The next section uses a case study to explore the links between Moreno Ocampo's prosecution of Bemba and an enhanced atmosphere of compliance in one rebel group in the CAR regarding international law's criminalization of sexual violence in conflict.

Case Study: Training a Rebel Group in the Central African Republic

> "I think we knew there were going to be cases of sexual violence. I don't think we knew that there were going to be this many."[86]
> —Phone interview with NGO worker (February 8, 2012)

A large international NGO that did not normally engage in providing IHL training ventured deep into the bush behind rebel lines to conduct two years of international law training for rebel forces engaged in ongoing civil conflict in the CAR. This case study covers those years, 2007 and 2008, and focuses on trainings conducted in "small towns" on the "front lines/just behind the lines of the fighting,"[87] located in the center and center-northwest of the country. To protect the anonymity of the NGO, this chapter cannot disclose its name or the name of the rebel group. At the time of writing, this particular rebel force has not been charged with any crimes at the ICC.

The CAR has been plagued by political instability and ongoing "low-level" conflicts[88] between government forces and rebels[89] since gaining independence from France in 1960. As a "least developed country (LDC), [the CAR] is ranked 178 out of 179 countries in the 2008 UNDP Human Development Index."[90] As of 2008, the United Nations stated that more than one million people had been negatively affected by ongoing instability and that almost two hundred thousand people had been internally displaced.[91] Unlike its problem-plagued neighbors—the Sudan, the DRC, and Uganda—the CAR has failed to garner much global interest.[92] This conflict and the substantial internal displacement it has created led to an agreement between the NGO and a United Nations agency to conduct work to improve the living conditions of those caught in the fighting.[93]

The NGO focused on providing health services with an emphasis on care to victims of sexual violence. To do so, they opened an office in a hospital "two hundred meters" from rebel-controlled territory.[94] The fighting had destroyed clinics in the rebel-held territory, and the rebels had set up roadblocks to keep women from accessing the hospital in African Union–patrolled territory where the NGO opened its program. When the NGO arrived, women and girls in the area were completely without health services and psychosocial sexual violence survivor services.[95] Without waiting for reporting to come out regarding this area—which would have been unrealistic given that the area was rebel-controlled and that the women and girls who had been attacked had little or no access to reporting structures—the NGO entered the CAR on the assumption that where there is conflict, there is also sexual violence. According to one NGO worker,

> A lot of people said we were wasting our time, but within two and a half weeks of setting up the office we were completely overwhelmed. We hadn't even had time to hire staff. We were running out of medicine. Within a year of opening we had seen over a thousand survivors of sexual violence. Most of the attacks had taken place within the previous year.[96]

The NGO operated from the perspective that providing rape kits and an office were not enough: real health services meant outreach, information, and access. This meant that beyond strategies such as locating their office in the maternity ward to allow women to access it without question, they had to work with the rebels to ensure women's access to the hospital. They built a relationship with the rebels and negotiated an end to the roadblocks. In the course of relationship building to facilitate services to survivors of sexual violence, the NGO workers saw an opportunity to train the rebels directly. While the NGO worker who ran the sexual health services had to remain distant from the rebels, given her role in the lives of sexual violence survivors, two other NGO workers worked closely with the rebels and provided international law training.

Complying with the Rome Statute Gave Combatants Legal and Political Legitimacy

A key factor in the NGO's ability to train the rebels was the fact that the rebels themselves wanted to be trained. The rebel leader wanted to be viewed as a "good rebel"[97] with legal and political legitimacy.[98] In the CAR, rebels are vying for political power, and it is not unusual for leaders of uprisings to assume the legitimate mantle of the state: current president François Bozizé Yangouvonda originally came to power after leading a 2003 coup.[99] Bozizé keeps a wary eye on threats to his rule and arrests rebel leaders.[100] When Bozizé seized control, he was condemned for doing so and criticized for lootings and rapes.[101] The Bozizé situation is not terribly unusual. For example, Gbagbo came to power in the Côte d'Ivoire by force in 2000.[102] Pre-Trial Chamber I confirmed the charges against Gbagbo on June 12, 2014.[103] In this context, it is not surprising that rebel forces would seek legal and political legitimacy and attempt to comply with the Rome Statute. The rebels in this case study were aware that other African rebel leaders had been arrested and wanted to avoid the same fate.[104] The ICC and international law figured prominently in the commander's idea of legitimacy. In the words of an interviewee, "He wanted to be a 'good rebel,' and the ICC was the most visible measure of whether he was doing so."[105] The principle of command, or superior, responsibility, delineated in article 28 of the Rome Statute,[106] has great potential for preventative effect, as exemplified by the Bemba case. During proceedings, ICC pretrial judges linked the duty of a commander to prevent crimes to the practice of instructing troops in legal prohibitions during armed conflicts. The Pre-Trial Chamber stated that the duty of a commander to take "all necessary measures" to prevent his or her troops from committing crimes might include instructing these troops in the prohibitions of the Rome Statute: the judges noted that while "Article 28 of the Statute does not define the specific measures required by the duty to prevent crimes," they nevertheless found "it appropriate to be guided by relevant factors such as measures: (i) to ensure that superior's forces are adequately trained in international humanitarian law."[107] Thus, the Rome Statute's principle of command responsibility has the potential to prompt leaders of fighting forces to instruct their troops in the law. Even if this instruction is done to discharge a duty or prepare a defense, it communicates the law and enhances the likelihood of compliance by subordinate fighters.

The rebel leader also viewed the legal trainings as a useful way to control his troops. As one NGO worker commented, "He actually told the officers, 'Rape is illegal in our movement and anyone who rapes will be punished.' I think for him it was an opportunity for putting some order in his movement." The added control the trainings afforded the rebel leader were further motivated by local politics. His movement was spread out over two geographical areas, and tension seemed to exist between him and the head of the other geographical division.[108] Consequently, it was even more important for this leader to have tight control over his own combatants.

What the Rebels Learned

"This was a very basic knowledge transfer."[109]
—Phone interview with Central
African Republic NGO worker (May 1, 2010)

The NGO chose to adapt a formal international law manual that it had used to train state-based combatants in workshop settings.[110] Workers adapted more than eighty pages of comprehensive international law manuals written in French and organized by subject matter—the rights of children, the rights of women, and explanations of concepts such as access to justice, basic due process protections and rights, and the law of armed conflict and criminal liability.[111] The manual's section on criminal liability explicitly referenced the ICC. The NGO personnel interviewed found the formality of the course to be ill-suited to training rebel forces. "It's fine if you're training a multinational force,"—the NGO also trained regional peacekeeping forces operating in the CAR—but it proved too sophisticated for rebel combatants.[112] The NGO adapted the training material and hired two male lawyers from the CAR to convey the material in the local language. These instructors, the NGO personnel, and the CAR lawyers met with various groups of rebels on at least a weekly basis. The groups changed frequently, which presented a practical challenge for the NGO. The NGO thus developed stand-alone sessions that addressed a single legal right at a time.[113]

The Setting: A Makeshift Classroom in the Forest

Working with the rebel forces, the NGO created various outdoor classrooms in rebel-controlled territory. Together, they chopped down trees and scraped the thick vegetation down to dirt to create small clearings.[114]

Clothed in mismatched garments rather than uniforms, the men dropped their guns by a specific tree as they entered the clearing and took their places on cramped log benches. The NGO had declared the classroom a weapons-free zone.[115] When rebels smoked marijuana in class, the staff made a rule prohibiting that as well.[116] A male lawyer from the CAR used a small chalkboard propped up on a wooden easel to draw pictures in colored chalk as he explained tenets of international law to the rebels. The rough-hewn classroom was a place of order, and the rebels generally followed the ground rules set by the NGO.

Teaching Prohibitions on Sexual Violence

The NGO workers initially addressed the topic of sexual violence with the rebels as an abuse that was not accepted.[117] They also aimed to impart a definition of rape by discussing what it means to rape.[118] This information generated curiosity and surprise among the rebel combatants. "This discussion regarding the meaning of rape was super interesting to them; with them it was an entirely new concept. The idea that forcing someone to have sex was not okay was kind of revolutionary."[119] The lack of understanding that sex by force was not sex but rather a violent crime was apparent in the responses in the classroom discussions:

> We spent a lot of time in our classes on the topic of what is rape? [We told them,] "Rape is when you have sex with someone and you use force to do that." This one guy—a real badass, a tough guy, completely covered in weapons type of guy—said in a really earnest way, confused way, "But, I've only *ever* had sex by force; that's what sex *is;* I don't get it." The soldiers really were listening. They were trying to follow the rules, and maybe they just didn't understand.[120]

This case study thus presents an example of rebel forces whose norms regarding sexual violence appeared to run counter to the tenets of the Rome Statute, inviting instruction in legal prohibitions that could change their actions. It illustrates the necessity both of criminalizing sexual violence under international law and of communicating the specificities of these crimes to those who might commit such acts in conflict. Like the data demonstrating the prevalence of sexual violence in conflict, which prompts a corollary of a prosecutorial focus on these crimes, this anecdote underscores the way in which law interacts with norms, beliefs, and behaviors.

Evaluating the Impact of the Trainings: New Norms,
New Language, New Concepts

In this case study, instructing combatants on the Rome Statute's prohibitions of sexual violence had several noticeable effects. First, the instruction in international law reshaped the internal norms and structure of the fighting force. Second, instruction in the Rome Statute provided the combatants with new rhetoric and concepts to discuss and understand as well as to explicitly prohibit sexual violence in conflict. Third, the trainings changed the way that the rebels interacted with the civilian population in at least three ways: they facilitated civilian access to health services—in particular, services for survivors of sexual violence; they allowed the NGO to correct misinformation about the NGO's activities and the ICC, a crucial effort in a tense conflict situation; and they facilitated a platform for the NGO to discuss better treatment and rights of civilians more generally. All of these outcomes, while modest, represent advances in ameliorating the substantial sexual violence that has occurred in the CAR.

A New Vocabulary for Discussing and
Prohibiting Sexual Violence

The NGO workers interviewed described an evolution in the dialogue they observed between the commander and the combatants. One interviewee said that the combatants employed their knowledge of international law in discussions with their commander:

> They would say, "I know international law. I know this is a right. I know how things are supposed to be. I know this is how we're supposed to deal with civilians." They'd talk about [international law.] They'd refer back to it. There is, of course, no way to know if this transferred into [changed] behavior.[121]

Another interviewee noted that the international law trainings "changed the rhetoric they used; the commander would declare absolute prohibitions on gender violence."[122] The rebels even held discussions on the topic when the NGO workers were not present. After the NGO workers returned from a Christmas holiday, some rebels were eager to report that they had held group discussions on the topic of sexual violence in the workers' absence.[123]

This chapter does not claim an absolute causal link between rhetoric and behavior. Nevertheless, social psychology research emphasizes the idea that language can help create a "hostile imagination," allowing for the dehumanization of others and facilitating violence against them.[124] Therefore, providing people with a vocabulary to conceptualize change—for example, a change in relationships between combatants and females in the area, a change in the social status of women and girls, or a change in what it means to be a good soldier—can be one tool for transforming attitudes and behaviors. The impact of this new vocabulary, derived from legal trainings, is enhanced by the status of the Rome Statute as legitimate law. A commander of a fighting force declaring an absolute prohibition on gender violence can be powerful. This declaration could influence the behavior of combatants who, while not necessarily fearful or cognizant of the prosecutor of the ICC, do fear reproach by their commander. The doctrine of command responsibility thus links the prosecutor to even the lowest-ranked combatant through a chain of liability. If the commander has control over these forces, the forces could theoretically be deterred from committing transgressions such as sexual violence.

Gained Access to Health Services for
Survivors of Sexual Violence

The NGO originally began working in the CAR to provide health services to survivors of sexual violence and came into contact with the rebels because they were blocking civilian access to these services. This contact then engendered training the rebels in international law practices and facilitated relationship building between the NGO workers and the rebels, particularly the group's leader. Developing this trust allowed the NGO workers to conduct outreach about sexual violence health services even in rebel-controlled territory. The NGO operated on the philosophy that simply providing rape kits was not enough; women and girls needed explanations about the services available before they would feel comfortable accessing these services. After establishing a rapport, the rebels allowed the NGO workers to conduct outreach and health trainings among the general population. Extensive outreach was necessary because "many women were attacked far from the main roads."[125]

When the ICC opened its investigation into the CAR, there was a moment when the rebels almost shut down this access for fear that they would become targets of the ICC investigation. The rebels had previously tested the NGO, claiming they had sent someone to verify that the NGO was providing only health services to victims rather than legal services or assistance to the ICC.[126] When the ICC opened an investigation into sexual violence in the CAR, the rebels realized that the patterns of violence documented by the hospital records could implicate them in crimes under the Court's jurisdiction. They preferred to shut the services down to avoid the risk. In response to this threat, the NGO called a meeting with the rebel leader and his fighters.[127] While many of the combatants opposed continued access to sexual violence services on the grounds that permitting access to such services would draw attention to the group, the rebel leader turned the conversation around, declaring that the men had to allow survivors access to health services and would do so.[128] In his view, his fighters had assumed such risks as prosecution when they decided to join an armed movement.[129] And, they would not shut down civilian health access to avoid such risks.[130] As a result of this strong relationship with the rebel leader and his efforts to remain legally and politically legitimate, access to the hospital remained open.

The Trainings Allowed the NGO to Correct Misinformation, Thereby Defusing Tension

Another way that instruction in the Rome Statute can change the content of conflict is by correcting misinformation. According to one interviewee, the media were the rebels' main source of information on the ICC, occasionally leading to problems. For example, the commander believed that women were reporting rape by the rebels to obtain money.

> Even in the case of the CAR, where [the NGO] was providing basic training on IHL and human rights, the reaction of the rebels to the ICC investigation stemmed more from what they heard through the media and less through our discussions. But we were, to a certain extent, able to provide accurate information in response to some of their misperceptions of the process.[131]

While media reports catalyzed fear of ICC prosecution in the rebels and this fear prompted legal training, these same reports led to confusion. The presence of the NGO, the regular weekly training sessions, and the trust and confidence between the commander and the NGO allowed the NGO to interject clarifications. Providing accurate information about the threat that the ICC did or did not present to the rebels was valuable in a tense combat area.

The Trainings Promoted Better Treatment
of the Civilian Population

The trainings in the Rome Statute and international law served as an entry
point for the NGO to suggest better rebel behavior toward the civilian
population. The high level of interest expressed by the rebels prompted the
NGO to expand its trainings:

> We approached the rebels and proposed this dialogue/training, but
> I will say that once we got a routine down, the rebels were very
> committed to the regular sessions and expressed disappointment
> [the] few times because of security I did have to call the commander
> and cancel. It was their interest, and the fact that they were coming
> in large numbers, that sparked us to increase the number of ses-
> sions/groups that we held each week. . . . [E]ventually, in coopera-
> tion with our [gender-based violence] team, [we] established a ses-
> sion just for the women among the rebels—their wives, girlfriends
> and some female soldiers. We used these sessions—both with the
> women and the men—to introduce other important information
> about HIV/AIDS, health service availability for the children living
> with them in the bush, and hygiene.[132]

The actions of the ICC prosecutor can thus create windows of opportunity
for other actors, such as NGOs, to ameliorate negative conduct that falls
below the level of crimes within the jurisdiction of the Rome Statute and
thus improve the lives of those living in conflict situations.

Among the factors that facilitated these outcomes is the rebel leader's
strong interest in political and legal legitimacy, which allowed the training
and kept the sexual violence health services up and running even when
the combatants wished to shut the clinic down. The role of the commander
was thus a crucial one. One NGO worker contrasted this situation with
her previous experience in Darfur, where the leadership was fluid and difficult to work with.[133] Another NGO worker commented that the pattern
of sexual violence in the CAR resembled opportunistic violence as opposed to rape as a weapon of war.[134] This interviewee distinguished this
from her experience in Darfur, where the evidence suggested to her that
rape was a deliberate tactic.[135] She hypothesized that because rape was not
the rebel commander's policy, it was easier to get access and acceptance for
the trainings and the support of the commander. Thus, if the commander
had instructed his subordinates to rape, the negotiations to prohibit sex-

ual violence would likely have taken a different course.[136] In this instance, legal prohibitions on sexual violence seemed to serve the rebel commander's need to maintain discipline, thereby facilitating the instruction and prohibition. If the commander had thought that sexual violence served his objectives, the ICC investigations and prosecutions might have had very different effects. This chapter does not purport to measure the total of these outcomes, but it does argue that they are, individually and together, markers of change and progress.

Conclusion: Taking the Necessary Steps toward Prevention

International criminal law's relationship to the prevention of sexual violence in conflict begins with the idea of compliance, which in turn centers on the notion of legitimacy. These concepts specific to law are parallel to concepts of obedience to authority and conformity in social science. A decade before the creation of the ICC, Thomas Franck wrote that

> in a community organized around rules, compliance [with international law] is secured—to whatever degree it is—at least in part by perception of a rule as legitimate by those to whom it is addressed. Their perception of legitimacy will vary in degree from rule to rule and time to time. It becomes a crucial factor, however, in the capacity of any rule to secure compliance when, as in the international system, there are no other compliance-inducing mechanisms. . . . Since the world is not about to create a global supersovereign with overriding enforcement powers, it might be encouraging to know that these are not the prerequisites of a developed, functioning international community. It would be even more helpful to know that the global system of rules could be further refined and developed, even in the absence of the Austinian factors, by augmenting the legitimacy of rules and institutions.[137]

Today, prosecution of international crimes provides an added compliance-inducing mechanism. However, the legitimacy of the rules and of the institutions that enforce the rules forms the bedrock of the legitimacy of the ICC's prosecutions. As Fatou Bensouda has stated, "We have no army, no police. We have one strength: our legitimacy."[138] It may strain the imagination to conceptualize efficacy without an international corollary to domestic criminal justice. And yet legitimacy, not enforcement mechanisms, is the hallmark of the ability of international law to exert compliance. As the case study of the rebel leader in the CAR illustrates, the compliance pull of an international law must attach to the desire of a political actor to be seen as legitimate under the law.

Luis Moreno Ocampo has worked to link the legitimacy of the ICC to the activities of fighting forces, arguing that he seeks to influence the behavior of military commanders through threat of prosecution.[139] When asked whether the court is a deterrent to those committing war crimes, Moreno Ocampo replied,

The legal advisor of NATO (North Atlantic Treaty Organisation), the most important military organisation, told me that they told their staff to imagine: in 15 years you are retired as a two-star general, on the beach with your family. Suddenly you're surrounded by policemen who handcuff you and you go to the ICC and the evidence is documentation from NATO. You have to be aware that if you commit crimes, you could be prosecuted. So that's it. Armies all over the world are adjusting to this.[140]

In a 2009 interview with Moreno Ocampo, a journalist writing in the *Wall Street Journal* posited that this threat to commanders is evidence that "the ICC's very existence is already changing the way Western nations fight wars."[141] In this interview, the prosecutor said that states are busying themselves with the task of compliance. "Six years ago, the challenge was—can a court without a state operate? Now the issue is how the states and other organizations will react to the global court."[142] This argument depends on the idea that law affects behavior. But can a court restructure the internal norms of fighting forces?

Social science research postulates that whether or not one can claim results from instructing fighting forces in international law, doing so is a known and necessary step for controlling violence in conflict and preventing atrocities. Direct instruction regarding a legal prohibition is a clear and requisite way to communicate expectations to combatants and thus shape their behavior. As the case study of the CAR explores in detail, a rebel leader used an NGO's legal trainings to convey his expectations to senior staff and rebel combatants under his command. Instructing combatants in prohibitions on sexual violence is necessary for two reasons: (1) sexual violence is pervasive in conflicts, and (2) conflict-related violence can spiral out of control with situations of authorized violence degenerating into those of prohibited violence. Punishment alone cannot prevent the problem of sexual violence in conflict; carefully planned instruction in these prohibitions prior to conflict is necessary.[143] Further, failure by leaders of armed forces to teach clear prohibitions on sexual violence may enhance the likelihood that those forces will commit sexual violence. A Red Cross study found that while

> violations of IHL may sometimes stem from orders giving by such an authority, they seem more frequently to be connected with a lack of any specific orders not to violate the law or an implicit authorization to behave in a reprehensible manner.[144]

These findings underscore the importance of leaders to specifically educate their combatants about the prohibition on sexual violence before combatants are deployed into combat.

Thus, through a sequence of events, all of them forming a necessary part of the chain, the Rome Statute and the ICC prosecutors have the power to influence the behavior of fighting forces and prevent sexual violence in conflict. The Rome Statute criminalizes acts of sexual violence and gender violence under international law in an unprecedented manner. The clarity and precision with which the Rome Statute details these crimes, the way in which the treaty was negotiated, and the large number of states parties to the Rome Statute, builds legitimacy for it and for the crimes it articulates. In addition, the centrality of sexual violence crimes in the strategies pursued by the ICC prosecutors—proven not only through policy statements but through prosecutions—activates the Rome Statute, communicating it as law in force, applicable to a large number of the world's combatants. Command responsibility links the actions of fighters to the prosecutor's ability to charge leaders with crimes before the ICC. This in turn creates incentives for these leaders to communicate the law criminalizing sexual violence to their troops. This formulation, which is profoundly innovative, heralds a new day for international law's response to sexual violence and perhaps, if we remain hopeful and vigilant, a new world in which women, girls, men, and boys are less threatened by these awful crimes.

NOTES

1. The first prosecutor of the International Criminal Court, Luis Moreno Ocampo, stated in a 2009 interview that the "idea" of the ICC is "changing the way the world is managing violence." *See* Patrick Smith, *Interview: Luis Moreno-Ocampo, ICC Prosecutor,*

AFRICA REPORT (Sept. 21, 2009), http://www.theafricareport.com/News-Analysis/interview-luis-moreno-ocampo-icc-prosecutor.html.

2. The CAR has been plagued by ongoing, "low-level" conflicts between government forces and rebel troops for the majority of the new millennium. *See, e.g.,* United Nations, *Central African Republic: A Silent Crisis Crying Out for Help,* http://www.un.org/events/tenstories/06/story.asp?storyID=300; *Central African Republic: Humanitarian Crisis in Central African Republic,* WFP.ORG, http://www.wfp.org/countries/central-african-republic.

3. *See, e.g., Thousands Fall Victim to Sexual Violence in Central African Republic—UN,* UN NEWS CENTRE (Feb. 22, 2008), http://www.un.org/apps/news/story.asp?NewsID=25725.

4. E-mail from NGO worker, with relationship to rebels, to author (Jan. 16, 2012) (on file with author).

5. Moreno Ocampo decided to open an investigation into the situation in the CAR on May 22, 2007. While the ICC's investigation covered 2002 and 2003, the Court also declared that it would monitor the current situation while collecting evidence regarding these crimes. Further, collecting evidence that can help determine which groups committed which crimes during the 2002–3 period might also include assessing current violence to look for patterns, signatures, and other indicators of responsibility. *See* International Criminal Court, *Prosecutor Opens Investigation in Central African Republic,* http://www.icc-cpi.int/menus/icc/press%20and%20media/press%20releases/2007/prosecutor%20opens%20investigation%20in%20the%20central%20african%20republic?lan=en-GB.

6. This chapter uses the phrase *fighting forces* broadly to mean both state and non-state combatants.

7. This chapter uses both *sexual violence* and *gender violence* because the Rome Statute and the prosecutors of the ICC use both terms. However, these terms are not strictly interchangeable. According to the definition in the Element of Crimes accompanying the Rome Statute, the "crime against humanity of sexual violence" occurs when "the perpetrator committed an act of a sexual nature against one or more persons or caused such person or persons to engage in an act of a sexual nature by force, or by threat of force or coercion, such as that caused by fear of violence, duress, detention, psychological oppression or abuse of power, against such person or persons or another person, or by taking advantage of a coercive environment or such person's or persons' incapacity to give genuine consent." Article 7(3) of the Rome Statute states that "for the purpose of this Statute, it is understood that the term 'gender' refers to the two sexes, male and female, within the context of society. The term 'gender' does not indicate any meaning different from the above." While speeches of members of the ICC Office of the Prosecutor often use these terms interchangeably, in at least one public statement, Moreno Ocampo sought to distinguish them, explaining, "In relation to the Statute, I would like to emphasise the relation between sexual crimes and this new concept of gender crimes in the Statute. Sexual crimes are crimes of violence or coercion. The concept of gender crimes added a different dimension to the analysis. The new concept emphasises that sexual crimes such as rape are crimes of gender inequality, enacted violently." This chapter adopts this definition. When it uses only the term *sexual violence,* it assumes that the acts of sexual violence referenced contained an element of "gender inequality," regardless of the sexes of the people perpetrating the act or being victimized by the act.

8. The Rome Statute enumerates sexual violence as a crime against humanity and as a war crime in articles 7 and 8. For example, as art. 7(1)(g) states, "For the purpose of this Statute, 'crime against humanity' means any of the following acts when committed as part of a widespread or systematic attack directed against any civilian population, with knowledge of the attack: . . . (g) Rape, sexual slavery, enforced prostitution, forced pregnancy, enforced sterilization, or any other form of sexual violence of comparable gravity." Similarly, with regard to "War crimes," art. 8(2)(b)(xxii) states, "For the purpose of this Statute, 'war crimes' means . . . [c]ommitting rape, sexual slavery, enforced prostitution, forced pregnancy, as defined in article 7, paragraph 2 (f), enforced sterilization, or any other form of sexual violence also constituting a grave breach of the Geneva Conventions." Moreover, article 7 sets forth additional definitions of these offenses, and the Elements of Crimes further explain the crime enumerated in articles 7 and 8. *See generally* Rome Statute of the International Criminal Court, 2187 U.N.T.S. 90 (July 7, 1998) (hereinafter Rome Statute); International Criminal Court, *Elements of Crimes,* ICC-ASP/1/3(part II-B)(Sept. 9, 2002), http://www.icc-cpi.int/NR/rdonlyres/336923D8-A6AD-40EC-AD7B-45BF9DE73D56/0/ElementsOfCrimesEng.pdf.

9. Article 7(1)(h) of the Rome Statute lists persecution on the grounds of gender as a crime against humanity.

10. Article 42(9) of the Rome Statute states, "The Prosecutor shall appoint advisers with legal expertise on specific issues, including, but not limited to, sexual and gender violence and violence against children," thereby establishing a structure within the Office of the Prosecutor for cultivating and receiving expert advice on sexual and gender based violence. Separately, article 54(1)(b) of the Rome Statute articulates that the "prosecutor shall . . . [t]ake appropriate measures to ensure the effective investigation and prosecution of crimes within the jurisdiction of the Court, and in doing so, respect the interests and personal circumstances of victims and witnesses, including age, gender as defined in article 7, paragraph 3, and health, and take into account the nature of the crime, in particular where it involves sexual violence, gender violence or violence against children." This article instructs the prosecutor to focus on sexual violence and gender violence as essential elements of crimes, thereby bringing these elements and crimes to the forefront of prosecutions in which such events have occurred.

11. *See* Fatou Bensouda, Prosecutor-Elect, ICC, *Gender Justice & the ICC: Progress & Reflections,* Speech at The ICC—Ten Year Review Conference: Justice for All? (Feb. 14, 2012), http://www.iccwomen.org/videos/webcasts/Justice-for-All.php.

12. The concept of legitimacy for law and legal institutions is discussed in more detail later in this chapter.

13. *See* Bensouda, *supra* note 11.

14. In addition to the conflicts mentioned in this chapter, for documentation of crimes of sexual violence throughout modern conflicts, see Human Rights Watch/Africa, *Shattered Lives: Sexual Violence during the Rwandan Genocide & Its Aftermath,* HRW.ORG n. 39 (Sept. 1996), http://www.hrw.org/reports/1996/Rwanda.htm# p341-72129, which enumerates a long list of rape in conflict by naming "a few" examples in a footnote: "During the Second World War, some 200,000 Korean women were forcibly held in sexual slavery to the Japanese army. During the armed conflict in Bangladesh in 1971, it is estimated that 200,000 civilian women and girls were victims of rape committed by Pakistani soldiers. Mass rape of women has been used since the beginning of the conflict in the Former Yugoslavia. Throughout the Somali conflict beginning in 1991,

rival ethnic factions have used rape against rival ethnic factions. During 1992 alone, 882 women were reportedly gang-raped by Indian security forces in Jammu and Kashmir. In Peru in 1982, rape of women by security forces was a common practice in the ongoing armed conflict between the Communist Party of Peru, the Shining Path, and government counterinsurgency forces. In Myanmar, in 1992, government troops raped women in a Rohingya Muslim village after the men had been inducted into forced labor. Under the former Haitian military regime of Lt. Gen. Raoul Cedras, rape was used as a tool of political repression against female activists or female relatives of opposition members."

15. *See, e.g.,* Oxfam Int'l, *Sexual Violence in Columbia: Instrument of War,* OXFAM.ORG (Sept. 9, 2009), http://www.oxfam.org/sites/www.oxfam.org/files/bp-sexual-violence-colombia.pdf.

16. "The phenomenon of sexual violence against women and children has reached truly genocidal proportions." Mr. Titinga Frédéric Pacéré, Advisory Services and Technical Cooperation in the Field of Human Rights Report Submitted by the Independent Expert on the Situation of Human Rights in the Democratic Republic of the Congo, E/CN.4/2005/120 (Feb. 7, 2005).

17. *See, e.g.,* Ian Fisher, *Iraqi Tells of U.S. Abuse, from Ridicule to Rape,* N.Y. TIMES (May 14, 2004), http://www.nytimes.com/2004/05/14/international/middleeast/14PRIS.html?pagewanted=all.

18. *See, e.g.,* Prosecutor v. Jean-Pierre Bemba Gombo, Case No. ICC-01/05/01/08, Decision Pursuant to Article 61(7)(a) and (b) of the Rome Statute on the Charges of the Prosecutor against Jean-Pierre Bemba Gombo, ¶¶71, 210 (June 15, 2009), http://www.icc-cpi.int/iccdocs/doc/doc699541.pdf (charging rape as a crime against humanity and as a war crime) (hereinafter Decision Pursuant to Article 61(7)(a) and (b) of the Rome Statute).

19. See, e.g., *Inquiry into "Rape & Torture" by UK Troops as Iraqis' Lawyer Claims 32 Cases Are Tip of the Iceberg,* DAILY MAIL ONLINE (Nov. 15, 2009), http://www.dailymail.co.uk/news/article-1228141/Rape-torture-inquiry-Iraqis-lawyer-claims-32-cases-tip-iceberg.html (noting accusations by people detained in Iraq by British troops); Duncan Gardham & Paul Cruickshank, *Abu Ghraib Abuse Photos "Show Rape,"* TELEGRAPH (May 27, 2009), http://www.telegraph.co.uk/news/worldnews/northamerica/usa/5395830/Abu-Ghraib-abuse-photos-show-rape.html (chronicling reports of rape at Abu Ghraib).

20. For example, the U.S. Army tried and convicted three soldiers of gang-raping and then murdering a fourteen-year-old Iraqi girl while serving in combat in Iraq in 2006. The soldiers were not tried or convicted for war crimes or crimes against humanity but rather for rape, conspiracy to commit rape, housebreaking with intent to commit rape, and felony murder. *See* Jim Frederick, *Civilian Trial Begins for Ex-Iraq Soldier,* TIME (Apr. 29, 2009), http://www.time.com/time/nation/article/0,8599,1894375,00.html#ixzz0niIYfedm. The longest sentence given was 110 years imprisonment. *See U.S. Soldier Sentenced to 100 Years,* BBC NEWS (Aug. 5, 2007), http://news.bbc.co.uk/2/hi/6930845.stm.

21. The International Committee of the Red Cross (ICRC), for example, notes that Rule 93 of Customary International Humanitarian Law is titled "Rape and Other Forms of Sexual Violence." *See* Int'l Committee of the Red Cross, *Customary IHL: Rule 93* (2005), http://www.icrc.org/customary-ihl/eng/docs/v1_rul_rule93. The ICRC cites state practice, the Leiber Code art. 44, common art. 3 of the Geneva Conventions, and other sources to establish this prohibition. *See id.* at n. 1.

22. *See* ICC, *About the Court*, ICC-CPI.INT (last visited Sept. 16, 2013), http://www.icc-cpi.int/en_menus/icc/about%20the%20court/Pages/about%20the%20court.aspx.

23. Article 5(g) of the statute of the ICTY and article 3(g) of the statute of the ICTR give these tribunals subject matter jurisdiction over rape as a crime against humanity. The ICTR statute article 4(e) also lists rape as a violation of article 3 common to the Geneva Conventions and Additional Protocol II.

24. Prosecutor v. Anto Furndžija, Case No. IT-95-17/1-T, Judgment ¶176 (Int'l Crim. Trib. for the Former Yugoslavia Dec. 10, 1998), http://www.icty.org/x/cases/furundzija/tjug/en/fur-tj981210e.pdf; Prosecutor v. Jean-Paul Akayesu, Case No. ICTR-96-4-T, Judgment ¶¶596, 687 (Sept. 1998), http://www.unictr.org/Portals/0/Case/English/Akayesu/judgement/akay001.pdf.

25. For example, the ICTY's website declares that the "ICTY took groundbreaking steps to respond to the imperative of prosecuting wartime sexual violence. Together with its sister tribunal for Rwanda, the Tribunal was among the first courts of its kind to bring explicit charges of wartime sexual violence, and to define gender crimes such as rape and sexual enslavement under customary law." *See Crimes of Sexual Violence*, ICTY. ORG (last visited Sept. 16, 2013), http://www.icty.org/sid/10312.

26. *See, e.g.,* U.N. Secretary-General, *Rep. of the Secretary-General Pursuant to Paragraph 2 of Security Council Resolution 808 (1993)*, ¶43, S/25704, (May 3, 1993), http://www.icty.org/x/file/Legal%20Library/Statute/statute_re808_1993_en.pdf.

27. At the ICTY and the ICTR, rape was charged as an act constituting *other* crimes established under customary international law rather than as itself a crime. As Catharine MacKinnon put it, "Rape under these statutes is thus not a free-standing crime but must be charged as an act of war, genocide, or crime against humanity. To reference only a few examples of how these two tribunals declared rape to constitute previously existing international crimes, the Akayesu trial chamber at the ICTR found rape and sexual violence to amount to crimes against humanity and to genocide, and the Čelebići case at the ICTY found rape to constitute torture as a crime under customary international law. See Prosecutor v. Akayesu, Case No. ICTR 96-4-T, Judgment, ¶¶692–97, 707, 731–33 (Sept. 2, 1998), available at http://www.unictr.org/Portals/0/Case/English/Akayesu/judgement/akay001.pdf; and Prosecutor v. Delalic et al., Case No. IT-96-21-T, Judgment, (Čelebići Case) ¶¶486–88, 495 (Feb. 20, 2001), http://www.icty.org/x/cases/mucic/acjug/en/cel-aj010220.pdf.

28. Additional preparatory documents leading up to the establishment of the ICTY, such as the EC Investigative Mission into the Treatment of Muslim Women in the Former Yugoslavia: Report to EC Foreign Ministers, Released Feb. 1993 by Udenrigsministeriat Ministry of Foreign Affairs Copenhagen, argued that rape committed systematically in the former Yugoslavia amounted to a war crime. ¶42: "The Mission is aware of work currently under way in the UN and elsewhere in this area. It notes existing provisions under the Geneva Conventions and Protocols for the protection of women against rape, enforced prostitution or any form of indecent assault. Practiced on the scale and for the purposes witnessed against Muslim Women in Bosnia-Hercegovina. The Mission believes there is now a strong case for clearly identifying these abuses as war crimes, irrespective of whether they occur in national or international conflicts."

29. "It is, of course, highly remarkable that so many definitions of rape have emerged from ICTY/R case law." ANNE-MARIE L. M. DE BROUWER, SUPRANATIONAL CRIMINAL

PROSECUTION OF SEXUAL VIOLENCE: THE ICC & THE PRACTICE OF THE ICTY & THE ICTR 127 (2005).

30. *See, e.g.,* Roelof Haveman, *Rape & Fair Trial in Supranational Criminal Law,* 9 MAASTRICHT J. OF EUR. & COMP. L. 263–78 (2002).

31. Customary international law, which consists of state practice and *opinio juris*—that states are following the law because they believe it to be the law—is one of the three sources of international law described in article 38 of the Statute of the International Court of Justice. For further support, see ALAN BOYLE & CHRISTINE CHINKIN, THE MAKING OF INTERNATIONAL LAW 234 (2007), stating that a "treaty does not 'make' customary law, but like soft law it may both codify existing law and contribute to the process by which new customary law is created and develops." This chapter argues that following the work of the ICTY and the ICTR, the widespread ratification of the Rome Statute is a strong indication that states consider its contents—and in particular, its new contents, such as sexual violence crimes—to have entered the corpus of customary international law. It may not yet have become customary international law, yet the belief of many states that it has is significant, including in the process of creating new norms.

32. The ICTY was officially established and its statute set forth in Security Council Resolution 827 of May 25, 1993. *See* S.C. Res. 827, U.N. Doc. S/RES/827 (May 25, 1993), http://daccess-dds-ny.un.org/doc/UNDOC/GEN/N93/306/28/IMG/N9330628. pdf?OpenElement. The ICTR was officially established and its statute set forth by Security Council Resolution 955. *See* S.C. Res. 955, U.N. Doc. S/RES/955 (Nov. 8, 1994), http://daccess-dds-ny.un.org/doc/UNDOC/GEN/N95/140/97/PDF/N9514097. pdf?OpenElement.

33. James Crawford, *The ILC's Articles on Responsibility of States for Internationally Wrongful Acts: A Retrospective,* 96 AM. J. INT'L L. 890 (2002), http://www.asil.org/ajil/ ilcsymp7.pdf.

34. Rome Statute, *supra* note 8, art. 7(1)(g).

35. *Id.*

36. *Id.* art. 9.

37. *See* Thomas M. Franck, *Legitimacy in the International System,* 82 AM. J. INT'L L. 705, 713 (1998).

38. *See* Margaret M. deGuzman, *An Expressive Rationale for the Thematic Prosecution of Sex Crimes,* in THEMATIC PROSECUTION OF INTERNATIONAL SEX CRIMES 11, 51 (Morten Bergsmo ed., 2012), http://www.fichl.org/fileadmin/fichl/documents/ FICHL_13_Web.pdf.

39. *See, e.g.,* GÉRARD PRUNIER, THE RWANDA CRISIS: HISTORY OF A GENOCIDE (1995) (detailing how ordinary civilians were instructed by civilian political leaders to rape and kill their civilian neighbors).

40. *See* PHILIP ZIMBARDO, THE LUCIFER EFFECT: UNDERSTANDING HOW GOOD PEOPLE TURN EVIL 8 (2007).

41. *See id.* at 10.

42. *See id.* at 8.

43. *See id.* at 258–96.

44. Zimbardo describes how self-serving biases inherent to all human beings obscure the reality of our moral flexibility and how much we are influenced by our surroundings.

As he notes, because "most people believe that they are less vulnerable to these self-serving biases than other people, even after being taught about them . . . [y]ou are convinced that you would be the good guard, the defiant prisoner, the resistor, the dissident, the nonconformist, and most of all, the Hero. Would that it were so, but heroes are a rare breed." *See id.* at 261.

45. *See* Ruth Seifert, *War & Rape: A Preliminary Analysis,* in MASS RAPE: THE WAR AGAINST WOMEN IN BOSNIA-HERZEGOVINA 58–65 (Alexandra Stiglmayer ed., 1994).

46. *See* Zimbardo, *supra* note 40, at 307–13.

47. *See, e.g.,* WORLD HEALTH ORGANIZATION, PREVENTING INTIMATE PARTNER & SEXUAL VIOLENCE AGAINST WOMEN: TAKING ACTION & GENERATING EVIDENCE 25–26 (2010), http://whqlibdoc.who.int/publications/2010/9789241564007_eng.pdf (hereinafter WHO Report).

48. *See* Sarnata Reynolds, *Deterring & Preventing Rape & Sexual Slavery during Periods of Armed Conflict,* 16 LAW & INEQ. 601, 607 (1998).

49. *See* Zimbardo, *supra* note 40, at 297–306.

50. *See id.* at 303–4.

51. *See id.* at 304–5.

52. *See id.* at 381–429.

53. *See id.* at 10–11.

54. Article 28, Responsibility of Commanders and Other Superiors, States: "In addition to other grounds of criminal responsibility under this Statute for crimes within the jurisdiction of the Court: (a) A military commander or person effectively acting as a military commander shall be criminally responsible for crimes within the jurisdiction of the Court committed by forces under his or her effective command and control, or effective authority and control as the case may be, as a result of his or her failure to exercise control properly over such forces, where: (i) That military commander or person either knew or, owing to the circumstances at the time, should have known that the forces were committing or about to commit such crimes; and (ii) That military commander or person failed to take all necessary and reasonable measures within his or her power to prevent or repress their commission or to submit the matter to the competent authorities for investigation and prosecution."

55. *See* Decision Pursuant to Article 61(7)(a) and (b) of the Rome Statute, *supra* note 18, at ¶438.

56. *See* Zimbardo, *supra* note 40, at 381–429.

57. Martha Minow, *Living Up to Rules: Holding Soldiers Responsible for Abusive Conduct & the Dilemma of the Superior Orders Defence,* 52 MCGILL L.J. 30, 35 (2007).

58. *See id.* at 36–37.

59. ICRC, *supra* note 21, at 206. *See* Daniel Munoz-Fresard, *The Roots of Behavior in War: Understanding & Preventing IHL Violations,* 853 INT'L REV. OF THE RED CROSS 206, 2006 (2004), http://www.icrc.org/eng/assets/files/other/irrc_853_fd_fresard_eng.pdf.

60. Laura T. Dickinson, *Military Lawyers on the Battlefield: An Empirical Account of International Law Compliance,* 104 AM. J. INT'L L. 1, 7 (2010), http://www.asil.org/ajil/Jan2010selectedpiece.pdf.

61. *See* Reynolds, *supra* note 48, at 604.

62. *See* WHO Report, *supra* note 47, at 6.

63. *See id.* at 18.

64. *See id.*

65. *See* YLVA I. BLONDEL, UNICEF, & OCHA, STRENGTHENING PREVENTION OF CONFLICT-RELATED SEXUAL VIOLENCE WITH NON-STATE ARMED GROUPS: A PRELIMINARY FRAMEWORK FOR KEY PREVENTION STRATEGIES 7 (2011), http://www.stoprapenow.org/uploads/advocacyresources/1352897743.pdf.

66. *See id.* at 5.

67. *See* Office of the Prosecutor, ICC, *Report on Prosecutorial Strategy* (Sept. 14, 2006), http://www.fidh.org/IMG/pdf/OTPProsecutorialStrategy_2006-2009.pdf.

68. *See* Bensouda, *supra* note 11.

69. *See* Fatou Bensouda, Deputy Prosecutor, ICC, *International Gender Justice Dialogue,* Keynote Address at the Women's Initiatives for Gender Justice and Nobel Women's Initiative (Apr. 19, 2010).

70. *See* Smith, *supra* note 1.

71. *See* Situation in Uganda, Case No. ICC-02/04-01/05, Warrant of Arrest for Joseph Kony, Issued on July 8, 2005, as Amended on September 27, 2005 (Sept. 27, 2005), http://www.iclklamberg.com/Caselaw/Uganda/Konyetal/PTCII/ICC-02-04-01-05-53_English%20Warrant.pdf.

72. *See* Prosecutor v. Germain Katanga, Case No. ICC-01/04-01/07, Warrant of Arrest for Germain Katanga (July 2, 2007), http://www.icc-cpi.int/iccdocs/doc/doc349648. PDF; Prosecutor v. Mathieu Ngudjolo Chui, Case No. ICC-01/04-02/07, Warrant of Arrest for Mathieu Ngudjolo Chui (July 6, 2007), http://www.icc-cpi.int/iccdocs/doc/doc453054.PDF.

73. *See* Prosecutor v. Callixte Mbarushimana, Case No. ICC-01/04-01/10, Warrant of Arrest for Callixte Mbarushimana (Sept. 28, 2010), http://www.icc-cpi.int/iccdocs/doc/doc954979.pdf.

74. *See* Prosecutor v. Bosco Ntaganda, Case No. ICC-01/04-02/06, Decision on the Prosecutor's Application under Article 58 (July 13, 2012), http://icc-cpi.int/iccdocs/doc/doc1441449.pdf.

75. Available at http://www.icc-cpi.int/iccdocs/doc/doc1441449.pdf.

76. See http://www.icc-cpi.int/en_menus/icc/situations%20and%20cases/situations/situation%20icc%200104/related%20cases/icc%200104%200206/Pages/icc%200104%200206.aspx.

77. *See* Prosecutor v. Ahmad Muhammad Harun ("Ahmad Harun") and Muhammad Al Abd-Al-Rahman ("Ali Kushayb"), Case No. ICC-02/05-01/07, Warrant of Arrest for Ahmad Harun (Apr. 27, 2007), http://www.icc-cpi.int/iccdocs/doc/doc279813.PDF.

78. *See* Prosecutor v. Ahmad Muhammad Harun ("Ahmad Harun") and Muhammad Al Abd-Al-Rahman ("Ali Kushayb"), Case No. ICC-02/05-01/07, Warrant of Arrest for Ali Kushayb (Apr. 27, 2007), http://www.icc-cpi.int/iccdocs/doc/doc279858.PDF.

79. *See* Prosecutor v. Omar Hassan Ahmad Al Bashir, Case No. ICC-02/05-01/09, Warrant of Arrest for Omar Hassan Ahmad Al Bashir (Mar. 4, 2009), http://www.icc-cpi.int/iccdocs/doc/doc639078.pdf.

80. *See* Bensouda, *supra* note 11.

81. More information is available at http://www.icc-cpi.int/menus/icc/situations%20and%20cases/situations/situation%20icc%200205/situation%20icc-0205?lan=en-GB.

82. *See* Situation in the Republic of Côte d'Ivoire, Case No. ICC-02/11, Warrant of Arrest for Laurent Koudou Gbagbo (Nov. 23, 2011), http://www.icc-cpi.int/iccdocs/doc/doc1276751.pdf.

83. *See* Prosecutor v. Francis Kirimi Muthaura, Uhuru Muigai Kenyatta, and Moham-

med Hussein Ali, Case No. ICC-01/09-02/11, Decision on the Confirmation of Charges Pursuant to Article 61(7)(a) and (b) of the Rome Statute (Jan. 23, 2012), http://www.icc-cpi.int/iccdocs/doc/doc1314543.pdf.

84. The rebel force discussed in this paper is not the same force over which Bemba had control. The rebel force cannot be named because it would jeopardize the need of the NGO that trained the force to remain anonymous. The name of the leader and the rebel group are on file with the author.

85. *See Interview: Luis Moreno-Ocampo, ICC Prosecutor,* STARAFRICA.COM (Sept. 21, 2009), http://www.starafrica.com/en/news/detail-news/view/interview-luis-moreno-ocampo-icc-prose-16651.html.

86. Telephone Interview with Former NGO Worker Who Helped Set Up Gender-Based Violence Health Program near Rebel-Held Area in the CAR (Feb. 8, 2012).

87. Interview with Former NGO Worker Who Conducted Trainings in the CAR (Apr. 24, 2010).

88. *See, e.g.,* United Nations, *supra* note 2.

89. *See Humanitarian Crisis in Central Africa Republic, supra* note 2.

90. *See id.*

91. *See Conflict in Central African Republic Uproots 300,000, UN Reports,* UN NEWS CENTRE, Jan. 17, 2008, http://www.un.org/apps/news/story.asp?NewsID=25320&Cr=car&Cr1=unicef.

92. The United Nations has called the situation in the CAR a "a silent crisis crying out for increased international donor support and media attention" and has noted that the world's attention is focused more on neighboring African conflicts (e.g., in the DRC) and on conflicts such as Iraq. *See, e.g.,* United Nations, *supra* note 2.

93. Telephone Interview with CAR NGO Personnel (May 1, 2010).

94. Telephone Interview from Feb. 8, 2012, *supra* note 86.

95. *See id.*

96. *See id.*

97. *See* Interview from Apr. 24, 2010, *supra* note 87.

98. *See id.;* Telephone Interview from May 1, 2010, *supra* note 93. Both interviewees spoke of how the rebel leader was seeking legitimacy via these trainings; how he was very savvy; and how he was in many ways using the trainings and his relationship with the NGO for his own advancement and the advancement of his cause.

99. *See Central African Republic: Rebel Leader Seizes Power, Suspends Constitution,* IRIN NEWS (Mar. 17, 2003), http://www.irinnews.org/report/42102/central-african-republic-rebel-leader-seizes-power-suspends-constitution.

100. *See, e.g., Central African Republic Rebels Demand Payment,* YAHOO NEWS (Jan. 6, 2012), http://news.yahoo.com/central-african-republic-rebels-demand-payment-165700252.html.

101. *See, e.g., CAR Coup Strongly Condemned,* BBC NEWS (Mar. 17, 2003), http://news.bbc.co.uk/2/hi/africa/2853429.stm (noting condemnation by the African Union and France).

102. *See, e.g., From Potentate to Prisoner,* ECONOMIST (Apr. 14, 2011), http://www.economist.com/node/18561015 (noting that Gbagbo "seized power from another unelected leader in 2000").

103. *See* http://www.icc-cpi.int/iccdocs/doc/doc1783399.pdf.

104. *See* Interview from Apr. 24, 2010, *supra* note 87.

105. E-mail from Former CAR NGO Worker (Apr. 16, 2010) (on file with author).

106. Article 28, Responsibility of Commanders and Other Superiors, *see supra* note 54.

107. *See* Decision Pursuant to Article 61(7)(a) and (b) of the Rome Statute, *supra* note 18, at ¶438.

108. *See* Telephone Interview from Feb. 8, 2012, *supra* note 86.

109. *See* Telephone Interview from May 1, 2010, *supra* note 93.

110. *See id.*

111. The gender-based violence specialist shared with the author the two training manuals that they adapted, one for 2007 and 2008. Because they are internal documents, they must remain confidential. The author read through the manuals, and all statements regarding the content of the manual are based on the author's reading.

112. *Id.*

113. *See* Telephone Interview from May 1, 2010, *supra* note 93.

114. The author viewed two confidential photographs of the classroom setting.

115. "The first day we set out a ground rule that guns got left at a certain tree. [The rebels] thought it was hilarious, and they'd try and sneak a gun in. I'd see someone with a small gun, like a pistol, and I'd remind them of the rule. It was a pretty bizarre place: they'd laugh and put it with the rest of the guns." Telephone Interview, *supra* note 93, May 1, 2010.

116. *See id.*

117. *See id.*

118. *See id.*

119. *See id.*

120. Interview, Apr. 24, 2010, *supra* note 87.

121. *See id.*

122. *See id.*

123. *See* Telephone Interview from Feb. 8, 2012, *supra* note 86.

124. *See* Zimbardo, *supra* note 40, at 11, 14, 402, 432.

125. *See* Telephone Interview from Feb. 8, 2012, *supra* note 86.

126. *See id.*

127. *See id.*

128. *See id.*

129. *See id.*

130. *See id.*

131. *See* E-mail, *supra* note 105.

132. *See id.*

133. *See* Telephone Interview from Feb. 8, 2012, *supra* note 86.

134. *See id.*

135. *See id.*

136. *See id.*

137. *See* Franck, *supra* note 37, at 706, 711.

138. Fatou Bensouda, Deputy Prosecutor, ICC, *The Rome Statute of the International Criminal Court & Its Incorporation of a Gender Perspective* (on file with the author).

139. *See* Smith, *supra* note 1.

140. *See id.*

141. *See* Daniel Schwammenthal, *Prosecuting American "War Crimes,"* WALL ST. J. (Nov. 26, 2009), http://online.wsj.com/article/SB10001424052748704013004574519253 095440312.html.

142. *See* Smith, *supra* note 1.

143. *See* Minow, *supra* note 57, at 36 ("Reliance on post hoc punishment based on a formal rule will always be at best a partial solution. . . . [T]he deterrent and pedagogical signals from punishments are insufficient to prevent future abuses. Advance planning and training are crucial to preventing atrocities.").

144. *See* Daniel Munoz-Fresard, *The Roots of Behavior in War: Understanding & Preventing IHL Violations,* 853 INT'L REV. OF THE RED CROSS 189, 194, 2006 (2004), http://www.icrc.org/eng/assets/files/other/irrc_853_fd_fresard_eng.pdf.

Education as a Tool in Preventing Violent Conflict

Suggestions for the Prosecutor of the International Criminal Court

Martha Minow

No one disputes that preventing genocide, crimes against humanity, and the crime of aggression would be better than punishing their perpetrators. Defenders of international criminal justice institutions suggest that indictments, arrests, prosecutions, and convictions can deter horrific violations of human rights, though formal criminal justice mechanisms never fully deter crimes. In addition, even more than other kinds of crimes, genocide and mass atrocity reflect political and personal motives that at best are only partially responsive to deterrence. The attitudes and actions of others—citizens, journalists, soldiers, bystanders—are likely to play a larger role in preventing and halting gross human rights violations at national and international levels. The unique structure creating the International Criminal Court (ICC) and its broad mandate to prevent as well as to punish offer a resource that could be pursued. A creature of a treaty that creates a body of member states, the ICC could provide a focal point for a mass movement for conflict-prevention education.

The first ICC prosecutor, Luis Moreno Ocampo, identified prevention as core to his mission and signaled strong interest in education as a means of preventing the crimes entrusted to the ICC. This chapter examines the relevant scope of the ICC prosecutor's authority and tools and argues that although the authority and means are limited, the ICC prosecutor can foster education as a prevention tool.

The ICC as a Resource for Prevention

As prosecutor, Moreno Ocampo emphasized the prevention mandate as equal to the duty to investigate and prosecute international crimes.[1] International criminal law historically tackles prevention of atrocities through prosecutions, trials, judgments, and punishment. Exemplified by the Nuremberg trials after World War II, the ad hoc International Criminal Tribunals for the Former Yugoslavia and Rwanda, and the Special Court for Sierra Leone, international criminal justice pursues prevention on four premises:

1. Incapacitation of alleged perpetrators in ongoing conflicts—if they can in fact be arrested and halted.[2] For example, Moreno Ocampo argued that enforcing the ICC's arrest warrant for onetime Sudanese government official Ahmad Haroun would prevent future crimes in Darfur.

2. Through plea-bargaining or other forms of formal or informal negotiations trading reduction of criminal sanction risks in exchange for cessation of conflicts, the operation of international criminal institutions can induce perpetrators currently engaged in mass atrocities to halt their actions.

3. Norm development—by articulating and elaborating norms at international and national levels, the international criminal process can engage leaders and members of civil society across the globe in the development of beliefs and priorities that they in turn can use to pressure governments to take appropriate actions to prevent further offenses.

4. Deterrence—by providing accountability and ending impunity for violations in the past and present, prosecutions and trials prevent future offenses. As U.N. secretary-general Kofi Annan explained, "We have little hope of preventing genocide, or reassuring those who live in fear of its recurrence, if people who have committed this most heinous of crimes are left at large, and not held to account. It is therefore vital that we build and maintain robust judicial systems, both national and international, so that, over time, people will see there is no impunity for such crimes."[3] Yet the emergence of international criminal justice—first after World War II and more recently—has not yet demonstrably deterred genocide, crimes against humanity, torture, or other gross violations of human rights.

Thus far, the ICC has pursued these ambitions through the familiar techniques of criminal law: indictments, arrests, prosecutions, trials, convictions, and punishment. The option of plea-bargaining or negotiation in the shadow of the courthouse is familiar in the United States but is rejected in many other parts of the world; a prosecutor might operate in this uncertain realm but would not have clear authority or political support to negotiate a deal. These tools are real but limited in producing prevention in the short term and even in the long term. Yet the existence and structure of the ICC may offer resources for sponsoring prevention efforts through education, and here, the prosecutor would be a likely and promising leader.

During his term as prosecutor, Moreno Ocampo identified two special features of the ICC that lift up education—devising and supporting direct instruction—as a distinct activity of the ICC.[4]

The first feature is the fact of the membership structure of the ICC. In this respect, the ICC differs from all other international criminal justice ventures. The Nuremberg trials emerged from the Charter of the International Military Tribunal announced by Franklin Roosevelt, Winston Churchill, and Joseph Stalin as victors after World War II. The ad hoc tribunals for the former Yugoslavia and Rwanda are creatures of the United Nations Security Council, so they indirectly reflect consent by member nations to the U.N. structure, and various countries have entered into agreements with the U.N. to carry out custodial sentences: the U.N. and Sierra Leone signed an agreement creating the Special Court for Sierra Leone. But the ICC is created by a treaty—known as the Rome Statute—and came into being by its own terms after 60 nations ratified the treaty. Currently 122 nations have joined. The treaty establishes not only the Court but also an Assembly of States Parties, which meets at least once a year. The assembly offers a potential venue for sharing information, for devising and testing educational programs, and for competition among countries for better programs. In short, it is a community with appointed representatives whose members have already signed onto the project of preventing genocide, crimes against humanity, war crimes, and the crime of aggression, and it has a forum ready-made for ongoing prevention efforts.

A second feature of the Court proceeds from the Rome Statute's inventive idea of complementarity and its elaboration by the Office of the Prosecutor (OTP). The complementarity principle holds that the ICC can proceed only in cases where states are unwilling or unable to do so, since the ultimate goal is to strengthen the responsibility, capacity, and commitment of member nations to punish and prevent genocide and gross violations of human rights.[5] In service of this goal, the OTP developed a policy of "positive complementarity," involving encouragement in support of genuine national prosecutions and limited assistance in the form of sharing information, expert advice and training, and connections with donors and development organizations.[6] This commitment to strengthen national responsibility and capacity and offer advice and assistance could undergird efforts by the OTP to promote prevention programs in member nations.

Even with these features, obvious limitations exist. "Positive complementarity" requires a strong reading of the principle designed to ensure constraints on the authority of the ICC and hence of its prosecutor. So some commentators—including member states—could well object to efforts to assert proactive power on this basis. Moreover, even modest efforts at sharing information and expert advice and training require time and money—already limited for the core functions of the ICC and the OTP. Also required would be specialized knowledge about pedagogy, curricula, and working within educational systems around the world in addition to expertise already within the ICC and the OTP. Even given these limitations, the visibility of the ICC and the capacity of the prosecutor to secure high-level attention within nation-states and in international media are compensating assets.

One approach, then, is to conceive of public education as a central activity for the prosecutor personally. Moreno Ocampo took on this role in part through his frequent speeches, appearances at conferences, and willingness to participate in documentaries and other media efforts.[7] His background in mass media equipped him to take on this public education role while also convincing him of the importance of media in raising consciousness and educating people. Speeches, conferences, and films may raise attention to the ICC and its activities, but educational efforts that are sustained and embedded in the lives of young people have greater prospects for altering behavior.

Why Turn to Education?

War, atrocity, genocide, torture, and rape may seem to be names of the problem, but in fact they are manifestations of an underlying problem: the easy availability of denigrating conceptions of "other people" as an outlet for fear and insecurity and a resource for unscrupulous leaders to manipulate. Dr. James Orbinski served as mission head of Médecins sans Frontières (Doctors without Borders) in Rwanda while the genocide was unfolding. When he learned that a hospital under Hutu control was sheltering several hundred Tutsi children, he went to the Hutu leader in charge and offered to take the children to a safer place. The leader refused. Dr. Orbinski asked, "Do you have children?" "Why yes," the leader replied, proudly pulling out photos. When Orbinski pointed out, "But these are children, too," the Hutu leader replied, "No, they are cockroaches." The next day, half of the children had been murdered.[8]

In the fall of 1992, residents of Billings, Montana, began finding anonymous fliers featuring racist, anti-Semitic, and other hateful images and words stuffed into mailboxes, under car windshield wipers, and into newspapers. Some white people disrupted services at an African American church; someone spray painted the home of a Native American family with swastikas and racist slurs, and someone threw a cinder block through a child's bedroom window that displayed a picture of a menorah. In response to the apparent surge in hate crimes, members of churches, civic leaders, government officials, and others organized an antihate campaign, Not in Our Town. The effort included an invitation for everyone in the community to paste on their windows the image of a menorah printed in a local newspaper, and thousands of people did so, standing against bigotry.[9] The movement generated a local and then national campaign against hatred and prompted production of a documentary film that aired on public television, a series of documentaries and teaching materials distributed throughout the country, and community efforts to combat group-based hatred.[10] Nevertheless, Billings experienced a resurgence of hateful graffiti and actions several years later, prompting renewed efforts to combat the problem.[11]

What can prevent people from thinking of other people's children as cockroaches, worthy of extermination? What practical and psychological shifts are necessary for people to band together against the targeting of some people as objects of hatred? What preventive investment is necessary to undertake the long-term work of overcoming prejudices and politicized differences?

It is common after intergroup conflict—whether local or international, interethnic or interracial—to hear calls for education. Education ideally offers the chance to shape the minds, hearts, and behaviors of succeeding generations. Educational programs on conflict resolution, human rights, tolerance, and peacemaking express the hope that if young people learn to respect others, to understand the costs of group hatreds, to avoid stereotypes, to develop tools for resolving disputes, to choose to stand up to demagogues, to be peacemakers, and to recognize and resist efforts of unscrupulous leaders to manipulate prejudices into violent hatreds, future atrocities might be prevented. Explicit programs can draw on historical examples to help people see the patterns of manipulation behind prior genocides and to alert them to the power of bystanders to either condone or resist violence.

After mass violence, the challenge is to avoid a "return to normal" after the conflict, for normal is what produced the conflict. Two anthropologists crystallized this insight when they wrote, "No glib appeal to 'our common humanity' can restore the confidence to inhabit each other's lives again. Instead, it is by first reformulating their notions of 'normality' as a changing norm that communities can respond to the destruction of trust in everyday life."[12] Educational change can be part of efforts to alter the conditions in which massive intergroup conflict arises.

Research over the past several decades indicates the power of educational efforts that combine contact among diverse groups with work on seeing things from other perspectives and collaboration.[13] Extensive studies also demonstrate the effectiveness of deliberate educational initiatives to enhance empathy.[14] Students can learn how to negotiate conflicts and draw on emotions as well as analysis in doing so.[15] Students can also learn about the historical contexts leading to prior atrocities and the roles that individuals, groups, laws, media, and politics can play in halting them.[16] And programs to train teachers to support such historical and perspective-taking learning can yield effective results.[17] Working with adolescents in conflict situations is especially crucial. In refugee camps and following periods of mass violence, a focus on the educational opportunities for young people matters not only to equip them for jobs but also to support attitudes and capacities that can prevent future violence. Obviously, the future lies in their hands. More subtly, studies of memory indicate that experiences formed in adolescence and early adulthood become the basis for the most enduring and vivid memories over people's lifetimes, but the shape of any memory is affected by the stories the individual learned with the context of their present.[18] Thus, adolescents who live through group conflict will likely hold onto those memories for the rest of their lives. But the meanings they attribute to those memories are affected by the collective narratives they learn and by emerging needs and interests in their adult lives. To prevent revenge as the response to the past and to prevent dehumanizing people in other groups, educational experiences for adolescents could be vital. Moreover, studies of human development indicate that people first develop strong commitments to abstract ideals during adolescence. The ideas that young people form about their national struggles will connect with their emerging notions of right and wrong, truth and fairness, identity and injustice and will deeply influence the rest of their lives. Varied strategies may help prevent mass violence and atrocity and quell the recruitment of people to join campaigns of hatred. No one should naively believe that education can prevent violent intergroup conflicts. But surely it can contribute to such an effort and perhaps can be one of many strategies for prevention.

A survey of educational efforts relevant to preventing genocide and gross violations of human rights locates several distinctive options. Educational programs for children and adolescents could focus on (1) conflict prevention and resolution, (2) direct experiences with positive intergroup contact; (3) human rights, (4) moral development, or (5) reflection on historical experiences and responses.[19]

Education in Conflict Prevention and Resolution

Teaching conflict resolution to young people ranges from skill training in negotiation and mediation to development of inclusive ideas of community and critique of instruction in bigotry or group-based indoctrination.[20] Experts believe that teaching students how to negotiate and communicate and how to mediate conflicts can enhance students' capacities to cooperate and to employ self-control, reducing incidents of aggression at school.[21]

Some programs involve students or mediators in their schools. Some efforts combine academic study of conflict resolution with skills training in communication and mediation. For example, one curriculum, Conflict and Communication, received support from George Soros's Open Society Institute for implementation in Central and Eastern European schools[22] and was implemented in Macedonia and Romania, and piloted in other Eastern European countries.[23] Using exercises to generate experiences, the curriculum engages students in practicing five steps toward resolving conflicts: (1) recognizing conflict; (2) examining one's own and others' feelings; (3) recognizing what oneself and others want from the conflict; (4) thinking of ideas to help both sides or parties get what they want at the same time; and (5) devising and acting on a plan to get there while strengthening the relationship with apparent opponents.[24]

Intergroup Contact

While conflict resolution programs seek to equip students to be peace-makers and mediators, intergroup contact initiatives proceed by giving students experiences with people in other groups as a way to overcome stereotypes through positive experiences while building relationships of equality and mutual acceptance.[25] Short-term experiential learning efforts bring together for a few weeks Palestinians and Israelis, teens from opposing sides in Northern Ireland, or suburban and urban adolescents in the United States.[26] Studies of long-term desegregation efforts in the United States and elsewhere show that casual, superficial contact—such as passing one another in the cafeteria—is much less likely to affect attitudes than joint school projects or experiences on the same sports team.[27] Seeds of Peace aims to empower children to break cycles of violence, to break down negative images of members of opposing groups, and to engage in critical reflection about themselves and their world. Staff leaders assign students to tables, bunks, and sports teams with a deliberate plan for encouraging interaction among members of different groups. Campers are given a chance to meet once a week with individuals from their own group, accompanied by teachers and representatives of their countries' ministries of education.[28] Seeds of Peace has expanded to include youth from Eastern Europe in its summer camp, programs for Greek and Turkish youth from Cyprus, and a year-round center in Jerusalem to help its alumni maintain their friendships.

Human Rights

An education program can instruct students about principles of universal human liberty and equality and historic and current efforts to build institutions and practices predicated on those principles. Such a program can draw people away from specific conflicts, oppressions, and injustices and toward commitments to broad ideals. Both human rights activists and human rights educators believe strongly that individuals, groups, nations, and the world can acknowledge the dignity and integrity of each person and toward that end can build a common language and set of institutions to improve the lives of all.

The United Nations and many nongovernmental organizations support ongoing human rights educational efforts.[29] The office of the U.N. High Commissioner for Human Rights produced a teaching guide, *ABC: Teaching Human Rights: Practical Activities for Primary & Secondary Schools,* which it distributes through its website.[30] The guide explicitly links instruction in human rights to prevention of violent intergroup conflict, urging educators to replace traditional, hierarchical instruction with teaching methods that are consonant with the content of the human rights of freedom of expression and equality. This means exposing and foreclosing the hypocrisy of a lecture on freedom of expression that begins with the instructor directing the students to shut up; it also means turning to experiential and hands-on learning that would be alien to many teachers around the world.[31]

Moral Reasoning

Direct instruction in tolerance and respect for others[32] can proceed by using ideas of psychological development[33] or paying attention to erroneous assumptions that generate intergroup distrust and hostility.[34] Students may learn such messages more effectively if adults in their community take a stand against hateful materials and create an unwelcome environment for the expression of hatred and bigotry.[35]

Comparative History and Self-Reflection

A fifth educational approach emphasizes inquiry into a period of one historical horror as a basis for involving students in thinking about their own situations and the importance of action to prevent violence and intergroup hatred.[36] The central goal is to promote young people's capacities for critical thinking, understanding, tolerance, caring and compassion, and action when needed to oppose injustice. Students can be invited to reflect on the choices made by historical actors and on personal choices, to see the dangers of indifference and consequences of stereotypes and hatred, and to learn from positive models of people who have made a real difference. External evaluations of one such program, Facing History and Ourselves, show that participating students demonstrate increased knowledge of historical content, greater capacity for moral reasoning, empathy, social interest, and improved self-perception.[37] Recent research about causes of genocides and about the roles of those who resist offer rich materials based on historical case studies.[38]

Each of these kinds of educational efforts offers ingredients that could make a real difference, though when taken alone, each has notable shortcomings. Conflict resolution and peace education can equip individuals with useful tools for mediating disputes and defusing their own conflicts. Yet without a fuller political and moral framework, such programs may fail to cultivate students' abilities to know when to engage in conflict—when to stand up in opposition to mistreatment or abuse of others or of themselves. If amplified by historical case studies and moral inquiry, insights worked out in conflict resolution theory and practice could equip students to prevent escalations of local conflicts while developing substantive commitments to justice and fairness.

Similarly, human rights education—and moral reasoning instruction—risk operating too abstractly to engage students' hearts and affect their aspirations and commitments. Abstract moral vocabularies risk operating at a level of remoteness that may not register in people's minds and lives. A review of moral instruction suggests that thicker language, grounded in particular narratives and echoed by practiced ritual, is more likely to resonate with children than is purely cognitive instruction.[39] If connected with hands-on conflict resolution activities and applications to rich historical contexts, education in both human rights and moral reasoning could motivate students and secure the kinds of lasting lessons that come when cognitive and emotional learning come together. Joint classes in subjects of practical importance—subjects such as computer technology or physics—could provide meaningful occasions for common constructive experiences but require resources to do well.

Sufficient resources for any form of education require political will. Even if a nation devotes resources to educate all children, political disputes over education make schooling design remote as a prevention tool precisely where violent conflict, past or incipient, hovers in the society. For nations with a history of genocide, civil war, or intergroup violence, even contemplation of school integration across group differences is fraught with risk. A hint of such controversy appeared in an exchange during a 2009 meeting held in Boston for teams representing divided cities—Mitrovica, which half of its residents think is in Kosovo and half think is in Serbia; Kirkuk, Iraq; Nicosia, Cyprus; and one Northern Irish town whose members cannot even agree on its name. Asked about prospects for integrating schools across religious and ethnic differences in Iraq, a government official replied, "We would go to war to stop that."[40]

Such reactions hint at the difficulty of developing and implementing effective educational efforts to prevent genocide and gross violations of human rights where communities are antagonistic and teach their children narratives of victimization and hatred that stoke intergroup conflicts. And none of the methods described here directly address trauma from conflict, which may be an immediate issue in particular communities.

What Can the OTP Do to Promote Education to Prevent Mass Atrocities?

Recognizing and supporting the particular and varied needs and desires of distinct nations is essential to any development of educational programs seeking to prevent genocide and gross violations of human rights. Despite the limitations on the ICC and the OTP, the Court's structure as the product of a treaty offers a genuine asset. The signatory nations have demonstrated at least sufficient political will to sign onto the project of international criminal justice and in so doing have agreed to create a body of member nations as well as to support and recognize the Court and its offices. The annual Assembly of States Parties offers an opportunity for the states parties to confer as well as to provide oversight for the Court and its operations.

The OTP is uniquely entrusted with initiating action, and the scope of authority includes prevention of as well as response to the crimes listed in the Rome Statute. The prosecutor could initiate a proposal that member nations commit to developing educational initiatives aimed at preventing genocide and gross violations of human rights. The work of the ICC itself could provide materials relevant to such education, but the prosecutor's charge to pursue prevention warrants a broader focus, reflecting research about causes of genocide, roles of bystanders and rescuers, contributions of information and institutions, and development of conflict-resolution skills and consciousness about the dynamics of propaganda and histories of group-based mass murders.[41]

The fact that there are many potential educational strategies that can prevent intergroup conflict and hatred could actually be an asset if the OTP seeks to promote efforts by member states. Each nation can pursue its own preferred approach, although without the push of international collaboration (and even international competition), reliance simply on national efforts could lead to little action or little effectiveness. The ICC prosecutor is a visible figure, charged with preventing genocide and with a role in communicating with the nations that have already committed by treaty to work to prevent genocide. The prosecutor could propose and organize a conference at which nations could learn about and share information on educational alternatives. The program could offer simple information exchange or take a more ambitious course by inviting member nations to compete to demonstrate the most effective approaches. The prosecutor could mobilize educators and funders to create resources to share or an arena where educators in member states could exchange curricula and ideas. More ambitiously, the prosecutor could develop a program with outside funding to subsidize the development and assessment of educational initiatives devoted to preventing genocide and mass violence. Over time, the prosecutor could work with the states parties to devise goals for adopting and evaluating educational programs within each nation and to ensure continuing evaluation and improvement of such efforts.

Prevention of the gravest violations of human rights is one of the most significant goals of international criminal justice. Despite the limitations of the ICC and the OTP, an untapped opportunity to promote education aimed at preventing mass violence and human rights violations would capitalize on the visibility of the institution, the structure of member states, and the commitment represented by the treaty establishing the ICC. No judge or other actor at the ICC is as well positioned as the prosecutor to take up the opportunity. Following Luis Moreno Ocampo's explorations of prevention and public education, his successors in the OTP could take up education and advance the vision of preventing mass violence.

NOTES

An earlier version of this chapter was presented as the Hesburgh Lecture in Ethics and Public Policy at the Kroc Center for International Peace Studies, University of Notre Dame, Mar. 12, 2010. Thanks to Luis Moreno Ocampo, Fernando Reimers, Cora True-Frost, and Alex Whiting for helpful comments.

1. See Luis Moreno Ocampo, *Speech: How Prosecution Can Lead to Prevention*, 29 LAW & INEQ. 477 (2011).

2. *See, e.g.,* Moreno Ocampo's remarks at the Global Conference on the Prevention of Genocide in 2007. Marie Winfield, *The Role of the ICC Prosecutor*, PREVENTION OF GENOCIDE BLOG (Oct. 10, 2007), http://lawiscool.com/2007/10/10/prevention-of-genocide/ (summarizing Moreno Ocampo's remarks and writing "Moreno Ocampo sees prevention and deterrence at the heart of the Rome Statute, which authorized the ICC. . . . He views the Darfur conflict as a testing model to see how law can be used to prevent atrocities. Enforcing the ICC's arrest warrant for Ahmad Haroun will prevent future crimes in Darfur, according to Moreno Ocampo."). In this discussion between Payam Akhavan and Moreno Ocampo, it was evident that a shift had taken place in terms of imagining the prosecution's role in current conflicts, including Darfur. Pursuant to this new role, Moreno Ocampo described a twofold function of the prosecutor's office: (1) the duty to investigate past and present crimes; and (2) to contribute to the prevention of crimes. *See id.*

3. *See* United Nations, *"Risk of Genocide Remains Frighteningly Real" Secretary-General Tells Human Rights Commission as He Launches Action Plan to Prevent Genocide* (Apr. 7, 2004), https://www.un.org/News/Press/docs/2004/sgsm9245.doc.htm.

4. I am grateful to Moreno Ocampo for conversations on this subject in Cambridge, Massachusetts, during the spring of 2009, Jan. 2010, and Jan. 2011.

5. Article 1 of the ICC Statute states that the Court "shall be complementary to na-

tional criminal jurisdictions." *See* Rome Statute of the International Criminal Court, art. 1, July 17, 1998, 2187 U.N.T.S. 90 (hereinafter Rome Statute). The concept of *complementarity* is implemented by article 17, which provides that the ICC, "shall determine that a case is inadmissible where:

> The case is being investigated or prosecuted by a State which has jurisdiction over it, unless the State is unwilling or unable genuinely to carry out the investigation or prosecution;
> The case has been investigated by a State which has jurisdiction over it and that State has decided not to prosecute the person concerned, unless the decision resulted from the unwillingness or inability of the State genuinely to prosecute;
> The person concerned has already been tried for conduct which is the subject of the complaint, and a trial by the Court is not permitted under article 20, paragraph 3; or
> The case is not of sufficient gravity to justify further action by the Court."

See id. art. 17(1).

6. *See* ICC, Office of the Prosecutor, *Prosecutorial Strategy 2009–2012,* at ¶¶16–17 (Feb. 1, 2010), http://www.icc-cpi.int/NR/rdonlyres/66A8DCDC-3650-4514-AA62-D229D1128F65/281506/OTPProsecutorialStrategy20092013.pdf.

7. *See, e.g.,* Marlow Stern, *"Prosecutor" Star Makes His Case,* DAILY BEAST (Oct. 5, 2011), http://www.thedailybeast.com/articles/2011/10/05/luis-moreno-ocampo-international-criminal-court-chief-on-libya-darfur-more.html; THE RECKONING: THE BATTLE FOR THE INTERNATIONAL CRIMINAL COURT (Skylight 2009), http://skylight.is/films/the-reckoning/.

8. Dr. James Orbinski, Professor, Univ. Toronto, Luncheon Address at the Conference on Justice, Memory, and Reconciliation (Feb. 16, 2000), http://www.nobelprize.org/nobel_prizes/peace/laureates/1999/msf-lecture.html (delivering Nobel Prize acceptance speech on behalf of Médecins sans Frontières).

9. *See* JANICE COHN, THE CHRISTMAS MENORAHS: HOW A TOWN FOUGHT HATE (1995); Janice I. Cohn, *The Town That Fought Hatred,* BELIEFNET (2005), http://www.beliefnet.com/Inspiration/2005/12/The-Town-That-Fought-Hatred.aspx#.

10. *See* the website of Not in Our Town, a national organization that grew out of the Montana effort (www.niot.org); Jo Clare Hartsig & Walter Wink, *Light in Montana: How One Town Said No to Hate,* in CIVIL PARTICIPATION & COMMUNITY ACTION SOURCEBOOK (Andy Nash ed., 2001), http://tech.worlded.org/docs/vera/montana.htm (describing the rise of hate crimes in Montana in the 1990s). Incidents revealing hatred of particular groups nonetheless continue. *See, e.g., Montana Men Face Possible Hate Crime Charges,* KTVQ NEWS (Jan. 2, 2014), http://www.ktvq.com/news/montana-men-face-possible-hate-crime-charges/.

11. *See* Jessica Higendorf, *Summit on Hate at RMC,* KULR8.COM (Nov. 16, 2013), http://www.kulr8.com/story/23990489/summit-on-hate-at-rmc.

12. *See* Veena Das & Arthur Kleinman, *Introduction,* in REMAKING A WORLD: VIOLENCE, SOCIAL SUFFERING, & RECOVERY 1, 23 (Veena Das et al. eds., 2002).

13. *See* Thomas F. Pettigrew & Linda R. Tropp, *A Meta-Analytic Test of Intergroup Contact Theory,* 90 J. PERSONALITY & SOC. PSYCHOL. 751 (2006) (reporting analysis of 713 samples in 515 studies).

14. *See* Theo Elfers et al., *Perspective Taking: A Review of Research & Theory Extending Selman's Developmental Model of Perspective Taking,* 54 ADVANCES IN PSYCHOL. RES. 229, 229–62 (Alexandra M. Columbus ed., 2008); Robert L. Selman & K. O. Yeats, *Social Competence in Schools,* 9 DEV. REV. 64 (1989).

15. *See* ROGER FISHER & DANIEL SHAPIRO, BEYOND REASON: USING EMOTIONS AS YOU NEGOTIATE (2009).

16. *See* MELINDA FINE, HABITS OF MIND (1995).

17. *See* Dennis Barr, *Continuing a Tradition of Research: On the Foundations of Democratic Education: The National Professional Development & Evaluation Project* (2010), http://www.facinghistory.org/sites/facinghistory.org/files/Continuing_a_Tradition_v93010_0.pdf.

18. *See* DANIEL L. SCHACTER, SEARCHING FOR MEMORY: THE BRAIN, THE MIND, THE PAST (1996).

19. The discussion of these alternatives draws on my prior work. *See* Martha Minow, *Education for Co-Existence,* 44 ARIZ. L. REV. 1, 1–29 (2002).

20. *See* Raymond Shonholtz, *Strengthening Transitional Democracies through Conflict Resolution: Conflict Resolution Education, Training, & Global Development,* 552 ANNALS 139 (1997).

21. *See* Alina Tugend, *Curriculum: Peaceable Playgrounds,* N.Y. TIMES (Nov. 11, 2001), http://www.nytimes.com/2001/11/11/education/curriculum-peaceable-playgrounds.html ("For a recent study by the University of Washington in Seattle, researchers watched students interact at the beginning and end of a year in six schools with conflict resolution programs and six without. In schools using programs, they found a 29 percent decline in incidents involving hitting and fighting and a 20 percent decline in verbal aggression like insulting and taunting. In schools without programs, physical aggression increased 41 percent and verbal aggression 22 percent.").

22. *See* DANIEL SHAPIRO, CONFLICT & COMMUNICATION: A GUIDE THROUGH THE LABYRINTH OF CONFLICT MANAGEMENT (1995). Thanks to Daniel Shapiro for conversations about the curriculum and the topics it reflects.

23. *Id.* at i.

24. *Id.* at 207.

25. *See* W. PAUL VOGT, TOLERANCE & EDUCATION: LEARNING TO LIVE WITH DIVERSITY & DIFFERENCE 151–76 (1997). The idea of social contact as a basis for positive outcomes began with Gordon Allport's work. *See* GORDON W. ALLPORT, THE NATURE OF PREJUDICE (1954). *See also* M. HEWSTONE & R. BROWN, EDS., CONTACT & CONFLICT IN ENCOUNTERS (1986) (building on Allport's work).

26. *See* Cynthia Cohen, *Engaging with the Arts to Promote Coexistence,* in IMAGINE COEXISTENCE (Antonia Chayes & Martha Minow eds., 2003).

27. *See id.* at 161 (reporting studies).

28. For a description by its founder, see JOHN WALLACH, THE ENEMY HAS A FACE: THE SEEDS OF PEACE EXPERIENCE (2000).

29. For information on just some of these groups, visit the websites for the Human Rights Education Associates (www.hrea.org) and the Human Rights Resource Center (www.hrusa.org).

30. *See* United Nations, *Teaching Human Rights: Practical Activities for Primary & Secondary Schools* (2004), http://visit.un.org/wcm/webdav/site/visitors/shared/docu ments/pdfs/Pub_United%20Nations_ABC_human%20rights.pdf.

31. *See id.* at 21 ("Already implicit above is the idea—central to this booklet—that teaching about human rights is not enough. The teacher will want to begin, and never to finish, teaching for human rights. Students will want not only to learn of human rights, but learn in them, for what they do to be of the most practical benefit to them. That is why the main part of the text consists of activities. The purpose of the activities is to create opportunities for students and teachers to work out from the basic elements that make up human rights such as life, justice, freedom, equity, and the destructive character of deprivation, suffering and pain—what they truly think and feel about a wide range of real world issues.").

32. *See* F. POWER, A. HIGGINS, & L. KOHLBERG, LAWRENCE KOLHBERG'S APPROACH TO MORAL EDUCATION (1989).

33. *See* THOMAS LICKONA, EDUCATING FOR CHARACTER: HOW OUR SCHOOLS CAN TEACH RESPECT & RESPONSIBILITY (1991). *See also* EDWARD F. DEROCHE & MARY M. WILLIAMS, CHARACTER EDUCATION: A GUIDE FOR SCHOOL ADMINISTRATORS (2001); JAMES DAVISON HUNTER, THE DEATH OF CHARACTER: MORAL EDUCATION IN AN AGE WITHOUT GOOD OR EVIL 116 (2000).

34. *See* DANIEL GOLEMAN, EMOTIONAL INTELLIGENCE: WHY IT CAN MATTER MORE THAN IQ (1995).

35. *See* JIM CARNES, ED., RESPONDING TO HATE AT SCHOOL: A GUIDE FOR TEACHERS, COUNSELORS, & ADMINISTRATORS (1999).

36. *See* MELINDA FINE, THE POLITICS & PRACTICE OF MORAL EDUCATION: A CASE STUDY (1991).

37. *See, e.g.,* Mary Brabaeck et al., *Human Rights Education through the "Facing History & Ourselves" Program,* 23 J. MORAL EDUC. 333 (1994); MARY T. GLYNN, AMERICAN YOUTH & THE HOLOCAUST: A STUDY OF FOUR MAJOR HOLOCAUST CURRICULA (1982); Betty Bardige, *Things So Finely Human: Moral Sensibilities at Risk in Adolescence,* in MAPPING THE MORAL DOMAIN: A CONTRIBUTION OF WOMEN'S THINKING TO PSYCHOLOGICAL THEORY & EDUCATION (C. Gilligan et al. eds., 1990).

38. *See, e.g.,* ALEXANDER HINTON, WHY DID THEY KILL?: CAMBODIA IN THE SHADOW OF GENOCIDE (2005); UNDERSTANDING GENOCIDE: THE SOCIAL PSYCHOLOGY OF THE HOLOCAUST (Leonard S. Newman & Ralph Erber eds., 2002); Jessica Casiro, *Argentine Rescuers: A Study on the "Banality of Good,"* 8 J. GENOCIDE RES. 437, 437–54 (2006), http://www.tandfonline.com/doi/pdf/10.1080/14623520601056281; Erwin Staub, *The Psychology of Bystanders, Perpetrators, & Heroic Helpers,* 17 INT'L J. INTERCULTURAL REL. 315, 315–41 (1993).

39. *See* HUNTER *supra* note 33, at 230.

40. *See* Kevin Baron, *"Divided Cities" Leaders to Gather, Advise Iraqis,* STARS & STRIPES (Mar. 21, 2009), http://www.stripes.com/news/divided-cities-leaders-to-gather-advise-iraqis-1.89330.

41. The work of initiatives such as Genocide Prevention Network, World without Genocide, Facing History and Ourselves, the U.N. High Commissioner for Human Rights, UNESCO's Human Rights Education Good Practices collection, and other programs would offer valuable resources in devising examples of and parameters for genocide prevention education.

Conclusion

Martha Minow, C. Cora True-Frost, and Alex Whiting

The International Criminal Court (ICC) is an instantiation of two modern ideas: that law can operate internationally, without a single sovereign, and that international criminal law, proceeding through the voluntary cooperation of nations and other actors, can produce accountability for the most heinous of crimes and in so doing deter their repetition. Even more than in a domestic circumstance, then, the ICC prosecutor represents a vision of law instead of vengeance and law instead of politics. Because the prosecutor's actions are crucial to launch a case, the post embodies in one person the ideas behind the ICC. It is not surprising, then, that Luis Moreno Ocampo, the first ICC prosecutor, became the focus of global attention on international criminal law as well as at times a lightning rod for controversy.

As the first in his office, the prosecutor—of course initially and foremost—had to establish his office within the legal and political constraints of the new Rome Statute system, further developing the cadre of international prosecutors coming from domestic jurisdictions and the ad hoc tribunals. In this regard, Moreno Ocampo performed a function that no other future prosecutor of the Court will have to undertake, building the office from nothing and showing that the Court can function. When he assumed office in June 2003, the ad hoc tribunals were bursting with activity. The ICC—the first permanent international criminal court with a distinct legal foundation, jurisdictional reach, structure, and set of rules—would also have to prove itself. Although Moreno Ocampo famously said in his inaugural speech that the ICC would be successful if it had *no* cases because that would indicate that complementarity was working and that national jurisdictions were prosecuting the cases themselves, everyone understood that this was an ambition for a faraway future and that the ICC would be measured, at least in its early years, by the success of its investigations and prosecutions. The work of the first prosecutor was necessarily shaped, therefore, by the imperative of quickly demonstrating that the Office of the Prosecutor (OTP) could investigate and prosecute atrocities.

Moreno Ocampo might have chosen many different approaches when launching his office within the existing institutional structure of the Rome Statute. Moreno Ocampo went beyond basic operating procedures, building the OTP's infrastructure and institutional foundation and by extension that of the Court. He also established three divisions and a team management structure within the office and developed clear and transparent practices and policies to guide future action.

Institution building was not Moreno Ocampo's sole task. He also focused on energetically applying the provisions of the Rome Statute to concrete matters. Although he frequently said that his mandate was to follow the letter of the law and to promote justice by prosecuting atrocities, he was also acutely aware of the Court's position as a court of last resort and the politically charged requirement that states cooperate with the Court's investigation and enforcement actions to develop and prosecute cases. He initiated relationships with the Security Council, with nongovernmental organizations, with member states, with nonmember states, with media, with academia, and with ordinary citizens to highlight the promise of international criminal law as well as to recruit the help without which that promise could not be realized.

The contributions in this book have explored in different ways the idea that the limitations of the prosecutor's powers in international criminal law are real constraints but also suggest strengths. First, these limitations allowed the prosecutor to focus on his core role: when demands for action fell outside of his narrow jurisdiction, he could say no, stay his hand, and protect his mandate and legitimacy. Along this line, he announced that he would not be drawn into political negotiations that might prioritize "peace" over "justice" but would instead keep his focus on the investigation and prosecution of Rome Statute crimes. He protected his independence, saying that he would apply the law to decide whether there were grounds for jurisdiction over a case even in the case of Security Council referral. Further, the limitations imposed by the Rome Statute necessarily required the prosecutor to cooperate with a wide array of other actors and institutions and thus afforded surprising opportunities for building coalitions and thus advancing international criminal law norms. At the same time, the constraints imposed by the statute and Rules of Procedure and

Evidence at times threatened to overwhelm the international criminal law project, sometimes leaving the prosecutor with few tools to combat instances of impunity. The prosecutions in the Kenya cases, for example, have been severely challenged by lack of cooperation by the government and the interference with witnesses (through threats and bribery) by supporters of the defendants. While the prosecutor can complain to the Security Council, and the OTP can attempt to prosecute those who interfere with witnesses when it has the requisite proof, these options are insufficient without sustained international support to assist with collecting the evidence necessary to prove the crimes, which has not necessarily been forthcoming.

The legal instruments also contained gaps resulting from unresolved disputes at Rome, unanticipated challenges, and spaces left open for discretion and prosecutorial independence. In addition to merely building the office, therefore, Moreno Ocampo could invent it, and invent he did. As Professor Jens Meierhenrich describes, Moreno Ocampo created the Jurisdiction, Complementarity and Cooperation Division within the OTP to focus and harmonize all complementarity and cooperation initiatives. As Christopher Stone discusses, Moreno Ocampo elevated the importance of the preliminary examination, using it as a tool to encourage countries to act as obligated by the Rome Statute, and accordingly invented the term *positive complementarity*. These innovations and others have been controversial in some quarters and have posed their own challenges, but through them, Moreno Ocampo sought to extend the office's impact, to transcend the constraints on his power. So far, his successor as prosecutor, Fatou Bensouda, has retained all of Moreno Ocampo's inventions. The chapters in this book have examined critically the choices made by the first prosecutor as well as the opportunities that lie ahead. As Professor Máximo Langer contends, the complementarity principle will require the OTP to explore further its relationship to national jurisdictions, particularly those seeking to exercise universal jurisdiction. While the Rome Statute privileges national prosecutions, the ICC has an important role to play in relation to national efforts.

Moreno Ocampo played other roles as well. In addition to creator, manager, inventor, and prosecutor, he was also a civil servant, a diplomat, and an educator. Although a legal actor, he operated always within a political environment. Thus, the prosecutor was forced to try to convince political actors to support his legal function, as he did when he persuaded the governments of some countries to refer themselves to the jurisdiction of the Court (rather than face a *proprio motu* investigation), when he urged governments to cooperate with investigations and arrests, or when he pressed governments to address impunity on their own, without ICC intervention. While performing these functions, Moreno Ocampo necessarily had to walk at the edge of his legal role, becoming vulnerable to criticism, particularly from those who might have an interest in undermining or discrediting the work of the OTP. In his contribution to the volume, Professor Robert H. Mnookin examines the unavoidable overlap between the spheres of peace and security, arguing that the prosecutor should sometimes find ways to delay or avoid prosecutions when there is a risk that they will interfere with peace but should do so without necessarily admitting to privileging peace over justice.

Given the (still) relative novelty of the international criminal justice project and the unquestionable novelty of his position, Moreno Ocampo also played the role of educator in everything he did. The Court's ambition is to cast a shadow in the world through the work it does, to inspire changes in political, military, and judicial norms. The core of the prosecutor's work is the select cases investigated and prosecuted by the office, but the project's success depends on the ability of the prosecutor and the Court to leverage the effects of these few cases on future practices. To that end, the prosecutor sought to engage all potential constituencies—governmental and nongovernmental—both to gain cooperation for the work of the OTP and to inculcate in future leaders the Court's central principles and values. Professor Martha Minow emphasizes this unique capacity to act as an educator in her discussion of how the office can broaden its mission to educate to help prevent conflict. Moreno Ocampo also pursued education in his public speeches and his participation on films documenting the work of the Court and its prosecutor.

Many of the chapters in this book describe how Moreno Ocampo was both cautious and bold. As Professor David Scheffer demonstrates, many of the fears about the prosecutor and the Court never came to pass. Even the prosecutor's worst critics would agree that the specter of the rogue prosecutor that haunted the Rome Statute negotiations was, in the end, only that. Moreno Ocampo used his *proprio motu* powers only twice and did not do so until 2010, when he opened an investigation into the post-election violence in Kenya, and 2011, when he turned to the situation in Côte d'Ivoire. The two referrals from the U.N. Security Council—in Sudan and Libya—arguably showed that Council members who once had anxieties about the ICC prosecutor were now willing to entrust him with new investigative responsibilities. Moreno Ocampo also used preliminary examinations to encourage countries to act against impunity, thereby promoting the Rome Statute's central aim of complementarity and allowing the OTP *not* to act. Within the ICC, Moreno Ocampo pressed his legal positions forcefully in Court and appealed adverse rulings when necessary, but as Professor Julie Rose O'Sullivan argues, he avoided direct criticism of the judges, understanding that doing so could undermine the institution as a whole. At the same time, Judge Patricia Wald contends that greater trust must be developed between the ICC judges and the prosecutor's office.

But as the first prosecutor of the global experiment that is the first permanent international court, Moreno Ocampo could not simply be cautious. As Professor Alex Whiting argues, caution is largely the privilege of more powerful and established prosecutors: had Moreno Ocampo been completely cautious, he would have risked becoming paralyzed in the face of the staggering challenges of investigating and prosecuting massive atrocities with few tools. Thus he moved quickly—some say too quickly—to bring cases to demonstrate the Court's relevance and maximize its impact. By the end of his tenure, the Court was investigating and prosecuting in seven different situations as well as monitoring seven preliminary investigations. Moreno Ocampo pushed forward with prosecutions of child soldier, sexual, and gender-based crimes. As Jessica Corsi shows, the prosecutor's relentless focus on sexual violence crimes shaped the discussion of these crimes and captured the attention of relevant actors in the world, including combatants. He relied heavily in his charging on the offense of crimes against humanity, at times risking a reaction from the Court's judges as he pushed the limits of this crime, according to Professor Leila Nadya Sadat. He focused on holding accountable those most responsible, bringing cases against heads of state in Libya and Sudan as well as a former head of state in Côte d'Ivoire. These bold choices underscored the ways in which the prosecutor's legal power was simultaneously broad and contingent, in many ways dependent on politics for implementation.

Despite facing significant resource and legal constraints, Moreno Ocampo established an institutional identity for the ICC, and the initial challenges have given way to new ones in many of which the "politics" of the Court are less central. These challenges now have more to do with the institution's core business, including how the OTP can investigate and prosecute mass atrocities with few tools and resources, particularly in light of the escalating demands of the jurisprudence of international criminal law. While such challenges may have seemed surmountable to many of those who participated in Rome, they now threaten to jeopardize the Court's credibility. In particular, Bensouda and subsequent prosecutors will need to focus first on complying with the increasingly rigorous procedural and substantive requirements of the corpus of international criminal law as articulated by the judges of the Court, particularly in light of the existing operational constraints. Second, as Professor C. Cora True-Frost argues, the new prosecutor will need to turn to the related issue of identifying and optimizing the supportive constituency of states and nongovernmental organizations to assist with investigation and enforcement. The judges have rejected a number of cases at both the confirmation and trial stages, making it clear that they will set a high bar for the scope and quality of the evidence presented by the prosecutor. At the same time, the OTP's resources have remained static even as it investigates more and more situations, raising urgent questions about its ability to fulfill its mission. Perhaps of even more concern is the question of whether the OTP can develop a constituency that will support its efforts to obtain evidence and have suspects arrested. The past experience of the ad hoc tribunals as well as that of the ICC has demonstrated that considerable international will is required for these international criminal institutions to succeed. Those tribunals, however, were time-limited and designed to terminate. In this fundamental respect, the ICC differs. The question going forward is not whether the institution will continue to exist. It will. But given its profound constraints and the odds against its mission, will it remain relevant, or will it become marginalized? That is the question for those following the first global prosecutor.

NOTE

The editors thank Kristin Flower, Paloma O'Connor, Chris Ramsdell, Kevin Rennells, and Melody Herr for fine assistance in producing this book.

Contributors

Jessica Lynn Corsi is a doctoral candidate in law at the University of Cambridge. She holds a bachelor's degree (cum laude) from Georgetown University's School of Foreign Service as well as a J.D. (cum laude) from Harvard Law School and a master's in law (prize in jurisprudence) from the University of Cambridge. Her Ph.D. dissertation is "Legal Fictions: Creating the Crime of Sexual Violence in International Law."

Máximo Langer is professor of law at the University of California, Los Angeles. He holds a bachelor of laws degree from the University of Buenos Aires Law School and a doctorate from Harvard Law School. His work has received numerous awards, including the 2007 Hessel Yntema Prize from the American Society of Comparative Law, the 2007 Margaret Popkin Award from the Latin American Studies Association, and the 2012 Deák Prize from the American Society of International Law. He has also taught at the University Torcuato DiTella School of Law in Argentina, Harvard Law School, the New York University School of Law, and the School of Law of Aix-Marseille University in France. He has also served on various boards and committees of the American Society of Comparative Law, the American Society of International Law, and the UCLA Latin American Institute, and he was the founding director of the UCLA Center for Argentina, Chile, and the Southern Cone. He serves on the executive editorial board of the *American Journal of Comparative Law* and is a co-organizer of the Comparative Law Work-in-Progress Workshop (cosponsored by the American Society of Comparative Law).

Jens Meierhenrich is associate professor of international relations at the London School of Economics and Political Science. His books include *The Legacies of Law: Long-Run Consequences of Legal Development in South Africa, 1652–2000* (2008), which won the American Political Science Association's 2009 Woodrow Wilson Foundation Award; *Lawfare: The Formation and Deformation of Gacaca Jurisdictions in Rwanda, 1994–2012* (2014); and *Genocide: A Reader* (2014). He has previously taught at Harvard University and served as a visiting professional in Trial Chamber II at the International Criminal Tribunal for the Former Yugoslavia and in the Office of the Prosecutor at the International Criminal Court. He recently edited a special issue of *Law and Contemporary Problems* on "The Practices of the International Criminal Court" (2013) and is presently at work on a genocide trilogy as well as an ethnography of the International Criminal Court.

Martha Minow is the Morgan and Helen Chu Dean and Professor of Law at Harvard Law School. Her books include *In Brown's Wake: Legacies of America's Constitutional Landmark* (2010); *Government by Contract* (co-edited, 2009); *Just Schools: Pursuing Equality in Societies of Difference* (co-edited, 2008); *Breaking the Cycles of Hatred: Memory, Law and Repair* (edited by Nancy Rosenblum with commentary by other authors, 2003); *Partners, Not Rivals: Privatization and the Public Good* (2002); *Engaging Cultural Differences: The Multicultural Challenge in Liberal Democracies* (co-edited 2002); *Between Vengeance and Forgiveness: Facing History After Genocide and Mass Violence* (1998); *Not Only for Myself: Identity, Politics and Law* (1997); *Law Stories* (co-edited 1996); *Narrative, Violence and the Law: The Essays of Robert M. Cover* (co-edited 1992); and *Making All the Difference: Inclusion, Exclusion, and American Law* (1990). She is the coeditor of two law school casebooks, *Civil Procedure: Doctrine, Practice and Context* (3rd ed. 2008) and *Women and the Law* (4th ed., 2007), and a reader, *Family Matters: Readings in Family Lives and the Law* (1993). She served on the Independent International Commission Kosovo and helped to launch Imagine Co-Existence, a program of the U.N. High Commissioner for Refugees to promote peaceful development in postconflict societies.

Robert H. Mnookin is the Samuel Williston Professor of Law at Harvard Law School, the chair of the Steering Committee of the Program on Negotiation at Harvard Law School, and the director of the Harvard Negotiation Research Project. He holds a bachelor's degree from Harvard College and a law degree from Harvard Law School. He served as a law clerk to Supreme Court justice John M. Harlan before practicing law and then moving into teaching. He has been a faculty member at Boalt Hall, University of California, Berkeley, as well as the Adelbert H. Sweet Professor

of Law at Stanford Law School and the director of the Stanford Center on
Conflict and Negotiation. He has also been a visiting fellow at Wolfson
College, University of Oxford; a visiting professor at Columbia Law
School; holder of the International Francqui Chair in Belgium; and a fellow at the Center for Advanced Study in the Behavioral Sciences at Stanford University. He is a fellow of the American Academy of Arts and Sciences and has served as a consultant to governments, international
agencies, major corporations, and law firms and as a neutral arbitrator or
mediator in numerous complex commercial disputes.

Luis Moreno Ocampo is an Argentine lawyer who served as the prosecutor of the International Criminal Court from 2003 to 2012. He previously
worked as a prosecutor in Argentina, combating corruption and prosecuting human rights abuses by senior military officials in the Trial of the
Juntas. He has also served as an associate professor of criminal law at the
University of Buenos Aires and a visiting professor at Stanford University
and Harvard Law School. He has acted as a consultant to the World Bank,
the Inter-American Development Bank, and the United Nations. He is a
former member of the advisory board of Transparency International and
a former president of its Latin America and Caribbean office. The founder
and president of Poder Ciudadano, Moreno Ocampo is a member of the
advisory board of the Project on Justice in Times of Transition and New
Tactics on Human Rights. He is currently a senior fellow at the Jackson
Institute for Global Affairs at Yale University.

Julie Rose O'Sullivan is a professor of law at Georgetown University Law
Center. She holds a bachelor's degree from Stanford University and a law
degree (summa cum laude) from Cornell Law School. She clerked for
Chief Judge Levin Campbell of the U.S. Court of Appeals for the First
Circuit and then for Justice Sandra Day O'Connor of the U.S. Supreme
Court. After five years in private practice, she became an assistant U.S. attorney with the Criminal Division of the U.S. Attorney's Office for the
Southern District of New York. She then served as associate counsel in the
Whitewater investigation before joining the Georgetown faculty. In 1995,
on appointment by the Supreme Court, she briefed and argued a case on
behalf of an indigent petitioner before the Court. She has taught international criminal law in London, Barcelona, and Dublin as well as at Georgetown, and in 2010, she served as a visiting professional at and a consultant
for the Office of the Prosecutor of the International Criminal Court. She

has written many articles and the leading casebook on white-collar crime as well as coauthored (with David Luban and David Stewart) a casebook on international and transnational criminal law.

Leila Nadya Sadat is the Henry H. Oberschelp Professor of Law at Washington University School of Law and director of the Whitney R. Harris World Law Institute. Sadat has received a bachelor's degree from Douglass College, a J.D. (summa cum laude) from Tulane Law School, a master's in law (summa cum laude) from Columbia University School of Law, and a diplôme d'études approfondies from the University of Paris I–Sorbonne. An award-winning and prolific scholar, she has served since December 2012 as special adviser for crimes against humanity to prosecutor Fatou Bensouda of the International Criminal Court. Sadat also serves as the director of the Crimes against Humanity Initiative, a multiyear project to draft a comprehensive convention addressing the punishment and prevention of such crimes. In 2001–3, she was a member of the U.S. Commission for International Religious Freedom; in 2011, she held the Alexis de Tocqueville Distinguished Fulbright Chair in Paris; and in 2012, she was elected to membership on the Council on Foreign Relations. She holds or has held leadership positions in the International Law Association (American Branch), the International Association of Penal Law, the American Law Institute, the American Society of International Law, the American Society of Comparative Law, and the International Law Students Association.

David Scheffer is the Mayer Brown/Robert A. Helman Professor of Law and director of the Center for International Human Rights at Northwestern University School of Law. He was the U.S. ambassador at large for war crimes issues (1997–2001) and led the U.S. delegation at the U.N. talks that established the International Criminal Court. Since January 2012, he has been the U.N. secretary-general's special expert on United Nations assistance to the Khmer Rouge trials. In 2013, he received the Berlin Prize, with a residential fellowship at the American Academy in Berlin. His book, *All the Missing Souls: A Personal History of the War Crimes Tribunals* (2012) was named Book of the Year by the American National Section of the International Association of Penal Law.

Christopher Stone has served as president of the Open Society Foundations since 2012. He received a bachelor's degree from Harvard University, a master's degree from the University of Cambridge, and a J.D. from Yale Law School. He previously worked with the Public Defender Service for the District of Columbia, served as president of the Vera Institute of Justice, and held the positions of Guggenheim Professor of the Practice of Criminal Justice at the John F. Kennedy School of Government and faculty director of the Hauser Center for Nonprofit Organizations at Harvard University. He founded the Neighborhood Defender Service of Harlem and served as a founding director of the New York State Capital Defender Office and of the Altus Global Alliance. He has also frequently served as an adviser to the Office of the Prosecutor of the International Criminal Court. As a result of his contributions to criminal justice reform in the United Kingdom, he was awarded an honorary Order of the British Empire.

C. Cora True-Frost is assistant professor at the Syracuse University College of Law. She earned a master's degree from Harvard Law School as a Gammon Fellow and a J.D./master's in public administration (magna cum laude) as one of two law fellows at Syracuse College of Law and the Maxwell School of Citizenship and Public Affairs. She was a Climenko Fellow and lecturer on law at Harvard Law School and worked at the Judicial Systems Monitoring Programme in East Timor. She also served as legal consultant to the Fofana defense team before the Special Court for Sierra Leone; led the NGO Working Group on Women, Peace, and Security at U.N. headquarters; and was a fellow at the Safra Foundation for Ethics and the Professions at Harvard University.

Patricia M. Wald is the first woman to be a judge on the U.S. Court of Appeals for the D.C. Circuit (where she held the position of chief judge from 1986 until 1991) and served as a judge for the International Criminal Tribunal for the Former Yugoslavia. She holds a law degree from Yale Law School. She served as a clerk for Judge Jerome Frank of the U.S. Court of Appeals for the Second Circuit, joined a private practice, and later worked at the U.S. Department of Justice's Office of Criminal Justice; the Neighborhood Legal Services Program in Washington, D.C.; the Center for Law and Social Policy; and the Mental Health Law Project, among others. She served in the Carter administration as an assistant attorney general before receiving appointment to the Court of Appeals. She has also been a member of the Iraq Intelligence Commission and has taken on countless leadership roles in professional associations, national commissions, and legal reform efforts in the United States and abroad. She currently serves on the U.S. government's Privacy and Civil Liberties Oversight Board. In 2013, President Barack Obama awarded Judge Wald the Presidential Medal of Freedom.

Alex Whiting is a professor of practice at Harvard Law School, where he focuses on domestic and international criminal law topics. He holds bachelor's and J.D. degrees from Yale University. From 2010 to 2013, he was the investigations coordinator and then prosecutions coordinator in the Office of the Prosecutor at the International Criminal Court. He previously served as an assistant clinical professor of law at Harvard Law School, as a senior trial attorney in the Office of the Prosecutor at the International Criminal Tribunal for the Former Yugoslavia, as an assistant U.S. attorney for the District of Massachusetts, and as a trial attorney in the criminal section of the Civil Rights Division in the U.S. Department of Justice. He has written on international criminal justice topics and has co-authored a casebook on international criminal law.

Index

Note: Locators in *italic* refer to figures, tables, or diagrams.